P9-CQO-717

PERL
IN A NUTSHELL

A Desktop Quick Reference

PERL
IN A NUTSHELL

A Desktop Quick Reference

Ellen Siever,
Stephen Spainhour & Nathan Patwardhan

O'REILLY®

Beijing · Cambridge · Farnham · Köln · Paris · Sebastopol · Taipei · Tokyo

Perl in a Nutshell

by Ellen Siever, Stephen Spainhour, and Nathan Patwardhan

Copyright © 1999 O'Reilly & Associates, Inc. All rights reserved.
Printed in the United States of America.

Published by O'Reilly & Associates, Inc., 101 Morris Street, Sebastopol, CA 95472.

Editor: Linda Mui

Production Editors: Nicole Gipson Arigo and Ellie Fountain Maden

Printing History:

> January 1999:   First Edition.

Nutshell Handbook, the Nutshell Handbook logo, and the O'Reilly logo are registered trademarks of O'Reilly & Associates, Inc. The association between the image of a camel and the topic of Perl is a trademark of O'Reilly & Associates.

Many of the designations used by manufacturers and sellers to distinguish their products are claimed as trademarks. Where those designations appear in this book, and O'Reilly & Associates, Inc. was aware of a trademark claim, the designations have been printed in caps or initial caps.

While every precaution has been taken in the preparation of this book, the publisher assumes no responsibility for errors or omissions, or for damages resulting from the use of the information contained herein.

This book is printed on acid-free paper with 85% recycled content, 15% post-consumer waste. O'Reilly & Associates is committed to using paper with the highest recycled content available consistent with high quality.

ISBN: 1-56592-286-7   [5/99]

Table of Contents

Part IV: CGI

Part V: Databases

Part VI: Network Programming

Part VII: Perl/Tk

Part VIII: Win32

Preface

Perl is a programming language that is *useful*. By this, we mean that people don't learn Perl just because they think they should, they learn Perl because they want to get something done.

This book is for Perl programmers who need to get things done. It's for readers who have dabbled a little in Perl and want a single reference for all their needs. This book is part reference, part guide to the world of Perl. We cover the language itself, but also the Perl modules that are most popular—modules for CGI, database manipulation, network programming, graphical interfaces, and Win32 integration.

How This Book Is Organized

This book has eight parts, as follows:

Part I, Getting Started

> Chapter 1, *Introduction to Perl*, gets you oriented to Perl and the Perl community.

> Chapter 2, *Installing Perl*, gives you some pointers on getting Perl and its modules installed on your machine. This chapter introduces you to the CPAN archive and discusses using the CPAN module to retrieve the latest versions of Perl modules.

> Chapter 3, *The Perl Interpreter*, is about using the *perl* program itself. It covers environment variables, command-line options, and the differences in executing the Unix and Win32 versions of Perl.

Part II, Language Basics

> Chapter 4, *The Perl Language*, is the turbo-charged tutorial/reference to the Perl language. If you've never programmed before, then you might need a tutorial that goes more slowly. But if you have some experience with other

programming languages, this chapter should teach you enough to start writing Perl programs.

Chapter 5, *Function Reference*, is a reference chapter for each of the built-in functions to Perl.

Chapter 6, *Debugging*, is about using the Perl debugger to help locate the rare errors in your programs.

Part III, Modules

Chapter 7, *Packages, Modules, and Objects*, gives a quick introduction to Perl packages, Perl modules, and object-oriented programming in Perl.

Chapter 8, *Standard Modules*, is a reference to each of the modules included in the standard Perl distribution.

Part IV, CGI

Chapter 9, *CGI Overview*, is a brief introduction to the concepts behind CGI programming.

Chapter 10, *The CGI.pm Module*, covers the very popular CGI.pm module, which is deemed essential by many CGI programmers.

Chapter 11, *Web Server Programming with mod_perl*, is about *mod_perl*, the Apache module that can be used to significantly improve CGI performance and also allows you to embed Perl code into the Apache server itself.

Part V, Databases

Chapter 12, *Databases and Perl*, gives a brief introduction to DBM databases in Perl, and provides a reference to DBI, the Database Independence package that gives you a consistent interface to many different database packages.

Part VI, Network Programming

Chapter 13, *Sockets*, explains socket programming and how to use the IO:Socket module.

Chapter 14, *Email Connectivity*, covers the Net::SMTP and Net::POP3 modules for sending and reading email, and also the Mail modules for manipulating email messages.

Chapter 15, *Usenet News*, explains the NNTP protocol and the Net::NNTP module for reading and posting Usenet news, and the News::Newsrc module for managing *.newsrc* files.

Chapter 16, *FTP*, explains the FTP protocol, the Net::FTP module for transfer-ring files by FTP, and the Net::Netrc module for managing *.netrc* files.

Chapter 17, *The LWP Library*, covers the most commonly used parts of the huge LWP library of modules for HTTP transactions.

Part VII, Perl/Tk

Chapter 18, *Perl/Tk*, is a reference to the Tk extension to Perl, for creating graphical user interfaces from within a Perl program.

Part VIII, Win32

Chapter 19, *Win32 Modules and Extensions*, talks about the many Perl modules for working with the Win32 operating systems.

Chapter 20, *PerlScript*, is about the ActiveX scripting tool, which is loosely based on Perl.

Typographical Conventions

Italics
are used for filenames, program names, URLs, command-line options, email addresses, replaceable text in syntax lines, and to introduce new terms.

Letter Gothic
is used for code snippets, method and function names, text to be typed literally, variables, constants, mail headers, and configuration directives.

Letter Gothic italics
are used for replaceable items in code examples.

How to Contact Us

We have tested and verified the information in this book to the best of our ability, but you may find that features have changed (or even that we have made mistakes!). Please let us know about any errors you find, as well as your suggestions for future editions, by writing to:

O'Reilly & Associates, Inc.
101 Morris Street
Sebastopol, CA 95472
1-800-998-9938 (in the U.S. or Canada)
1-707-829-0515 (international/local)
1-707-829-0104 (FAX)

You can also send us messages electronically. To be put on the mailing list or request a catalog, send email to:

info@oreilly.com

To ask technical questions or comment on the book, send email to:

bookquestions@oreilly.com

We have a web site for the book, where we'll list errata and any plans for future editions. You can access this page at:

http://www.oreilly.com/catalog/perlnut/

Acknowledgments

Many thanks to everyone who helped out on this book. Thanks to Larry Wall, Randal Schwartz, Tom Christiansen, and Sriram Srinivasan for their excellent books on Perl. Some material in this book is adapted from theirs; for that, we are very grateful.

Thanks also to all the reviewers of this book, who include Randal Schwartz, Tom Christiansen, Graham Barr, Clinton Wong, and Erik Olson. Without their help, this book wouldn't be nearly as helpful as it is.

We'd like to thank Linda Mui, our editor, and Val Quercia, who kept us on track, for all their support.

Finally, since this book shares the camel image with *Programming Perl*, it occurs to us that someone might confuse it with the True Camel. So let's try to nip that in the bud: if you insist on giving this book a cute animal-related nickname, we encourage you to call it the "Camel head" or "Camel nut" or something else that makes the difference clear.

PART I

Getting Started

CHAPTER 1

Introduction to Perl

Computer languages differ not so much in what they make possible, but in what they make easy. Perl is designed to make the easy jobs easy, without making the hard jobs impossible. Perl makes it easy to manipulate numbers, text, files, directories, computers, networks, and programs. It also makes it easy to develop, modify, and debug your own programs portably, on any modern operating system.

Perl is especially popular with systems programmers and web developers, but it also appeals to a much broader audience. Originally designed for text processing, it has grown into a sophisticated, general-purpose programming language with a rich software development environment complete with debuggers, profilers, cross-referencers, compilers, interpreters, libraries, syntax-directed editors, and all the rest of the trappings of a "real" programming language.

There are many reasons for Perl's success. For starters, Perl is freely available and freely redistributable. But that's not enough to explain the Perl phenomenon, since many other freeware packages fail to thrive. Perl is not just free; it's also fun. People feel like they can be creative in Perl, because they have freedom of expression.

Perl is both a very simple language and a very rich language. It's a simple language in that the types and structures are simple to use and understand, and it borrows heavily from other languages you may already be familiar with. You don't have to know everything there is to know about Perl before you can write useful programs.

However, Perl is also a rich language, and there is much to learn about it. That's the price of making hard things possible. Although it will take some time for you to absorb all that Perl can do, somewhere down the line you will be glad that you have access to the extensive capabilities of Perl.

What's Perl Good For?

Perl has the advantage of being easy to learn if you just want to write simple scripts—thus its appeal to the ever-impatient system administrator and the deadline-driven CGI developer. However, as you become more ambitious, Perl lets you act on those ambitions. Chapter 2, *Installing Perl*, covers how to get and install Perl, and Chapter 3, *The Perl Interpreter*, through Chapter 6, *Debugging*, cover the basics of the Perl language, its functions, and how to use the Perl debugger.

On top of the Perl language itself, however, are the Perl modules. You can think of modules as add-ons to the Perl language that allow you to streamline tasks by providing a consistent API. Perl itself is fun to use, but the modules lend Perl even more flexibility and enormous power. Furthermore, anyone can write and distribute a Perl module. Some modules are deemed important enough or popular enough to be distributed with Perl itself, but very few are actually written by the core Perl developers themselves. Chapter 7, *Packages, Modules, and Objects*, introduces you to Perl modules, and Chapter 8, *Standard Modules*, covers the standard modules that are distributed with Perl itself.

The most popular Perl module is CGI.pm, which gives a simple interface to developing CGI (common gateway interface) applications in Perl. While Perl itself is indispensable for many different tasks, its text-manipulation features make it perfect for CGI development on the Web. In fact, the resurgence of Perl over the past few years must be credited to its popularity as a CGI language. Chapter 10, *The CGI.pm Module*, and Chapter 11, *Web Server Programming with mod_perl*, talk about using Perl for CGI, including *mod_perl*, which merges Perl into the Apache web server.

Database interconnectivity is one of the most important functions of any programming language today, and Perl is no exception. DBI is a suite of modules that provide a consistent database-independent interface for Perl. Chapter 12, *Databases and Perl*, covers both DBI and DBM (the more primitive but surprisingly effective database interface built directly into Perl).

The Internet doesn't start and stop at CGI. Network programming is another of Perl's strengths, with a robust sockets interface and several modules for writing clients and servers for all sorts of Internet services—not only the Web, but also email, news, FTP, etc. Chapter 13, *Sockets*, through Chapter 17, *The LWP Library*, cover the modules for developing fully functional Internet applications in Perl.

Perl programs are traditionally command-line–based, but the Perl/Tk extension can provide Perl programs with graphical user interfaces, for both Unix and Microsoft Windows. Chapter 18, *Perl/Tk*, gives a complete reference to Perl/Tk.

Finally, although Perl is primarily developed for Unix, recent releases of Perl for Windows 95 and Windows NT are gaining popularity, both for CGI and system administration tasks. Chapter 19, *Win32 Modules and Extensions*, covers the Win32 modules for Perl. Web developers on Win32 machines can use a variation of Perl called PerlScript, for JavaScript-like programming over the Web. Chapter 20, *PerlScript*, gives an introduction to PerlScript and summarizes its syntax and functions.

As you may have noticed, this section entitled "What's Perl Good For" has sneakily become a description of the contents of this book. This book aims at being a general-purpose reference to all things Perl.

Perl Development

Software doesn't grow on trees. Perl is free because of the donated efforts of several generous persons who have devoted large chunks of their spare time to the development, maintenance, and evangelism of Perl.

Perl itself was created by Larry Wall, in an effort to produce reports for a bug-reporting system. Larry designed a new scripting language for this purpose, and then released it to the Internet, thinking that someone else might find it useful. In the spirit of freeware, other people suggested improvements and even ways to implement them, and Perl transformed from a cute scripting language into a robust programming language.

Today, Larry does little actual development himself, but he is the ringleader of a core development team known as the Perl Porters. The Porters determine which new features should be added and which pesky bugs should be fixed. To keep it from being a free-for-all, there is generally one person who is responsible for delivering the next release of Perl, with several "development releases" in the interim.

Which Platforms Support Perl?

While Perl was developed on Unix and is closely entwined with Unix culture, it also has a strong following on the Windows and Macintosh platforms. Perl gives Windows 95, Windows NT, Macintosh, and even VMS users the opportunity to take advantage of the scripting power that Unix users take for granted.

Most Unix machines will have Perl already installed, since it's one of the first things a Unix system administrator will build for a new machine (and is in fact distributed with the operating system on some versions of Unix, such as Linux and FreeBSD). For Windows NT, Windows 95, and Macintosh, there are binary distributions of Perl that you can download for free. See Chapter 2 for information on installing Perl.

Although there is some history of other platforms not being treated seriously by the Perl community, Perl is becoming increasingly friendly to non-Unix platforms. The Win32 ports of Perl are quite stable, and as of Perl 5.005, are integrated wholly with core Perl. MacPerl integration is expected with Perl 5.006.

Perl Resources

Paradoxically, the way in which Perl helps you the most has almost nothing to do with Perl itself, and everything to do with the people who use Perl. While people start using Perl because they need it, they continue using Perl because they love it.

The result is that the Perl community is one of the most helpful in the world. When Perl programmers aren't writing their own programs, they spend their time helping others write theirs. They discuss common problems and help devise solutions. They develop utilities and modules for Perl, and give them away to the world at large.

The comp.lang.perl.* Newsgroups

The central meeting place for Perl aficionados is Usenet. If you're not familiar with Usenet, it's a collection of special-interest groups (called *newsgroups*) on the Internet. For most anyone using a modern browser, Usenet access is as simple as a selecting a menu option on the browser. Perl programmers should consider subscribing to the following newsgroups:

comp.lang.perl.announce
> A moderated newsgroup with announcements about new utilities or products related to Perl.

comp.lang.perl.misc
> The general-purpose newsgroup devoted to non–CGI-related Perl programming questions.

comp.lang.perl.moderated
> A moderated newsgroup intended to be a forum for more controlled, restrained discussions about Perl.

comp.lang.perl.modules
> A newsgroup devoted to using and developing Perl modules.

comp.lang.perl.tk
> A newsgroup concentrating on Perl/Tk, the graphical extension to Perl.

comp.infosystems.www.authoring.cgi
> A newsgroup for CGI questions in general, but mostly Perl-related ones.

At some point, it seems like every Perl programmer subscribes to *comp.lang.perl.misc*. You may eventually abandon it if the discussion becomes too detailed, too belligerent, or too bizarre for your taste. But you'll likely find yourself coming back from time to time, either to ask a question or just to check out the latest buzz.

One bit of advice, however: before posting questions to *comp.lang.perl.misc* (or any newsgroup, for that matter), you should read the group for a few days and read the FAQ (Frequently Asked Questions list—see the next section). The *comp.lang.perl.** newsgroups are a wonderful resource if you have an interesting or unusual question, but no one can save you if you ask something that's covered in the FAQ.

By the way, if you're a first-time poster to *comp.lang.perl.misc*, you shouldn't be surprised if you receive an email message listing various resources on Perl that you may not know about. This is done via an "auto-faq" service, which scans all postings and sends this helpful email to anyone who hasn't posted earlier.

Frequently Asked Questions Lists (FAQs)

A FAQ is a Frequently Asked Questions list, with answers. FAQs are traditionally associated with Usenet newsgroups, but the term has since been adopted by web sites, technical support departments, and even health care pamphlets. In general, FAQs are written and maintained on a volunteer basis by dedicated (and generous) members of the community. The *comp.lang.perl.misc* FAQ (also known as the Perl FAQ) is maintained by Tom Christiansen and Nathan Torkington.

The Perl FAQ was created to minimize traffic on the *comp.lang.perl.misc* newsgroup, when it became clear that the same questions were being asked over and over again. However, the FAQ has transcended into a general-purpose starting point for learning anything about Perl.

The FAQ is distributed in several different formats, including HTML, PostScript, and plain ASCII text. You can find the FAQ at several places:

- The main source is located at *http://www.perl.com/perl/faq/*.

- On CPAN, you can find it in */CPAN/doc/FAQs/FAQ/*. (See Chapter 2 for more information on CPAN.)

- On a semi-regular basis, the latest version of the FAQ is posted on *comp.lang.perl.misc*.

In addition to the *comp.lang.perl.misc* FAQ, there are also several niche FAQs that are Perl-related. They are:

Perl CGI Programming FAQ
   http://www.perl.com/CPAN-local/doc/FAQs/cgi/perl-cgi-faq.html

Perl/TK FAQ
   http://w4.lns.cornell.edu/~pvhp/ptk/ptkTOC.html

Perl for Win32 FAQ
   http://www.ActiveState.com/support/faqs/win32/

Perl for the Mac FAQ
   http://www.perl.com/CPAN/doc/FAQs/mac/MacPerlFAQ.html

Mailing Lists

Several mailing lists are focused on more specialized aspects of Perl. Like Usenet newsgroups, mailing lists are discussion groups, but the discussion takes place over email. In general, mailing lists aren't as convenient as newsgroups, since a few hundred mail messages a day about Perl can become intrusive to any but the most obsessive Perl hackers. However, because mailing lists tend to have much smaller and more focused distributions, you'll find that they can sometimes be much more interesting and helpful than newsgroups.

There are tons of mailing lists for Perl users and developers alike. Some are specific to a particular module or distribution, such as the mailing lists for users of CGI.pm, LWP, DBI, or *mod_perl*. Other mailing lists discuss using Perl on non-Unix platforms such as Windows, Macintosh or VMS. Still more mailing lists are devoted to the development and advocacy of Perl in general. To find a mailing list for your topic, look in the documentation or README of a module distribution, look in the Perl FAQ, or just ask someone.

Many of these mailing lists also have a "digest" version, which means that instead of receiving individual email messages all day long, you receive a few "digests" of the messages on a regular basis. Digests of a mailing list might be preferable to the minute-by-minute onslaught of email throughout the day, depending on how involved you are in the discussion.

www.perl.com

There are countless web pages devoted to Perl, but probably the most useful entry site to Perl resources is *www.perl.com*. Formerly maintained by Tom Christiansen, *www.perl.com* is now maintained by Tom with help from O'Reilly & Associates (the publisher of this book). From *www.perl.com*, you can access Perl documentation, news, software, FAQs, articles, and (of course) Perl itself.

The Perl Institute (www.perl.org)

Although the URLs are similar, don't confuse *www.perl.com* with the Perl Institute, *www.perl.org*. The Perl Institute is a member-supported organization for Perl programmers to help drive Perl development and improve Perl's visibility. Membership dues range from $32 for students to $4096 for corporate sponsors (yes, all membership fees are a power of $2).

Perl Mongers

User groups for Perl call themselves "Perl Mongers," and have been sprouting up in major cities over the past few years. They range from small groups of Perl aficionados socializing at cafes, to large organizations sponsoring guest speakers. Cities with Perl Mongers groups currently include New York, London, Amsterdam, Boston, Chicago, Philadelphia, and Boulder.

The Perl Journal

The *Perl Journal*, published by Jon Orwant, is a quarterly publication with articles and news about Perl. You can find the *Perl Journal* in some technical bookstores. You can also subscribe by sending email to *subscriptions@tpj.com* or by visiting *www.tpj.com*.

Perl Conferences

For years, Usenix has devoted tracks of its conferences to Perl. However, starting in 1997, O'Reilly & Associates has been hosting conferences dedicated entirely to Perl. You can learn more about Perl conferences from *www.perl.com*.

Books

There are many books written on Perl. In fact, the current popularity of Perl is often credited to the original publication of *Programming Perl*, also known as "The Camel" (because of the animal on its cover),* by Larry Wall and Randal Schwartz. The Camel is also published by O'Reilly & Associates. The Camel isn't the best place to start if you're just learning Perl from scratch, but it's essential if you want to really understand Perl and not just dabble in it.

Other Perl books published by O'Reilly & Associates are *Learning Perl* ("The Llama"), *Advanced Perl Programming, Perl Cookbook, Managing Regular Expressions, Learning Perl on Win32 Systems, Learning Perl/Tk, Web Client Programming with Perl*, and *CGI Programming with Perl.*

See *http://www.perl.com/* for an archive of reviews of Perl-related books.

---

* The first edition of *Programming Perl* is also known as the Pink Camel, because of the color of the spine. The second edition is known as the Blue Camel, and is written by Larry Wall, Tom Christiansen, and Randal Schwartz.

CHAPTER 2

Installing Perl

The best things in life are free. So is Perl. Although you can get a bundled Perl distribution on CD-ROM, most people download Perl from an online archive. CPAN, the Comprehensive Perl Archive Network, is the main distribution point for all things Perl. Whether you are looking for Perl itself, for a module, or for documentation about Perl, CPAN is the place to go, at *http://www.perl.com/CPAN/*. The ongoing development and enhancement of Perl is very much a cooperative effort, and CPAN is the place where the work of many individuals comes together.

The CPAN Architecture

CPAN represents the development interests of a cross-section of the Perl community. It contains Perl utilities, modules, documentation, and (of course) the Perl distribution itself. CPAN was created by Jarkko Hietaniemi and Andreas König.

The home system for CPAN is *funet.fi*, but CPAN is also mirrored on many other sites around the globe. This ensures that anyone with an Internet connection can have reliable access to CPAN's contents at any time. Since the structure of all CPAN sites is the same, a user searching for the current version of Perl can be sure that the *latest.tar.gz* file is the same on every site.

The easiest way to access CPAN is to utilize the CPAN multiplex service at *www.perl.com*. The multiplexor tries to connect you to a local, fast machine on a large bandwidth hub. To use the multiplexor, go to *http://www.perl.com/CPAN/*; the multiplexor will automatically route you to a site based on your domain.

If you prefer, you can choose a particular CPAN site, instead of letting the multiplexor choose one for you. To do that, go to the URL *http://www.perl.com/CPAN* (no trailing slash). When you omit the trailing slash, the CPAN multiplexor presents a menu of CPAN mirrors from which you select the one you want. It remembers your choice next time.

If you want to use anonymous FTP, the following machines should have the Perl source code plus a copy of the CPAN mirror list:

```
ftp.perl.com
ftp.cs.colorado.edu
ftp.cise.ufl.edu
ftp.funet.fi
ftp.cs.ruu.nl
```

The location of the top directory of the CPAN mirror differs on these machines, so look around once you get there. It's often something like */pub/perl/CPAN*.

If you don't have reliable Internet access, you can also get CPAN on CD as part of O'Reilly's *Perl Resource Kit.* In addition to CPAN itself, the *Perl Resource Kit* CD includes a tool for simple installation and update of Perl modules. See *http://perl.oreilly.com/* for more information.

How Is CPAN Organized?

CPAN materials are grouped into categories, including Perl modules, distributions, documentation, announcements, ports, scripts, and contributing authors. Each category is linked to related categories. For example, links to a graphing module written by an author appear in both the module and the author areas.

Since CPAN provides the same offerings worldwide, the directory structure has been standardized; files are located in the same place in the directory hierarchy at all CPAN sites. All CPAN sites use *CPAN* as the root directory, from which the user can select a specific Perl item.

From the *CPAN* directory you have the following choices:

```
CPAN.html       CPAN info page; lists what's available
                in CPAN and describes each of the modules
ENDINGS         Description of the file extensions, such as .tar, .gz, and .zip
MIRRORED BY     A list of sites mirroring CPAN
MIRRORING.FROM  A list of sites mirrored by CPAN
README          A brief description of what you'll find on CPAN
README.html     An HTML-formatted version of the README file
RECENT          Recent additions to the CPAN site
RECENT.DAY      Recent additions to the CPAN site (daily)
RECENT.html     An HTML-formatted list of recent additions
RECENT.WEEK     Recent additions to the CPAN site (weekly)
ROADMAP         What you'll find on CPAN and where
ROADMAP.html    An HTML-formatted version of ROADMAP
SITES           An exhaustive list of CPAN sites
SITES.html      An HTML-formatted version of SITES
authors         A list of CPAN authors
clpa            An archive of comp.lang.perl.announce
doc             Various Perl documentation, FAQs, etc.
indices         All that is indexed.
latest.tar.gz   The latest Perl distribution sources
misc            Misc Perl stuff like Larry Wall quotes and gifs
modules         Modules for Perl version 5
other-archives  Other things yet uncategorized
ports           Various Perl ports
scripts         Various scripts appearing in Perl books
src             The Perl sources from various versions
```

To get the current Perl distribution, click on *latest.tar.gz*. For ports to other systems, click on *ports*. The *modules* link is the one you want if you're looking for a Perl module—from there you can get a full list of the modules, or you can access the modules directly by author, by CPAN category, or by module. (The section "Getting and Installing Modules" later in this chapter talks about installing modules.) Click on *doc* for Perl documentation, FAQs, etc.

Installing Perl

Most likely your system administrator is responsible for installing and upgrading Perl. But if you are the system administrator, or you want to install Perl on your own system, sooner or later you will find yourself installing a new version of Perl.

 If you have been running Perl, and you are now going to install Perl 5.005, you need to be aware that it is not binary-compatible with older versions. This means that you must rebuild and reinstall any dynamically loaded extensions that you built under earlier versions.

Specific installation instructions come in the *README* and *INSTALL* files of the Perl distribution kit. If you don't already have the Perl distribution, you can download it from CPAN—the latest Unix distribution is in *latest.tar.gz*. The information in this section is an overview of the installation process. The gory details are in the *INSTALL* file, which you should look at before starting, especially if you haven't done an installation before. Note that operating systems other than Unix may have special instructions; if so, follow those instructions instead of what's in this section or in *INSTALL*. Look for a file named *README.xxx*, where *xxx* is your OS name.

In addition to Perl itself, the standard distribution includes a set of core modules that are automatically installed with Perl. See the "Getting and Installing Modules" section later in this chapter for how to install modules that are not bundled with Perl; Chapter 8, *Standard Modules*, describes the standard modules in some detail.

Installing on Unix

Typically, you'll get the Perl kit packed as either a *tar* file or as a set of *shar* (shell archive) scripts; in either case, the file will be in a compressed format. If you got your version of Perl directly from CPAN, it is probably in "tar-gzipped" format; *tar* and *gzip* are popular Unix data-archiving formats. In any case, once you've downloaded the distribution, you need to uncompress and unpack it. The filename indicates what kind of compression was used. A *.Z* extension indicates you need to *uncompress* the file first, while a *.gz* extension indicates you need to *gunzip* the file. You then unpack the file as appropriate, read the *README* and *INSTALL* files, and run a massive shell script called *Configure*, which tries to figure out everything about your system and creates the file *Config.pm* to store the information. After this is done, you do a series of "makes" to find header file dependencies, to compile Perl (and *a2p*, which translates *awk* scripts to Perl), to run regression tests, and to install Perl in your system directories.

One common problem is not making sure that Perl is linked against all the libraries it needs to build correctly. Also, you should say "yes" when *Configure* asks if you want dynamic loading, if your system supports it. Otherwise, you won't be able to install modules that use XS, which provides an interface between Perl and C.

If you are running Linux, some Linux distributions might not include a complete MakeMaker, which you need for installing modules. To be safe, you should make sure everything is there; one way to do that is to check the *Config.pm* file. If MakeMaker is not correctly installed, you might need to build Perl yourself.

It's possible you'll get a compiled (binary) copy of Perl, rather than the source. In that case, make sure you get *suidperl*, *a2p*, *s2p*, and the Perl library routines. Install these files in the directories that your version was compiled for. Note that binary distributions of Perl are made available because they're handy, not because you are restricted from getting the source and compiling it yourself. The people who give you the binary distribution ought to provide you with some form of access to the source, if only a pointer to where *they* got the source. See the *Copying* file in the distribution for more information.

Perl examples

The Perl source distribution comes with some sample scripts in the *eg/* subdirectory. Feel free to browse among them and use them. They are not installed automatically, however, so you need to copy them to the appropriate directory and possibly fix the #! line to point to the right interpreter.

The files in the *t/* and *lib/* subdirectories, although arcane in spots, can also serve as examples.

Patches

Since Perl is constantly being honed and improved, patches are sometimes made available through CPAN. Your distribution is likely to have had most of the patches applied already—run `perl -v` to check the patch level of your distribution. Patches are sent out with complete instructions on how to apply them using *patch*, which is available from the GNU project.

Installing on Win32

You need to obtain and install a copy of Perl yourself, unless you have had the good fortune of having a system administrator install Perl on your system.

For Perl 5.004, there are two different distributions for Win32 systems. The first is Perl for Win32, which was developed by ActiveState Tool Corporation. The second is actually the standard Perl distribution—Perl 5.004 added support for Win32 systems to the standard Perl distribution. In Perl 5.004, the two versions are largely compatible, with some of the Perl 5.004 code being based on the ActiveState port. However, there are also some differences: using either the ISAPI version of Perl or

PerlScript with 5.004 requires the ActiveState distribution. On the other hand, the Win32 ports of *mod_perl* or Perl/Tk require the "native" (or standard) version of 5.004.

With Perl 5.005, this scenario has changed, and the two versions have been merged. If you look on CPAN, you'll see that there still seem to be two versions—the ActiveState distribution, now known as ActivePerl, and the standard distribution. The difference is that they are now based on the same source code. Get ActivePerl if you want to install from a binary distribution or get the standard distribution to build Perl from the source code.

ActivePerl

The canonical source for the ActivePerl distribution at the time of this writing is at *http://www.activestate.com/*. Included in the distribution are:

Perl for Win32
    Binary for the core Perl distribution

Perl for ISAPI
    IIS plug-in for use with ISAPI-compliant web servers

PerlScript
    ActiveX scripting engine

Perl Package Manager
    Manager for Perl modules and extensions

The ActivePerl binary comes as a self-extracting executable that uses the standard Win32 InstallShield setup wizard to guide you through the installation process. By default, Perl is installed into the directory *C:\Perl\version*, where *version* is the current version number (e.g., 5.005). Unless you choose to customize your setup, the default installation does not modify your registry other than to add an entry so you can uninstall Perl. For information on customizing your installation, see the Win32 FAQ on the ActiveState web site. The installation also associates the file extension *.pl* with Perl and adds the directory into which you installed Perl to your PATH environment variable.

Standard Perl distribution

The standard Perl distribution is available from CPAN, where you'll find binary and source distributions for Perl 5.004 for both Windows NT and Windows 95, and the source distribution for Perl 5.005. You can get the binary for Perl 5.004 as either a *.tar.gz* file or a *.zip* file. The source distributions come as *.tar.gz* files, which you can extract using a utility that supports *gzip* files, *tar* files, and long filenames. Ports of both GNU *gzip* and *tar* are available for the various Win32 platforms, or you can use a graphical *zip* archive program such as WinZip. Make sure you preserve the directory structure when you unpack the distribution.

To install from the source, you need the Microsoft Visual C++ compiler, the Borland C++ compiler, or Mingw32 with either EGCS or GCC. You also need a *make* utility. Microsoft Visual C++ comes with *nmake*, or you can use *dmake*.* Once you have the distribution, start by reading the file *README.win32*. Next, edit the file *Makefile* in the *win32* subdirectory of the distribution and make sure that you're happy with the values for the install drive and directory.

Then execute the following commands from the *win32* subdirectory of the distribution to build, test, and install the distribution. This example assumes that you have the proper environment variables (LIB, INCLUDE, etc.) set up for your compiler and that *nmake* is your make program.

```
> nmake          Build all of Perl
> nmake test     Test your distribution
> nmake install  Install to target directory, as specified in the Makefile
```

Assuming everything is now built correctly, you just need to add the *bin* subdirectory of the installation target directory to your path. For example, if you installed the Perl distribution to *C:\Perl*, you'll want to add *C:\Perl\bin* to your path.

Finally, restart your machine so the environment changes take effect, and you're ready to go.

If you want to install the Perl 5.004 binary, you can do so either from the command line or from Windows. To install from the command line, *cd* to the top level of the directory into which you unpacked Perl and type:

```
% install
```

From a window, click on the *install.bat* icon. That should initiate the installation, but if it doesn't, it will put you into the command shell in the correct directory. At that point, type:

```
> perl\bin\perl install.bat
```

The setup script then asks you a few questions such as where you want to install Perl and whether you want to install HTML versions of the documentation. It then confirms your responses and does the installation. When it's done, it gives you some information about setting environment variables and then terminates. At that point, you can start running Perl scripts.

A word of warning: Windows 95 users can expect significantly different functionality from their Perl distribution than Windows NT users. For various reasons, some of the Win32 modules don't work on Windows 95. The functionality required to implement them may be missing on Windows 95, or bugs in Windows 95 may prevent them from working correctly.

Getting and Installing Modules

As you'll see when you look at the lists of modules and their authors on CPAN, many users have made their modules freely available. If you find an interesting problem and are thinking of writing a module to solve it, check the *modules* directory on CPAN first to see if there is a module there that you can use. The chances

---

* See the file *README.win32* for information on obtaining Mingw32 and a Win32 *dmake* port.

are good that there is either a module already that does what you need, or perhaps one that you can extend, rather than starting from scratch.*

Before you download a module, you might also check your system to see if it's already installed. The following command searches the libraries in the @INC array and prints the names of all modules it finds:

```
find `perl -e 'print "@INC"'` -name '*.pm' -print
```

Locating modules

If you start from the *modules* directory on CPAN, you'll see that the modules are categorized into three subdirectories:

by-authors	*Modules by author's registered CPAN name*
by-category	*Modules by subject matter (see below)*
by-module	*Modules by namespace (i.e., MIME)*

If you know what module you want, you can go directly to it by clicking on the *by-module* entry. If you are looking for a module in a particular category, you can find it through the *by-category* subdirectory. If you know the author, click on *by-author*. However, if you aren't familiar with the categories and you want to find out if there is a module that performs a certain task, you might want to get the file *00modlist.long.html*, also in the *modules* directory. That file is the "Perl 5 Modules List." It contains a list of all the modules, by category, with a brief description of the purpose of each module and a link to the author's CPAN directory for downloading.

Here is a list of the categories; there are currently 22 categories, plus one for modules that don't fit anywhere else:

```
02_Perl_Core_Modules
03_Development_Support
04_Operating_System_Interfaces
05_Networking_Devices_Inter_Process
06_Data_Type_Utilities
07_Database_Interfaces
08_User_Interfaces
09_Interfaces_to_Other_Languages
10_File_Names_Systems_Locking
11_String_Processing_Language_Text_Process
12_Option_Argument_Parameter_Processing
13_Internationalization_and_Locale
14_Authentication_Security_Encryption
15_World_Wide_Web_HTML_HTTP_CGI
16_Server_and_Daemon_Utilities
17_Archiving_and_Compression
18_Images_Pixmap_Bitmap_Manipulation
19_Mail_and_Usenet_News
20_Control_Flow_Utilities
21_File_Handle_Input_Output
22_Microsoft_Windows_Modules
```

---

* If you are interested in writing and contributing modules, there are several places that serve as good starting points for learning to do that—see the *perlmodlib* manpage, the "Perl 5 Module List," and the "Perl Authors Upload Server" (*http://www.perl.com/CPAN/modules/04pause.html*).

```
23_Miscellaneous_Modules
99_Not_In_Modulelist
```

If you are in the *by-categories* subdirectory and have selected an area from which you'd like to download a module, you'll find a list of the files in the directory. *tar* files have a *.tar.gz* extension, and README files have a *.readme* extension. You'll generally find a README file for each module; take a look at it before you decide to download the file.

Here's a sample directory listing from category 15:

```
ANDK
CGI-Out-96.081401.readme
CGI-Out-96.081401.tar.gz
CGI-Response-0.03.readme
CGI-Response-0.03.tar.gz
CGI-modules-2.75.readme
CGI-modules-2.75.tar.gz
CGI-modules-2.76.readme
CGI-modules-2.76.tar.gz
CGI.pm-2.32.readme
CGI.pm-2.33.readme
CGI.pm-2.34.readme
CGI.pm-2.35.readme
CGI.pm-2.35.tar.gz
CGI.pm-2.36.readme
CGI.pm-2.36.tar.gz
CGI_Imagemap-1.00.readme
CGI_Imagemap-1.00.tar.gz
CGI_Lite-1.62.pm.gz
DOUGM
LDS
MGH
MIKEH
MUIR
SHGUN
```

You'll notice that multiple versions are sometimes listed—for example, CGI.pm has versions 2.35 and 2.36 available. Generally this is to ease the transition to a new version of the module.

Select the *.readme* file of the most current archive and review its contents carefully. README files often give special instructions about building the module; they warn you about other modules needed for proper functioning and if the module can't be built under certain versions of Perl. If you're satisfied with what you read, download the file.

Module Installation

If you're running the standard distribution of Perl, either on a Unix or Win32 system, and you want to install a module, this section explains how to do it. If you are running the ActiveState Win32 port, see the next section.

Before installing modules, you should understand at least a little about *make*. *make* is a command designed to automate compilations; it guarantees that programs are compiled with the correct options and are linked to the current version of program modules and libraries. But it's not just for programmers—*make* is useful for any situation where there are dependencies among a group of related files.

make uses a file known as a Makefile, which is a text file that describes the dependencies and contains instructions that tell *make* what to do. A Perl programmer who writes a module creates a file called *Makefile.PL* that comes with the module when you download it. *Makefile.PL* is a Perl script that uses another module, ExtUtils::MakeMaker (generally just referred to as MakeMaker), to generate a Makefile specific to that module on your system.

Before you can actually install the module, you need to decide where it should go. Modules can be installed either globally, for everyone to use, or locally, for your own use. Most system administrators install popular software, including Perl modules, to be globally available. In that case, the modules are generally installed in a branch of the *lib* directory with the rest of the Perl libraries.

If you have root privileges or write access to the locations where Perl modules are installed on your system, you can proceed to move the downloaded module file to the correct directory and run *gunzip* and *tar* to unpack it. Then *cd* to the module directory and check any README or INSTALL files, and check the MANIFEST file to be sure everything is there. If all is well, you can then run the following to complete the installation:

```
% perl Makefile.PL
% make
% make test
% make install
```

It's possible that you'll need to customize *Makefile.PL* before running it. If so, see the discussion of ExtUtils::MakeMaker in Chapter 8.

If you are going to install the module locally (for example, if you don't have permission to install globally or you want to test it locally before installing it for general use), you need to pass a PREFIX argument to Perl when you run *Makefile.PL* to generate the Makefile. This argument tells MakeMaker to use the directory following PREFIX as the base directory when installing the module.

For example, to install a module in the directory */home/mydir/Perl/Modules*, the PREFIX argument would look like this:

```
% perl Makefile.PL PREFIX=/home/mydir/Perl/Modules
```

Then follow the remaining steps as above:

```
% make
% make test
% make install
```

The module is now available, but when you write Perl code to use the module, there's another detail to take care of. Since Perl looks in system-wide directories as specified in the special array @INC, it won't find local modules unless you tell it where they are. Instead, you'll receive an error message like the following:

```
Can't locate <ModuleName>.pm in @INC.
BEGIN failed--compilation aborted.
```

Thus, if you installed the module in */home/mydir/Perl/Modules*, you need to tell Perl to look in that location with the command use lib '*path*':

```
#!/usr/local/bin/perl -w
use lib '/home/mydir/Perl/Modules';
use ModuleName;
```

Installing Modules with ActiveState Perl

Prior to Perl 5.005, ActiveState's Perl for Win32 did not support the use of Make-Maker. If you are running Perl 5.004 (or earlier), this prevents you from installing some modules. Others can be installed manually by making sure all the files that come in the module distribution are placed in the correct libraries. The documentation that comes with the module may help you determine if you can install it and what you need to do.

With 5.005, you can now use MakeMaker to install the modules, or you can use the Perl Package Manager that comes with ActivePerl.

Using MakeMaker

To install a module using MakeMaker, follow the procedure described earlier for installing when you are running the standard distribution, replacing *make* with *nmake* or *dmake* as appropriate.

Using the Perl Package Manager

The Perl Package Manager (PPM) provides a command-line interface for obtaining and installing Perl modules and extensions. To run PPM, connect to the site (such as CPAN or the CD that comes with the *Perl Resource Kit for Win32*) that contains the modules you are interested in, and type:

```
perl ppm.pl
```

The PPM prompt appears, and you can begin to enter PPM commands. The available commands are:

help *[command]*
    Prints the list of commands and what they do, or help for a particular command.

install *packages*
    Installs the specified packages.

quit
    Leaves the Perl Package Manager.

remove *packages*
    Removes the specified packages from the system.

search
    Searches for information about available packages.

set Sets or displays current options.

verify
> Verifies that your current installation is up-to-date.

Installing Modules with the CPAN Module

If you are just getting and installing one or a few modules, it's not a big problem to do it manually. But if you don't want to deal with doing it all manually, or if you are maintaining an entire Perl installation, there is an easier way—you can use the CPAN module. The CPAN module (*CPAN.pm*) can be used interactively from the command line to locate, download, and install Perl modules, or to identify modules and authors. *CPAN.pm* was designed to automate the installation of Perl modules; it includes searching capabilities and the ability to retrieve files from one or more of the mirrored CPAN sites and unpack them in a dedicated directory.

To run the CPAN module interactively, enter:

```
% perl -MCPAN -eshell
```

The first time you use the CPAN module, it takes you through a series of setup questions and writes a file called *MyConfig.pm* in a subdirectory of your home directory that defaults to ˜/.*cpan/CPAN/MyConfig.pm*. After that, whenever you use the CPAN module for downloading other modules, it uses the *.cpan* directory as the general build and cache directory, saved as cpan_home in the configuration file. If ReadLine support is available (i.e., Term::ReadKey and Term::ReadLine are installed), you can use command history and command completion as you enter commands.

When the module runs and is ready for you to enter commands, you'll see the prompt:

```
cpan>
```

You can then enter h to get a brief help message, or just start entering commands. The commands are all methods in the CPAN::Shell package. For commands that can operate on modules, bundles, authors, or distributions, *CPAN.pm* treats arguments containing a slash (/) as distributions, arguments beginning with Bundle:: as bundles, and everything else as modules or authors.

The following is a listing of the interactive CPAN modules:

?

> ?

> Displays brief help message. Same as h command.

!

> ! *perl-code*
> evals a Perl command.

---

a *[authorlist]*

Searches for CPAN authors. Arguments can be strings to be matched exactly or regular expressions, which must be enclosed in slashes and are matched in case-insensitive fashion. With no arguments, it returns a list of all authors, by CPAN ID. With arguments, it returns a list of authors if there is more than one that matches the criteria, or it returns additional information if a single author is returned. String and regular expression arguments can be combined in the same command.

```
cpan> a /^nv/ LWALL
Author          NVPAT (Nathan V. Patwardhan)
Author          LWALL (Larry Wall. Author of Perl. Busy man.)

cpan> a /^nv/
Author id = NVPAT
    EMAIL       nvp@ora.com
    FULLNAME    Nathan V. Patwardhan
```

autobundle

autobundle *[bundlelist]*

Writes a bundle file containing a list of all modules that are both available from CPAN and currently installed within @INC. The file is written to the *Bundle* subdirectory of cpan_home with a name that contains the current date and a counter; for example, *Snapshot_1998_04_27_00.pm*. You can then use that file as input to the install command to install the latest versions of all the modules on your system:

```
perl -MCPAN -e 'install Bundle::Snapshot_1998_04_27_00'
```

b

b *[bundlelist]*

Searches for CPAN bundles. Arguments are the same as for the a command except they specify bundles. With a single argument, it displays details about the bundle; with multiple arguments, it displays a list.

clean

clean *[arglist]*

Does a *make clean* in the distribution file's directory. *arglist* can include one or more modules, bundles, distributions, or one of the values "r" or "u" to reinstall or uninstall.

d

d *[distriblist]*

Displays information about module distributions for the distribution(s) specified in *distriblist.* Arguments are the same as for the a command. Displays
details for a single argument, or a list if the output consists of multiple distributions.

force

force *method [arglist]*

Takes as a first argument the method to invoke, which can be one of make,
test, or install, and executes the command from scratch for each argument
in *arglist.* The arguments may be modules or distributions.

h

h

Displays brief help message. Same as ?.

i

i *[arglist]*

Displays information about the arguments specified in *arglist,* which can be
any of authors, modules, bundles, or distributions. Arguments and output are
the same as for a.

install

install *[arglist]*

Installs the arguments specified in *arglist,* which can be modules or distributions. Implies test. For a distribution, install is run unconditionally. For a
module, *CPAN.pm* checks to see if the module is up-to-date, and if so, prints
a message to that effect and does not do the install. Otherwise, it finds and
processes the distribution that contains the module.

look

look *arg*

Takes one argument, which is a module or distribution, gets and untars the
distribution file if necessary, changes to the appropriate directory, and opens
a subshell process in that directory.

m

m *[arglist]*

Displays information about modules. Arguments are the same as for the a command. Displays details for a single module, or a list if there is more than one in the output.

make

make *[arglist]*

Unconditionally runs a *make* on each argument in *arglist*, which can be a module or a distribution. For a module, *CPAN.pm* finds and processes the distribution that contains the module.

o

o *type [option] [value]*

Sets and queries options. Takes the following arguments:

type
> Type of options to set or query. The possible values are:
>
> debug
>> Debugging options. Prints CPAN module options for debugging the package.
>
> conf
>> Configuration options. Lists or sets values for CPAN module configuration variables kept in the hash %CPAN::Config. Here are the configuration variables from %CPAN::Config:

Variable	Content
build_cache	Size of cache for directories to build modules
build_dir	Locally accessible directory to build modules
index_expire	Number of days before refetching index files
cpan_home	Local directory reserved for this package
gzip	Location of external program *gzip*
inactivity_timeout	Breaks an interactive *Makefile.PL* after inactivity_timeout seconds of inactivity (set to 0 to never break)
inhibit_startup_message	If true, does not print startup message
keep_source	If set, keeps source in local directory

$\rightarrow$

keep_source_where	Where to keep source
make	Location of external *make* program
make_arg	Arguments to always pass to *make*
make_install_arg	Same as make_arg for *make install*
makepl_arg	Arguments to always pass to *perl Makefile.PL*
pager	Location of external *more* program (or other pager)
tar	Location of external *tar* program
unzip	Location of external *unzip* program
urllist	Arrayref to nearby CPAN sites (or equivalent locations such as CD-ROM)

option

The CPAN module configuration option or options; used with conf. Can be one or more scalar or list options from the table above.

value

Value to be set for a configuration option.

The possibilities for o conf are:

o conf *scalaropt*
Prints current value of scalar option

o conf *scalaropt value*
Sets scalar option to *value*

o conf *listopt*
Prints current value of list option in MakeMaker format

o conf *listopt* [shift|pop]
Shifts or pops the array in *listopt* variable

o conf *listopt* [unshift|push|splice] *list*
Works like the corresponding Perl functions to modify the array in *listopt* based on *list*

---

q

q

Quits the CPAN module shell subroutine.

---

r

r

Recommendations for reinstallation. With no argument, lists all distributions that are out of date. With an argument, tells you whether that module or distribution is out of date.

---

readme

readme *arglist*

Finds and displays the README file for modules or distributions in *arglist*.

recompile

recompile

Runs full *make/test/install* cycle over all installed dynamically loadable modules with force in effect. Useful for completing a network installation on systems after the first installation, where the CPAN module would otherwise declare the modules already up-to-date.

reload

reload *arg*

Reloads index files or re-evals *CPAN.pm* itself. *arg* may be:

cpan
> Re-eval *CPAN.pm*.

index
> Reload index of files.

test

test

Runs the *make test* command.

u

u

Lists all uninstalled distributions.

Documentation

Perl documentation is written in a language known as *pod* (plain old documentation). Pod is a set of simple tags that can be processed to produce documentation in the style of Unix manpages. There are also several utility programs available that process pod text and generate output in different formats. Pod tags can be intermixed with Perl commands, or they can be saved in a separate file, which usually has a *.pod* extension. The pod tags and the utility programs that are included in the Perl distribution are described in Chapter 4, *The Perl Language*.

Installing the Documentation

On Unix, the standard Perl installation procedure generates manpages for the Perl documentation from their pod format, although your system administrator might also choose to install the documentation as HTML files. You can also use this procedure to generate manpages for CPAN modules when you install them. You might need to modify your MANPATH environment variable to include the path to the Perl manpages, but then you should be able to read the documentation with the *man* command. In addition, Perl comes with its own command, *perldoc*, which formats the pod documentation and displays it. *perldoc* is particularly useful for reading module documentation, which might not be installed as manpages; you can also use it for reading the core Perl documentation.

The ActiveState Win32 port comes with documentation in HTML format; you can find it in the */docs* subdirectory of the distribution. Documentation specific to ActiveState's Perl for Win32 is installed in the */docs/Perl-Win32* subdirectory.

The native Win32 port installs the *perldoc* command for formatting and reading Perl documentation; it also provides an option during installation for the documentation to be formatted and saved as HTML files.

The Perl Manpages

Perl comes with lots of online documentation. To make life easier, the manpages have been divided into separate sections so you don't have to wade through hundreds of pages of text to find what you are looking for. You can read them with either the *man* command or with *perldoc*. Run `man perl` or `perldoc perl` to read the top-level page. That page in turn directs you to more specific pages. Or, if you know which page you want, you can go directly there by using:

```
% man perlvar
```

or:

```
% perldoc perlvar
```

The following table lists the sections in a logical order for reading through them:

Section	Description
perl	Overview (the top level)
perldelta	Changes since previous version
perlfaq	Frequently asked questions
perltoc	Table of contents for Perl documentation
perldata	Data structures
perlsyn	Syntax
perlop	Operators and precedence
perlre	Regular expressions
perlrun	Execution and options
perlfunc	Builtin functions
perlvar	Predefined variables
perlsub	Subroutines

Section	Description
perlmod	How modules work
perlmodlib	How to write and use modules
perlmodinstall	How to install modules from CPAN
perlform	Formats
perllocale	Locale support
perlref	References
perldsc	Data structures introduction
perllol	Data structures: lists of lists
perltoot	OO tutorial
perlobj	Objects
perltie	Objects hidden behind simple variables
perlbot	OO tricks and examples
perlipc	Interprocess communication
perldebug	Debugging
perldiag	Diagnostic messages
perlsec	Security
perltrap	Traps for the unwary
perlport	Portability guide
perlstyle	Style guide
perlpod	Plain old documentation
perlbook	Book information
perlembed	Embedding Perl in your C or C++ application
perlapio	Internal IO abstraction interface
perlxs	XS application programming interface
perlxstut	XS tutorial
perlguts	Internal functions for those doing extensions
perlcall	Calling conventions from C
perlhist	History records

PART II

Language Basics

CHAPTER 3

The Perl Interpreter

The *perl* executable, normally installed in */usr/bin* or */usr/local/bin* on your machine, is also called the *perl interpreter*. Every Perl program must be passed through the Perl interpreter in order to execute. The first line in many Perl programs is something like:

```
#!/usr/bin/perl
```

For Unix systems, this #! (hash-bang or shebang) line tells the shell to look for the */usr/bin/perl* program and pass the rest of the file to that program for execution. Sometimes you'll see different pathnames to the Perl executable, such as */usr/local/bin/perl*. You might see *perl5* instead of *perl* on sites that still depend on older versions of Perl. Or you'll see command-line options tacked on the end, such as the notorious *-w* switch, which produces warning messages. But almost all Perl programs on Unix start with some variation of this line.

If you get a mysterious "Command not found" error on a Perl program, it's often because the path to the Perl executable is wrong. When you download Perl programs off the Internet, copy them from one machine to another, or copy them out of a book (like this one!), the first thing you should do is make sure that the #! line points to the location of the Perl interpreter on your system.

So what does the Perl interpreter do? It compiles the program internally into a parse tree and then executes it immediately. Perl is commonly known as an interpreted language, but this is not strictly true. Since the interpreter actually does convert the program into byte code before executing it, it is sometimes called an *interpreter/compiler*, if anything at all.* Although the compiled form is not stored

---

* So do you call something a Perl "script" or a Perl "program"? Typically, the word "program" is used to describe something that needs to be compiled into assembler or byte code before executing, as in the C language, and the word "script" is used to describe something that runs through an interpreter, as in the Bourne shell. For Perl, you can use either phrase and not worry about offending anyone.

as a file, release 5.005 of Perl includes a working version of a standalone Perl compiler.

What does all this brouhaha mean for you? When you write a Perl program, you can just give it a correct #! line at the top of the script, make it executable with chmod +x, and run it. For 95% of Perl programmers in this world, that's all you'll care about.

Command Processing

In addition to specifying a #! line, you can also specify a short script directly on the command line. Here are some of the possible ways to run Perl:

- Issue the *perl* command, writing your script line by line via *−e* switches on the command line:

  ```
  perl -e 'print "Hello, world\n"'     #Unix
  perl -e "print \"Hello, world\n\""   #Win32
  ```

- Issue the *perl* command, passing Perl the name of your script as the first parameter (after any switches):

  ```
  perl testpgm
  ```

- On Unix systems that support the #! notation, specify the Perl command on the #! line, make your script executable, and invoke it from the shell (as described above).

- Pass your script to Perl via standard input. For example, under Unix:

  ```
  echo "print 'Hello, world'" | perl -
  ```

  or (unless ignoreeof is set):

  ```
  % perl
  print "Hello, world\n";
  ^D
  ```

- On Win32 systems, you can associate an extension (e.g., *.plx*) with a file type and double-click on the icon for a Perl script with that file type. If you are using the ActiveState version of Win32 Perl, the installation script normally prompts you to create the association.

- On Win32 systems, if you double-click on the icon for the Perl executable, you'll find yourself in a command-prompt window, with a blinking cursor. You can enter your Perl commands, indicating the end of your input with CTRL-Z, and Perl will compile and execute your script.

Perl parses the input file from the beginning, unless you've specified the *−x* switch (see the section "Command-Line Options" below). If there is a #! line, it is always examined for switches as the line is being parsed. Thus, switches behave consistently regardless of how Perl was invoked.

After locating your script, Perl compiles the entire script into an internal form. If there are any compilation errors, execution of the script is not attempted. If the script is syntactically correct, it is executed. If the script runs off the end without hitting an `exit` or `die` operator, an implicit `exit(0)` is provided to indicate successful completion.

Command-Line Options

Perl expects any command-line options, also known as *switches* or *flags*, to come first on the command line. The next item is usually the name of the script, followed by any additional arguments (often filenames) to be passed into the script. Some of these additional arguments may be switches, but if so, they must be processed by the script, since Perl gives up parsing switches as soon as it sees either a non-switch item or the special -- switch that terminates switch processing.

A single-character switch with no argument may be combined (bundled) with the switch that follows it, if any. For example:

```
#!/usr/bin/perl -spi.bak
```

is the same as:

```
#!/usr/bin/perl -s -p -i.bak
```

Perl recognizes the switches listed in Table 3-1.

Table 3-1: Perl Switches

Switch	Function
--	Terminates switch processing, even if the next argument starts with a minus. It has no other effect.
−0[*octnum*]	Specifies the record separator ($/) as an octal number. If *octnum* is not present, the null character is the separator. Other switches may precede or follow the octal number.
−a	Turns on autosplit mode when used with −*n* or −*p*. An implicit `split` of the @F array is inserted as the first command inside the implicit `while` loop produced by −*n* or −*p*. The default field delimiter is whitespace; a different field delimiter may be specified using −*F*.
−c	Causes Perl to check the syntax of the script and then exit without executing it. More or less equivalent to having `exit(0)` as the first statement in your program.
−d	Runs the script under the Perl debugger. See Chapter 6, *Debugging*.
−d:*foo*	Runs the script under the control of a debugging or tracing module installed in the Perl library as Devel::*foo*. For example, −*d:DProf* executes the script using the Devel::DProf profiler. See also the section on DProf in Chapter 6.

Table 3–1: Perl Switches (continued)

Switch	Function
−Dnumber *−Dlist*	Sets debugging flags. (This only works if debugging was compiled into the version of Perl you are running.) You may specify either a number that is the sum of the bits you want, or a list of letters. To watch how Perl executes your script, for instance, use *−D14* or *−Dslt*. Another useful value is *−D1024* (*−Dx*), which lists your compiled syntax tree. And *−D512* (*−Dr*) displays compiled regular expressions. The numeric value of the flags is available internally as the special variable $^D. Here are the assigned bit values:

Bit	Letter	Meaning
1	p	Tokenizing and parsing
2	s	Stack snapshots
4	l	Label stack processing
8	t	Trace execution
16	o	Object method lookup
32	c	String/numeric conversions
64	P	Print preprocessor command for −P
128	m	Memory allocation
256	f	Format processing
512	r	Regular expression processing
1,024	x	Syntax tree dump
2,048	u	Tainting checks
4,096	L	Memory leaks (not supported any more)
8,192	H	Hash dump—usurps *values*
16,384	X	Scratchpad allocation
32,768	D	Cleaning up

Switch	Function
−e commandline	May be used to enter one or more lines of script. If *−e* is used, Perl does not look for the name of a script in the argument list. Multiple *−e* commands may be given to build up a multiline script. (Make sure to use semicolons where you would in a normal program.)
−Fpattern	Specifies the pattern to split on if *−a* is also in effect. The pattern may be surrounded by //, " ", or ' '; otherwise it is put in single quotes.
−h	Prints a summary of Perl's command-line options.

Table 3-1: Perl Switches (continued)

Switch	Function
-i[extension]	Specifies that files processed by the <> construct are to be edited in-place. Perl does this by renaming the input file, opening the output file by the original name, and selecting that output file as the default for `print` statements. The extension, if supplied, is added to the name of the old file to make a backup copy. If no extension is supplied, no backup is made.
-Idirectory	Directories specified by *-I* are prepended to @INC, which holds the search path for modules. If *-P* is also specified, to invoke the C preprocessor, *-I* tells the preprocessor where to search for include files. By default, it searches */usr/include* and */usr/lib/perl*.
-l[octnum]	Enables automatic line-end processing. This switch has two effects: first, when it's used with *-n* or *-p*, it causes the line terminator to be automatically chomped, and second, it sets $\ to the value of *octnum* so any print statements will have a line terminator of ASCII value *octnum* added back on. If *octnum* is omitted, $\ is set to the current value of $/, which is typically a newline. So, to trim lines to 80 columns, say this: `perl -lpe 'substr($_, 80) = ""'`
-m[-]module *-M[-]module* *-M[-]'module* ... *-[mM][-]module* *arg[,arg]...* *-mmodule*	Executes use *module* before executing your script.
-Mmodule	Executes use *module* before executing your script. The command is formed by interpolation, so you can use quotes to add extra code after the module name, for example, *-M'module qw(foo bar)'*. If the first character after the *-M* or *-m* is a minus (-), then the use is replaced with no. You can also say *-m module=foo,bar* or *-Mmodule=foo,bar* as a shortcut for *-M'module qw(foo bar)'*. This avoids the need to use quotes when importing symbols. The actual code generated by *-Mmodule=foo,bar* is:

Table 3-1: Perl Switches (continued)

Switch	Function
	`use module split(/,/, q{foo,bar})` The = form removes the distinction between −*m* and −*M*.

−*n*	Causes Perl to assume the following loop around your script, which makes it iterate over filename arguments:
	
	    `LINE: while (<>) {`
	      `. . .` `# your script goes here`
	
	By default, the lines are not printed. See −*p* to have lines printed. BEGIN and END blocks may be used to capture control before or after the implicit loop.

−*p*	Causes Perl to assume the following loop around your script, which makes it iterate over filename arguments:
	
	    `LINE: while (<>) {`
	      `. . .` `# your script goes here } continue {`
	      `print; }`
	
	The lines are printed automatically. To suppress printing, use the −*n* switch. If both are specified, the −*p* switch overrides −*n*. BEGIN and END blocks may be used to capture control before or after the implicit loop.

−*P*	Causes your script to be run through the C preprocessor before compilation by Perl. (Since both comments and *cpp* directives begin with the # character, you should avoid starting comments with any words recognized by the C preprocessor such as `if`, `else`, or `define`.)
−*s*	Enables some rudimentary parsing of switches on the command line after the script name but before any filename arguments or the `--` switch terminator. Any switch found there is removed from `@ARGV`, and a variable of the same name as the switch is set in the Perl script. No switch bundling is allowed, since multicharacter switches are allowed.
−*S*	Makes Perl use the PATH environment variable to search for the script (unless the name of the script starts with a slash). Typically this is used to emulate #! startup on machines that don't support #!.

Table 3-1: Perl Switches (continued)

Switch	Function
-T	Forces "taint" checks to be turned on. Ordinarily, these checks are done only when running setuid or setgid. It's a good idea to turn them on explicitly for programs run on another user's behalf, such as CGI programs.
-u	Causes Perl to dump core after compiling your script. You can then take this core dump and turn it into an executable file by using the *undump* program (not supplied). This speeds startup at the expense of some disk space (which you can minimize by stripping the executable). If you want to execute a portion of your script before dumping, use Perl's dump operator instead. Note: availability of *undump* is platform-specific; it may not be available for a specific port of Perl.
-U	Allows Perl to do unsafe operations. Currently, the only "unsafe" operations are the unlinking of directories while running as superuser and running setuid programs with fatal taint checks turned into warnings.
-v	Prints the version and patch level of your Perl executable.
-V	Prints a summary of the major Perl configuration values and the current value of @INC.
-V:name	Prints the value of the named configuration variable to STDOUT.
-w	Prints warnings about identifiers that are mentioned only once and scalar variables that are used before being set. Also warns about redefined subroutines and references to undefined filehandles or to filehandles opened as read-only that you are attempting to write on. Warns you if you use a non-number as though it were a number, if you use an array as though it were a scalar, if your subroutines recurse more than 100 levels deep, etc.
-x [directory]	Tells Perl to extract a script that is embedded in a message, by looking for the first line that starts with #! and contains the string "perl". Any meaningful switches on that line after the word "perl" are applied. If a directory name is specified, Perl switches to that directory before running the script. The script must be terminated with _ _END_ _ or _ _DATA_ _ if there is trailing text to be ignored. (The script can process any or all of the trailing text via the DATA filehandle if desired.)

Environment Variables

Environment variables are used to set user preferences. Individual Perl modules or programs are always free to define their own environment variables, and there is also a set of special environment variables that are used in the CGI environment (see Chapter 9, *CGI Overview*).

Perl uses the following environment variables:

HOME
> Used if `chdir` has no argument.

LOGDIR
> Used if `chdir` has no argument and HOME is not set.

PATH
> Used in executing subprocesses and in finding the script if *−S* is used.

PATHEXT
> On Win32 systems, if you want to avoid typing the extension every time you execute a Perl script, you can set the PATHEXT environment variable so that it includes Perl scripts. For example:
>
> ```
> > set PATHEXT=%PATHEXT%;.PLX
> ```
>
> This setting lets you type:
>
> ```
> > myscript
> ```
>
> without including the file extension. Take care when setting PATHEXT permanently—it also includes executable file types like *.com, .exe, .bat,* and *.cmd.* If you inadvertently lose those extensions, you'll have difficulty invoking applications and script files.

PERL5LIB
> A colon-separated list of directories in which to look for Perl library files before looking in the standard library and the current directory. If PERL5LIB is not defined, PERLLIB is used. When running taint checks, neither variable is used. The script should instead say:
>
> ```
> use lib "/my/directory";
> ```

PERL5OPT
> Command-line options (switches). Switches in this variable are taken as if they were on every Perl command line. Only the *−[DIMUdmw]* switches are allowed. When running taint checks, this variable is ignored.

PERLLIB
> A colon-separated list of directories in which to look for Perl library files before looking in the standard library and the current directory. If PERL5LIB is defined, PERLLIB is not used.

PERL5DB

The command used to load the debugger code. The default is:

```
BEGIN { require 'perl5db.pl' }
```

PERL5SHELL

On Win32 systems, may be set to an alternative shell for Perl to use internally to execute "backtick" commands or the system function.

PERL_DEBUG_MSTATS

Relevant only if your Perl executable was built with –DDEBUG-GING_MSTATS. If set, causes memory statistics to be dumped after execution. If set to an integer greater than one, it also causes memory statistics to be dumped after compilation.

PERL_DESTRUCT_LEVEL

Relevant only if your Perl executable was built with –DDEBUGGING. Controls the behavior of global destruction of objects and other references.

Perl also has environment variables that control how Perl handles data specific to particular natural languages. See the *perllocale* manpage.

The Perl Compiler

A native-code compiler for Perl is now (as of Perl 5.005) part of the standard Perl distribution. The compiler allows you to distribute Perl programs in binary form, which enables easy packaging of Perl-based programs without having to depend on the source machine having the correct version of Perl and the correct modules installed. After the initial compilation, running a compiled program should be faster to the extent that it doesn't have to be recompiled each time it's run. However, you shouldn't expect that the compiled code itself will run faster than the original Perl source or that the executable will be smaller—in reality, the executable file is likely to be significantly bigger.

This initial release of the compiler is still considered to be a beta version. It's distributed as an extension module, B, that comes with the following backends:

Bytecode

Translates a script into platform-independent Perl byte code.

C   Translates a Perl script into C code.

CC Translates a Perl script into optimized C code.

Deparse

Regenerates Perl source code from a compiled program.

Lint

Extends the Perl *-w* option. Named after the Unix Lint program-checker.

Showlex

Shows lexical variables used in functions or files.

Xref

Creates a cross-reference listing for a program.

Once you've generated the C code with either the C or the CC backend, you run the *cc_harness* program to compile it into an executable. There is also a *byteperl* interpreter that lets you run the code you've generated with the Bytecode backend.

Here's an example that takes a simple "Hello world" program and uses the CC backend to generate C code:

```
% perl -MO=CC,-ohi.c hi.pl
hi.pl syntax OK
% perl cc_harness -O2 -ohi hi.c
gcc -B/usr/ccs/bin/ -D_REENTRANT -DDEBUGGING -I/usr/local/include
-I/usr/local/lib/perl5/sun4-solaris-thread/5.00466/CORE -O2 -ohi hi.c
-L/usr/local/lib /usr/local/lib/perl5/sun4-solaris-thread/5.00466/CORE/libperl.a
-lsocket -lnsl -lgdbm -ldl -lm -lposix4 -lpthread -lc -lcrypt
% hi
Hi there, world!
```

The compiler also comes with a frontend, *perlcc*. You can use it to compile code into a standalone executable, or to compile a module (a *.pm* file) into a shared object (an *.so* file) that can be included in a Perl program via *use*. For example:

```
% perlcc a.p        # compiles into the executable 'a'
% perlcc A.pm       # compiles into A.so
```

The following options can be used with *perlcc*:

−*argv arguments*
> Used with −*run* or −*e*. Passes the string *arguments* to the executable as @ARGV.

−*C c_code_name*
> Gives the name *c_code_name* to the generated C code that is to be compiled. Only valid if you are compiling one file on the command line.

−*e perl_line_to_execute*
> Works like *perl* −*e* to compile "one-liners." The default is to compile and run the code. With −*o*, it saves the resulting executable.

−*gen*
> Creates the intermediate C code but doesn't compile the results; does an implicit −*sav*.

−*I include_directories*
> Adds directories inside *include_directories* to the compilation command.

−*L library_directories*
> Adds directories in *library_directories* to the compilation command.

−*log logname*
> Opens a log file (for append) for saving text from a compile command.

−*mod*
> Tells *perlcc* to compile the files given at the command line as modules. Usually used with module files that don't end with *.pm*.

−*o executable_name*
> Gives the name *executable_name* to the executable that is to be compiled. Only valid if compiling one file on the command line.

−prog

> Tells *perlcc* to compile the files given at the command line as programs. Usually used with program files that don't end with a *.p*, *.pl*, or *.bat* extension.

−regex rename_regex

> Provides the rule *rename_regex* for creating executable filenames, where *rename_regex* is a Perl regular expression.

−run

> Immediately run the generated Perl code. Note that the rest of @ARGV is interpreted as arguments to the program being compiled.

−sav

> Tells Perl to save the intermediate C code.

−verbose verbose_level

> Compile verbosely, setting *verbose_level* to control the degree of verbosity. *verbose_level* can be given as either a sum of bits or a list of letters. Values are:

Bit	Letter	Action
1	g	Code generation errors to STDERR.
2	a	Compilation errors to STDERR.
4	t	Descriptive text to STDERR.
8	f	Code generation errors to file. Requires *−log*.
16	c	Compilation errors to file. Requires *−log*.
32	d	Descriptive text to file. Requires *−log*.

> With *−log*, the default level is 63; otherwise the default level is 7.

There are two environment variables that you can set for *perlcc*: PERL_SCRIPT_EXT and PERL_MODULE_EXT. These can be used to modify the default extensions that *perlcc* recognizes for programs and for modules. The variables take colon-separated Perl regular expressions.

The modules that comprise the compiler are described in Chapter 8, *Standard Modules*. Also see the documentation that comes with the compiler, which includes more complete information on installing and using it.

Threads

Perl 5.005 also includes the first release of a native multithreading capability, which is distributed with Perl as a set of modules. Since this is an initial release, the threads modules are considered to be beta software and aren't automatically compiled in with Perl. Therefore, the decision to use the threads feature has to be made during installation, so it can be included in the build of Perl. Or you might want to build a separate version of Perl for testing purposes.

Chapter 8 describes the individual Thread modules. For information on what threads are and how you might use them, see the article "Threads" in the Summer 1998 issue of *The Perl Journal*. There is also an explanation of threads in the book *Programming with Perl Modules* from O'Reilly's Perl Resource Kit, Win32 Edition.

CHAPTER 4

The Perl Language

This chapter is a quick and merciless guide to the Perl language itself. If you're try-ing to learn Perl from scratch, and you'd prefer to be taught rather than to have things thrown at you, then you might be better off with *Learning Perl* by Randal Schwartz and Tom Christiansen, or *Learning Perl on Win32 Systems* by Randal Schwartz, Erik Olson, and Tom Christiansen. However, if you already know some other programming languages and just want to hear the particulars of Perl, this chapter is for you. Sit tight, and forgive us for being terse: we have a lot of ground to cover.

If you want a more complete discussion of the Perl language and its idiosyncrasies (and we mean *complete*), see *Programming Perl* by Larry Wall, Tom Christiansen, and Randal Schwartz.

Program Structure

Perl is a particularly forgiving language, as far as program layout goes. There are no rules about indentation, newlines, etc. Most lines end with semicolons, but not everything has to. Most things don't have to be declared, except for a couple of things that do. Here are the bare essentials:

Whitespace
> Whitespace is required only between items that would otherwise be confused as a single term. All types of whitespace—spaces, tabs, newlines, etc.—are equivalent in this context. A comment counts as whitespace. Different types of whitespace are distinguishable within quoted strings, formats, and certain line-oriented forms of quoting. For example, in a quoted string, a newline, a space, and a tab are interpreted as unique characters.

Semicolons
> Every simple statement must end with a semicolon. Compound statements contain brace-delimited blocks of other statements and do not require

terminating semicolons after the ending brace. A final simple statement in a block also does not require a semicolon.

Declarations

Only subroutines and report formats need to be explicitly declared. All other user-created objects are automatically created with a null or 0 value unless they are defined by some explicit operation such as assignment. The *−w* command-line switch will warn you about using undefined values.

You may force yourself to declare your variables by including the use strict pragma in your programs (see Chapter 8, *Standard Modules*, for more information on pragmas and strict in particular). This makes it an error to not explicitly declare your variables.

Comments and documentation

Comments within a program are indicated by a pound sign (#). Everything following a pound sign to the end of the line is interpreted as a comment.

Lines starting with = are interpreted as the start of a section of embedded documentation (pod), and all subsequent lines until the next =cut are ignored by the compiler. See the "Pod" section later in this chapter for more information on pod format.

Data Types and Variables

Perl has three basic data types: *scalars*, *arrays*, and *hashes*.

Scalars are essentially simple variables. They are preceded by a dollar sign ($). A scalar is either a number, a string, or a reference. (A reference is a scalar that points to another piece of data. References are discussed later in this chapter.) If you provide a string where a number is expected or vice versa, Perl automatically converts the operand using fairly intuitive rules.

Arrays are ordered lists of scalars that you access with a numeric subscript (subscripts start at 0). They are preceded by an "at" sign (@).

Hashes are unordered sets of key/value pairs that you access using the keys as subscripts. They are preceded by a percent sign (%).

Numbers

Perl stores numbers internally as either signed integers or double-precision floating-point values. Numeric literals are specified in any of the following floating-point or integer formats:

```
12345             # integer
-54321            # negative integer
12345.67          # floating point
6.02E23           # scientific notation
0xffff            # hexadecimal
0377              # octal
4_294_967_296     # underline for legibility
```

Since Perl uses the comma as a list separator, you cannot use a comma for improving legibility of a large number. To improve legibility, Perl allows you to use an underscore character instead. The underscore only works within literal numbers specified in your program, not in strings functioning as numbers or in data read from somewhere else. Similarly, the leading 0x for hex and 0 for octal work only for literals. The automatic conversion of a string to a number does not recognize these prefixes—you must do an explicit conversion.

String Interpolation

Strings are sequences of characters. String literals are usually delimited by either single (') or double quotes ("). Double-quoted string literals are subject to backslash and variable interpolation, and single-quoted strings are not (except for \' and \\, used to put single quotes and backslashes into single-quoted strings). You can embed newlines directly in your strings.

Table 4-1 lists all the backslashed or escape characters that can be used in double-quoted strings.

Table 4-1: Double-Quoted String Representations

Code	Meaning
\n	Newline
\r	Carriage return
\t	Horizontal tab
\f	Form feed
\b	Backspace
\a	Alert (bell)
\e	ESC character
\033	ESC in octal
\x7f	DEL in hexadecimal
\cC	CTRL-C
\\	Backslash
\"	Double quote
\u	Force next character to uppercase
\l	Force next character to lowercase
\U	Force all following characters to uppercase
\L	Force all following characters to lowercase
\Q	Backslash all following non-alphanumeric characters
\E	End \U, \L, or \Q

Table 4-2 lists alternative quoting schemes that can be used in Perl. They are useful in diminishing the number of commas and quotes you may have to type, and also allow you to not worry about escaping characters such as backslashes when there are many instances in your data. The generic forms allow you to use any non-alphanumeric, non-whitespace characters as delimiters in place of the slash

(/). If the delimiters are single quotes, no variable interpolation is done on the pattern. Parentheses, brackets, braces, and angle brackets can be used as delimiters in their standard opening and closing pairs.

Table 4-2: Quoting Syntax in Perl

Customary	Generic	Meaning	Interpolates
' '	q//	Literal	No
" "	qq//	Literal	Yes
` `	qx//	Command	Yes
( )	qw//	Word list	No
//	m//	Pattern match	Yes
s///	s///	Substitution	Yes
y///	tr///	Translation	No

Lists

A list is an ordered group of scalar values. A literal list can be composed as a comma-separated list of values contained in parentheses, for example:

```
(1,2,3)                 # array of three values 1, 2, and 3
("one","two","three")   # array of three values "one", "two", and "three"
```

The generic form of list creation uses the quoting operator qw// to contain a list of values separated by white space:

```
qw/snap crackle pop/
```

Variables

A variable always begins with the character that identifies its type: $, @, or %. Most of the variable names you create can begin with a letter or underscore, followed by any combination of letters, digits, or underscores, up to 255 characters in length. Upper- and lowercase letters are distinct. Variable names that begin with a digit can only contain digits, and variable names that begin with a character other than an alphanumeric or underscore can contain only that character. The latter forms are usually predefined variables in Perl, so it is best to name your variables beginning with a letter or underscore.

Variables have the undef value before they are first assigned or when they become "empty." For scalar variables, undef evaluates to zero when used as a number, and a zero-length, empty string ("") when used as a string.

Simple variable assignment uses the assignment operator (=) with the appropriate data. For example:

```
$age = 26;              # assigns 26 to $age
@date = (8, 24, 70);    # assigns the three-element list to @date
```

```
%fruit = ('apples', 3, 'oranges', 6);
 # assigns the list elements to %fruit in key/value pairs
```

Scalar variables are always named with an initial $, even when referring to a scalar value that is part of an array or hash.

Every variable type has its own namespace. You can, without fear of conflict, use the same name for a scalar variable, an array, or a hash (or, for that matter, a filehandle, a subroutine name, or a label). This means that $foo and @foo are two different variables. It also means that $foo[1] is an element of @foo, not a part of $foo.

Arrays

An array is a variable that stores an ordered list of scalar values. Arrays are preceded by an "at" (@) sign.

```
@numbers = (1,2,3);        # Set the array @numbers to (1,2,3)
```

To refer to a single element of an array, use the dollar sign ($) with the variable name (it's a scalar), followed by the index of the element in square brackets (the *subscript operator*). Array elements are numbered starting at 0. Negative indexes count backwards from the last element in the list (i.e., −1 refers to the last element of the list). For example, in this list:

```
@date = (8, 24, 70);
```

$date[2] is the value of the third element, 70.

Hashes

A hash is a set of key/value pairs. Hashes are preceded by a percent (%) sign. To refer to a single element of a hash, you use the hash variable name followed by the "key" associated with the value in curly brackets. For example, the hash:

```
%fruit = ('apples', 3, 'oranges', 6);
```

has two values (in key/value pairs). If you want to get the value associated with the key apples, you use $fruit{'apples'}.

It is often more readable to use the => operator in defining key/value pairs. The => operator is similar to a comma, but it's more visually distinctive, and it also quotes any bare identifiers to the left of it:

```
%fruit = (
    apples  => 3,
    oranges => 6
);
```

Scalar and List Contexts

Every operation that you invoke in a Perl script is evaluated in a specific context, and how that operation behaves may depend on which context it is being called in. There are two major contexts: *scalar* and *list*. All operators know which context they are in, and some return lists in contexts wanting a list, and scalars in contexts

---

wanting a scalar. For example, the `localtime` function returns a nine-element list in list context:

```
($sec,$min,$hour,$mday,$mon,$year,$wday,$yday,$isdst) = localtime();
```

But in a scalar context, `localtime` returns the number of seconds since January 1, 1970:

```
$now = localtime();
```

Statements that look confusing are easy to evaluate by identifying the proper context. For example, assigning what is commonly a list literal to a scalar variable:

```
$a = (2, 4, 6, 8);
```

gives $a the value 8. The context forces the right side to evaluate to a scalar, and the action of the comma operator in the expression (in the scalar context) returns the value farthest to the right.

Another type of statement that might be confusing is the evaluation of an array or hash variable as a scalar, for example:

```
$b = @c;
```

When an array variable is evaluated as a scalar, the number of elements in the array is returned. This type of evaluation is useful for finding the number of elements in an array. The special $#*array* form of an array value returns the index of the last member of the list (one less than the number of elements).

If necessary, you can force a scalar context in the middle of a list by using the `scalar` function.

Declarations and Scope

In Perl, only subroutines and formats require explicit declaration. Variables (and similar constructs) are automatically created when they are first assigned.

Variable declaration comes into play when you need to limit the scope of a variable's use. You can do this in two ways:

- *Dynamic scoping* creates temporary objects within a scope. Dynamically scoped constructs are visible globally, but only take action within their defined scopes. Dynamic scoping applies to variables declared with `local`.

- *Lexical scoping* creates private constructs that are only visible within their scopes. The most frequently seen form of lexically scoped declaration is the declaration of `my` variables.

Therefore, we can say that a `local` variable is *dynamically scoped*, whereas a `my` variable is *lexically scoped*. Dynamically scoped variables are visible to functions called from within the block in which they are declared. Lexically scoped variables, on the other hand, are totally hidden from the outside world, including any called subroutines unless they are declared within the same scope.

See the "Subroutines" section later in this chapter for further discussion.

Statements

A simple statement is an expression evaluated for its side effects. Every simple statement must end in a semicolon, unless it is the final statement in a block.

A sequence of statements that defines a scope is called a *block*. Generally, a block is delimited by braces, or { }. Compound statements are built out of expressions and blocks. A conditional expression is evaluated to determine whether a statement block will be executed. Compound statements are defined in terms of blocks, not statements, which means that braces are required.

Any block can be given a label. *Labels* are identifiers that follow the variable-naming rules (i.e., they begin with a letter or underscore, and can contain alphanumerics and underscores). They are placed just before the block and are followed by a colon, like SOMELABEL here:

```
SOMELABEL: {
    ...statements...
    }
```

By convention, labels are all uppercase, so as not to conflict with reserved words. Labels are used with the loop-control commands next, last, and redo to alter the flow of execution in your programs.

Conditionals and Loops

The if and unless statements execute blocks of code depending on whether a condition is met. These statements take the following forms:

```
if (expression) {block} else {block}

unless (expression) {block} else {block}

if (expression1) {block}
elsif (expression2) {block}
    ...
elsif (lastexpression) {block}
else {block}
```

while loops

The while statement repeatedly executes a block as long as its conditional expression is true. For example:

```
while (<INFILE>) {
    print OUTFILE, "$_\n";
    }
```

This loop reads each line from the file opened with the filehandle INFILE and prints them to the OUTFILE filehandle. The loop will cease when it encounters an end-of-file.

If the word while is replaced by the word until, the sense of the test is reversed. The conditional is still tested before the first iteration, though.

The while statement has an optional extra block on the end called a continue block. This block is executed before every successive iteration of the loop, even if the main while block is exited early by the loop control command next. However, the continue block is not executed if the main block is exited by a last statement. The continue block is always executed before the conditional is evaluated again.

for loops

The for loop has three semicolon-separated expressions within its parentheses. These three expressions function respectively as the initialization, the condition, and the re-initialization expressions of the loop. The for loop can be defined in terms of the corresponding while loop:

```
for ($i = 1; $i < 10; $i++) {
    ...
}
```

is the same as:

```
$i = 1;
while ($i < 10) {
    ...
}
continue {
    $i++;
}
```

foreach loops

The foreach loop iterates over a list value and sets the control variable (var) to be each element of the list in turn:

```
foreach var (list) {
    ...
}
```

Like the while statement, the foreach statement can also take a continue block.

Modifiers

Any simple statement may be followed by a single modifier that gives the statement a conditional or looping mechanism. This syntax provides a simpler and often more elegant method than using the corresponding compound statements. These modifiers are:

```
statement if EXPR;
statement unless EXPR;
statement while EXPR;
statement until EXPR;
```

For example:

```
$i = $num if ($num < 50); # $i will be less than 50
$j = $cnt unless ($cnt < 100); # $j will equal 100 or greater
$lines++ while <FILE>;
print "$_\n" until /The end/;
```

The conditional is evaluated first with the while and until modifiers except when applied to a do {} statement, in which case the block executes once before the conditional is evaluated. For example:

```
do {
    $line = <STDIN>;
    ...
} until $line eq ".\n";
```

For more information on do, see Chapter 5, *Function Reference*.

Loop control

You can put a label on a loop to give it a name. The loop's label identifies the loop for the loop-control commands next, last, and redo.

```
LINE: while (<SCRIPT>) {
    print;
    next LINE if /^#/;        # discard comments
    }
```

The syntax for the loop-control commands is:

```
last label
next label
redo label
```

If the label is omitted, the loop-control command refers to the innermost enclosing loop.

The last command is like the break statement in C (as used in loops); it immediately exits the loop in question. The continue block, if any, is not executed.

The next command is like the continue statement in C; it skips the rest of the current iteration and starts the next iteration of the loop. If there is a continue block on the loop, it is always executed just before the conditional is about to be evaluated again.

The redo command restarts the loop block without evaluating the conditional again. The continue block, if any, is not executed.

goto

Perl supports a goto command. There are three forms: goto *label*, goto *expr*, and goto &*name*.

The goto *label* form finds the statement labeled with *label* and resumes execution there. It may not be used to go inside any construct that requires initialization, such as a subroutine or a foreach loop.

The goto *expr* form expects the expression to return a label name.

The goto &*name* form substitutes a call to the named subroutine for the currently running subroutine.

Special Variables

Some variables have a predefined and special meaning in Perl. They are the variables that use punctuation characters after the usual variable indicator ($, @, or %), such as $_. The explicit, long-form names shown are the variables' equivalents when you use the English module by including "use English;" at the top of your program.

Global Special Variables

The most commonly used special variable is $_, which contains the default input and pattern-searching string. For example, in the following lines:

```
foreach ('hickory','dickory','doc') {
        print;
}
```

The first time the loop is executed, "hickory" is printed. The second time around, "dickory" is printed, and the third time, "doc" is printed. That's because in each iteration of the loop, the current string is placed in $_, and is used by default by print. Here are the places where Perl will assume $_ even if you don't specify it:

- Various unary functions, including functions like ord and int, as well as the all file tests (-f, -d) except for -t, which defaults to STDIN.

- Various list functions like print and unlink.

- The pattern-matching operations m//, s///, and tr/// when used without an =~ operator.

- The default iterator variable in a foreach loop if no other variable is supplied.

- The implicit iterator variable in the grep and map functions.

- The default place to put an input record when a line-input operation's result is tested by itself as the sole criterion of a while test (i.e., <filehandle>). Note that outside of a while test, this will not happen.

The following is a complete listing of global special variables:

$_
$ARG
    The default input and pattern-searching space.

$.
$INPUT_LINE_NUMBER
$NR The current input line number of the last filehandle that was read. An explicit close on the filehandle resets the line number.

$/
$INPUT_RECORD_SEPARATOR
$RS The input record separator; newline by default. If set to the null string, it treats blank lines as delimiters.

`$,`
`$OUTPUT_FIELD_SEPARATOR`
`$OFS`
> The output field separator for the `print` operator.

`$\`
`$OUTPUT_RECORD_SEPARATOR`
`$ORS`
> The output record separator for the `print` operator.

`$"`
`$LIST_SEPARATOR`
> Like "`$,`" except that it applies to list values interpolated into a double-quoted string (or similar interpreted string). Default is a·space.

`$;`
`$SUBSCRIPT_SEPARATOR`
`$SUBSEP`
> The subscript separator for multidimensional array emulation. Default is "`\034`".

`$^L`
`$FORMAT_FORMFEED`
> What a format outputs to perform a formfeed. Default is "`\f`".

`$:`
`$FORMAT_LINE_BREAK_CHARACTERS`
> The current set of characters after which a string may be broken to fill continuation fields (starting with ^) in a format. Default is " `\n-`".

`$^A`
`$ACCUMULATOR`
> The current value of the `write` accumulator for `format` lines.

`$#`
`$OFMT`
> Contains the output format for printed numbers (deprecated).

`$?`
`$CHILD_ERROR`
> The status returned by the last pipe close, backtick (` `` `) command, or `system` operator.

`$!`
`$OS_ERROR`
`$ERRNO`
> If used in a numeric context, yields the current value of the `errno` variable, identifying the last system call error. If used in a string context, yields the corresponding system error string.

`$@`
`$EVAL_ERROR`
> The Perl syntax error message from the last `eval` command.

$$
$PROCESS_ID
$PID

> The pid of the Perl process running this script.

$<
$REAL_USER_ID
$UID

> The real user ID (uid) of this process.

$>
$EFFECTIVE_USER_ID
$EUID

> The effective uid of this process.

$(
$REAL_GROUP_ID
$GID

> The real group ID (gid) of this process.

$)
$EFFECTIVE_GROUP_ID
$EGID

> The effective gid of this process.

$0
$PROGRAM_NAME

> Contains the name of the file containing the Perl script being executed.

$[

> The index of the first element in an array and of the first character in a sub-
> string. Default is 0.

$]
$PERL_VERSION

> Returns the version plus patchlevel divided by 1000.

$^D
$DEBUGGING

> The current value of the debugging flags.

$^E
$EXTENDED_OS_ERROR

> Extended error message on some platforms.

$^F
$SYSTEM_FD_MAX

> The maximum system file descriptor, ordinarily 2.

$^H Contains internal compiler hints enabled by certain pragmatic modules.

$^I
$INPLACE_EDIT
> The current value of the inplace-edit extension. Use undef to disable inplace editing.

$^M The contents of $^M can be used as an emergency memory pool in case Perl dies with an out-of-memory error. Use of $^M requires a special compilation of Perl. See the INSTALL document for more information.

$^O
$OSNAME
> Contains the name of the operating system that the current Perl binary was compiled for.

$^P
$PERLDB
> The internal flag that the debugger clears so that it doesn't debug itself.

$^T
$BASETIME
> The time at which the script began running, in seconds since the epoch.

$^W
$WARNING
> The current value of the warning switch, either true or false.

$^X
$EXECUTABLE_NAME
> The name that the Perl binary itself was executed as.

$ARGV
> Contains the name of the current file when reading from <ARGV>.

Global Special Arrays and Hashes

@ARGV
> The array containing the command-line arguments intended for the script.

@INC
> The array containing the list of places to look for Perl scripts to be evaluated by the do, require, or use constructs.

@F The array into which the input lines are split when the −a command-line switch is given.

%INC
> The hash containing entries for the filename of each file that has been included via do or require.

%ENV
> The hash containing your current environment.

%SIG
> The hash used to set signal handlers for various signals.

Global Special Filehandles

ARGV

> The special filehandle that iterates over command line filenames in @ARGV. Usually written as the null filehandle in <>.

STDERR

> The special filehandle for standard error in any package.

STDIN

> The special filehandle for standard input in any package.

STDOUT

> The special filehandle for standard output in any package.

DATA

> The special filehandle that refers to anything following the __END__ token in the file containing the script. Or, the special filehandle for anything following the __DATA__ token in a required file, as long as you're reading data in the same package __DATA__ was found in.

_ (underscore)

> The special filehandle used to cache the information from the last stat, lstat, or file test operator.

Global Special Constants

__END__

> Indicates the logical end of your program. Any following text is ignored, but may be read via the DATA filehandle.

__FILE__

> Represents the filename at the point in your program where it's used. Not interpolated into strings.

__LINE__

> Represents the current line number. Not interpolated into strings.

__PACKAGE__

> Represents the current package name at compile time, or undefined if there is no current package. Not interpolated into strings.

Regular Expression Special Variables

For more information on regular expressions, see the "Regular Expressions" section later in this chapter.

$digit

> Contains the text matched by the corresponding set of parentheses in the last pattern matched. For example, $1 matches whatever was contained in the first set of parentheses in the previous regular expression.

`$&`

`$MATCH`

> The string matched by the last successful pattern match.

`` $` ``

`$PREMATCH`

> The string preceding whatever was matched by the last successful pattern match.

`$'`

`$POSTMATCH`

> The string following whatever was matched by the last successful pattern match.

`$+`

`$LAST_PAREN_MATCH`

> The last bracket matched by the last search pattern. This is useful if you don't know which of a set of alternative patterns was matched. For example:

```
/Version: (.*)|Revision: (.*)/ && ($rev = $+);
```

Filehandle Special Variables

Most of these variables only apply when using formats. See the "Formats" section later in this chapter.

`$|`

`$OUTPUT_AUTOFLUSH`

> If set to nonzero, forces an `fflush(3)` after every `write` or `print` on the currently selected output channel.

`$%`

`$FORMAT_PAGE_NUMBER`

> The current page number of the currently selected output channel.

`$=`

`$FORMAT_LINES_PER_PAGE`

> The current page length (printable lines) of the currently selected output channel. Default is 60.

`$-`

`$FORMAT_LINES_LEFT`

> The number of lines left on the page of the currently selected output channel.

`$~`

`$FORMAT_NAME`

> The name of the current report format for the currently selected output channel. Default is the name of the filehandle.

`$^`

`$FORMAT_TOP_NAME`

> The name of the current top-of-page format for the currently selected output channel. Default is the name of the filehandle with `_TOP` appended.

Operators

Table 4-3 lists all the Perl operators from highest to lowest precedence and indicates their associativity.

Table 4-3: Perl Associativity and Operators, Listed by Precedence

Associativity	Operators
Left	Terms and list operators (leftward)
Left	-> (method call, dereference)
Nonassociative	++ -- (autoincrement, autodecrement)
Right	** (exponentiation)
Right	! ~ \ and unary + and - (logical not, bit-not, reference, unary plus, unary minus)
Left	=~ !~ (matches, doesn't match)
Left	* / % x (multiply, divide, modulus, string replicate)
Left	+ - . (addition, subtraction, string concatenation)
Left	<< >> (left bit-shift, right bit-shift)
Nonassociative	Named unary operators and file-test operators
Nonassociative	< > <= >= lt gt le ge (less than, greater than, less than or equal to, greater than or equal to, and their string equivalents)
Nonassociative	== != <=> eq ne cmp (equal to, not equal to, signed comparison, and their string equivalents)
Left	& (bit-and)
Left	| ^ (bit-or, bit-xor)
Left	&& (logical AND)
Left	|| (logical OR)
Nonassociative	.. ... (range)
Right	?: (ternary conditional)
Right	= += -= *= and so on (assignment operators)
Left	, => (comma, arrow comma)
Nonassociative	List operators (rightward)
Right	not (logical not)
Left	and (logical and)
Left	or xor (logical or, xor)

You can make your expressions clear by using parentheses to group any part of an expression. Anything in parentheses will be evaluated as a single unit within a larger expression.

With very few exceptions, Perl operators act upon scalar values only, not upon list values.

Terms that take highest precedence in Perl include variables, quote and quotelike operators, any expression in parentheses, and any function whose arguments are in parentheses.

A list operator is a function that can take a list of values as its argument. List operators take highest precedence when considering what's to the left of them. They have considerably lower precedence when looking at their right side, which is the expected result.

Also parsed as high-precedence terms are the do{} and eval{} constructs, as well as subroutine and method calls, the anonymous array and hash composers ([] and {}), and the anonymous subroutine composer sub{}.

A unary operator is a function that takes a single scalar value as its argument. Unary operators have a lower precedence than list operators because they only expect and take one value.

The Arrow Operator

The arrow operator is a dereference operator. It can be used for references to arrays, hashes, code references, or for calling methods on objects. See the discussion of references in Chapter 7, *Packages, Modules, and Objects.*

Unary Operators

Unary ! performs logical negation, that is, "not." The not operator is a lower-precedence version of !.

Unary - performs arithmetic negation if the operand is numeric. If the operand is an identifier, then a string consisting of a minus sign concatenated with the identifier is returned. Otherwise, if the string starts with a plus or minus, a string starting with the opposite sign is returned.

Unary ~ performs bitwise negation, that is, one's complement. For example, on a 32-bit machine, ~0xFF is 0xFFFFFF00. If the argument to ~ is a string instead of a number, a string of identical length is returned, but with all the bits of the string complemented.

Unary + has no semantic effect whatsoever, even on strings. It is syntactically useful for separating a function name from a parenthesized expression that would otherwise be interpreted as the complete list of function arguments.

Unary \ creates a reference to whatever follows it (see "References and Complex Data Structures" later in this chapter). Do not confuse this behavior with the behavior of backslash within a string. The \ operator may also be used on a parenthesized list value in a list context, in which case it returns references to each element of the list.

Arithmetic Operators

Binary ** is the exponentiation operator. Note that it binds even more tightly than unary minus, so -2**4 is -(2**4), not (-2)**4. Note also that ** has right associativity, so:

```
$e = 2 ** 3 ** 4;
```

evaluates to 2 to the 81st power, not 8 to the 4th power.

The * (multiply) and / (divide) operators work exactly as you might expect, multiplying or dividing their two operands. Division is done in floating-point mode, unless integer mode in enabled (via use integer).

The % (modulus) operator converts its operands to integers before finding the remainder according to integer division. For the same operation in floating-point mode, you may prefer to use the fmod( ) function from the POSIX module (see Chapter 8).

Comparison Operators

Relational operators

Perl has two classes of relational operators. One class operates on numeric values, and the other operates on string values. String comparisons are based on the ASCII collating sequence. Relational operators are nonassociative, so $a < $b < $c is a syntax error.

Numeric	String	Meaning
>	gt	Greater than
>=	ge	Greater than or equal to
<	lt	Less than
<=	le	Less than or equal to

Equality operators

The equal and not-equal operators return 1 for true, and "" for false (just as the relational operators do). The <=> and *cmp* operators return −1 if the left operand is less than the right operand, 0 if they are equal, and +1 if the left operand is greater than the right.

Numeric	String	Meaning
==	eq	Equal to
!=	ne	Not equal to
<=>	cmp	Comparison, with signed result

Autoincrement and Autodecrement

If placed before a variable, the ++ and -- operators increment or decrement the variable before returning the value, and if placed after, they increment or decrement the variable after returning the value.

Assignment Operators

Perl recognizes the following operators for assigning a value to a variable:

```
=    **=    +=    *=    &=    <<=    &&=
           -=    /=    |=    >>=    ||=
           .=    %=    ^=
                 x=
```

Each operator requires a variable on the left side and some expression on the right side. For the simple assignment operator, =, the value of the expression is stored into the designated variable. For the other operators, Perl evaluates the expression:

```
$var OP= $value
```

as if it were written:

```
$var = $var OP $value
```

except that $var is evaluated only once. For example:

```
$a += 2; # same as $a = $a + 2
```

Pattern Match Operators

Binary =~ binds a scalar expression to a pattern match, substitution, or translation. These operations search or modify the string $_ by default.

Binary !~ is just like =~ except the return value is negated in the logical sense. The following expressions are functionally equivalent:

```
$string !~ /pattern/
not $string =~ /pattern/
```

See the section "Regular Expressions" later in this chapter.

File Test Operators

A file test operator is a unary operator that tests a filename or a filehandle.

Operator	Meaning
-r	File is readable by effective uid/gid.
-w	File is writable by effective uid/gid.
-x	File is executable by effective uid/gid.
-o	File is owned by effective uid.

Operator	Meaning
-R	File is readable by real uid/gid.
-W	File is writable by real uid/gid.
-X	File is executable by real uid/gid.
-O	File is owned by real uid.
-e	File exists.
-z	File has zero size.
-s	File has non-zero size (returns size).
-f	File is a plain file.
-d	File is a directory.
-l	File is a symbolic link.
-p	File is a named pipe (FIFO).
-S	File is a socket.
-b	File is a block special file.
-c	File is a character special file.
-t	Filehandle is opened to a tty.
-u	File has setuid bit set.
-g	File has setgid bit set.
-k	File has sticky bit set.
-T	File is a text file.
-B	File is a binary file (opposite of -T).
-M	Age of file (at startup) in days since modification.
-A	Age of file (at startup) in days since last access.
-C	Age of file (at startup) in days since inode change.

Logical Operators

Perl provides the && (logical AND) and || (logical OR) operators. They evaluate from left to right testing the truth of the statement.

Example	Name	Result
$a && $b	And	$a if $a is false, $b otherwise
$a || $b	Or	$a if $a is true, $b otherwise

For example, an oft-appearing idiom in Perl programs is:

```
open(FILE, "somefile") || die "Cannot open somefile: $!\n";
```

In this case, Perl first evaluates the open function. If the value is true (because somefile was successfully opened), the execution of the die function is unnecessary and is skipped.

Perl also provides lower-precedence and and or operators that are more readable.

Bitwise Operators

Perl has bitwise AND, OR, and XOR (exclusive OR) operators: &, |, and ^. These operators work differently on numeric values than they do on strings. If either operand is a number, then both operands are converted to integers, and the bitwise operation is performed between the two integers. If both operands are strings, these operators do bitwise operations between corresponding bits from the two strings.

Miscellaneous Operators

Range operator

The .. range operator is really two different operators depending on the context. In a list context, it returns a list of values counting (by ones) from the left value to the right value.

In a scalar context, .. returns a Boolean value. It is false as long as its left operand is false. Once the left operand is true, the range operator stays true until the right operand is true, after which the range operator becomes false again. The right operand is not evaluated while the operator is in the false state, and the left operand is not evaluated while the operator is in the true state.

The alternate version of this operator, ..., does not test the right operand immediately when the operator becomes true; it waits until the next evaluation.

Conditional operator

Ternary ?: is the conditional operator. It works much like an if-then-else statement, but it can safely be embedded within other operations and functions.

```
test_expr ? if_true_expr : if_false_expr
```

If the test_expr is true, only the if_true_expr is evaluated. Otherwise, only the if_false_expr is evaluated. Either way, the value of the evaluated expression becomes the value of the entire expression.

Comma operator

In a list context, "," is the list argument separator and inserts both its arguments into the list. In scalar context, "," evaluates its left argument, throws that value away, then evaluates its right argument and returns that value.

The => operator is mostly just a synonym for the comma operator. It's useful for documenting arguments that come in pairs. It also forces any identifier to the left of it to be interpreted as a string.

String operator

The concatenation operator "." is used to add strings together:

```
print 'abc' . 'def';        # prints abcdef
print $a . $b;              # concatenates the string values of $a and $b
```

Binary x is the string repetition operator. In scalar context, it returns a concatenated string consisting of the left operand repeated the number of times specified by the right operand.

```
print '-' x 80;                     # prints row of dashes
print "\t" x ($tab/8), ' ' x ($tab%8);    # tabs over
```

In list context, if the left operand is a list in parentheses, the x works as a list replicator rather than a string replicator. This is useful for initializing all the elements of an array of indeterminate length to the same value:

```
@ones = (1) x 80;           # a list of 80 1s
@ones = (5) x @ones;        # set all elements to 5
```

Regular Expressions

Regular expressions are used several ways in Perl. They're used in conditionals to determine whether a string matches a particular pattern. They're also used to find patterns in strings and replace the match with something else.

The ordinary pattern match operator looks like /pattern/. It matches against the $_ variable by default. If the pattern is found in the string, the operator returns true ("1"); if there is no match, a false value ("") is returned.

The substitution operator looks like s/pattern/replace/. This operator searches $_ by default. If it finds the specified pattern, it is replaced with the string in replace. If pattern is not matched, nothing happens.

You may specify a variable other than $_ with the =~ binding operator (or the negated !~ binding operator, which returns true if the pattern is not matched). For example:

```
$text =~ /sampo/;
```

Pattern-Matching Operators

The following list defines Perl's pattern-matching operators. Some of the operators have alternative "quoting" schemes and have a set of modifiers that can be placed directly after the operators to affect the match operation in some way.

m/pattern/gimosx
> Searches a string for a pattern match. Modifiers are:

Modifier	Meaning
g	Match globally, i.e., find all occurrences.
i	Do case-insensitive pattern matching.

Modifier	Meaning
m	Treat string as multiple lines.
o	Only compile pattern once.
s	Treat string as single line.
x	Use extended regular expressions.

If / is the delimiter, then the initial m is optional. With the m, you can use any pair of non-alphanumeric, non-whitespace characters as delimiters.

?pattern?

This operator is just like the m/*pattern*/ search, except it matches only once.

qr/*pattern*/imosx

Creates a precompiled regular expression from *pattern*, which can be passed around in variables and interpolated into other regular expressions. The modifiers are the same as those for m// above.

s/*pattern*/*replacement*/egimosx

Searches a string for *pattern*, and replaces any match with the *replacement* text. Returns the number of substitutions made, which can be more than one with the /g modifier. Otherwise, it returns false (0). If no string is specified via the =~ or !~ operator, the $_ variable is searched and modified. Modifiers are:

Modifier	Meaning
e	Evaluate the right side as an expression.
g	Replace globally, i.e., all occurrences.
i	Do case-insensitive pattern matching.
m	Treat string as multiple lines.
o	Only compile pattern once.
s	Treat string as single line.
x	Use extended regular expressions.

Any non-alphanumeric, non-whitespace delimiter may replace the slashes. If single quotes are used, no interpretation is done on the replacement string (the /e modifier overrides this, however).

tr/*pattern1*/*pattern2*/cds
y/*pattern1*/*pattern2*/cds

This operator scans a string, character by character, and replaces all occurrences of the characters found in *pattern1* with the corresponding character in *pattern2*. It returns the number of characters replaced or deleted. If no string is specified via the =~ or !~ operator, the $_ string is translated. Modifiers are:

Modifier	Meaning
c	Complement *pattern1*.
d	Delete found but unreplaced characters.
s	Squash duplicate replaced characters.

Regular Expression Syntax

The simplest kind of regular expression is a literal string. More complicated patterns involve the use of *metacharacters* to describe all the different choices and variations that you want to build into a pattern. Metacharacters don't match themselves, but describe something else. The metacharacters are:

Metacharacter	Meaning
\	Escapes the character(s) immediately following it
.	Matches any single character except a newline (unless /s is used)
^	Matches at the beginning of the string (or line, if /m used)
$	Matches at the end of the string (or line, if /m used)
*	Matches the preceding element 0 or more times
+	Matches the preceding element 1 or more times
?	Matches the preceding element 0 or 1 times
{ . . . }	Specifies a range of occurrences for the element preceding it
[. . .]	Matches any one of the class of characters contained within the brackets
(. . .)	Groups regular expressions
|	Matches either the expression preceding or following it

The "." (single dot) is a wildcard character. When used in a regular expression, it can match any single character. The exception is the newline character (\n), except when you use the /s modifier on the pattern match operator. This modifier treats the string to be matched against as a single "long" string with embedded newlines.

The ^ and $ metacharacters are used as anchors in a regular expression. The ^ matches the beginning of a line. This character should only appear at the beginning of an expression to match the line beginning. The exception to this is when the /m (multi-line) modifier is used, in which case it will match at the beginning of the string and after every newline (except the last, if there is one). Otherwise, ^ will match itself, unescaped, anywhere in a pattern, except if it is the first character in a bracketed character class, in which case it negates the class.

Similarly, $ will match the end of a line (just before a newline character) only if it is at the end of a pattern, unless /m is used, in which case it matches just before every newline and at the end of a string. You need to escape $ to match a literal dollar sign in all cases, because if $ isn't at the end of a pattern (or placed right before a) or]), Perl will attempt to do variable interpretation. The same holds true for the @ sign, which Perl will interpret as an array variable start unless it is backslashed.

The *, +, and ? metacharacters are called *quantifiers*. They specify the number of times to match something. They act on the element immediately preceding them, which could be a single character (including the .), a grouped expression in parentheses, or a character class. The { . . . } construct is a generalized modifier.

You may put two numbers separated by a comma within the braces to specify minimum and maximum numbers that the preceding element can match.

Parentheses are used to group characters or expressions. They also have the side effect of remembering what they matched so you can recall and reuse patterns with a special group of variables.

The | is the alternation operator in regular expressions. It matches either what's on its left side or right side. It does not only affect single characters. For example:

```
/you|me|him|her/
```

looks for any of the four words. You should use parentheses to provide boundaries for alternation:

```
/And(y|rew)/
```

This will match either "Andy" or "Andrew".

Escaped Sequences

The following table lists the backslashed representations of characters that you can use in regular expressions:

Code	Matches
\a	Alarm (beep)
\n	Newline
\r	Carriage return
\t	Tab
\f	Formfeed
\e	Escape
\007	Any octal ASCII value
\x7f	Any hexadecimal ASCII value
\cx	Control-x

Character Classes

The [. . .] construct is used to list a set of characters (a *character class*) of which *one* will match. Brackets are often used when capitalization is uncertain in a match:

```
/[tT]here/
```

A dash (-) may be used to indicate a range of characters in a character class:

```
/[a-zA-Z]/;  # match any single letter
/[0-9]/;     # match any single digit
```

To put a literal dash in the list you must use a backslash before it (\-).

By placing a ^ as the first element in the brackets, you create a negated character class, i.e., it matches any character not in the list. For example:

```
/[^A-Z]/; matches any character other than an uppercase letter
```

Some common character classes have their own predefined escape sequences for your programming convenience:

Code	Matches
\d	A digit, same as [0-9]
\D	A nondigit, same as [^0-9]
\w	A word character (alphanumeric), same as [a-zA-Z_0-9]
\W	A nonword character, [^a-zA-Z_0-9]
\s	A whitespace character, same as [\t\n\r\f]
\S	A non-whitespace character, [^ \t\n\r\f]

These elements match any single element in (or not in) their class. A \w matches only one character of a word. Using a modifier, you can match a whole word, for example, with \w+. The abbreviated classes may also be used within brackets as elements of other character classes.

Anchors

Anchors don't match any characters; they match places within a string. The two most common anchors are ^ and $, which match the beginning and end of a line, respectively. This table lists the anchoring patterns used to match certain boundaries in regular expressions:

Assertion	Meaning
^	Matches at the beginning of the string (or line, if /m used)
$	Matches at the end of the string (or line, if /m used)
\b	Matches at word boundary (between \w and \W)
\B	Matches except at word boundary
\A	Matches at the beginning of the string
\Z	Matches at the end of the string or before a newline
\z	Matches only at the end of the string
\G	Matches where previous m//g left off

The $ and \Z assertions can match not only at the end of the string, but also one character earlier than that, if the last character of the string happens to be a newline.

Quantifiers

Quantifiers are used to specify how many instances of the previous element can match. For instance, you could say "match any number of a's, including none" (a*), or match between five and ten instances of the word "owie" ((owie){5,10}).

Quantifiers, by nature, are greedy. That is, the way the Perl regular expression "engine" works is that it will look for the biggest match possible (the farthest to the right) unless you tell it not to. Say you are searching a string that reads:

```
a whatever foo, b whatever foo
```

and you want to find a and foo with something in between. You might use:

```
/a.*foo/
```

A `.` followed by a `*` looks for any character, any number of times, until foo is found. But since Perl will look as far to the right as possible to find foo, the first instance of foo is swallowed up by the greedy `.*` expression.

All the quantifiers therefore have a notation that allows for minimal matching, so they are non-greedy. This notation uses a question mark immediately following the quantifier to force Perl to look for the earliest available match (farthest to the left). The following table lists the regular expression quantifiers and their non-greedy forms:

Maximal	Minimal	Allowed Range
{n,m}	{n,m}?	Must occur at least n times but no more than m times
{n,}	{n,}?	Must occur at least n times
{n}	{n}?	Must match exactly n times
*	*?	0 or more times (same as {0,})
+	+?	1 or more times (same as {1,})
?	??	0 or 1 time (same as {0,1})

Pattern Match Variables

Parentheses not only serve to group elements in a regular expression, they also remember the patterns they match. Every match from a parenthesized element is saved to a special, read-only variable indicated by a number. You can recall and reuse a match by using these variables.

Within a pattern, each parenthesized element saves its match to a numbered variable, in order starting with 1. You can recall these matches within the expression by using \1, \2, and so on.

Outside of the matching pattern, the matched variables are recalled with the usual dollar-sign, i.e., $1, $2, etc. The dollar sign notation should used in the replacement expression of a substitution and anywhere else you might want to use them in your program. For example, to implement "i before e, except after c":

```
s/([^c])ei/$1ie/g;
```

The backreferencing variables are:

$+   Returns the last parenthesized pattern match

$&   Returns the entire matched string

$`   Returns everything before the matched string

$'   Returns everything after the matched string

Backreferencing with these variables will slow down your program noticeably for all regular expressions.

Extended Regular Expressions

Perl defines an extended syntax for regular expressions. The syntax is a pair of parentheses with a question mark as the first thing within the parentheses. The character after the question mark gives the function of the extension. The extensions are:

(?#text)
> A comment. The text is ignored.

(?: . . .)
> This groups things like "(. . .)" but doesn't make backreferences.

(?= . . .)
> A zero-width positive lookahead assertion. For example, /\w+(?=\t)/ matches a word followed by a tab, without including the tab in $&.

(?! . . .)
> A zero-width negative lookahead assertion. For example, /foo(?!bar)/ matches any occurrence of "foo" that isn't followed by "bar".

(?<= . . .)
> A zero-width positive lookbehind assertion. For example, /(?<=bad)boy/ matches the word boy that follows bad, without including bad in $&. This only works for fixed-width lookbehind.

(?<!= . . .)
> A zero-width negative lookbehind assertion. For example, /(?<!=bad)boy/ matches any occurrence of "boy" that doesn't follow "bad". This only works for fixed-width lookbehind.

(?> . . .)
> Matches the substring that the standalone pattern would match if anchored at the given position.

(?(condition)yes-pattern|no-pattern)
(?(condition)yes-pattern)
> Matches a pattern determined by a condition. The *condition* should be either an integer, which is "true" if the pair of parentheses corresponding to the integer has matched, or a lookahead, lookbehind, or evaluate, zero-width assertion. The *no-pattern* will be used to match if the condition was not meant, but it is also optional.

(?imsx-imsx)
> One or more embedded pattern-match modifiers. Modifiers are switched off if they follow a – (dash). The modifiers are defined as follows:

Modifier	Meaning
i	Do case-insensitive pattern matching
m	Treat string as multiple lines
s	Treat string as single line
x	Use extended regular expressions

Subroutines

Subroutines are declared using one of these forms:

```
sub name {block}
sub name (proto) {block}
```

Prototypes allow you to put constraints on the arguments you provide to your subroutines.

You can also create anonymous subroutines at run-time, which will be available for use through a reference:

```
$subref = sub {block};
```

Calling Subroutines

The ampersand (&) is the identifier used to call subroutines. Most of the time, however, subroutines can be used in an expression just like built-in functions. To call subroutines directly:

```
name(args);               # & is optional with parentheses
name args;                # Parens optional if predeclared/imported
&name;                    # Passes current @_ to subroutine
```

To call subroutines indirectly (by name or by reference):

```
&$subref(args);           # & is not optional on indirect call
&$subref;                 # Passes current @_ to subroutine
```

Passing Arguments

All arguments to a subroutine are passed as a single, flat list of scalars, and return values are returned the same way. Any arrays or hashes passed in these lists will have their values interpolated into the flattened list.

Any arguments passed to a subroutine come in as the array @_.

You may use the explicit return statement to return a value and leave the subroutine at any point.

Passing References

If you want to pass more than one array or hash into or out of a function and have them maintain their integrity, then you will want to pass references as arguments. The simplest way to do this is to take your named variables and put a backslash in front of them in the argument list:

```
@returnlist = ref_conversion(\@temps1, \@temps2, \@temps3);
```

This sends references to the three arrays to the subroutine (and saves you the step of creating your own named references to send to the function). The references to the arrays are passed to the subroutine as the three-member @_ array. The subroutine will have to dereference the arguments so that the data values may be used.

Returning references is a simple matter of returning scalars that are references. This way you can return distinct hashes and arrays.

Private and Local Variables

Any variables you use in the function that aren't declared private are global variables. In subroutines, you'll often want to use variables that won't be used anywhere else in your program, and you don't want them taking up memory when the subroutine is not being executed. You also might not want to alter variables in subroutines that might have the same name as global variables.

The my function declares variables that are *lexically scoped* within the subroutine. Lexically scoped variables are private variables that only exist within the block or subroutine in which they are declared. Outside of their scope, they are invisible and can't be altered in any way.

To scope multiple variables at once, use a list in parentheses. You can also assign a variable in a my statement:

```
my @list = (44, 55, 66);
my $cd = "orb";
```

Dynamic variables are visible to other subroutines called from within their scope. Dynamic variables are defined with local, and they are not private variables, but rather they are global variables with temporary values. When a subroutine is executed, the global value is hidden away, and the local value is used. Once the scope is exited, the original global value is used. Most of the time you will want to use my to localize parameters in a subroutine.

Prototypes

Prototypes allow you to design your subroutines to take arguments with constraints on the number of parameters and types of data. To declare a function with prototypes, use the prototype symbols in the declaration line, like this:

```
sub addem ($$) {
}
```

In this case, the function expects two scalar arguments. The following table gives the various prototype symbols:

Symbol	Meaning
$	Scalar
@	List
%	Hash
&	Anonymous subroutine
*	Typeglob

A backslash placed before one of these symbols forces the argument to be that exact variable type. For instance, a function that requires a hash variable would be declared like this:

```
sub hashfunc (\%);
```

Unbackslashed @ or % symbols act exactly alike, and will eat up all remaining arguments, forcing list context. A $ likewise forces scalar context on an argument, so taking an array or hash variable for that parameter would probably yield unwanted results.

A semicolon separates mandatory arguments from optional arguments. For example:

```
sub newsplit (\@$;$);
```

requires two arguments: an array variable and a scalar. The third scalar is optional. Placing a semicolon before @ and % is not necessary since lists can be null.

A typeglob prototype symbol (*) will always turn its argument into a reference to a symbol table entry. It is most often used for filehandles.

References and Complex Data Structures

A Perl reference is a fundamental data type that "points" to another piece of data or code. A reference knows the location of the information and what type of data is stored there.

A reference is a scalar and can be used anywhere a scalar can be used. Any array element or hash value can contain a reference (a hash key cannot contain a reference), and this is how nested data structures are built in Perl. You can construct lists containing references to other lists, which can contain references to hashes, and so on.

Creating References

You can create a reference to an existing variable or subroutine by prefixing it with a backslash:

```
$a = "fondue";
@alist = ("pitt", "hanks", "cage", "cruise");
%song = ("mother" => "crying", "brother" => "dying");
sub freaky_friday { s/mother/daughter/ }
```

```
# Create references
$ra = \$a;
$ralist = \@alist;
$rsong = \%song;
$rsub = \&freaky_friday; # '&' required for subroutine names
```

References to scalar constants are created similarly:

```
$pi = \3.14159;
$myname = \"Charlie";
```

Note that all references are prefixed by a $, even if they refer to an array or hash. All references are scalars, thus you can copy a reference to another scalar or even reference another reference:

```
$aref = \@names;
$bref = $aref;  # both refer to @names
$cref = \$aref; # $cref is a reference to $aref
```

Because arrays and hashes are collections of scalars, you can create references to individual elements by prefixing their names with backslashes:

```
$star = \$alist[2];       # refers to third element of @alist
$action = \$song{mother}; # refers to the 'mother' value of %song
```

Referencing anonymous data

It is also possible to take references to literal data not stored in a variable. This data is called *anonymous* because it is not bound to any named variable.

To create a reference to a scalar constant, simply backslash the literal string or number.

To create a reference to an anonymous array, place the list of values in square brackets:

```
$shortbread = [ "flour", "butter", "eggs", "sugar" ];
```

This creates a reference to an array, but the array is only available through the reference $shortbread.

A reference to an anonymous hash uses curly braces around the list of elements:

```
$cast =  { host     => "Space Ghost",
           musician => "Zorak",
           director => "Moltar" };
```

Dereferencing

Dereferencing returns the value a reference points to. The general method of dereferencing uses the reference variable substituted for the regular name part of a variable. If $r is a reference, then $$r, @$r, or %$r retrieve the value being referred to, depending on whether $r is pointing to a scalar, array, or hash. A reference can be used in all the places where an ordinary data type can be used.

When a reference is accidentally evaluated as a plain scalar, it returns a string that indicates what type of data it points to and the memory address of the data.

If you just want to know which type of data is being referenced, use ref, which returns one of the following strings if its argument is a reference. Otherwise, it returns false.

```
SCALAR
ARRAY
HASH
CODE
GLOB
REF
```

Arrow dereferencing

References to arrays, hashes, and subroutines can be dereferenced using the -> operator. This operator dereferences the expression to its left, which must resolve to an array or hash, and accesses the element represented by the subscripted expression on its right. For example, these three statement are equivalent:

```
$$arrayref[0] = "man";
${$arrayref}[0] = "man";
$arrayref->[0] = "man";
```

The first statement dereferences $arrayref first and then finds the first element of that array. The second uses braces to clarify this procedure. The third statement uses the arrow notation to do the same thing.

The arrow dereferencing notation can only be used to access a single scalar value. You cannot use arrow operators in expressions that return either slices or whole arrays or hashes.

Filehandles

A filehandle is the name for an I/O connection between your Perl process and the operating system. Filehandle names are like label names, but use their own namespace. Like label names, the convention is to use all uppercase letters for file-handle names.

Every Perl program has three filehandles that are automatically opened: STDIN, STDOUT, and STDERR. By default, the print and write functions write to STD-OUT. Additional filehandles are created using the open function:

```
open (DATA, "numbers.txt");
```

DATA is the new filehandle that is attached to the external file, which is now opened for reading. You can open filehandles for reading, writing, and appending to external files and devices. To open a file for writing, prefix the filename with a greater-than sign:

```
open(OUT, ">outfile");
```

To open a file for appending, prefix the filename with two greater-than signs:

```
open(LOGFILE, ">>error_log");
```

The open function returns true if the file is successfully opened, and false if it failed to open. Opening a file can fail for any number of reasons: a file does not exist, is write-protected, or you don't have permission for a file or directory. However, a filehandle that has not been successfully opened can still be read from (giving you an immediate EOF) or written to, with no noticeable effects.

You should always check the result of open immediately and report an error if the operation does not succeed. The warn function can report an error to standard error if something goes wrong, and die can terminate your program and tell you what went wrong. For example:

```
open(LOGFILE, "/usr/httpd/error_log")
        || warn "Could not open /usr/httpd/error_log.\n";
open(DATA, ">/tmp/data") || die "Could not create /tmp/data\n.";
```

Once the file is opened, you can access the data using the diamond operator, <filehandle>. This is the line-input operator. When used on a filehandle in a scalar context, it will return a line from a filehandle as a string. Each time it is called it will return the next line from the filehandle, until it reaches the end-of-file. The operator keeps track of which line it is on in the file, unless the filehandle is closed and reopened, resetting the operator to the top-of-file.

For example, to print any line containing the word "secret.html" from the LOGFILE filehandle:

```
while (<LOGFILE>) {
        print "$_\n" if /secret\.html/;
}
```

In a list context, the line-input operator returns a list in which each line is an element. The empty <> operator reads from the ARGV filehandle, which reads the array of filenames from the Perl command line. If @ARGV is empty, the operator resorts to standard input.

A number of functions send output to a filehandle. The filehandle must already be opened for writing, of course. In the previous example, print wrote to the STDOUT filehandle, even though it wasn't specified. Without a filehandle, print defaults to the currently selected output filehandle, which will be STDOUT until you open and select another one in your program. See the select function (filehandle version) for more information.

If your program involves more than a couple of open filehandles, you should be safe and specify the filehandles for all of your IO functions:

```
print LOGFILE "====== Generated report $date ======"
```

To close a filehandle, use the close function. Filehandles are also closed when the program exits.

Formats

Formats are a mechanism for generating formatted reports for outputting data. Formats are defined with the format keyword. The general form looks like:

```
format name =
...template lines...
...argument line...
.
```

Most of your format names will be the same as the filehandle names for which they are used. The default format for a filehandle is the one with the same name.

The format definition is like a subroutine definition. It doesn't contain immediately executed code and can therefore be placed anywhere in the file with the rest of the program; they are commonly placed near the end of the file with subroutine definitions. To output to a format, use the write function instead of print.

The template lines contain literal text and fieldholders. Fieldholders contain symbols that describe the size and positioning of the area on the line where data is output. An argument line immediately follows a template line that contains the fields to be replaced by data. The argument line is a list of variables (or expressions), separated by commas, which fill the fields in the previous line in the order they are listed.

Here's an example of a template line with two fieldholders, and the argument line that follows:

```
Hello, my name is @<<<<<<<<<< and I'm @<< years old.
$name, $age
```

The fieldholders are the @<<<<<<<<<< and @<<, which specify left-justified text fields with 11 and 3 characters, respectively.

Most fieldholders start with @. The characters following the @ indicate the type of field, while the number of characters (including the @) indicate the field width. The following fieldholder characters determine the positioning of text fields:

<<<< (left angle-brackets)
> A left-justified field; if the value is shorter than the field width, it will be padded on the right with spaces.

>>>> (right angle-brackets)
> A right-justified field; if the value is too short, it gets padded on the left with spaces.

|||| (vertical bars)
> A centered field; if the value is too short, it gets padded on both sides with spaces, enough on each side to make the value mostly centered within the field.

Another kind of fieldholder is a *fixed-precision numeric field*. This field also begins with @, and is followed by one or more hashmarks (###) with an optional dot (indicating a decimal point). For example:

```
format MONEY =
Assets: @#####.## Liabilities: @######.## Net: @#####.##
$assets, $liabilities, $assets-$liabilities
```

The multiline fieldholder allows you to include a value that may have many lines of information. This fieldholder is denoted by @* on a line by itself. The next line

---

defines the value that will be substituted into the field, which in this case may be an expression that results in a value that contains many newlines.

Another kind of fieldholder is a *filled field*. This fieldholder allows you to create a filled paragraph, breaking the text into conveniently sized lines at word boundaries, wrapping the lines as needed. A filled field is denoted by replacing the @ marker in a text fieldholder with a caret (^<<<, for example). The corresponding value for a filled field (on the following line of the format) must be a scalar variable containing text, rather than an expression that returns a scalar value. When Perl is filling the filled field, it takes the value of the variable and removes as many words as will fit in the field. Subsequent calls for the variable in a filled field will continue where the last one left off.

If the variable's contents are exhausted before the number of fields, you will simply end up with blank lines. You can suppress blank lines by placing a tilde (~) on the line. Any line that contains a tilde character is not output if the line would have otherwise printed blank (i.e., just whitespace). The tilde itself always prints as a blank and can be placed anywhere a space could have been placed in the line.

If the text in the variable is longer than what can be filled in the fields, output only continues until the fields run out. The shortcut to get the string to print until its end is to use two consecutive tildes (~~) on a line. This causes the line to be repeated automatically until the result is a completely blank line (which will be suppressed).

Default values for format parameters all relate to the format of the currently selected filehandle. The currently selected filehandle starts out as STDOUT, which makes it easy to print things on the standard output. However, you can change the currently selected filehandle with the select function, which takes a single filehandle (or a scalar variable containing the name of a filehandle) as an argument. Once the currently selected filehandle is changed, it affects all future operations that depend on the currently selected filehandle.

Pod

Pod is a simple, but surprisingly capable, text formatter that uses tags to tell a translator how to format the text. The tags serve several purposes:

- They tell the formatter how to lay out text on the page.

- They provide font and cross-reference information.

- They start and stop parsing of code.

The last item is indicative of one of pod's most useful features — that it can be intermixed with Perl code. While it can be difficult to force yourself to go back and write documentation for your code after the fact, with Perl you can simply intermingle the documentation with the code, and do it all at once. It also lets you use the same text as both code documentation and user documentation if you wish.

A pod translator reads a file paragraph by paragraph, ignoring text that isn't pod, and converting it to the proper format. Paragraphs are separated from each other by blank lines (not just by a newline). The various translators recognize three kinds of paragraphs:

Command

> Commands begin with =, followed immediately by the command identifier:
>
> ```
> =cut
> ```
>
> They can also be followed by text:
>
> ```
> =head2 Second-level head
> ```
>
> A blank line signals the end of the command.

Text

> A paragraph consisting of a block of text, generally filled and possibly justified, depending on the translator. For example, a command like =head2 is probably going to be followed with a text paragraph:
>
> ```
> =head2 Pod
>
> Pod is a simple, but surprisingly capable, text formatter that uses
> tags to tell a translator how to format the text.
> ```

Verbatim

> A paragraph that is to be reproduced as-is, with no filling or justification. To create a verbatim paragraph, indent each line of text with at least one space:
>
> ```
> Don't fill this paragraph. It's supposed
> to look exactly like this on the page.
> There are blanks at the beginning of each line.
> ```

Paragraph tags

The following paragraph tags are recognized as valid pod commands:

=back

=back

Moves left margin back to where it was before the last =over. Ends the innermost =over/=back block of indented text. If there are multiple levels of indent, one =back is needed for each level.

=begin

=begin *format*

Starts a block of text that is to be passed directly to a particular formatter rather than being treated as pod. For example:

```
=begin html
```

$\rightarrow$

A =begin/=end block is like =for except that it doesn't necessarily apply to a single paragraph.

=cut

=cut

Indicates the end of pod text. Tells the compiler that there isn't any more pod (for now) and to start compiling again.

=end

=end

Ends a =begin block. Tells the translator to treat what follows as pod again.

=for

=for *format*

Indicates a format change, for the next paragraph only.

=head1

=head1 *text*

text following the tag is formatted as a top-level heading. Generally all upper-case.

=head2

=head2 *text*

text following the tag is formatted as a second-level heading.

=item

=item *text*

Starts a list. Lists should always be inside an over/back block. Many translators use the value of *text* on the first =item to determine the type of list:

=item *

> Bulleted list. An asterisk (*) is commonly used for the bullet, but can be replaced with any other single character. Followed by a blank line and then the text of the bulleted item:
>
>   =item *
>
>   This is the text of the bullet.

=item *n*

> Numbered list. Replace *n* with 1 on the first item, 2 on the second, and so on—pod does not automatically generate the numbers.

$\rightarrow$

=item *text*

> Definition list. Formats *text* as the term and the following paragraph as the body of the list item. For example:

```
=item <HTML>

Indicates the beginning of an HTML file
```

> The exact appearance of the output depends on what translator you use, but it will look pretty much like this:

```
<HTML>
      Indicates the beginning of an HTML file
```

=over

=over *n*

Specifies the beginning of a list, where *n* indicates the depth of the indent. For example, =over 4 will indent four spaces. Another =over before a =back creates nested lists. The =over tag should be followed by at least one =item.

=pod

=pod

Indicates the beginning of pod text. A translator starts to pay attention when it sees this tag, and the compiler ignores everything from there to the next =cut.

Interior sequences

In addition to the paragraph tags, pod has a set of tags that apply within text, either in a paragraph or a command. These interior sequences are:

Sequence	Function
B<*text*>	Makes text bold, usually for switches and programs
C<*code*>	Literal code
E<*escape*>	Named character:
E<gt>	Literal >
E<lt>	Literal <
E<*html*>	Non-numeric HTML entity
E<*n*>	Character number *n*, usually an ASCII character
F<*file*>	Filename
I<*text*>	Italicize *text*, usually for emphasis or variables
L<*name*>	Link (cross-reference) to *name*:
L<*name*>	Manpage
L<*name*/*ident*>	Item in a manpage
L<*name*/"*sec*">	Section in another manpage
L<"*sec*">	Section in this manpage; quotes are optional
L</"*sec*">	Same as L<"*sec*">
S<*text*>	*text* has non-breaking spaces

→

Sequence	Function
X<index>	Index entry
Z<>	Zero-width character

Pod Utilities

As mentioned earlier, a number of utility programs have been written to convert files from pod to a variety of output formats. Some of the utilities are described here, particularly those that are part of the Perl distribution. Other programs are available on CPAN.

perldoc

perldoc *[options] docname*

Formats and displays Perl pod documentation. Extracts the documentation from pod format and displays it. For all options except *–f*, *docname* is the name of the manpage, module, or program containing pod to be displayed. For *–f*, it's the name of a built-in Perl function to be displayed.

Options

–f function
: Formats and displays documentation for the specified Perl function.

–h Displays help message.

–l Displays full path to the module.

–m Displays entire module, both code and pod text, without formatting the pod.

–t Displays using text formatter instead of nroff. Faster, but output is less fancy.

–u Unformatted. Finds and displays the document without formatting it.

–v Verbose. Describes search for the file, showing directories searched and where file was found.

perldoc applies switches found in the PERLDOC environment variable before those from the command line. It searches directories specified by the PERL5LIB, PERLLIB (if PERL5LIB isn't defined), and PATH environment variables.

pod2fm

pod2fm *[options] file*

Translates pod to FrameMaker format.

Options

-book [bookname]

> If set, creates FrameMaker book file. If not specified, *bookname* defaults to perl; filename extension is *.book* in either case.

-[no]doc

> Whether to convert a MIF-format *.doc* output file to binary FrameMaker format. Default is *-doc*.

-format type

> Which format to copy from the template document specified with the *-template* option. Type can be a comma-separated list, and *-format* can also be specified more than once. Legal types are:

Type	Description
all	All types (the default)
Character	Character formats
Paragraph	Paragraph formats
Page	Master page layouts
Reference	Reference page layouts
Table	Table formats
Variables	Variable definitions
Math	Math definitions
Cross	Cross-reference definitions
Color	Color definitions
Conditional	Conditional text definitions
Break	Preserves page breaks; controls how the other types are used
Other	Preserves other format changes; controls how the other types are used

-[no]index

> Whether to generate an index. Defaults to *-noindex*.

-[no]lock

> Whether to lock file as read-only so you can use hypertext marker feature. Defaults to *-nolock*.

-[no]mmlonly

> Whether to stop execution after generating the MML version of the file. Default is *-nommlonly*.

-[no]open

> Whether to try to open the book after creating it; requires the *-book* option.

-template document

> Specifies a template document for *pod2fm* to copy a format for use in formatting the output. *document* is the path to the template document.

-[no]toc

> Whether to generate a table of contents. Defaults to *-notoc*.

pod2html

pod2html *[options] inputfile*

Translates files from pod to HTML format. Wrapper around the standard module Pod::Html; see Chapter 8 for the options, which are passed to Pod::Html as arguments.

pod2latex

pod2latex *inputfile*

Translates files from pod to LaTeX format. Writes output to a file with *.tex* extension.

pod2man

pod2man *[options] inputfile*

Translates pod directives in file *inputfile* to Unix manpage format. Converts pod-tagged text to nroff source that can be viewed by the *man* command, or troff for typesetting.

Options

--center=string
> Sets centered header to *string*. Defaults to "User Contributed Perl Documentation" unless *--official* flag is set, in which case it defaults to "Perl Programmers Reference Guide."

--date=string
> Sets left-hand footer string to *date*.

--fixed=font
> Specifies the fixed-width font to use for code examples.

--lax
> If set, ignores missing sections.

--official
> If set, uses default header as shown for *--center* above.

--release=rel
> Sets centered footer. Defaults to current Perl release.

--section=manext
> Sets manpage section for nroff .TH macro. Default is 3 (functions) if filename ends in *.pm*, otherwise 1 (user commands).

pod2text

pod2text < *input*

Translates pod to text and displays it. A wrapper around the Pod::Text module.

Options

--help
Displays help information

--htmlroot=name
Sets base URL for the HTML files to *name*.

--index
Generates index at top of the HTML file (default).

--infile=name
Converts pod file *name*. Default is to take input from STDIN.

--libpods=name: ... :name
List of page names (e.g., "perlfunc") that contain linkable =items.

--outfile=name
Creates HTML file *name*. Default is to send output to STDOUT.

--podroot=name
Uses *name* as base directory for finding library pods.

--podpath=name: ... :name
List of *podroot* subdirectories with pod files whose HTML-converted forms can be linked to in cross-references.

--netscape
Uses Netscape HTML directives when applicable.

--noindex
Does not generate index at top of the HTML file.

--nonetscape
Does not use Netscape HTML directives (default).

--norecurse
Does not recurse into subdirectories specified in *podpath*.

--recurse
Recurses into subdirectories specified in *podpath* (default).

--title=title
Specifies title for the resulting HTML file.

--verbose
Displays progress messages.

CHAPTER 5

Function Reference

This chapter gives a brief description of Perl's built-in functions. Each description gives the syntax of the function, with the types and order of its arguments.

Required arguments are shown in italics, separated by commas. If an argument must be a specific variable type, that variable's identifier will be used (i.e., a percent sign for a hash, *%hash*). Optional arguments are placed in brackets. Do not actually use the brackets in your function calls unless you really want to use an anonymous hash reference.

There are different ways to use a built-in function. For starters, any argument that requires a scalar value can be made up of any expression that returns one. For example, you can obtain the square root of the first value in an array:

```
$root = sqrt (shift @numbers);
```

shift removes the first element of @numbers and returns it to be used by sqrt.

Many functions take a list of scalars for arguments. Any array variable or other expression that returns a list can be used for all or part of the arguments. For example:

```
chmod (split /,/ <FILELIST>); # an expression returns a list
chmod 0755, @executables;     # array used for part of arguments
```

In the first line, the split expression reads a string from a filehandle and splits it into a list. The list provides proper arguments for chmod. The second line uses an array that contains a list of filenames for chmod to act upon.

Parentheses are not required around a function's arguments. However, without parentheses, functions are viewed as operators in an expression (the same is true of predeclared subroutines). If you use a function in a complex expression, you may want to use parentheses for clarity. See Chapter 4, *The Perl Language*, for more about precedence in Perl expressions.

Perl Functions by Category

Here are Perl's functions and function-like keywords, arranged by category. Note that some functions appear under more than one heading.

Scalar manipulation
> chomp, chop, chr, crypt, hex, index, lc, lcfirst, length, oct, ord, pack, q//, qq//, reverse, rindex, sprintf, substr, tr///, uc, ucfirst, y///

Regular expressions and pattern matching
> m//, pos, qr//, quotemeta, s///, split, study

Numeric functions
> abs, atan2, cos, exp, hex, int, log, oct, rand, sin, sqrt, srand

Array processing
> pop, push, shift, splice, unshift

List processing
> grep, join, map, qw//, reverse, sort, unpack

Hash processing
> delete, each, exists, keys, values

Input and output
> binmode, close, closedir, dbmclose, dbmopen, die, eof, fileno, flock, format, getc, print, printf, read, readdir, rewinddir, seek, seekdir, select, syscall, sysread, sysseek, syswrite, tell, telldir, truncate, warn, write

Fixed-length data and records
> pack, read, syscall, sysread, syswrite, unpack, vec

Filehandles, files, and directories
> chdir, chmod, chown, chroot, fcntl, glob, ioctl, link, lstat, mkdir, open, opendir, readlink, rename, rmdir, stat, symlink, sysopen, umask, unlink, utime

Flow of program control
> caller, continue, die, do, dump, eval, exit, goto, last, next, redo, return, sub, wantarray

Scoping
> caller, import, local, my, package, use

Miscellaneous
> defined, dump, eval, formline, local, my, prototype, reset, scalar, undef, wantarray

Processes and process groups
> alarm, exec, fork, getpgrp, getppid, getpriority, kill, pipe, qx//, setpgrp, setpriority, sleep, system, times, wait, waitpid

Library modules
> do, import, no, package, require, use

Classes and objects
> bless, dbmclose, dbmopen, package, ref, tie, tied, untie, use

Low-level socket access
> accept, bind, connect, getpeername, getsockname, getsockopt, listen, recv, send, setsockopt, shutdown, socket, socketpair

System V interprocess communication
> msgctl, msgget, msgrcv, msgsnd, semctl, semget, semop, shmctl, shmget, shmread, shmwrite

Fetching user and group information
> endgrent, endhostent, endnetent, endpwent, getgrent, getgrgid, getgrnam, getlogin, getpwent, getpwnam, getpwuid, setgrent, setpwent

Fetching network information
> endprotoent, endservent, gethostbyaddr, gethostbyname, gethostent, getnetbyaddr, getnetbyname, getnetent, getprotobyname, getprotobynumber, getprotoent, getservbyname, getservbyport, getservent, sethostent, setnetent, setprotoent, setservent

Time
> gmtime, localtime, time, times

Language
Basics

Perl Functions in Alphabetical Order

---

abs

abs *value*

Returns the absolute value of its argument (or $_ if omitted).

---

accept

accept *newsocket, genericsocket*

Readies a server process to accept socket connections from clients. Execution is suspended until a connection is made, at which time the *newsocket* filehandle is opened and attached to the newly made connection. The function returns the connected address if the call succeeds, or returns false otherwise (and it puts the error code into $!). *genericsocket* must be a filehandle already opened via the socket function and bound to one of the server's network addresses.

---

alarm

alarm *n*

Sends a SIGALRM signal to the executing Perl program after *n* seconds. On some older systems, alarms go off at the "top of the second," so, for instance,

$\rightarrow$

an alarm 1 may go off anywhere between 0 to 1 seconds from now, depending on when in the current second it is. An alarm 2 may go off anywhere from 1 to 2 seconds from now. And so on.

Each call disables the previous timer, and an argument of 0 may be supplied to cancel the previous timer without starting a new one. The return value is the number of seconds remaining on the previous timer.

atan2

atan2 *y, x*

Returns the arctangent of y/x in the range $-\pi$ to π. A quick way to get an approximate value of π is to say:

```
$pi = atan2(1,1) * 4;
```

For the tangent operation, you may use the POSIX::tan() function, or use the familiar relation:

```
sub tan { sin($_[0]) / cos($_[0]) }
```

bind

bind *socket, address*

Attaches an address to an already opened socket specified by the *socket* filehandle. The function returns true for success, false otherwise (and puts the error code into $!). *address* should be a packed address of the proper type for the socket.

binmode

binmode *filehandle*

Arranges for the file to be treated in binary mode on operating systems that distinguish between binary and text files. It should be called after open but before any I/O is done on the filehandle. The only way to reset binary mode on a filehandle is to reopen the file.

binmode has no effect under Unix, Plan9, or other systems that use a single \n (newline) character as a line delimiter. On systems such as Win32 or MS-DOS, binmode is needed to prevent the translation of the line delimiter characters to and from \n.

bless

bless *$ref, [classname]*

Looks up the item pointed to by reference *ref* and tells the item that it is now an object in the *classname* package—or the current package if no *classname* is specified. It returns the reference for convenience, since a bless is often the last thing in a constructor function. (Always use the two-argument version

$\rightarrow$

if the constructor doing the blessing might be inherited by a derived class. In such cases, the class you want to bless your object into will normally be found as the first argument to the constructor in question.)

Language
Basics

caller

caller [*n*]

Returns information about the stack of current subroutine calls. Without an argument, it returns the package name in a scalar context, and in a list context, it returns the package name, filename, and line number that the currently executing subroutine was called from:

```
($package, $filename, $line) = caller;
```

With an argument it evaluates *n* as the number of stack frames to go back before the current one. It also reports some additional information that the debugger uses to print a stack trace:

```
$i = 0;
while (($pack, $file, $line, $subname, $hasargs,
        $wantarray, $evaltext, $is_require) = caller($i++)) {
    ...
}
```

Furthermore, when called from within the DB package, caller returns more detailed information: it sets the list variable @DB::args to be the argument passed in the given stack frame.

chdir

chdir *dirname*

Changes the working directory to *dirname*, if possible. If *dirname* is omitted, it changes to the home directory. The function returns 1 upon success, 0 otherwise (and puts the error code into $!).

chmod

chmod *mode, filelist*

Changes the permissions of a list of files. The first argument must be the permissions mode given in its octal number representation. The function returns the number of files successfully changed. For example:

```
$cnt = chmod 0755, 'file1', 'file2';
```

will set $cnt to 0, 1, or 2, depending on how many files got changed (in the sense that the operation succeeded, not in the sense that the bits were different afterward).

chomp

> chomp *$var*
> chomp *@list*

Removes any line-ending characters of a string in $*var*, or each string in @*list*, that correspond to the current value of $/ (not just any last character, as chop does). chomp returns the number of characters deleted. If $/ is empty (in paragraph mode), chomp removes all newlines from the selected string (or strings, if chomping a *list*). If no argument is given, the function chomps the $_ variable.

chop

> chop *$var*
> chop *@list*

Chops off the last character of a string contained in the variable $*var* (or strings in each element of a @*list*) and returns the character chopped. The chop operator is used primarily to remove the newline from the end of an input record, but is more efficient than s/\n$//. If no argument is given, the function chops the $_ variable.

chown

> chown *uid, gid, files*

Changes the owner and group of a list of files. The first two arguments must be the *numerical* uid and gid, in that order. The function returns the number of files successfully changed.

On most systems, you are not allowed to change the ownership of the file unless you're the superuser, although you should be able to change the group to any of your secondary groups. On insecure systems, these restrictions may be relaxed, but this is not a portable assumption.

chr

> chr *number*

Returns the character represented by *number* in the character set. For example, chr(65) is "A" in ASCII.

chroot

> chroot *dirname*

Changes the root directory for the current process to *dirname*—the starting point for pathnames beginning with "/". This directory is inherited across exec calls and by all subprocesses. There is no way to undo a chroot. Only the superuser can use this function.

close

close *filehandle*

Closes the file, socket, or pipe associated with the given filehandle. You don't have to close *filehandle* if you are immediately going to do another open on it, since the next open will close it for you. However, an explicit close on an input file resets the line counter ($.), while the implicit close done by open does not. Closing a pipe will wait for the process executing on the pipe to complete, and it prevents the script from exiting before the pipeline is finished. Closing a pipe explicitly also puts the status value of the command executing on the pipe into $?.

filehandle may be an expression whose value gives a real filehandle name. It may also be a reference to a filehandle object returned by some of the object-oriented I/O packages.

Language
Basics

closedir

closedir *dirhandle*

Closes a directory associated with the given directory handle opened by opendir.

connect

connect *socket, address*

Initiates a connection with another process that is waiting at an accept on the filehandle *socket*. The function returns true for success, false otherwise (and puts the error code into $!). *address* is a packed network address of the proper type for *socket*.

To disconnect a socket, use either close or shutdown.

cos

cos *num*

Returns the cosine of *num* (expressed in radians). For the inverse cosine operation, you may use the POSIX::acos() function, or use this relation:

```
sub acos { atan2( sqrt(1 - $_[0] * $_[0]), $_[0] ) }
```

crypt

crypt *string, salt*

Used by the passwd function on Unix systems to produce a unique 13-character string (stored in the system's password file) from the first 8 characters of the given *string* and the 2-character *salt*. The Perl function operates the same way, and returns a 13-character string with the first 2 characters being the *salt*. crypt uses a modified version of the Data Encryption Standard, which

→

produces a one-way encryption; the resulting string cannot be decrypted to determine the original string. crypt can be used to check that a password is correct by comparing the string from the function to the string found in */etc/passwd* (if you have permission to do this):

```
if (crypt ($guess, $pass) eq $pass) {
      # guess is correct
   }
```

The variable $pass is the password string from the password file. crypt merely uses the first two characters from this string for the *salt* argument.

dbmclose

dbmclose *%hash*

Breaks the binding between a DBM file and a hash.

This function is actually just a call to untie with the proper arguments, but is provided for backward compatibility with older versions of Perl.

dbmopen

dbmopen *%hash, dbname, mode*

Binds a DBM file (*dbname*) to a hash (*%hash*). *dbname* is the name of the database without the *.dir* or *.pag* extension. If the database does not exist, and a valid *mode* is specified, the database is created with the permissions specified by *mode* (as modified by the umask). To prevent creation of the database if it doesn't exist, you may specify a *mode* of undef, and the function will return a false value if it can't find an existing database. If your system supports only the older DBM functions, you may have only one dbmopen in your program.

Values assigned to the hash prior to the dbmopen are not accessible. If you don't have write access to the DBM file, you can only read the hash variables, not set them.

This function is actually just a call to tie with the proper arguments, but is provided for backward compatibility with older versions of Perl.

defined

defined *expr*

Returns a Boolean value saying whether the scalar value resulting from *expr* has a real value or not. If no argument is given, defined checks $_.

A scalar that contains no valid string, numeric, or reference value is known as the undefined value, or undef for short. Many operations return the undefined value under exceptional conditions, such as end of file, uninitialized variable, system error, and such. This function allows you to distinguish between an undefined null string and a defined null string when you're using operators that might return a real null string.

$\rightarrow$

You can use defined to see if a subroutine exists, that is, if the subroutine definition has been successfully parsed. However, using defined on an array or a hash is not guaranteed to produce intuitive results, and should be avoided.

delete

delete *$hash{key}*
delete *@hash{@keys}*

Deletes the specified *key* or *keys* and associated values from the specified *hash*. (It doesn't delete a file. See unlink for that.) Deleting from $ENV{} modifies the environment. Deleting from a hash that is bound to a (writable) DBM file deletes the entry from the DBM file.

For normal hashes, the delete function returns the value (not the key) that was deleted, but this behavior is not guaranteed for tied hashes, such as those bound to DBM files. To test whether a hash element has been deleted, use exists.

die

die *message*

Prints *message* to the standard error output and exits the Perl program with a nonzero exit status. *message* can be a list value, like the arguments to print, from which the elements are concatenated into a single string for output. If *message* does not end with a newline (\n), the current script filename, line number, and input line number (if any) are appended to the message with a newline. With no argument, the function outputs the string Died as its default.

die exits the programs with the current value of the $! variable, which contains the text describing the most recent operating system error value. This value can be used in the *message* to describe what the problem may have been.

die behaves differently inside an eval statement. It places the error message in the $@ variable and aborts the eval, which returns an undefined value. This use of die can raise runtime exceptions that can be caught at a higher level of the program.

do

do *{block}*

Executes the sequence of commands in the *block* and returns the value of the last expression evaluated. When modified by a loop modifier, Perl executes the *block* once before testing the loop condition. (On other statements, the loop modifiers test the conditional first.)

dump

dump *label*

During program execution, causes an immediate core dump after code previous to it has already been executed. Primarily, this is so that you can use the undump program to turn your core dump into an executable binary after having initialized all your variables at the beginning of the program. dump arranges for the revived binary, when run, to begin by executing a goto *label* (with all the restrictions that goto suffers). Think of the operation as a goto with an intervening core dump and reincarnation. If *label* is omitted, the function arranges for the program to restart from the top. Please note that any files opened at the time of the dump will not be open any more when the program is reincarnated. See also the *−u* command-line switch.

The undump program is not available on all systems, and may not be compatible with specific ports of Perl.

each

each *%hash*

Returns a two-element list consisting of the key and value for the next element of a hash. With successive calls to each, you can iterate over the entire hash. Entries are returned in an indeterminate order. When the hash is entirely read, a null list is returned. The next call to each after that will start a new iteration. The iterator can be reset either by reading all the elements from the hash, or by calling the keys function in scalar context. You must not add elements to the hash while iterating over it, although you are permitted to use delete. In a scalar context, each returns just the key.

There is a single iterator for each hash, shared by all each, keys, and values function calls in the program. This means that after a keys or values call, the next each call will start again from the beginning.

endgrent

endgrent

Closes the groups file (usually */etc/group* on Unix systems) if open. Not implemented on Win32 systems.

endhostent

endhostent

Closes the hosts file (usually */etc/hosts* on Unix systems) if open. Not implemented on Win32 systems.

endnetent

endnetent

Closes the networks file (usually */etc/networks* on Unix systems) if open. Not implemented on Win32 systems.

endprotoent

endprotoent

Closes the prototypes file (usually */etc/prototypes* on Unix systems) if open. Not implemented on Win32 systems.

endpwent

endpwent

Closes the password file (*/etc/passwd* or equivalent on Unix systems) if open. Not implemented on Win32 systems.

endservent

endservent

Closes the services file (usually */etc/services* on Unix systems) if open. Not implemented on Win32 systems.

eof

eof *filehandle*
eof( )

Returns true if the next read on *filehandle* will return end-of-file, or if *filehandle* is not open. *filehandle* may be an expression whose value gives the real filehandle name. An eof without an argument returns the end-of-file status for the last file read. Empty parentheses ( ) may be used in connection with the combined files listed on the command line. That is, inside a while (<>) loop, eof( ) will detect the end of only the last of a group of files. Use eof(ARGV) or eof (without the parentheses) to test *each* file in a while (<>) loop. For example, the following code inserts dashes just before the last line of the *last* file:

```
while (<>) {
    if (eof()) {
        print "-" x 30, "\n";
    }
    print;
}
```

eval

eval *string*
eval {*block*}

Evaluates the expression or code in its argument at runtime as a separate Perl program within the context of the larger script. Any variable settings remain afterward, as do any subroutine or format definitions. The code of the eval is treated as a block, so any locally scoped variables declared within the eval last only until the eval is done. (See also local and my.) The value returned from an eval is the value of the last expression evaluated. Like subroutines, you may also use the return function to return a value and exit the eval.

With eval *string*, the contents of *string* are compiled and executed at runtime. For example:

```
$a = 3, $b = 4;
$c = '$a * $b';
print (eval "$c"); # prints 12
```

The string form of eval is useful for executing strings produced at runtime from standard or other dynamic input sources. If the string produces an error, either from syntax or at runtime, the eval exits with the undefined value and places the error in $@. If *string* is omitted, the operator evaluates $_.

The block form of eval is used in Perl programs to handle runtime errors (exceptions). The code in *block* is compiled only once during the compilation of the main program. If there is a syntax error in the block it will produce an error at compile time. If the code in *block* produces a runtime error (or if a die statement is encountered), the eval exits, and the error is placed in $@. For example, the following code can be used to trap a divide-by-zero error at runtime:

```
eval {
    $a = 10; $b = 0;
    $c = $a / $b;      # causes runtime error
                       # trapped by eval
};
print $@;              # Prints "Illegal division by 0 at try.pl line 3"
```

As with any code in a block, a final semicolon is not required.

exec

exec *command*

Terminates the currently running Perl script and executes the program named in *command*. The Perl program does not resume after the exec unless the exec cannot be run and produces an error. Unlike system, the executed *command* is not forked off into a child process. An exec completely replaces the script in its current process.

command may be a scalar containing a string with the name of the program to run and any arguments. This string is checked for shell metacharacters, and if there are any, passes the string to /bin/sh/ -c for parsing. Otherwise, the

$\rightarrow$

string is read as a program command, bypassing any shell processing. The first word of the string is used as the program name, with any remaining words used as arguments.

command may also be a list value where the first element is parsed as the program name and remaining elements as arguments. For example:

```
exec 'echo', 'Your arguments are: ', @ARGV;
```

The exec function is not implemented for Perl on Win32 platforms.

exists

exists *$hash{$key}*

Returns true if the specified hash key exists, even if the corresponding value is undefined.

exit

exit *status*

Exits the current Perl process immediately with that value given by *status*. This could be the entire Perl script you are running, or only a child process created by fork. Here's a fragment that lets a user exit the program by typing x or X:

```
$ans = <STDIN>;
exit 0 if $ans =~ /^[Xx]/;
```

If *status* is omitted, the function exits with 0. You shouldn't use exit to abort a subroutine if there's any chance that someone might want to trap whatever error happened. Use die instead, which can be trapped by an eval.

exp

exp *num*

Returns *e* to the power of *num*. If *num* is omitted, it gives exp($_). To do general exponentiation, use the ** operator.

fcntl

fcntl *filehandle, function, arg*

Calls the file control *function* (with the function-specific *arg*) to use on the file or device opened with *filehandle*. fcntl calls Unix's fcntl function (not available on Win32 platforms). If the function is not implemented, the program exits with a fatal error. fcntl sets file descriptors for a filehandle. This built-in command is usable when you use the Fcntl module in the standard distribution:

```
use Fcntl;
```

→

This module imports the correct *function* definitions. See the description of the Fcntl module in Chapter 8, *Standard Modules*.

The return value of fcntl (and ioctl) is as follows:

System call returns	Perl returns
-1	Undefined value
0	String "0 but true"
Anything else	That number

Thus Perl returns true on success and false on failure, yet you can still easily determine the actual value returned by the operating system.

fileno

fileno *filehandle*

Returns the file descriptor for a filehandle. (A file descriptor is a small integer, unlike the filehandle, which is a symbol.) It returns undef if the handle is not open. It's useful for constructing bitmaps for select, and for passing to certain obscure system calls if syscall is implemented. It's also useful for double-checking that the open function gave you the file descriptor you wanted.

flock

flock *filehandle, operation*

Establishes or removes a lock on a file opened with *filehandle*. This function calls one of the Unix functions flock, lockf, or the locking capabilities of fcntl, whichever your system supports. If none of these functions exist on your system, flock will produce a fatal error.

operation is the type of locking function to perform. The number by each operation name is the argument that Perl's flock takes by default. You may also use the operation names if you explicitly import them from the Fcntl module with use Fcntl ':flock'.

LOCK_SH (1)
    Establishes a shared lock on the file (read lock).

LOCK_EX (2)
    Establishes an exclusive lock on the file (write lock).

LOCK_UN (8)
    Removes a lock from the file.

LOCK_NB (4)
    Prevents flock from blocking while trying to establish a lock with LOCK_SH or LOCK_EX and instructs it to return immediately. LOCK_NB must be *or*ed with the other operation as an expression for the operation argument, i.e., (LOCK_EX | LOCK_NB).

fork

fork

Spawns a child process that executes the code immediately following the `fork` call until the process is terminated (usually with an `exit`). The child process runs parallel to the parent process and shares all the parent's variables and open filehandles. The function returns the child pid to the parent process and 0 to the child process on success. If it fails, it returns the undefined value to the parent process, and no child process is created. If you `fork` your child processes, you'll have to `wait` on their zombies when they die. See the `wait` function for more information. The `fork` function is unlikely to be implemented on any operating system not resembling Unix, unless it purports POSIX compliance.

Language
Basics

---

formline

formline *picture, variables*

Internal function used by formats, although you may also call it. It formats a list of values (*variables*) according to the contents of *picture*, placing the output into the format output accumulator, $^A. When a `write` is done, the contents of $^A are written to some filehandle, but you could also read $^A yourself and set $^A back to "". Note that a format typically does one `formline` per line of form, but the `formline` function itself doesn't care how many newlines are embedded in the *picture*. This means that the ˜ and ˜˜ tokens will treat the entire *picture* as a single line. Thus, you may need to use multiple formlines to implement a single record-format, like the format compiler.

Be careful if you put double quotes around the picture, since an @ character may be taken to mean the beginning of an array name. `formline` always returns true. See "Formats" in Chapter 4 for more information.

---

getc

getc *filehandle*

Returns the next byte from the input file attached to *filehandle*. At end-of-file, it returns a null string. If *filehandle* is omitted, the function reads from STDIN. This operator is very slow, but is occasionally useful for single-character input from the keyboard.

---

getgrent

getgrent

Returns the next entry from the system's group file (usually */etc/group* on Unix systems) starting from the top. Returns null when EOF is reached. The return value from `getgrent` in list context is:

```
($name, $passwd, $gid, $members)
```

$\rightarrow$

where $members contains a space-separated list of the login names of the members of the group. In scalar context, getgrent returns only the group name.

getgrgid

getgrgid *gid*

Retrieves a group file (*/etc/group*) entry by group number *gid*. The return value in list context is:

```
($name, $passwd, $gid, $members)
```

where $members contains a space-separated list of the login names of the members of the group. If you want to do this repeatedly, consider caching the data in a hash using getgrent. In scalar context, getgrgid returns only the group name.

getgrnam

getgrnam *name*

Retrieves a group file entry by the group name *name*. The return value in list context is:

```
($name, $passwd, $gid, $members)
```

where $members contains a space-separated list of the login names of the members of the group. In scalar context, getgrnam returns only the numeric group ID.

gethostbyaddr

gethostbyaddr *address,* [*addrtype*]

Retrieves the hostname (and alternate addresses) of a packed binary network *address.* (*addrtype* indicates the type of address given. Since gethostbyaddr is used almost solely for Internet IP addresses, *addrtype* is not needed.) The return value in list context is:

```
($name, $aliases, $addrtype, $length, @addrs)
```

where @addrs is a list of packed binary addresses. In the Internet domain, each address is four bytes long and can be unpacked by saying something like:

```
($a, $b, $c, $d) = unpack('C4', $addrs[0]);
```

In scalar context, gethostbyaddr returns only the hostname.

gethostbyname

gethostbyname *name*

Retrieves the address (and other names) of a network hostname. The return value in list context is:

```
($name, $aliases, $addrtype, $length, @addrs)
```

where @addrs is a list of raw addresses. In scalar context, gethostbyname returns only the host address.

gethostent

gethostent

Retrieves the next entry from your system's network hosts file (usually */etc/hosts* on Unix). The return value from gethostent is:

```
($name, $aliases, $addrtype, $length, @addrs)
```

where @addrs is a list of raw addresses. Scripts that use this function should not be considered portable.

getlogin

getlogin

Returns the current login from */etc/utmp* (Unix systems only), if any. If null, use getpwuid. For example:

```
$login = getlogin || getpwuid($<) || "Intruder!!";
```

getnetbyaddr

getnetbyaddr *address*, [*addrtype*]

Retrieves the network name or names of the given network *address*. (*addrtype* indicates the type of address. Often this function is used for IP addresses, where the type is not needed.) The return value in list context is:

```
($name, $aliases, $addrtype, $net)
```

In scalar context, getnetbyaddr returns only the network name.

getnetbyname

getnetbyname *name*

Retrieves the network address of a network *name*. The return value in list context is:

```
($name, $aliases, $addrtype, $net)
```

In scalar context, getnetbyname returns only the network address.

getnetent

getnetent

Retrieves the next line from your */etc/networks* file, or system equivalent. The
return value in list context is:

```
($name, $aliases, $addrtype, $net)
```

In scalar context, getnetent returns only the network name.

getpeername

getpeername *socket*

Returns the packed socket address of the other end of the *socket* connection.
For example:

```
use Socket;
$hersockaddr = getpeername SOCK;
($port, $heraddr) = unpack_sockaddr_in($hersockaddr);
$herhostname = gethostbyaddr($heraddr, AF_INET);
$herstraddr = inet_ntoa($heraddr);
```

getpgrp

getpgrp *pid*

Returns the current process group for the specified process ID (*pid*). Use a
pid of 0 for the current process. Invoking getpgrp will produce a fatal error if
used on a machine that doesn't implement the getpgrp system call. If *pid* is
omitted, the function returns the process group of the current process (the
same as using a *pid* of 0). On systems implementing this operator with the
POSIX getpgrp(2) system call, *pid* must be omitted or, if supplied, must be 0.

getppid

getppid

Returns the process ID of the parent process. On the typical Unix system, if
your parent process ID changes to 1, your parent process has died and you've
been adopted by the *init* program.

getpriority

getpriority *type, id*

Returns the current priority for a process, a process group, or a user. *type* indicates which of these three process types to return. (The type identifiers are
system-specific. Consult the manpage for getpriority.) The *id* gives the specific ID of the corresponding process type in *type*: a process ID, a processgroup ID, or a user ID. The value 0 in *who* gives the priority for the current
process, process group, or user.

$\rightarrow$

The priority will be an integer value. Lower values indicate higher priority (negative values may be returned on some systems). Invoking `getpriority` will produce a fatal error if used on a machine that doesn't implement the `getpriority` system call.

getprotobyname

getprotobyname *name*

Translates a protocol name to its corresponding number. The return value in list context is:

```
($name, $aliases, $protocol_number)
```

In scalar context, `getprotobyname` returns only the protocol number.

getprotobynumber

getprotobynumber *number*

Translates a protocol number to its corresponding name. The return value in list context is:

```
($name, $aliases, $protocol_number)
```

In scalar context, `getprotobynumber` returns only the protocol name.

getprotoent

getprotoent

Retrieves the next line from the */etc/protocols* file (on some Unix systems). Returns null at the end of the file. The return value from `getprotoent` is:

```
($name, $aliases, $protocol_number)
```

In scalar context, `getprotoent` returns only the protocol name.

getpwent

getpwent

Retrieves the next line from the */etc/passwd* file (or its equivalent coming from some server somewhere). Returns null at the end of the file. The return value in list context is:

```
($name,$passwd,$uid,$gid,$quota,$comment,$gcos,$dir,$shell)
```

Some machines may use the quota and comment fields for other purposes, but the remaining fields will always be the same. To set up a hash for translating login names to uids, do this:

$\rightarrow$

```
while (($name, $passwd, $uid) = getpwent) {
    $uid{$name} = $uid;
}
```

In scalar context, `getpwent` returns only the username.

getpwnam

getpwnam *name*

Retrieves the *passwd* file entry of a user, *name*. The return value in list context is:

```
($name,$passwd,$uid,$gid,$quota,$comment,$gcos,$dir,$shell)
```

If you want to do this repeatedly, consider caching the data in a hash using `getpwent`.

In scalar context, `getpwnam` returns only the numeric user ID.

getpwuid

getpwuid *uid*

Retrieves the *passwd* file entry with the user ID *uid*. The return value in list context is:

```
($name,$passwd,$uid,$gid,$quota,$comment,$gcos,$dir,$shell)
```

If you want to do this repeatedly, consider slurping the data into a hash using `getpwent`.

In scalar context, `getpwuid` returns the username.

getservbyname

getservbyname *name, proto*

Translates a service (port) name to its corresponding port number. *proto* is a protocol name such as "tcp". The return value in list context is:

```
($name, $aliases, $port_number, $protocol_name)
```

In scalar context, `getservbyname` returns only the service port number.

getservbyport

getservbyport *port, proto*

Translates a service (port) number to its corresponding names. *proto* is a protocol name such as "tcp". The return value in list context is:

```
($name, $aliases, $port_number, $protocol_name)
```

In scalar context, `getservbyport` returns only the service port name.

getservent

getservent

Retrieves the next listing from the */etc/services* file or its equivalent. Returns null at the end of the file. The return value in list context is:

```
($name, $aliases, $port_number, $protocol_name)
```

In scalar context, getservent returns only the service port name.

getsockname

getsockname *socket*

Returns the packed socket address of this end of the *socket* connection.

getsockopt

getsockopt *socket, level, optname*

Returns the value of the socket option *optname*, or the undefined value if there is an error. *level* identifies the protocol level used by *socket*. Options vary for different protocols. See also setsockopt.

glob

glob *expr*

Performs filename expansion (globbing) on *expr*, returning the next successive name on each call. If *expr* is omitted, $_ is globbed instead. This is the internal function implementing the <*> operator, except that it may be easier to type this way.

The glob function is not related to the Perl notion of typeglobs, other than that they both use a * to represent multiple items.

gmtime

gmtime *expr*

Converts a time string as returned by the time function to a nine-element list with the time correct for Greenwich Mean Time zone (a.k.a. GMT, UTC, etc.). Typically used as follows:

```
($sec,$min,$hour,$mday,$mon,$year,$wday,$yday,$isdst) =
        gmtime(time);
```

All list elements are numeric and come straight out of a C language struct tm. In particular this means that $mon has the range 0..11, $wday has the range 0..6, and the year has had 1,900 subtracted from it. (You can remember which ones are 0-based because those are the ones you're always using

$\rightarrow$

as subscripts into 0-based arrays containing month and day names.) If *expr* is omitted, it does gmtime(time). For example, to print the current month in London:

```
$london_month = (qw(Jan Feb Mar Apr May Jun
          Jul Aug Sep Oct Nov Dec))[(gmtime)[4]];
```

The Perl library module Time::Local contains a subroutine, timegm( ), that can convert in the opposite direction.

In scalar context, gmtime returns a ctime(3)-like string based on the GMT time value.

---

goto

goto *label*
goto *&name*

Finds the statement labeled with *label* (or an expression that evaluates to a label) and resumes execution there. It may not be used to go into any construct that requires initialization, such as a subroutine or a foreach loop. It also can't be used to go into a construct that is optimized away. It can be used to go almost anywhere else within the dynamic scope, including out of subroutines, but for that purpose it's usually better to use some other construct such as last or die.

goto *&name* substitutes a call to the named subroutine for the currently running subroutine. This is used by AUTOLOAD subroutines that wish to load another subroutine and then pretend that this subroutine—and not the original one—had been called in the first place (except that any modifications to @_ in the original subroutine are propagated to the replacement subroutine). After the goto, not even caller will be able to tell that the original routine was called first.

---

grep

grep *expr, list*
grep {*block*} *list*

Evaluates *expr* or *block* in a Boolean context for each element of *list*, temporarily setting $_ to each element in turn. In list context, it returns a list of those elements for which the expression is true. Mostly used like Unix *grep* where *expr* is a search pattern, and list elements that match are returned. In scalar context, grep returns the number of times the expression was true.

For example, presuming @all_lines contains lines of code, this example weeds out comment lines:

```
@code_lines = grep !/^#/, @all_lines;
```

hex

hex *hexnum*

Converts a hexadecimal string *hexnum* into its equivalent decimal value. If *hexnum* is omitted, it interprets $_. The following code sets $number to 4,294,906,560:

```
$number = hex("ffff12c0");
```

To do the inverse function, use:

```
sprintf "%lx", $number;   # (That's a letter 'l', not a one.)
```

Language
Basics

index

index *string, substr,* [*start*]

Returns the position of the first occurrence of *substr* in *string*. The *start*, if specified, specifies the position to start looking in the string. Positions are integer numbers based at 0. If the substring is not found, the index function returns -1.

int

int *num*

Returns the integer portion of *num*. If *num* is omitted, the function uses $_.

ioctl

ioctl *filehandle, function, arg*

Calls the ioctl Unix system call to perform *function* (with the function-specific *arg*) on the file or device opened with *filehandle*. See fcntl for a description of return values.

join

join *char, list*

Joins the separate strings of *list* into a single string with fields separated by the value of *char*, and returns the string. For example:

```
$_ = join ':', $login,$passwd,$uid,$gid,$gcos,$home,$shell;
```

To do the opposite, see split. To join things together into fixed-position fields, see pack.

keys

keys *%hash*

Returns a list consisting of all the keys of the named hash. The keys are returned in an apparently random order, but it is the same order that either the `values` or `each` function produces (assuming that the hash has not been modified between calls).

In scalar context, `keys` returns the number of elements of the hash (and resets the `each` iterator).

`keys` can be used as an lvalue to increase the number of hash buckets allocated for the hash:

```
keys %hash = 200;
```

kill

kill *sig, processes*

Sends a signal, *sig*, to a list of *processes*. You may use a signal name in quotes (without a `SIG` on the front). This function returns the number of processes successfully signaled. If the signal is negative, the function kills process groups instead of processes.

last

last *label*

Immediately exits the loop identified by *label*. If *label* is omitted, the command refers to the innermost enclosing loop.

lc

lc *string*

Returns a lowercase version of *string* (or `$_` if omitted). This is the internal function implementing the `\L` escape in double-quoted strings.

lcfirst

lcfirst *string*

Returns a version of *string* (or `$_` if omitted) with the first character lowercased. This is the internal function implementing the `\l` escape in double-quoted strings.

length

length *val*

Returns the length in bytes of the scalar value *val*. If *val* is omitted, the function returns the length of $_.

Do not try to use length to find the size of an array or hash. Use scalar @*array* for the size of an array, and scalar keys %*hash* for the size of a hash.

link

link *oldfile, newfile*

Creates a Unix hard link from a new filename, *newfile*, to an existing file, *oldfile*, on the same filesystem. The function returns 1 for success, 0 otherwise (and puts the error code into $!). This function is unlikely to be implemented on non-Unix systems. See also symlink.

listen

listen *socket, queuesize*

Tells the operating system that you are ready to accept connections on *socket* and sets the number of waiting connections to *queuesize*. If the queue is full, clients trying to connect to the socket will be refused connection.

local

local *vars*

Declares one or more global variables *vars* to have temporary values within the innermost enclosing block, subroutine, eval, or file. The new value is initially undef for scalars and () for arrays and hashes. If more than one variable is listed, the list must be placed in parentheses, because the operator binds more tightly than a comma. All the listed variables must be legal lvalues, that is, something you could assign to. This operator works by saving the current values of those variables on a hidden stack and restoring them upon exiting the block, subroutine, or eval, or file.

Subroutines called within the scope of a local variable will see the localized inner value of the variable. The technical term for this process is "dynamic scoping." Use my for true private variables.

localtime

localtime *val*

Converts the value returned by time to a nine-element list with the time corrected for the local time zone. It's typically used as follows:

$\rightarrow$

```
($sec,$min,$hour,$mday,$mon,$year,$wday,$yday,$isdst) =
        localtime(time);
```

All list elements are numeric. The element $mon (month) has the range $0..11$,
and $wday (weekday) has the range $0..6$. The year has had 1,900 subtracted
from it. (You can remember which ones are 0-based because those are the
ones you're always using as subscripts into 0-based arrays containing month
and day names.) If *val* is omitted, it does localtime(time). For example, to
get the name of the current day of the week:

```
$thisday = (Sun,Mon,Tue,Wed,Thu,Fri,Sat)[(localtime)[6]];
```

The Perl library module Time::Local contains a subroutine, timelocal(), that
can convert in the opposite direction.

In scalar context, localtime returns a ctime(3)-like string based on the localtime value.

log

log *num*

Returns logarithm (base *e*) of *num*. If *num* is omitted, the function uses $_.

lstat

lstat *file*

Like stat, returns information on *file*, except that if *file* is a symbolic link,
lstat returns information about the link; stat returns information about the
file pointed to by the link. (If symbolic links are unimplemented on your system, a normal stat is done instead.)

map

map {*block*} *list*
map *expr, list*

Evaluates the *block* or *expr* for each element of *list* (locally setting $_ to each
element) and returns the list value composed of the results of each such evaluation. It evaluates *block* or *expr* in a list context, so each element of *list* may
produce zero, one, or more elements in the returned value. These are all flattened into one list. For instance:

```
@words = map { split ' ' } @lines;
```

splits a list of lines into a list of words. Often, though, there is a one-to-one
mapping between input values and output values:

```
@chars = map chr, @nums;
```

This statement translates a list of numbers to the corresponding characters.

mkdir

mkdir *filename, mode*

Creates the directory specified by *filename*, with permissions specified by the numeric *mode* (as modified by the current umask). If it succeeds, it returns 1; otherwise, it returns 0 and sets $! (from the value of errno).

msgctl

msgctl *id, cmd, arg*

Calls the msgctl system call, which is used to perform different control operations on IPC message queues. See the msgctl documentation on your system for details. If *cmd* is &IPC_STAT, then *arg* must be a variable that will hold the returned msqid_ds structure. The return values work like those of fnctl: the undefined value for error, "0 but true" for zero, or the actual return value otherwise. On error, it puts the error code into $!. Before calling, you should say:

```
require "ipc.ph";
require "msg.ph";
```

This function is available only on machines supporting System V IPC.

msgget

msgget *key, flags*

Calls the System V IPC msgget system call. See the msgget documentation on your system for details. The function returns the message queue ID, or the undefined value if there is an error. On error, it puts the error code into $!. Before calling, you should say:

```
require "ipc.ph";
require "msg.ph";
```

This function is available only on machines supporting System V IPC.

msgrcv

msgrcv *id, var, size, type, flags*

Calls the System V IPC msgrcv system call to receive a message from message queue *id* into variable *var* with a maximum message size of *size*. When a message is received, the message type will be the first thing in *var*, and the maximum length of *var* is *size* plus the size of the message type. The function returns true if successful, or false if there is an error. On error, it puts the error code into $!. Before calling, you should say:

```
require "ipc.ph";
require "msg.ph";
```

This function is available only on machines supporting System V IPC.

msgsnd

msgsnd *id, msg, flags*

Calls the System V IPC msgsnd system call to send the message *msg* to the message queue *id*. *msg* must begin with the long integer message type. You can create a message like this:

```
$msg = pack "L a*", $type, $text_of_message;
```

The function returns true if successful, or false if there is an error. On error, it puts the error code into $!. Before calling, you should say:

```
require "ipc.ph";
require "msg.ph";
```

This function is available only on machines supporting System V IPC.

my

my *vars*

Declares one or more private variables to exist only within the innermost enclosing block, subroutine, eval, or file. The new value is initially undef for scalars and () for arrays and hashes. If more than one variable is listed, the list must be placed in parentheses, because the operator binds more tightly than a comma. Only simple scalars or complete arrays and hashes may be declared this way. The variable name may not be package-qualified, because package variables are all global, and private variables are not related to any package.

Unlike local, this operator has nothing to do with global variables, other than hiding any other variable of the same name from view within its scope. (A global variable can always be accessed through its package-qualified form or a symbolic reference, however.) A private variable is not visible until the statement *after* its declaration. Subroutines called from within the scope of such a private variable cannot see the private variable unless the subroutine is also textually declared within the scope of the variable.

next

next *label*

Immediately jumps to the next iteration of the loop identified by *label* or the innermost enclosing loop, if there is no argument. If there is a continue block, it will be executed immediately after the next, before the loop is reiterated.

no

no *Module list*

Effectively "undoes" the use function. Used to deactivate pragmas (compiler directives) for sections of your program. For instance:

```
no strict 'refs'
```

allows soft references to the end of the block scope, if:

```
use strict 'refs'
```

was previously invoked.

oct

oct *ostring*

Interprets *ostring* as an octal string and returns the equivalent decimal value. (If *ostring* happens to start off with 0x, it is interpreted as a hex string instead.) The following will handle decimal, octal, and hex in the standard notation:

```
$val = oct $val if $val =~ /^0/;
```

If *ostring* is omitted, the function interprets $_. To perform the inverse function on octal numbers, use:

```
$oct_string = sprintf "%lo", $number;
```

open

open *filehandle, filename*

Opens the file given by *filename*, and associates it with *filehandle*. If *filehandle* is omitted, the scalar variable of the same name as the *filehandle* must contain the filename. (And you must also be careful to use "or die" after the statement rather than "|| die", because the precedence of || is higher than list operators like open.)

If *filename* is preceded by either < or nothing, the file is opened for input (read-only). If *filename* is preceded by >, the file is opened for output. If the file doesn't exist, it will be created; if the file exists, it will be overwritten with output using >. Preceding the filename with >> opens an output file for appending. For both read and write access, use a + before either < or >.

A filehandle may also be attached to a process by using a piped command. If the filename begins with |, the filename is interpreted as a command to which output is to be piped. If the filename ends with a |, the filename is interpreted as a command which pipes input to you. You may not have an open command that pipes both in and out.

Any pipe command containing shell metacharacters is passed to the shell for execution; otherwise, it is executed directly by Perl. The filename "–" refers to

$\rightarrow$

STDIN, and ">-" refers to STDOUT. open returns non-zero upon success, the undefined value otherwise. If the open involved a pipe, the return value happens to be the process ID of the subprocess.

opendir

opendir *dirhandle, directory*

Opens a *directory* for processing by readdir, telldir, seekdir, rewinddir, and closedir. The function returns true if successful. Directory handles have their own namespace separate from filehandles.

ord

ord *expr*

Returns the numeric ASCII value of the first character of *expr*. If *expr* is omitted, it uses $_. The return value is always unsigned. If you want a signed value, use unpack('c', *expr*). If you want all the characters of the string converted to a list of numbers, use unpack('C*', *expr*) instead.

pack

pack *template, list*

Takes a list of values and packs it into a binary structure, returning the string containing the structure. The *template* is a sequence of characters that give the order and type of values, as follows:

Character	Meaning
a	An ASCII string, will be null padded
A	An ASCII string, will be space padded
b	A bit string, low-to-high order (like vec())
B	A bit string, high-to-low order
c	A signed char value
C	An unsigned char value
d	A double-precision float in the native format
f	A single-precision float in the native format
h	A hexadecimal string, low nybble first
H	A hexadecimal string, high nybble first
i	A signed integer value
I	An unsigned integer value
l	A signed long value
L	An unsigned long value
n	A short in "network" (big-endian) order
N	A long in "network" (big-endian) order
p	A pointer to a string

$\rightarrow$

Character	Meaning
P	A pointer to a structure (fixed-length string)
s	A signed short value
S	An unsigned short value
v	A short in "VAX" (little-endian) order
V	A long in "VAX" (little-endian) order
u	A uuencoded string
w	A BER compressed integer
x	A null byte
X	Back up a byte
@	Null-fill to absolute position

Language Basics

Each character may optionally be followed by a number that gives a repeat count. Together the character and the repeat count make a field specifier. Field specifiers may be separated by whitespace, which will be ignored. With all types except a and A, the pack function will gobble up that many values from the *list*. Saying * for the repeat count means to use however many items are left. The a and A types gobble just one value, but pack it as a string of length *count*, padding with nulls or spaces as necessary. (When unpacking, A strips trailing spaces and nulls, but a does not.) Real numbers (floats and doubles) are in the native machine format only; due to the multiplicity of floating formats around, and the lack of a standard network representation, no facility for interchange has been made.

The same template may generally also be used in the unpack function. If you want to join variable length fields with a delimiter, use the join function.

package

package *namespace*

Declares that the rest of the innermost enclosing block, subroutine, eval or file belongs to the indicated *namespace*. (The scope of a package declaration is thus the same as the scope of a local or my declaration.) All subsequent references to unqualified global identifiers will be resolved by looking them up in the declared package's symbol table. A package declaration affects only global variables—including those you've used local on—but not lexical variables created with my.

Typically you would put a package declaration as the first thing in a file that is to be included by the require or use operator, but you can put one anywhere that a statement would be legal. When defining a class or a module file, it is customary to name the package the same name as the file, to avoid confusion. (It's also customary to name such packages beginning with a capital letter, because lowercase modules are, by convention, interpreted as pragmas.)

pipe

pipe *readhandle, writehandle*

Opens a pair of connected pipes. This call is almost always used right before a fork, after which the pipe's reader should close *writehandle*, and the writer should close *readhandle*. (Otherwise the pipe won't indicate EOF to the reader when the writer closes it.) Note that if you set up a loop of piped processes, deadlock can occur unless you are very careful. In addition, note that Perl's pipes use standard I/O buffering, so you may need to set $| on your *writehandle* to flush after each output command, depending on the application—see select *filehandle*.

pop

pop *@array*

Treats an array like a stack, popping and returning the last value of the array, shortening the array by one element. If *array* is omitted, the function pops @ARGV (in the main program), or @_ (in subroutines).

If there are no elements in the array, pop returns the undefined value. See also push and shift. If you want to pop more than one element, use splice.

pos

pos *$scalar*

Returns the location in *scalar* where the last m//g search over *scalar* left off. It returns the offset of the character *after* the last one matched. This is the offset where the next m//g search on that string will start. Remember that the offset of the beginning of the string is 0. For example:

```
$grafitto = "fee fie foe foo";
while ($grafitto =~ m/e/g) {
    print pos $grafitto, "\n";
}
```

prints 2, 3, 7, and 11, the offsets of each of the characters following an "e". The pos function may be assigned a value to tell the next m//g where to start.

print

print [*filehandle*] *list*

Prints a string or a comma-separated list of strings to the specified *filehandle*. If no filehandle is given, the function prints to the currently open filehandle (STDOUT initially). The function returns 1 if successful, 0 otherwise. *filehandle* may be a scalar variable name (unsubscripted), in which case the variable contains either the name of the actual filehandle or a reference to a filehandle object from one of the object-oriented filehandle packages. *filehandle* may also be a block that returns either kind of value:

$\rightarrow$

```
print { $OK ? "STDOUT" : "STDERR" } "stuff\n";
print { $iohandle[$i] } "stuff\n";
```

If *list* is also omitted, $_ is printed. Note that, because print takes a list, anything in the *list* is evaluated in list context.

printf

printf [*filehandle*] *format, list*

Prints a formatted string of the elements in *list* to *filehandle* or, if omitted, the currently selected output filehandle. This is similar to the C library's printf and fprintf functions, except that the * field width specifier is not supported. The function is exactly equivalent to:

```
print filehandle sprintf(format, list);
```

printf and sprintf use the same format syntax, but sprintf only returns a string; it doesn't print to a filehandle. The *format* string contains text with embedded field specifiers into which the the elements of *list* are substituted in order, one per field. Field specifiers follow the form:

```
%m.nx
```

A percent sign begins each field, and *x* is the type of field. The optional *m* gives the minimum field width for appropriate field types (negative *m* left-justifies). The .*n* gives the precision for a specific field type, such as the number of digits after a decimal point for floating-point numbers, the maximum length for a string, and the minimum length for an integer.

Field specifiers (*x*) may be the following:

Code	Meaning
%	Percent sign
c	Character
d	Decimal integer
e	Exponential format floating-point number
E	Exponential format floating-point number with uppercase E
f	Fixed-point format floating-point number
g	Floating-point number, in either exponential or fixed decimal notation
G	Like g with uppercase E (if applicable)
ld	Long decimal integer
lo	Long octal integer
lu	Long unsigned decimal integer
lx	Long hexadecimal integer
o	Octal integer
s	String
u	Unsigned decimal integer
x	Hexadecimal integer

$\rightarrow$

Code	Meaning
X	Hexadecimal integer with uppercase letters
p	The Perl value's address in hexadecimal
n	Special value that stores the number of characters output so far into the next variable in the parameter list

prototype

prototype *function*

Returns the prototype of a function as a string, or undef if the function has no prototype. *function* is the name of the function or a reference to it.

push

push *@array, list*

Pushes the elements of *list* onto the end of *array*. The length of *array* increases by the length of *list*. The function returns this new length. See also pop and unshift.

q/*string*/

q/*string*/
qq/*string*/
qx/*string*/
qw/*strings*/

Generalized forms of quoting. q// is equivalent to using single quotes (literal, no variable interpolation). qq// is equivalent to double quotes (literal, interpolated). qx// is equivalent to using backticks for commands (interpolated). And qw// is equivalent to splitting a single-quoted string on whitespace.

quotemeta

quotemeta *expr*

Returns the value of *expr* (or $_ if not specified) with all non-alphanumeric characters backslashed. This is the internal function implementing the \Q escape in interpolative contexts (including double-quoted strings, backticks, and patterns).

rand

rand *num*

Returns a random fractional number between 0 and the value of *num*. (*num* should be positive.) If *num* is omitted, the function returns a value between 0 and 1 (including 0, but excluding 1). See also srand.

$\rightarrow$

To get an integral value, combine this with `int`, as in:

```
$roll = int(rand 6) + 1;        # $roll is now an integer between 1 and 6
```

read

read *filehandle*, $*var*, *length*, [*offset*]

Attempts to read *length* bytes of data into variable *var* from the specified *file-handle*. The function returns the number of bytes actually read, or 0 at end-of-file. It returns the undefined value on error. *var* will grow or shrink to the length actually read. The *offset*, if specified, says where in the variable to start putting bytes, so that you can do a read into the middle of a string.

To copy data from the filehandle FROM into the filehandle TO, you could say:

```
while (read FROM, $buf, 16384) {
    print TO $buf;
}
```

Note that the opposite of read is simply print, which already knows the length of the string you want to write and can write a string of any length.

Perl's read function is actually implemented in terms of standard I/O's fread function, so the actual read system call may read more than *length* bytes to fill the input buffer, and fread may do more than one system read in order to fill the buffer. To gain greater control, specify the real system call using sys-read.

readdir

readdir *dirhandle*

Reads directory entries from a directory handle opened by opendir. In scalar context, this function returns the next directory entry, if any; otherwise, it returns an undefined value. In list context, it returns all the rest of the entries in the directory, which will of course be a null list if there are none.

readline

readline **filehandle*

Reads a line or lines from the specified *filehandle*. (A typeglob of the filehandle name should be supplied.) Returns one line per call in a scalar context. Returns a list of all lines until the end-of-file in list context.

readlink

readlink *name*

Returns the name of a file pointed to by the symbolic link *name*. *name* should evaluate to a filename, the last component of which is a symbolic link.

→

If it is not a symbolic link, or if symbolic links are not implemented, or if some system error occurs, the undefined value is returned, and you should check the error code in $!. If *name* is omitted, the function uses $_.

readpipe

readpipe *cmd*

Executes *cmd* as a system command and returns the collected standard output of the command. In a scalar context, the output is returned as a single, possibly multiline string. In list context, a list of output lines is returned.

recv

recv *socket,* $*var, len, flags*

Receives a message on a socket. It attempts to receive *len* bytes of data into variable *var* from the specified *socket* filehandle. The function returns the address of the sender, or the undefined value if there's an error. *var* will grow or shrink to the length actually read. The function takes the same flags as the recv(2) system call.

redo

redo [*label*]

Restarts a loop block identified by *label* without re-evaluating the conditional. The continue block, if any, is not executed. If the *label* is omitted, the command refers to the innermost enclosing loop.

ref

ref $*var*

Returns a string indicating the type of the object referenced if *var* is a reference; returns the null string otherwise. Built-in types include:

```
REF
SCALAR
ARRAY
HASH
CODE
GLOB
```

If the referenced object has been blessed into a package, that package name is returned instead. You can think of ref as a "typeof" operator.

rename

rename *oldname, newname*

Changes the name of a file from *oldname* to *newname*. It returns 1 for success, 0 otherwise (and puts the error code into $!). It will not work across

$\rightarrow$

filesystem boundaries. If there is already a file named *newname*, it will be destroyed.

require

require *filename*
require *num*
require *package*

Asserts a dependency of some kind depending on its argument. (If an argument is not supplied, $_ is used.)

If the argument is a string *filename*, this function includes and executes the Perl code found in the separate file of that name. This is similar to performing an `eval` on the contents of the file, except that `require` checks to see that the library file has not been included already. The function also knows how to search the include path stored in the @INC array.

If `require`'s argument is a number *num*, the version number of the currently executing Perl binary (as known by $]) is compared to *num*, and if smaller, execution is immediately aborted. Thus, a script that requires Perl version 5.003 can have as its first line:

```
require 5.003;
```

and earlier versions of Perl will abort.

If `require`'s argument is a package name, `require` assumes an automatic *.pm* suffix, making it easy to load standard modules. This is like use, except that it happens at runtime, not compile time, and the `import` routine is not called.

reset

reset *expr*

Used at the top of a loop or in a `continue` block at the end of a loop, to clear global variables or reset `??` searches so that they work again. *expr* is a list of single characters (hyphens are allowed for ranges). All scalar variables, arrays, and hashes beginning with one of those letters are reset to their pristine state. If *expr* is omitted, one-match searches (?*PATTERN*?) are reset to match again. The function resets variables or searches for the current package only. It always returns 1.

Lexical variables (created by `my`) are not affected. Use of `reset` is vaguely deprecated.

return

return *expr*

Returns from a subroutine (or `eval`) with the value of *expr*. (In the absence of an explicit `return`, the value of the last expression evaluated is returned.) Use of `return` outside of a subroutine or `eval` will result in a fatal error.

$\rightarrow$

The supplied expression will be evaluated in the context of the subroutine invocation. That is, if the subroutine was called in a scalar context, *expr* is also evaluated in scalar context. If the subroutine was invoked in a list context, then *expr* is also evaluated in list context, and can return a list value. A return with no argument returns the undefined value in scalar context, and a null list in list context. The context of the subroutine call can be determined from within the subroutine by using the (misnamed) wantarray function.

reverse

reverse *list*

Returns a list value consisting of the elements of *list* in the opposite order. This is fairly efficient because it just swaps the pointers around. In scalar context, the function concatenates all the elements of *list* together and returns the reverse of that, character by character.

rewinddir

rewinddir *dirhandle*

Sets the current position to the beginning of the directory for the readdir routine on *dirhandle*. The function may not be available on all machines that support readdir.

rindex

rindex *str, substr, [position]*

Works just like index except that it returns the position of the last occurrence of *substr* in *str* (a reverse index). The function returns -1 if not found. *position*, if specified, is the rightmost position that may be returned—how far in the string the function can search.

rmdir

rmdir *name*

Deletes the directory specified by *name* if it is empty. If it succeeds, it returns 1; otherwise, it returns 0 and puts the error code into $!. If *name* is omitted, the function uses $_.

scalar

scalar *expr*

Forces an expression *expr* to be evaluated in scalar context.

seek

seek *filehandle, offset, whence*

Positions the file pointer for *filehandle*, just like the fseek(3) call of standard I/O. The first position in a file is at offset 0, not offset 1, and offsets refer to byte positions, not line numbers. The function returns 1 upon success, 0 otherwise. For handiness, the function can calculate offsets from various file positions for you. The value of *whence* specifies which of three file positions your *offset* is relative to: 0, the beginning of the file; 1, the current position in the file; or 2, the end of the file. *offset* may be negative for a *whence* of 1 or 2.

Language
Basics

seekdir

seekdir *dirhandle, pos*

Sets the current position for the readdir routine on *dirhandle*. *pos* must be a value returned by telldir. This function has the same caveats about possible directory compaction as the corresponding system library routine.

select

select *filehandle*

Returns the currently selected output filehandle, and if *filehandle* is supplied, sets that as the current default filehandle for output. This has two effects: first, a write or a print without a filehandle argument will default to this *filehandle*. Second, special variables related to output will refer to this output filehandle.

select

select *rbits, wbits, ebits, timeout*

The four-argument select operator is totally unrelated to the previously described select operator. This operator is for discovering which (if any) of your file descriptors are ready to do input or output, or to report an exceptional condition. It calls the select(2) system call with the bitmasks you've specified, which you can construct using fileno and vec, like this:

```
$rbits = $wbits = $ebits = "";
vec($rbits, fileno(STDIN), 1) = 1;
vec($wbits, fileno(STDOUT), 1) = 1;
$ein = $rin | $win;
```

The select call blocks until one or more file descriptors is ready for reading, writing, or reporting an error condition. *timeout* is given in seconds and tells select how long to wait.

semctl

semctl *id, semnum, cmd, arg*

Calls the System V IPC system call semctl(2). If *cmd* is &IPC_STAT or &GETALL, then *arg* must be a variable which will hold the returned semid_ds structure or semaphore value array. The function returns like ioctl: the undefined value for error, 0 but true for zero, or the actual return value otherwise. On error, it puts the error code into $!. Before calling, you should say:

```
require "ipc.ph";
require "sem.ph";
```

This function is available only on machines supporting System V IPC.

semget

semget *key, nsems, size, flags*

Calls the System V IPC system call semget(2). The function returns the semaphore ID, or the undefined value if there is an error. On error, it puts the error code into $!. Before calling, you should say:

```
require "ipc.ph";
require "sem.ph";
```

This function is available only on machines supporting System V IPC.

semop

semop *key, opstring*

Calls the System V IPC system call semop(2) to perform semaphore operations such as signaling and waiting. *opstring* must be a packed array of semop structures. You can make each semop structure by saying pack("s*", $semnum, $semop, $semflag). The number of semaphore operations is implied by the length of *opstring*. The function returns true if successful, or false if there is an error. On error, it puts the error code into $!. Before calling, you should say:

```
require "ipc.ph";
require "sem.ph";
```

This function is available only on machines supporting System V IPC.

send

send *socket, msg, flags, [dest]*

Sends a message *msg* on a socket. It takes the same flags as the system call of the same name—see send(2). On unconnected sockets you must specify a destination *dest* to send to, in which case send works like sendto(2). The function returns the number of bytes sent, or the undefined value if there is an error. On error, it puts the error code into $!.

$\rightarrow$

(Some non-Unix systems improperly treat sockets as different objects than ordinary file descriptors, with the result that you must always use send and recv on sockets rather than the standard I/O operators.)

sethostent

sethostent *stayopen*

Opens the hosts file (usually */etc/hosts* on Unix systems) and resets the "current" selection to the top of the file. *stayopen*, if non-zero, keeps the file open across calls to other functions. Not implemented on Win32 systems.

setgrent

setgrent

Opens the groups file (usually */etc/group* on Unix systems) and resets the top of the file as the starting point for any read and/or write functions on the file (with the proper permissions). This function will reset the getgrent function back to retrieve group entries from the start of the group file. Not implemented on Win32 systems.

setnetent

setnetent *stayopen*

Opens the networks file (usually */etc/group*) and resets the "current" selection to the top of the file. *stayopen*, if non-zero, keeps the file open across calls to other functions. Not implemented on Win32 systems.

setpgrp

setpgrp *pid, pgrp*

Sets the current process group *pgrp* for the specified *pid* (use a *pid* of 0 for the current process). Invoking setpgrp will produce a fatal error if used on a machine that doesn't implement setpgrp(2). Some systems will ignore the arguments you provide and always do setpgrp(0, $$). Fortunately, those are the arguments you usually provide. (For better portability, use the setpgid() function in the POSIX module, or if you're really just trying to daemonize your script, consider the POSIX::setsid() function as well.)

setpriority

setpriority *which, who, priority*

Sets the current *priority* for a process, a process group, or a user. *which* must indicate one of these types: PRIO_PROCESS, PRIO_PGRP, or PRIO_USER. *who* therefore identifies the specific process, process group, or user with its ID. *priority* is an integer number that will be added to or subtracted from the current priority; the lower the number, the higher the priority. The interpretation

$\rightarrow$

of a given priority may vary from one operating system to the next. See `set-priority` on your system. Invoking `setpriority` will produce a fatal error if used on a machine that doesn't implement `setpriority`.

setprotoent

setprotoent *stayopen*

Opens the prototypes file (usually */etc/prototypes*) and resets the "current" selection to the top of the file. *stayopen*, if non-zero, keeps the file open across calls to other functions. Not implemented on Win32 systems.

setpwent

setpwent

Opens the password file (usually */etc/passwd*) and resets the top of the file as the starting point for any read and/or write functions on the file (with the proper permissions). This function will reset the `getpwent` function back to retrieve group entries from the start of the group file. Not implemented on Win32 systems.

setservent

setservent *stayopen*

Opens the services file (usually */etc/services*) and resets the "current" selection to the top of the file. *stayopen*, if non-zero, keeps the file open across calls to other functions. Not implemented on Win32 systems.

setsockopt

setsockopt *socket, level, optname, optval*

Sets the socket option requested (*optname*) to the value *optval*. The function returns undefined if there is an error. *optval* may be specified as `undef` if you don't want to pass an argument. *level* specifies the protocol type used on the socket.

shift

shift *@array*

Removes the first value of *@array* and returns it, shortening the array by 1 and moving everything down. If there are no elements in the array, the function returns the undefined value. If *@array* is omitted, the function shifts @ARGV (in the main program), or @_ (in subroutines). See also `unshift`, `push`, `pop`, and `splice`. The `shift` and `unshift` functions do the same thing to the left end of an array that `pop` and `push` do to the right end.

shmctl

shmctl *id, cmd, arg*

Calls the System V IPC system call, shmctl(2), for performing operations on shared memory segments. If *cmd* is &IPC_STAT, then *arg* must be a variable that will hold the returned shmid_ds structure. The function returns like ioctl: the undefined value for error, "0 but true" for zero, or the actual return value otherwise. On error, it puts the error code into $!. Before calling, you should say:

```
require "ipc.ph";
require "shm.ph";
```

This function is available only on machines supporting System V IPC.

shmget

shmget *key, size, flags*

Calls the System V IPC system call, shmget(2). The function returns the shared memory segment ID, or the undefined value if there is an error. On error, it puts the error code into $!. Before calling, you should say:

```
require "ipc.ph";
require "shm.ph";
```

This function is available only on machines supporting System V IPC.

shmread

shmread *id, var, pos, size*

Reads from the shared memory segment *id* starting at position *pos* for size *size* (by attaching to it, copying out, and detaching from it). *var* must be a variable that will hold the data read. The function returns true if successful, or false if there is an error. On error, it puts the error code into $!. This function is available only on machines supporting System V IPC.

shmwrite

shmwrite *id, string, pos, size*

Writes to the shared memory segment ID starting at position *pos* for size *size* (by attaching to it, copying in, and detaching from it). If *string* is too long, only *size* bytes are used; if *string* is too short, nulls are written to fill out *size* bytes. The function returns true if successful, or false if there is an error. On error, it puts the error code into $!. This function is available only on machines supporting System V IPC.

shutdown

shutdown *socket, how*

Shuts down a socket connection in the manner indicated by *how*. If *how* is 0, further receives are disallowed. If *how* is 1, further sends are disallowed. If *how* is 2, everything is disallowed.

(This function will not shut down your system; you'll have to execute an external program to do that. See system.)

sin

sin *num*

Returns the sine of *num* (expressed in radians). If *num* is omitted, it returns the sine of $_.

sleep

sleep *n*

Causes the script to sleep for *n* seconds, or forever if no argument is given. It may be interrupted by sending the process a SIGALRM. The function returns the number of seconds actually slept. On some systems, the function sleeps till the "top of the second," so, for instance, a sleep 1 may sleep anywhere from 0 to 1 second, depending on when in the current second you started sleeping.

socket

socket *socket, domain, type, protocol*

Opens a socket of the specified kind and attaches it to filehandle *socket*. *domain*, *type*, and *protocol* are specified the same as for socket(2). Before using this function, your program should contain the line:

```
use Socket;
```

This setting gives you the proper constants. The function returns true if successful.

socketpair

socketpair *sock1, sock2, domain, type, prtcl*

Creates an unnamed pair of sockets in the specified *domain* and of the specified *type*. *domain*, *type*, and *protocol* are specified the same as for socketpair(2). If socketpair is unimplemented, invoking this function yields a fatal error. The function returns true if successful.

This function is typically used just before a fork. One of the resulting processes should close *sock1*, and the other should close *sock2*. You can use

$\rightarrow$

these sockets bidirectionally, unlike the filehandles created by the pipe function.

sort

sort [*code*] *list*

Sorts a *list* and returns the sorted list value. By default (without a *code* argument), it sorts in standard string comparison order (undefined values sorting before defined null strings, which sort before everything else). *code*, if given, may be the name of a subroutine or a code block (anonymous subroutine) that defines its own comparison mechanism for sorting elements of *list*. The routine must return to the sort function an integer less than, equal to, or greater than 0, depending on how the elements of the list are to be ordered. (The handy <=> and cmp operators can be used to perform three-way numeric and string comparisons.)

The normal calling code for subroutines is bypassed, with the following effects: the subroutine may not be a recursive subroutine, and the two elements to be compared are passed into the subroutine as $a and $b, not via @_. The variables $a and $b are passed by reference, so don't modify them in the subroutine.

Do not declare $a and $b as lexical variables (with my). They are package globals (though they're exempt from the usual restrictions on globals when you're using use strict). You do need to make sure your sort routine is in the same package though, or else you must qualify $a and $b with the package name of the caller.

In versions preceding 5.005, Perl's sort is implemented in terms of C's qsort(3) function. Some qsort(3) versions will dump core if your sort subroutine provides inconsistent ordering of values. As of 5.005, however, this is no longer true.

splice

splice @*array*, *pos*, [*n*], [*list*]

Removes *n* number of elements from @*array* starting at position *pos*, replacing them with the elements of *list*, if provided. The function returns the elements removed from the array. The array grows or shrinks as necessary. If *n* is omitted, the function removes everything from *pos* onward.

split

split /*pattern*/, *string*, [*limit*]

Scans a *string* for delimiters that match *pattern*, and splits the string into a list of substrings, returning the resulting list value in list context, or the count of substrings in scalar context. The delimiters are determined by repeated pattern matching, using the regular expression given in *pattern*, so the delimiters may be of any size, and need not be the same string on every match. If the

→

pattern doesn't match at all, `split` returns the original string as a single substring. If it matches once, you get two substrings, and so on.

If *limit* is specified and is not negative, the function splits into no more than that many fields. If *limit* is negative, it is treated as if an arbitrarily large *limit* has been specified. If *limit* is omitted, trailing null fields are stripped from the result (which potential users of pop would do well to remember). If `string` is omitted, the function splits the `$_` string. If *pattern* is also omitted, the function splits on whitespace, `/\s+/`, after skipping any leading whitespace.

If the *pattern* contains parentheses, then the substring matched by each pair of parentheses is included in the resulting list, interspersed with the fields that are ordinarily returned. Here's a simple case:

```
split /([-,])/, "1-10,20";
```

that produces the list value:

```
(1, '-', 10, ',', 20)
```

---

sprintf

sprintf *format, list*

Returns a string formatted by the `printf` conventions. The *format* string contains text with embedded field specifiers into which the elements of *list* are substituted, one per field. Field specifiers are roughly of the form:

```
%m.nx
```

where the *m* and *n* are optional sizes whose interpretation depends on the type of field, and *x* is one of the following:

Code	Meaning
%	Percent sign
c	Character
d	Decimal integer
e	Exponential format floating-point number
E	Exponential format floating-point number with uppercase E
f	Fixed-point format floating-point number
g	Floating-point number, in either exponential or fixed decimal notation
G	Like g with uppercase E (if applicable)
ld	Long decimal integer
lo	Long octal integer
lu	Long unsigned decimal integer
lx	Long hexadecimal integer
o	Octal integer
s	String
u	Unsigned decimal integer

$\rightarrow$

Code	Meaning
x	Hexadecimal integer
X	Hexadecimal integer with uppercase letters
p	The Perl value's address in hexadecimal
n	Special value that stores the number of characters output so far into the next variable in the parameter list.

m is typically the minimum length of the field (negative for left-justified), and *n* is precision for exponential formats and the maximum length for other formats. Padding is typically done with spaces for strings and zeroes for numbers. The * character as a length specifier is not supported.

sqrt

sqrt *num*

Returns the square root of *num*, or $_ if omitted. For other roots such as cube roots, you can use the ** operator to raise something to a fractional power.

srand

srand *expr*

Sets the random number seed for the rand operator so that rand can produce a different sequence each time you run your program. If *expr* is omitted, a default seed is used that is a mix of difficult-to-predict, system-dependent values. If you call rand and you haven't called srand yet, rand calls srand with the default seed.

stat

stat *file*

Returns a 13-element list giving the statistics for a *file*, indicated by either a filehandle or an expression that gives its name. It's typically used as follows:

```
($dev,$ino,$mode,$nlink,$uid,$gid,$rdev,$size,
    $atime,$mtime,$ctime,$blksize,$blocks)
         = stat $filename;
```

Not all fields are supported on all filesystem types. Here are the meanings of the fields:

Field	Meaning
dev	Device number of filesystem
ino	Inode number
mode	File mode (type and permissions)
nlink	Number of (hard) links to the file
uid	Numeric user ID of file's owner

→

Field	Meaning
gid	Numeric group ID of file's owner
rdev	The device identifier (special files only)
size	Total size of file, in bytes
atime	Last access time since the epoch
mtime	Last modification time since the epoch
ctime	Inode change time (not creation time!) since the epoch
blksize	Preferred blocksize for file system I/O
blocks	Actual number of blocks allocated

$dev and $ino, taken together, uniquely identify a file. The $blksize and $blocks are likely defined only on BSD-derived filesystems. The $blocks field (if defined) is reported in 512-byte blocks. Note that $blocks*512 can differ greatly from $size for files containing unallocated blocks, or "holes," which aren't counted in $blocks.

If stat is passed the special filehandle consisting of an underline, no actual stat is done, but the current contents of the stat structure from the last stat or stat-based file test (the -x operators) is returned.

study

study *scalar*

This function takes extra time to study *scalar* ($_ if unspecified) in anticipation of doing many pattern matches on the string before it is next modified. You may have only one study active at a time—if you study a different scalar, the first is "unstudied."

sub

sub *name* [*proto*] {*block*}
sub [*proto*] *name*

Declares and defines a subroutine. *name* is the name given to the subroutine; *block* is the code to be executed when the subroutine is called. Without *block*, this statement only declares a subroutine, which must be defined at some later point in your program. *proto* is a sequence of symbols that places constraints on the arguments that the subroutine will receive. See "Subroutines" in Chapter 4.

substr

substr *string, pos,* [*n, replacement*]

Extracts and returns a substring *n* characters long, starting at character position *pos*, from a given *string*. If *pos* is negative, the substring starts that far from the end of the string instead. If *n* is omitted, everything to the end of the string is returned. If *n* is negative, the length is calculated to leave that many characters off the end of the string.

→

You can use substr() as an lvalue—replacing the delimited substring with a new string—if *string* is given as an lvalue. You can also specify a *replacement* string in the fourth parameter to replace the substring. The original extracted substring is still returned.

symlink

symlink *oldfile, newfile*

Creates a new filename symbolically linked to the old filename. The function returns 1 for success, 0 otherwise. On systems that don't support symbolic links, it produces a fatal error at runtime. Be careful if you supply a relative symbolic link, since it'll be interpreted relative to the location of the symbolic link itself, not your current working directory. See also link and readlink.

syscall

syscall *list*

Calls the system call specified as the first element of the list, passing the remaining elements as arguments to the system call. The function produces a fatal error if syscall(2) is unimplemented. The arguments are interpreted as follows: if a given argument is numeric, the argument is passed as a C integer. If not, a pointer to the string value is passed.

sysopen

sysopen *filehandle, filename, mode,* [*perms*]

Opens the file given by *filename* and associates it with *filehandle*. This function calls open(2) with the parameters *filename, mode,* and *perms.*

The possible values and flag bits of the *mode* parameter are system-dependent; they are available via the Fcntl library module. However, for historical reasons, some values are universal: zero means read-only, one means write-only, and two means read/write.

If the file named by *filename* does not exist, and sysopen creates it (typically because *mode* includes the O_CREAT flag), then the value of *perms* specifies the permissions of the newly created file. If *perms* is omitted, the default value is 0666, which allows read and write for all. This default is reasonable: see umask.

The FileHandle module provides a more object-oriented approach to sysopen. See also open.

sysread

sysread *filehandle, scalar, length,* [*offset*]

Reads *length* bytes of data into variable *scalar* from the specified *filehandle*. The function returns the number of bytes actually read, or 0 at EOF. It returns

$\rightarrow$

the undefined value on error. *scalar* will grow or shrink to the length actually read. The *offset*, if specified, says where in the string to start putting the bytes, so that you can read into the middle of a string that's being used as a buffer. You should be prepared to handle the problems (like interrupted system calls) that standard I/O normally handles for you.

sysseek

sysseek *filehandle, offset, whence*

A variant of seek() that sets and gets the file's system read/write position using the lseek(2) system call. It's the only reliable way to seek before a sysread() or syswrite(). Returns the new position, or undef on failure. Arguments are the same as for seek.

system

system *list*

Executes any program on the system for you. It does exactly the same thing as exec *list* except that it does a fork first, and then, after the exec, it waits for the execed program to complete. That is, it runs the program for you, and returns when it's done, unlike exec, which never returns (if it succeeds). Note that argument processing varies depending on the number of arguments, as described for exec. The return value is the exit status of the program as returned by the wait(2) call. To get the actual exit value, divide by 256. (The lower eight bits are set if the process died from a signal.) See exec.

syswrite

syswrite *filehandle, scalar, length, [offset]*

Writes *length* bytes of data from variable *scalar* to the specified *filehandle*. The function returns the number of bytes actually written, or the undefined value on error. You should be prepared to handle the problems that standard I/O normally handles for you, such as partial writes. The *offset*, if specified, says where in the string to start writing from, in case you're using the string as a buffer, for instance, or you need to recover from a partial write.

Do not mix calls to print (or write) and syswrite on the same filehandle unless you really know what you're doing.

tell

tell *filehandle*

Returns the current file position (in bytes, 0-based) for *filehandle*. This value is typically fed to the seek function at some future time to get back to the current position. If *filehandle* is omitted, the function returns the position of the file last read. File positions are only meaningful on regular files. Devices, pipes, and sockets have no file position.

telldir

telldir *dirhandle*

Returns the current position of the readdir routines on a directory handle (*dirhandle*). This value may be given to seekdir to access a particular location in a directory. The function has the same caveats about possible directory compaction as the corresponding system library routine. This function may not be implemented everywhere that readdir is. Even if it is, no calculation may be done with the return value. It's just an opaque value, meaningful only to seekdir.

Language
Basics

tie

tie *variable, classname, list*

Binds a *variable* to a package class, *classname*, that will provide the implementation for the variable. Any additional arguments (*list*) are passed to the "new" method of the class (meaning TIESCALAR, TIEARRAY, or TIEHASH). Typically these are arguments such as might be passed to the dbm_open(3) function of C, but this is package-dependent. The object returned by the "new" method is also returned by the tie function, which can be useful if you want to access other methods in *classname*. (The object can also be accessed through the tied function.)

A class implementing a hash should provide the following methods:

```
TIEHASH $class, LIST
DESTROY $self
FETCH $self, $key
STORE $self, $key, $value
DELETE $self, $key
EXISTS $self, $key
FIRSTKEY $self
NEXTKEY $self, $lastkey
```

A class implementing an ordinary array should provide the following methods:

```
TIEARRAY $classname, LIST
DESTROY $self
FETCH $self, $subscript
STORE $self, $subscript, $value
```

A class implementing a scalar should provide the following methods:

```
TIESCALAR $classname, LIST
DESTROY $self
FETCH $self,
STORE $self, $value
```

Unlike dbmopen, the tie function will not use or require a module for you—you need to do that explicitly yourself.

tied

tied *variable*

Returns a reference to the object underlying *variable* (the same value that was originally returned by the tie call which bound the variable to a package). It returns the undefined value if *variable* isn't tied to a package. So, for example, you can use:

```
ref tied %hash
```

to find out which package your hash is currently tied to.

time

time

Returns the number of non-leap seconds since January 1, 1970, UTC. The returned value is suitable for feeding to gmtime and localtime, and for comparison with file modification and access times returned by stat, and for feeding to utime.

times

times

Returns a four-element list giving the user and system CPU times, in seconds (possibly fractional), for this process and for the children of this process:

```
($user, $system, $cuser, $csystem) = times;
```

For example, to time the execution speed of a section of Perl code:

```
$start = (times)[0];
...
$end = (times)[0];
printf "that took %.2f CPU seconds\n", $end - $start;
```

truncate

truncate *file, length*

Truncates a *file* (given as a filehandle or by name) to the specified length. The function produces a fatal error if truncate(2) or an equivalent isn't implemented on your system.

uc

uc *string*

Returns an uppercased version of *string* (or $_ if *string* is omitted). This is the internal function implementing the \U escape in double-quoted strings. POSIX setlocale(3) settings are respected.

ucfirst

ucfirst *string*

Returns a version of *string* (or $_ if *string* is omitted) with the first character uppercased. This is the internal function that implements the \u escape in double-quoted strings. POSIX setlocale(3) settings are respected.

umask

umask *expr*

Sets the umask for the process to *expr* and returns the old one. (The umask tells Unix which permission bits to disallow when creating a file.) If *expr* is omitted, the function merely returns the current umask. For example, to ensure that the "other" bits are turned on and that the "user" bits are turned off, try something like:

```
umask((umask() & 077) | 7);
```

undef

undef *expr*

Undefines the value of *expr*, which must be an lvalue. Use only on a scalar value, an entire array or hash, or a subroutine name (using the & prefix). Any storage associated with the object will be recovered for reuse (though not returned to the system, for most versions of Unix). The undef function will probably not do what you expect on most special variables. The function always returns the undefined value. This is useful because you can omit the *expr*, in which case nothing gets undefined, but you still get an undefined value that you could, for instance, return from a subroutine to indicate an error.

You may use undef as a placeholder on the left side of a list assignment, in which case the corresponding value from the right side is simply discarded. Apart from that, you may not use undef as an lvalue.

unlink

unlink *list*

Deletes a *list* of files. (Under Unix, it will remove a link to a file, but the file may still exist if another link references it.) If *list* is omitted, it unlinks the file given in $_. The function returns the number of files successfully deleted. Note that unlink will not delete directories unless you are the superuser and the −U flag is supplied to Perl. Even if these conditions are met, be warned that unlinking a directory can inflict serious damage on your filesystem. Use rmdir instead.

unpack

unpack *template, string*

Takes a string (*string*) representing a data structure and expands it into a list value, returning the list value. (unpack does the reverse of pack.) In a scalar context, it can be used to unpack a single value. The *template* has much the same format as in the pack function—it specifies the order and type of the values to be unpacked. (See pack for a more detailed description of *template*.)

unshift

unshift *@array, list*

Prepends the elements of *list* to the front of the array, and returns the new number of elements in the array.

untie

untie *variable*

Breaks the binding between a variable and a package. See tie.

use

use *Module list*
use *version*
use *Module version list*

If the first argument is a number, it is treated as a version number. If the version of Perl is less than *version*, an error message is printed and Perl exits. This provides a way to check the Perl version at compilation time, instead of waiting for runtime.

If *version* appears between *Module* and *list*, then use calls the version method in class *Module* with *version* as an argument.

Otherwise, use imports some semantics into the current package from the named *Module*, generally by aliasing certain subroutine or variable names into your package. It is exactly equivalent to the following:

```
BEGIN { require Module; import Module list; }
```

The BEGIN forces the require and import to happen at compile time. The require makes sure that the module is loaded into memory if it hasn't been yet. The import is not a built-in function—it's just an ordinary static method call into the package named by *Module* to tell the module to import the list of features back into the current package. The module can implement its import method any way it likes, though most modules just choose to derive their import method via inheritance from the Exporter class that is defined in the Exporter module.

$\rightarrow$

If you don't want your namespace altered, explicitly supply an empty list:

```
use Module ();
```

That is exactly equivalent to the following:

```
BEGIN { require Module; }
```

Because this is a wide-open interface, pragmas (compiler directives) are also implemented this way. See Chapter 8 for descriptions of the currently implemented pragmas. These pseudomodules typically import semantics into the current block scope, unlike ordinary modules, which import symbols into the current package. (The latter are effective through the end of the file.)

There's a corresponding declaration, no, that "unimports" any meanings originally imported by use, but that have since become less important:

```
no integer;
no strict 'refs';
```

Language Basics

utime

utime *atime, mtime, files*

Changes the access time (*atime*) and modification time (*mtime*) on each file in a list of *files*. The first two elements must be the *numerical* access and modification times, in that order. The function returns the number of files successfully changed. The inode change time of each file is set to the current time. Here's an example of a utime command:

```
#!/usr/bin/perl
$now = time;
utime $now, $now, @ARGV;
```

To read the times from existing files, use stat.

values

values *%hash*

Returns a list consisting of all the values of the named hash. The values are returned in an apparently random order, but it is the same order as either the keys or each function would produce on the same hash. To sort the hash by its values, see the example under keys. Note that using values on a hash that is bound to a very large DBM file is going to produce a very large list, causing you to have a very large process, and leaving you in a bind. You might prefer to use the each function, which will iterate over the hash entries one by one without reading them all into a single list.

vec

vec *string, offset, bits*

Treats a *string* as a vector of unsigned integers, and returns the value of the element specified by *offset* and *bits*. The function may also be assigned to,

$\rightarrow$

which causes the element to be modified. The purpose of the function is to provide very compact storage of lists of small integers. The integers may be very small—vectors can hold numbers that are as small as one bit, resulting in a bitstring.

The *offset* specifies how many elements to skip over to find the one you want. *bits* is the number of bits per element in the vector, so each element can contain an unsigned integer in the range $0..(2**bits)-1$. *bits* must be one of 1, 2, 4, 8, 16, or 32. As many elements as possible are packed into each byte, and the ordering is such that vec($vectorstring,0,1) is guaranteed to go into the lowest bit of the first byte of the string. To find out the position of the byte in which an element is going to be put, you have to multiply the *offset* by the number of elements per byte. When *bits* is 1, there are eight elements per byte. When *bits* is 2, there are four elements per byte. When *bits* is 4, there are two elements (called nybbles) per byte. And so on.

Regardless of whether your system is big-endian or little-endian, vec($foo, 0, 8) always refers to the first byte of string $foo. See select for examples of bitmaps generated with vec.

Vectors created with vec can also be manipulated with the logical operators |, &, ^, and ~, which will assume a bit vector operation is desired when the operands are strings. A bit vector (*bits* == *1*) can be translated to or from a string of 1s and 0s by supplying a b* template to unpack or pack. Similarly, a vector of nybbles (*bits* == *4*) can be translated with an h* template.

wait

wait

Waits for a child process to terminate and returns the pid of the deceased process, or -1 if there are no child processes. The status is returned in $?. If you get zombie child processes, you should be calling either this function or waitpid. A common strategy to avoid such zombies is:

```
$SIG{CHLD} = sub { wait };
```

If you expected a child and didn't find it, you probably had a call to system, a close on a pipe, or backticks between the fork and the wait. These constructs also do a wait(2) and may have harvested your child process. Use waitpid to avoid this problem.

waitpid

waitpid *pid, flags*

Waits for a particular child process *pid* to terminate and returns the pid when the process is dead, or -1 if there are no child processes or if the *flags* specify non-blocking and the process isn't dead yet. The status of the dead process is returned in $?. To get valid flag values say this:

```
use POSIX "sys_wait_h";
```

→

On systems that implement neither the waitpid(2) nor the wait4(2) system call, *flags* may be specified only as 0. In other words, you can wait for a specific *pid*, but you can't do it in non-blocking mode.

wantarray

wantarray

Returns true if the context of the currently executing subroutine is looking for a list value. The function returns false if the context is looking for a scalar. May also return undef if a subroutine's return value is not going to be used at all.

warn

warn *msg*

Produces a message on STDERR just like die, but doesn't try to exit or throw an exception. For example:

```
warn "Debug enabled" if $debug;
```

If the message supplied is null, the message "Something's wrong" is used. As with die, a message not ending with a newline will have file and line number information automatically appended. The warn operator is unrelated to the *−w* switch.

write

write *filehandle*

Writes a formatted record (possibly multiline) to the specified *filehandle*, using the format associated with that filehandle—see "Formats" in Chapter 4. By default, the format for a filehandle is the one having the same name as the filehandle.

If *filehandle* is unspecified, output goes to the current default output filehandle, which starts out as STDOUT but may be changed by the select operator. If the *filehandle* is an expression, then the expression is evaluated to determine the actual *filehandle* at runtime.

Note that write is *not* the opposite of read. Use print for simple string output. If you want to bypass standard I/O, see syswrite.

CHAPTER 6

Debugging

Of course everyone writes perfect code on the first try, but on those rare occasions when something goes wrong and you're having trouble with your Perl script, there are several things you can try:

- Run the script with the −w switch, which prints warnings about possible problems in your code.

- Use the Perl debugger.

- Use another debugger, or a profiler such as the Devel::DProf module.

The major focus of this chapter is the Perl debugger, which provides an interactive Perl environment. The chapter also describes the use of the DProf module and the *dprofpp* program that comes with it; together they can provide you with a profile of your Perl script. If you've ever used any debugger, and you understand concepts such as breakpoints and backtraces, you'll have no trouble learning to use the Perl debugger. Even if you haven't used another debugger, the command descriptions and some experimenting should get you going.

The Perl Debugger

To run your script under the Perl source debugger, invoke Perl with the −*d* switch:

```
perl -d myprogram
```

This works like an interactive Perl environment, prompting for debugger commands that let you examine source code, set breakpoints, get stack backtraces, change the values of variables, etc. If your program takes any switches or arguments, you must include them in the command:

```
perl -d myprogram myinput
```

In Perl, the debugger is not a separate program as it is in the typical compiled environment. Instead, the *–d* flag tells the compiler to insert source information into the parse trees it's about to hand off to the interpreter. That means your code must first compile correctly for the debugger to work on it—the debugger won't run until you have fixed all compiler errors.

After your code has compiled, and the debugger has started up, the program halts right before the first runtime executable statement (but see the section "Using the Debugger" below regarding compile time statements) and waits for you to enter a debugger command. Whenever the debugger halts and shows you a line of code, it always displays the line it's about to execute, rather than the one it has just executed.

Any command not recognized by the debugger is directly executed as Perl code in the current package. In order to be recognized by the debugger, the command must start at the beginning of the line, otherwise the debugger assumes it's for Perl.

Debugger Commands

The debugger understands the following commands:

---

a

    a *[line] command*

    Sets an action to be done before the *line* is executed. The following steps are taken:

- Checks for a breakpoint at this line.

- Prints the line if necessary.

- Performs any actions associated with the line.

- Prompts the user if at a breakpoint or in single-step mode.

- Evaluates the line.

For example, the following prints the value of $foo (and "DB FOUND") every time line 53 is passed:

```
a 53 print "DB FOUND $foo\n"
```

A

    A

    Deletes all installed actions.

b

b *[line] [condition]*

Sets a breakpoint at *line*, which must begin an executable statement. If *line* is omitted, sets a breakpoint on the line that is about to be executed. *condition*, if given, is evaluated each time the statement is reached, and a breakpoint is taken if *condition* is true:

```
b 237 $x > 30
b 33 /pattern/i
```

b

b *subname [condition]*

Sets a (possibly conditional) breakpoint at the first line of the named subroutine.

b

b load *filename*

Sets a breakpoint on `requireing` the given file.

b

b postpone *subname [condition]*

Sets a (possibly conditional) breakpoint at the first line of subroutine *subname* after it has been compiled.

b

b compile *subname*

Stops after the subroutine has been compiled.

c

c *[line | sub]*

Continues, optionally inserting a one-time-only breakpoint at the specified line or subroutine.

d

d *[line]*

Deletes the breakpoint at the specified *line*. If *line* is omitted, deletes the breakpoint on the line that is about to be executed.

D

D

Deletes all installed breakpoints.

f

f *filename*

Switches to viewing a different file.

h

h *[command]*

Prints a help message, listing the available debugger commands.

If you supply another debugger command as an argument to the h command, it prints out the description for just that command. The command h h produces a more compact help listing designed to fit on one screen.

H

H *[-number]*

Displays last *number* commands. If *number* is omitted, it lists all previous commands. Only commands longer than one character are listed.

l

l *[linespec]*

If *linespec* is omitted, lists the next few lines. Otherwise lists the lines specified by *linespec*, which can be one of the following:

line
> Lists the single line *line*.

min+incr
> Lists *incr*+1 lines starting at *min*.

min-max
> Lists lines *min* through *max*.

subname
> Lists the first few lines from subroutine *subname*.

Also see the w and – commands.

L

L

Lists all breakpoints and actions for the current file.

m

m *expr*

`eval`s the expression in array context and prints methods callable on the first element of the result.

m

m *class*

Prints methods callable via the given class.

n

n

Next. Passes over subroutine calls and executes the next statement at this level.

O

O *[opt[=val]] [opt"val"] [opt?]*

Sets or queries option values. If omitted, *val* defaults to 1. *opt?* displays the value of option *opt*. *opt* can be abbreviated to the shortest unique string, and multiple options can be specified. The possible options are:

`AutoTrace`
: Affects printing of messages at every possible breaking point.

`frame`
: Enables printing of messages on entry and exit from subroutines.

`inhibit_exit`
: Enables stepping off the end of the script.

`maxTraceLen`
: Gives the maximum length of evals/args listed in the stack trace.

`ornaments`
: Affects the appearance of the command line on the screen.

`pager`
: Specifies the program to use for output of pager-piped commands (those beginning with a | character). Default value is `$ENV{PAGER}`.

`PrintRet`
: Enables printing of return value after `r` command.

`recallCommand, ShellBang`
: Specifies the characters used to recall previous commands or spawn a shell. By default, these are both set to `!`.

→

The following options affect what happens with the V, X, and x commands:

arrayDepth, hashDepth
> Prints only to depth *n* (" " for all).

compactDump, veryCompact
> Changes style of array and hash dumps.

DumpDBFiles
> Dumps arrays holding debugged files.

DumpPackages
> Dumps symbol tables of packages.

globPrint
> Specifies whether to print contents of globs.

quote, HighBit, undefPrint
> Changes style of string dump.

signalLevel, warnLevel, dieLevel
> Specifies level of verbosity.

tkRunning
> Runs Tk while prompting (with ReadLine).

During startup, debugger options are initialized from $ENV{PERLDB_OPTS}. You can set the additional initialization options TTY, noTTY, ReadLine, and NonStop there. See the section called "Customizing the Debugger," later in this chapter, for more information.

---

p

p *expr*

Same as print DB::OUT *expr* in the current package. In particular, does not dump nested data structures and objects, unlike the x command. The DB::OUT handle is opened to */dev/tty* (or perhaps an editor window) no matter where standard output may have been redirected to.

---

q

q *or* ^D

Quits the debugger.

---

r

r

Returns from current subroutine.

R

R

Restarts the debugger. As much as possible of your history is maintained across the sessions, but some internal settings and command-line options may be lost.

s

s *[expr]*

Single steps. Executes until it reaches the beginning of another statement, descending into subroutine calls. If an expression is supplied that includes a function call, the function is also single-stepped.

S

S *[[!]pattern]*

Lists subroutine names matching (or, if ! is specified, not matching) *pattern*. If *pattern* is omitted, lists all subroutines.

t

t

Toggles trace mode.

t

t *expr*

Traces through execution of *expr*.

T

T

Produces a stack backtrace. For example:

```
DB<2> T
$ = main::infested called from file `Ambulation.pm' line 10
@ = Ambulation::legs(1, 2, 3, 4) called from file `camel_flea' line 7
$ = main::pests('bactrian', 4) called from file `camel_flea' line 4
```

The left-hand character ($ or @) tells whether the function was called in a scalar or list context. The example shows three lines because it was three functions deep when the stack backtrace ran.

v

v

Shows versions of loaded modules.

V

V *[pkg [vars]]*

Displays all (or some) variables in package *pkg* using a data pretty-printer (which displays keys and their values for hashes, makes control characters printable, prints nested data structures in a legible fashion, and so on). *pkg* defaults to the main package. Make sure you enter the identifiers without a type specifier such as $ or @, like this:

```
V DB filename line
```

In place of a variable name, you can use ~*pattern* or !*pattern* to print existing variables whose names either match or don't match the specified regular expression.

w

w *[line]*

Lists a window of a few lines around the given *line*, or lists the current line if *line* is omitted.

x

x *expr*

evals the expression in a list context and dumps out the result in a pretty-printed fashion. Unlike the print command above, prints nested data structures recursively.

X

X *[vars]*

Same as V *currentpackage* [*vars*].

<CR>

<CR>

Repeats last n or s command.

−

−

Lists the previous few lines.

.

.

Returns debugger pointer to the last-executed line and prints it out.

/pattern/

/pattern/

Searches forward for *pattern*; final / is optional.

?pattern?

?pattern?

Searches backward for *pattern*; final ? is optional.

<

< [command]

Sets a Perl command to run before every debugger prompt. A multiline *command* may be entered by backslashing the newlines. With no *command*, the list of actions is reset.

<<

<< [command]

Adds to the list of Perl commands to run before each debugger prompt.

>

> [command]

Sets a Perl command to run after the prompt when you've just given a command to return to executing the script. A multiline *command* may be entered by backslashing the newlines.

>>

>> [command]

Adds to the list of Perl commands to run after each debugger prompt.

{

{ *[commandline]*

Sets a debugger command to run before each prompt.

{{

{{ *[commandline]*

Adds to the list of debugger commands to run before each prompt.

!

! *[number]*

Reruns a previous command (defaults to the last command executed).

!

! *−number*

Reruns *number*th-to-last command.

!

! *pattern*

Reruns last command that started with *pattern*. See O recallCommand.

!!

!! *cmd*

Runs *cmd* in a subprocess (which reads from DB::IN and writes to DB::OUT). See O shellBang.

|

| *dbcmd*

Runs specified debugger command, piping DB::OUT to $ENV{PAGER}.

| |

| | *dbcmd*

Same as | *dbcmd*, but DB::OUT is temporarily selected as well. Often used with commands that would otherwise produce long output, such as:

```
|V main
```

=

= *[alias value]*

Defines a command alias. If *alias* and *value* are omitted, lists all current aliases.

---

command

command

Executes *command* as a Perl statement. A semicolon is not needed at the end.

Using the Debugger

If you have any compile time executable statements (code within a BEGIN block or a use statement), they are not stopped by the debugger, although requires are.

The debugger prompt is something like this:

```
DB<8>
```

or even this:

```
DB<<17>>
```

where the number in angle brackets is the command number. A *csh*-like history mechanism lets you access previous commands by number. For example, !17 repeats command number 17. The number of angle brackets indicates the depth of the debugger. You get more than one set of brackets, for example, if you're already at a breakpoint and then you print out the result of a function call that itself also has a breakpoint.

If you want to enter a multiline command, such as a subroutine definition with several statements, you can use a backslash to escape the newline that would normally end the debugger command:

```
DB<1> sub foo { \
cont:    print "fooline\n"; \
cont: }

DB<2> foo
fooline
```

You can maintain limited control over the Perl debugger from within your Perl script. You might do this, for example, to set an automatic breakpoint at a certain subroutine whenever a particular program is run under the debugger. Setting $DB::single to 1 causes execution to stop at the next statement, as though you'd used the debugger's s command. Setting $DB::single to 2 is equivalent to typing the n command, and the $DB::trace variable can be set to 1 to simulate the t command.

Once you are in the debugger, you can terminate the session by entering q or CTRL-D at the prompt. You can also restart the debugger with R.

Customizing the Debugger

You can do some customizing by setting up a *.perldb* file with initialization code. When it starts up, the debugger reads and processes this file. For instance, you can set up aliases like these:

```
$DB::alias{'len'}  = 's/^len(.*)/p length($1)/';
$DB::alias{'stop'} = 's/^stop (at|in)/b/';
$DB::alias{'ps'}   = 's/^ps\b/p scalar /';
$DB::alias{'quit'} = 's/^quit\b.*/exit/';
```

You can also use this file to set options and to define a subroutine, &afterinit, to be executed after the debugger is initialized.

After the configuration file has been processed, the debugger consults the environment variable PERLDB_OPTS and parses its contents as arguments to the O opt=val debugger command.

While any options can be set in PERLDB_OPTS, the following options can *only* be specified at startup. If you want to set them in your configuration file, call &parse_options("opt=val").

TTY The TTY to use for debugging I/O.

noTTY
>   If set, goes in NonStop mode. On an interrupt, if TTY is not set, it uses the value of noTTY or */tmp/perldbtty$$* to find the TTY using Term::Rendezvous. The current variant is to have the name of the TTY in this file.

ReadLine
>   If false, a dummy ReadLine is used so that you can debug ReadLine applications.

NonStop
>   If true, no interaction is performed until an interrupt.

LineInfo
>   File or pipe to print line number information to. If it's a pipe, then a short, *emacs*-like message is used.

For example, if you create the following *.perldb* file:

```
&parse_options("NonStop=1 LineInfo=db.out");
sub afterinit { $trace = 1; }
```

your script will run without human intervention, putting trace information into the file *db.out*.

The Perl Profiler

You can supply an alternative debugger for Perl to run, by invoking your script with the *-d:module* switch. One of the most popular alternative debuggers for Perl is DProf, the Perl profiler. As of this writing, DProf was not included with the standard Perl distribution, but it is expected to be included soon.

Meanwhile, you can fetch the Devel::DProf module from CPAN. Once it has been properly installed on your system, you can use it to profile the Perl program in *testpgm* by typing:

```
perl -d:DProf testpgm
```

As your script runs, DProf gathers profile information. When the script terminates, the profiler dumps the gathered information to a file called *tmon.out*. A tool such as *dprofpp*, which is supplied with the Devel::DProf package, can be run to interpret the profile. If you run *dprofpp* against the *tmon.out* file created by DProf in the example above, you'll see something like the following:

```
% dprofpp tmon.out
Total Elapsed Time =     0.15 Seconds
    User+System Time =     0.1 Seconds
Exclusive Times
%Time Seconds    #Calls sec/call Name
 30.0  0.030          1   0.0300 Text::Wrap::CODE(0x175f08)
 20.0  0.020          1   0.0200 main::CODE(0xc7880)
 20.0  0.020          1   0.0200 main::CODE(0xfe480)
 10.0  0.010          1   0.0100 Text::Wrap::CODE(0x17151c)
 10.0  0.010         10   0.0010 Text::Tabs::expand
 0.00  0.000          1   0.0000 lib::CODE(0xfe5b8)
 0.00  0.000          3   0.0000 Exporter::export
 0.00  0.000          1   0.0000 Config::FETCH
 0.00  0.000          1   0.0000 lib::import
 0.00  0.000          1   0.0000 Text::Wrap::CODE(0x171438)
 0.00  0.000          3   0.0000 vars::import
 0.00  0.000          3   0.0000 Exporter::import
 0.00  0.000          2   0.0000 strict::import
 0.00  0.000          1   0.0000 Text::Wrap::CODE(0x171684)
 0.00  0.000          1   0.0000 lib::CODE(0xfe4d4)
```

The output shows the fifteen subroutines that use the most time—you can then focus your efforts on those subroutines where tuning the code will have the greatest effect. This output is an example of running the *dprofpp* command with the default option set. The following are the options that are available:

-a Sorts output alphabetically by subroutine name.

-E Default. Displays all subroutine times exclusive of child subroutine times.

-F Forces generation of fake exit timestamps if *dprofpp* reports that the profile is garbled. Useful only if *dprofpp* determines that the profile is garbled due to missing exit timestamps.

-I Displays all subroutine times inclusive of child subroutine times.

-l Sorts by number of calls to the subroutines.

−O cnt
> Shows only *cnt* subroutines. The default is fifteen.

−p script
> Profiles the given script and then interprets its profile data, combining the usual two steps into one.

−Q Used with *−p*, profiles the script and then quits without interpreting the data.

−q Does not display column headers.

−r Displays elapsed real times.

−s Displays system times only.

−T Displays subroutine calls, but not subroutine statistics.

−t Displays subroutine call tree, but not subroutine statistics. A subroutine called multiple times is only shown once, with a repeat count.

−U Displays unsorted output.

−u Displays user times only.

−V Prints the *dprofpp* version number.

−v Sorts by average time spent in subroutines during each call.

−z Default. Sorts by amount of user and system time used, so that the first few lines should show which subroutines are using the most time.

The perlbug Program

As you develop and debug your own code, it's possible that you'll run into a bug in Perl itself—if you do, the best way to report it is with the *perlbug* program. *perlbug* is a Perl program designed to automate the process of reporting bugs in the Perl standard distribution and the standard modules. It works interactively, prompting you for the information needed and generating an email message addressed to *perlbug@perl.com*. (If the bug you found is in one of the non-standard Perl ports, see the documentation for that port to find out how to report bugs.) When you run *perlbug*, it prompts you to include all relevant information, making it easier for the Perl developers to reproduce and track down the bug. If you come up with a patch to resolve the problem, include that too.

Don't use *perlbug* as a way to get help debugging your code (see the list of newsgroups and other resources in Chapter 1, *Introduction to Perl*, for that), but if you believe you've found a bug in Perl itself, *perlbug* is the way to report it.

To run *perlbug*, simply enter the command, with any options you want to include. For example:

```
% perlbug -t
```

The possible options are:

−a address
> Email address to send report to. Default is *perlbug@perl.com*.

−b body
> Body of report. If not included on the command line or in a file, you are given a chance to edit it.

−C Don't send a copy to your Perl administrator.

−c address
> Email address where copy should be sent. Default is your Perl administrator.

−d Data mode. (The default if you redirect or pipe input.) Prints your configuration data, without mailing anything. Use with *−v* to get more complete data.

−e editor
> Editor to use. Defaults to your default editor or to *vi*.

−f file
> File containing prepared body of report.

−b Prints help message.

−ok
> Reports successful build on this system to Perl porters. Forces *−S* and *−C*; forces and supplies values for *−s* and *−b*. Use with *−v* to get more complete data. Only reports if this system is less than 60 days old.

−okay
> Like *−ok* but will report on systems older than 60 days.

−r address
> Return address. If not specified on the command line, *perlbug* prompts for it.

−S Send without asking for confirmation.

−s subject
> Subject to include. If not specified on command line, *perlbug* prompts for it.

−t Test mode. Target address defaults to *perlbug-test@perl.com*.

−v Verbose. Includes verbose configuration data in report.

PART III

Modules

CHAPTER 7

Packages, Modules,
and Objects

Over the years, Perl has evolved from a utilitarian scripting tool into a sophisticated object-oriented programming language. Many people continue to use Perl just for simple scripts, and Perl will continue to make simple tasks easy. However, Perl can also make difficult tasks possible, by writing reusable code and using object-oriented programming techniques.

This chapter explains what Perl modules are and how to use them in your programs. Modules are written to accomplish tasks that either aren't implemented by Perl's built-in functions, or that could be done better. We say modules are "reusable" because anyone who needs to accomplish the same task can use that module instead of writing the code from scratch. As you write more and more Perl code, you'll undoubtedly find yourself using many of the modules other Perl programmers have provided. You may also find yourself writing modules and making them available for others to use.

The remainder of this book describes a significant portion of the functionality that's present in publicly available Perl modules. You'll find that a number of *standard* or *core* modules are distributed with Perl; many of these modules are discussed in Chapter 8, *Standard Modules*. Scores of other modules are available on CPAN, and virtually any task you'd like to accomplish in Perl is implemented in a module found there. For unbundled modules, you'll need to install the module on your system, and then integrate it into your program with the use function.

The use function is often the key to working with modules. For example, to bring the functionality of the popular CGI module into your program, you need to install the CGI.pm module (the .pm stands for Perl module) and put this line near the top of your program:

```
use CGI;
```

Now your program can make use of the many functions and variables made available by the CGI module.

Packages (from which modules are built) are also the mechanism by which Perl's object-oriented features are implemented. But object-oriented programming isn't for everyone, and there's nothing in packages that forces the programmer to work with the object-oriented paradigm.

Namespaces and Packages

A namespace does what it says: it *stores* names (or identifiers), including names of variables, subroutines, filehandles, and formats. Each namespace has its own *symbol table*, which is basically a hash with a key for each identifier.

The default namespace for programs is main, but you may define other namespaces and variables and use them in your program. Variables in different namespaces can even have the same name, but they are completely distinct from one another.

In Perl, a namespace is held in a *package*. By convention, package names start with a capital letter, and you should follow that convention when you create your own packages.

Each package starts with a package declaration. The package call takes one argument, the name of the package. Within the scope of a package declaration, all regular identifiers are created within that package (except for my variables).

From inside one package, you can refer to variables from another package by "qualifying" them with the package name. To do this, place the name of the package followed by two colons (::) before the identifier's name, i.e., $Package::varname.

If the package name is null, the main package is assumed. For example, $var and $::var are the same as $main::var.

Packages may be nested inside other packages. However, the package name must still be fully qualified. For example, if the package Province is declared inside the package Nation, a variable in the Province package is called as $Nation::Province::var. You cannot use a "relative" package name such as $Province::var within the Nation package for the same thing.

The default main namespace contains all other packages within it.

Modules

A *module* is a package defined in a file whose name is the same as the package. Perl locates modules by searching the @INC array, which contains a list of library directories. Perl's use of @INC is roughly comparable to the Unix shell's use of the PATH environment variable to locate executable programs. @INC is defined when Perl is built, and can be supplemented with the –I command-line option to Perl or with use lib within a program.

When you refer to *ModuleName* in your program, Perl searches in the directories listed in @INC for the module file *ModuleName.pm*, and uses the first one it finds. When you refer to a module embedded in another package, such as

`ParentPackage::ModuleName`, Perl looks for a *ParentPackage/* subdirectory in the @INC path, and for a *ModuleName.pm* file in that subdirectory.

Every Perl installation includes a central *lib* directory. The actual pathname of this directory varies from system to system, but it's commonly */usr/lib/perl* or */usr/local/lib/perl*. Looking at the central *lib* directory for your Perl distribution, you'll see something like this:

```
% ls -aF /usr/local/lib/perl
./                I18N/          bigfloat.pl      less.pm
../               IO/            bigint.pl        lib.pm
AnyDBM_File.pm    IPC/           bigrat.pl        locale.pm
AutoLoader.pm     Math/          blib.pm          look.pl
AutoSplit.pm      Net/           cacheout.pl      man/
Benchmark.pm      Pod/           chat2.pl         newgetopt.pl
Bundle/           Search/        complete.pl      open2.pl
CGI/              SelectSaver.pm constant.pm      open3.pl
CGI.pm            SelfLoader.pm  ctime.pl         perl5db.pl
CPAN/             Shell.pm       diagnostics.pm   pod/
CPAN.pm           Symbol.pm      dotsh.pl         pwd.pl
Carp.pm           Sys/           dumpvar.pl       shellwords.pl
    ...
```

When you request the `AnyDBM_File` module, it uses *AnyDBM_File.pm*. When you request the `Math::Complex` module, it looks for *Math/Complex.pm*.

A module can be included in your program with `use` or `require`. Both `use` and `require` read in a module file for use with your program.

```
require Module;
```

or:

```
use Module;
```

`use` can also take a list of strings naming entities that you want to import from the module. The list only has to include entities that are not automatically exported by the module. You don't have to provide this list at all if the module automatically exports all the entities you need.

```
use Module qw(const1 const2 func1 func2 func3);
```

The difference between `use` and `require` is that `use` pulls in the module at compile time. This means that functions like *func1* or *func2* can be used as predeclared list operators throughout the file. The `require` call does not necessarily load the module during compilation, so you must explicitly qualify its routines with the package name.

Object-Oriented Perl

In Perl circles, modules and object-oriented programming are often spoken of in the same breath. But just because the programmer has written a package and a subroutine doesn't mean that the code is objectified.

A module that describes a class must contain a special subroutine to create an object. (Each object that is created is an *instance* of a class.) This subroutine is called a *constructor*. (Often the constructor is named new, but Create is also used in Win32 classes.) The constructor creates a new object and returns a reference to it. This reference is a regular scalar variable, except that it refers to some underlying object that knows what class it belongs to. In your programs, you will use the reference to manipulate the object.

Methods are subroutines that expect an object reference as a first argument, such as:

```
sub in_class {
    my $class = shift; # object reference
    my ($this, $that) = @_; # params
}
```

Methods may be invoked like this:

```
PackageName->constructor(args)->method_name(args);
```

or:

```
$object = PackageName->constructor(args);
$object->method_name(args);
```

Objects have a specific set of available methods within their class, but they also inherit methods from their parent class, if they have one.

Objects are destroyed when the last reference to them goes away. You can control this capture before the object is destroyed with the DESTROY method. The DESTROY method should be defined somewhere in the class. You do not call DESTROY explicitly; it will be called at an appropriate time. Object references contained in the current object will be freed when the current object is freed. Most of the time you won't need to explicitly destroy an object, but there are occasions where you should, such as when you are done with a socket object.

Object Syntax

Perl uses two forms of syntax for invoking methods on objects. For both types of syntax, the object reference or class name is given as the first argument. A method that takes a class name is called a *class method*, and one that takes an object reference is called an *instance method*.

Class methods provide functionality for the entire class, not just for a single object that belongs to the class. Class methods expect a class name as their first argument. Following this explanation, a constructor is an example of a class method:

```
sub new {
    my $self = {};
    bless $self;
    return $self;
}
```

On the other hand, an instance method expects an object reference as its first argument. An instance method will shift the first argument and use this argument as a reference:

```
sub instance_method {
    my $self = shift;
    my($one, $two, $three) = @_;
    # do stuff
}
```

Here is an example of a constructor creating a new object and returning a reference:

```
$tri = new Triangle::Right (side1 => 3, side2 => 4);
```

This example creates a new right-triangle object and references it with $tri. The parameters are given as a hash-style list. This is common for constructors, as they set initial parameters for an object that is probably just a hash. Now that we have an object, we can invoke some method on it. Suppose Triangle::Right defines a method, hypot, that returns the length of the hypotenuse for a given right-triangle object. It would be used like this:

```
$h = hypot $tri;
print "The hypotenuse is: $h.\n";
```

In this particular example, there happens to be no additional arguments to the hypot method, but there could have been.

With the arrow (–>) notation, the left side of the arrow must be an object reference or a class name, while the right side of the arrow must be a method defined for that object. Any arguments must follow the method inside of parentheses. For example:

```
$obj->method(args)
CLASS->method(args)
```

You have to use parentheses because this form can't be used as a list operator, although the first type of method syntax can.

The examples given above would look like this using the arrow syntax:

```
$tri = Triangle::Right->new(side1 => 3, side2 => 4);
$h = $tri->hypot();
print "The hypotenuse is: $h.\n";
```

The arrow syntax provides a helpful visual relationship between the object and its method, but both forms of syntax do the same thing. Precedence for the arrow syntax is left to right, exactly the same as the dereferencing operator. This allows you to chain together objects and methods if you want to simplify things. You just have to make sure you have an object to the left of the arrow and a method to the right:

```
%sides = (side1 => 3, side2 => 4);
$h = Triangle::Right->new(%sides)->hypot();
print "The hypotenuse is: $h.\n";
```

In this example, you never assign a variable name to the right-triangle object; the reference is passed directly to the hypot method.

CHAPTER 8

Standard Modules

We've talked about the extent to which Perl benefits from user contributions. In fact, many contributed modules are so generally useful that they are now distributed with Perl itself. This chapter describes these "standard modules"—if you are running Perl 5.005, all these modules are already available to you. If you are running an earlier version of Perl, and you find that a module you want isn't on your system, or if you simply don't find what you need among the modules in this chapter, check CPAN for one that does what you want.

While this chapter primarily covers standard Perl modules called at execution time from your program, it also covers the "pragmatic" modules that affect the compilation phase. (A pragma is a compiler directive that provides hints to the compiler.) By convention, the names of the pragmatic modules are all lowercase, while the names of other modules begin with an uppercase letter and are of mixed case.

The Win32-specific modules are not included in this chapter, but are described in Chapter 19, *Win32 Modules and Extensions*.

The following table provides a quick look at the standard modules and what they do:

Module	Function
AnyDBM_File	Provides framework for multiple DBMs
attrs	Sets or gets attributes of a subroutine
AutoLoader	Loads functions only on demand
AutoSplit	Splits a module for autoloading
autouse	Postpones load of modules until a function is used
B	Perl compiler and tools
base	Establishes IS-A relationship with base class at compile time
Benchmark	Checks and compares running times of code
blib	Uses MakeMaker's uninstalled version of a package

Module	Function
Carp	Generates error messages
CGI	Simple Common Gateway Interface class
CGI::Apache	Sets up environment to use CGI with Perl-Apache API
CGI::Carp	CGI routines for writing to HTTPD (or other) error log
CGI::Cookie	CGI interface to Netscape (HTTP/1.1) cookies
CGI::Fast	CGI interface for FastCGI
CGI::Push	Interface for server push operations
CGI::Switch	Tries multiple constructors and returns the first available CGI object
Class::Struct	Declares struct-like datatypes as Perl classes
Config	Accesses Perl configuration information
constant	Perl pragma to declare constants
CPAN	Queries, downloads, and builds Perl modules from CPAN sites
CPAN::FirstTime	Utility for CPAN::Config file initialization
CPAN::Nox	Wrapper around *CPAN.pm* without using any XS module
Cwd	Gets pathname of current working directory
Data::Dumper	Returns Perl data structures as strings
DB_File	Accesses Berkeley DB
Devel::SelfStubber	Generates stubs for a selfloading module
diagnostics	Forces verbose warning diagnostics
DirHandle	Supplies object methods for directory handles
DynaLoader	Automatic dynamic loading of Perl modules
English	Uses English or *awk* names for punctuation variables
Env	Imports environment variables
Errno	System errno constants from *errno.h* include file
Exporter	Default import method for modules
ExtUtils::Command	Utilities to replace common Unix commands
ExtUtils::Embed	Utilities for embedding Perl in C/C++ applications
ExtUtils::Install	Installs files from here to there
ExtUtils::Installed	Inventory management of installed modules
ExtUtils::Liblist	Determines libraries to use and how to use them
ExtUtils::MakeMaker	Creates a Makefile for a Perl extension
ExtUtils::Manifest	Utilities to write and check a MANIFEST file
ExtUtils::Miniperl	Writes the C code for *perlmain.c*
ExtUtils::Mkbootstrap	Makes a bootstrap file for use by DynaLoader
ExtUtils::Mksymlists	Writes linker option files for dynamic extension
ExtUtils::MM_OS2	Methods to override Unix behavior in ExtUtils::Make-Maker
ExtUtils::MM_Unix	Methods used by ExtUtils::MakeMaker
ExtUtils::MM_VMS	Methods to override Unix behavior in ExtUtils::Make-Maker
ExtUtils::MM_Win32	Methods to override Unix behavior in ExtUtils::Make-Maker
ExtUtils::Packlist	Manages *.packlist* files
ExtUtils::testlib	Adds *blib/** directories to @INC

Module	Function
Fatal	Replaces functions with equivalents that succeed or die
Fcntl	Loads the C *fcntl.h* defines
fields	Perl pragma to provide compile-time verified class fields
File::Basename	Parses file specifications
File::CheckTree	Runs many tests on a collection of files
File::Compare	Compares files or filehandles
File::Copy	Copies files or filehandles
File::DosGlob	DOS-like globbing with enhancements
File::Find	Traverses a file tree
File::Path	Creates or removes a series of directories
File::Spec	Portably performs operations on filenames
File::stat	By-name interface to Perl's built-in `stat` functions
FileCache	Keeps more files open than the system permits
FileHandle	Supplies object methods for filehandles
FindBin	Locates directory of original Perl script
GDBM_File	Tied access to GDBM library
Getopt::Long	Extended processing of command-line options
Getopt::Std	Processes single-character options with option clustering
I18N::Collate	Compares 8-bit scalar data according to the current locale
integer	Does arithmetic in integer instead of double
IO	Loads various IO modules
IO::File	Supplies object methods for filehandles
IO::Handle	Supplies object methods for I/O handles
IO::Pipe	Supplies object methods for pipes
IO::Seekable	Supplies seek-based methods for I/O objects
IO::Select	Object-oriented interface to the select system call
IO::Socket	Object interface to socket communications
IPC::Msg	System V Msg IPC object class
IPC::Open2	Opens a process for both reading and writing
IPC::Open3	Opens a process for reading, writing, and error handling
IPC::Semaphore	System V Semaphore IPC object class
IPC::SysV	System V IPC constants
less	Perl pragma to request less of something from the compiler
lib	Manipulates `@INC` at compile time
locale	Perl pragma to use and avoid POSIX locales for built-in operations
Math::BigFloat	Arbitrary-length floating-point math package
Math::BigInt	Arbitrary-length integer math package
Math::Complex	Complex numbers package
Math::Trig	Trigonometric functions
NDBM_File	Tied access to NDBM files
Net::hostent	By-name interface to Perl's built-in `gethost*` functions

Module	Function
Net::netent	By-name interface to Perl's built-in getnet* functions
Net::Ping	Checks whether a host is online
Net::protoent	By-name interface to Perl's built-in getproto* functions
Net::servent	By-name interface to Perl's built-in getserv* functions
ODBM_File	Tied access to ODBM files
Opcode	Disables named opcodes when compiling Perl code
ops	Restricts unsafe operations when compiling
overload	Overloads Perl's mathematical operations
Pod::Functions	Used in converting from pod to HTML
Pod::Html	Module to convert pod files to HTML
Pod::Text	Converts pod data to formatted ASCII text
POSIX	Perl interface to IEEE Std 1003.1
re	Perl pragma to alter regular expression behavior
Safe	Creates safe namespaces for evaluating Perl code
SDBM_File	Tied access to SDBM files
Search::Dict	Searches for key in dictionary file
SelectSaver	Saves and restores selected filehandle
SelfLoader	Loads functions only on demand
Shell	Runs shell commands transparently within Perl
sigtrap	Enables stack backtrace on unexpected signals
Socket	Loads the C *socket.h* defines and structure manipulators
strict	Restricts unsafe constructs
subs	Predeclares subroutine names
Symbol	Generates anonymous globs; qualifies variable names
Sys::Hostname	Tries every conceivable way to get hostname
Sys::Syslog	Perl interface to Unix syslog(3) calls
Term::Cap	Terminal capabilities interface
Term::Complete	Word completion module
Term::ReadLine	Interface to various ReadLine packages
Test	Framework for writing test scripts
Test::Harness	Runs Perl standard test scripts with statistics
Text::Abbrev	Creates an abbreviation table from a list
Text::ParseWords	Parses text into a list of tokens
Text::Soundex	The soundex algorithm described by Knuth
Text::Tabs	Expands and unexpands tabs
Text::Wrap	Wraps text into a paragraph
Thread	Multithreading support
Thread::Queue	Thread-safe queues
Thread::Semaphore	Thread-safe semaphores
Thread::Signal	Starts a thread that runs signal handlers reliably
Thread::Specific	Thread-specific keys
Tie::Array	Base class definitions for tied arrays
Tie::Handle	Base class definitions for tied handles
Tie::Hash, Tie::StdHash	Base class definitions for tied hashes
Tie::RefHash	Uses references as hash keys
Tie::Scalar, Tie::StdScalar	Base class definitions for tied scalars

Module	Function
Tie::SubstrHash	Fixed-table-size, fixed-key-length hashing
Time::gmtime	By-name interface to Perl's built-in `gmtime` function
Time::Local	Computes time from local and GMT time
Time::localtime	By-name interface to Perl's built-in `localtime` function
Time::tm	Internal object used by Time::gmtime and Time::localtime
UNIVERSAL	Base class for all classes (blessed references)
User::grent	By-name interface to Perl's built-in `getgr*` functions
User::pwent	By-name interface to Perl's built-in `getpw*` functions
vars	Predeclares global variable names
vmsish	Enables VMS-specific language features

In the remainder of this chapter, the modules are arranged in alphabetical order for easy reference. For more detail about a module, use the *perldoc* command to read the manpage for that module (see Chapter 4, *The Perl Language*, for information on *perldoc*).

AnyDBM_File

Provides a single DBM (Database Manager) interface regardless of the DBM implementation you use. The module inherits from the various DBM packages; by default, it inherits from NDBM_File. If it doesn't find NDBM_File, the default search order is: DB_File, GDBM_File, SDBM_File (which comes with Perl), and finally ODBM_File. You can override this default order by redefining @ISA:

```
@AnyDBM_File::ISA = qw(DB_File GDBM_File NDBM_File);
```

However, an explicit `use` takes priority over the @ISA ordering.

Perl's `dbmopen` function actually just calls `tie` to bind a hash to AnyDBM_File. The effect is to bind the hash to one of the specific DBM classes that AnyDBM_File inherits from.

attrs

Sets or gets the attributes of subroutines. Attributes are set for a subroutine at compile time; therefore, setting an invalid attribute results in a compile-time error. During execution, when you call `attrs::get` on a subroutine reference or name, it returns the list of attributes that are set. Note that `attrs::get` is not exported. For example:

```
sub test {
    use attrs qw(locked method);
    ...
}
@a = attrs::get(\&foo);
```

The valid attributes are:

`locked`

> Meaningful only when the subroutine or method is to be called by multiple threads. When set on a subroutine that also has the method attribute set, invoking that subroutine implicitly locks its first argument before execution. On a non-method subroutine, a lock is taken on the subroutine itself before execution. The lock semantics are identical to one taken explicitly with the `lock` operator immediately after entering the subroutine.

`method`

> The invoking subroutine is a method.

AutoLoader

Delays the loading of functions until they are used. Each function is placed in a file that has the same name as the function, with an *.al* extension. The files are stored in a subdirectory of the *auto/* directory that is named after the package. For example, the function `GoodStuff::whatever` is loaded from the file *auto/Good-Stuff/whatever.al*. Should always be `use`d and not `required`.

A module using the AutoLoader has the special marker `__END__` prior to the declarations for the subroutine to be autoloaded. Any code before this marker is loaded and compiled when the module is used, but at the marker, Perl stops parsing the file.

Later, during execution, when a subroutine that isn't yet in memory is called, the `AUTOLOAD` function attempts to find it in a directory relative to the location of the module file. For example, if *POSIX.pm* is in the directory */usr/local/lib/perl5*, then the AutoLoader looks for POSIX subroutines in */usr/local/lib/perl5/auto/POSIX/*.al*.

AutoSplit

Splits a program or module into files that the AutoLoader can handle. It can be called from a program or from the command line:

```
# from a program
use AutoSplit;
autosplit_modules(@ARGV)

# from the command line
perl -MAutoSplit -e 'autosplit(FILE, DIR, KEEP, CHECK, MODTIME)' ...

# another interface
perl -MAutoSplit -e 'autosplit_lib_modules(@ARGV)' ...
```

AutoSplit is used by MakeMaker as well as the standard Perl libraries. It operates on a file, splitting off subroutines that come after the `__END__` marker and storing them as described above for AutoLoader, creating any necessary directories along the way. AutoSplit has two functions:

autosplit

autosplit *(file, dir, keep, check, modtime)*

Splits the module into files. Each file is given the name of the subroutine it contains, with *.al* appended. `autosplit` also creates the file *autosplit.ix*, which serves as both a forward declaration of all package routines and as a timestamp showing when the hierarchy was last updated. Takes the following arguments:

file Filename of program or module to be split.

dir Name of directory hierarchy in which to store the split files.

keep
  If false, pre-existing *.al* files in the *auto* directory that are no longer part of the module are deleted.

check
  If true, checks to be sure the module being split includes a `use AutoLoader` statement. If the statement is missing, `autosplit` doesn't process the module.

modtime
  If true, only splits the module if it is newer than *autosplit.ix*.

autosplit_lib_modules

autosplit_lib_modules *(@ARGV)*

Takes a list of modules that are assumed to be in a *lib* subdirectory of the current directory, processes them as described above for `autosplit`, and stores the resulting file in the directory *lib/auto*. Used in building Perl.

autouse

Pragma for postponing the loading of a module from compile time to execution time. The module isn't loaded until one of its subroutines is used; the subroutines all have to be exported by the module.

```
use autouse module => qw(sub1 [sub2 ...])
```

Use with care, since problems that might otherwise be found during compilation won't crop up until your program is already executing.

B

The Perl compiler. To use the compiler, you don't need to use this module. See the O module, which is the user frontend to the compiler; also see the compiler section of Chapter 3, *The Perl Interpreter*. The B module provides the classes for implementing backends for the compiler. If you plan to write a new backend, read the B manpage for the details of the module.

B::Asmdata

Contains autogenerated data about Perl ops; used to generate bytecode. Any changes made to this file will be lost.

B::Assembler

Assembles Perl bytecode.

B::Bblock

Walks the basic blocks of a program. Invoked as:

```
perl -MO=Bblock[,options] filename
```

B::Bytecode

The bytecode backend for the Perl compiler. Takes Perl source code and generates platform-independent bytecode that can be run with the *byteperl* executable or can be loaded via the byteload_fh function in the B module. Compiling with the Byte-code backend won't speed up execution of your program, but it may improve start-up time. Invoke as:

```
perl -MO=Bytecode[,options] program
```

where *program* is the name of the Perl script to compile. Any non-option arguments are treated as the names of objects to be saved; the main program is assumed if there are no extra arguments. Possible options are:

-- Forces end of options.

−Dopts
: Debug options, which can be either concatenated or specified separately. Possible options are:

  a Tells the bytecode assembler to include assembler source in its output as bytecode comments.

  b Prints debugging information about bytecompiler progress.

  C Prints each CV from the final walk through the symbol tree.

  o Prints each OP as it's processed.

−fopt
: Forces individual optimizations on or off. Preceding an optimization with no- turns that option off (e.g., no-compress-nullops). Possible values of *opt* are:

  bypass-nullops
  : If op->op_next ever points to a NULLOP, replaces the op_next field with the first non-NULLOP in the path of execution.

`compress-nullops`
> Fills in only the necessary fields of ops that have been optimized away by Perl's internal compiler.

`omit-sequence-numbers`
> Leaves out the code to fill in the op_seq field for all ops that are used only by Perl's internal compiler.

`strip-syntax-tree`
> Leaves out the code to fill in the internal syntax tree pointers. Use of this option breaks any goto `label` statements and prevents later recompiling or disassembling of the resulting program.

−*m* Compiles as a module rather than as a standalone program.

−*ofilename*
> Sends output to *filename* instead of STDOUT.

−*O[n]*
> Sets the optimization level to *n*, where *n* is an integer. *n* defaults to 1. −O1 sets −fcompress-nullops −fomit-sequence-numbers, and −O6 adds −fstrip-syntax-tree.

−*S* Outputs bytecode assembler source instead of assembling it into bytecode.

B::C

The C backend for the Perl compiler. Generates C source code from Perl source; the generated code corresponds to Perl's internal structures for running the program. Compiling with the C backend won't speed up execution of your program, but it may improve start-up time. Invoke as:

```
perl -MO=C[,options] program
```

where *program* is the name of the Perl script to compile. Any non-option arguments are treated as the names of objects to be saved; the main program is assumed if there are no extra arguments. Possible options are:

−− Forces end of options.

−*Dopts*
> Debug options, which can be either concatenated or specified separately. Possible options are:

A   Prints AV information on saving.

c   Prints COPs as they are processed, including file and line number.

C   Prints CV information on saving.

M   Prints MAGIC information on saving.

o   Prints each OP as it's processed.

–fopt

> Forces individual optimizations on or off. Possible values of *opt* are:
>
> cog Copy-on-grow; PVs are declared and initialized statically.
>
> no-cog
> > No copy-on-grow.

–ofilename

> Sends output to *filename* instead of to STDOUT.

–O[n]

> Sets optimization level, where *n* is an integer. *n* defaults to 1. Currently, values of 1 and higher set cog.

–uPackname

> Forces apparently unused subroutines from package *Packname* to be compiled, letting programs use eval "foo()" even if subroutine foo isn't seen to be used at compile time. You can specify multiple *–u* options.

–v Compiles verbosely.

B::CC

The CC backend for the Perl compiler. Generates optimized C source code that corresponds to your program's flow. The initial version included in Perl 5.005 actually includes few optimizations, but this will change. Programs compiled with this backend may both start up and execute slightly faster. Invoke as:

```
perl -MO=C[,options] program
```

where *program* is the name of the Perl script to compile. Any non-option arguments are treated as the names of objects to be saved; the main program is assumed if there are no extra arguments. Possible options are:

> –– Forces end of options.

–Dopts

> Debug options, which can be either concatenated or specified separately. Possible options are:
>
> 1 Outputs the filename and line number of each original line of Perl code as it is processed.
>
> O Outputs each OP as it is compiled.
>
> p Outputs the contents of the shadow pad of lexicals as it is loaded for each sub or for the main program.
>
> q Outputs the name of each fake PP function in the queue as it's about to be processed.
>
> r Writes debugging output to STDERR instead of as comments in the C output.

s   Outputs the contents of the shadow stack at each OP.

t   Outputs timing information of the stages of compilation.

–fopt
    Forces individual optimizations on or off. Possible values of *opt* are:

    `freetmps-each-bblock`
        Runs FREETMPS at the end of each basic block instead of at the end of each statement. `freetmps-each-loop` and `freetmps-each-bblock` are mutually exclusive.

    `freetmps-each-loop`
        Runs FREETMPS at the end of each loop instead of at the end of each statement. `freetmps-each-loop` and `freetmps-each-bblock` are mutually exclusive.

    `omit-taint`
        Doesn't generate code for handling Perl's tainting mechanism.

–mModulename
    Generates source for an XSUB module instead of for an executable.

–ofilename
    Sends output to *filename* instead of to STDOUT.

–O[n]
    Sets optimization level, where *n* is an integer. *n* defaults to 1. Currently, –O1 sets –ffreetmps-each-bblock, and –O2 sets –ffreetmps-each-loop.

–uPackname
    Forces apparently unused subroutines from package *Packname* to be compiled, permitting programs to use `eval "foo()"` even if subroutine foo isn't seen to be used at compile time. You can specify multiple *–u* options.

–v   Compiles verbosely.

B::Debug

Walks the Perl syntax tree, printing debug information about ops. Invoke as:

```
perl -MO=Debug[,exec] filename
```

If exec is specified, walks in execution order rather than in syntax order.

B::Deparse

Perl compiler backend that generates Perl source code from the internal compiled structure of a program. The output won't be exactly the same as the original program, but it will be close. Invoke as:

```
perl -MO=Deparse[,options] program
```

program is the name of the program to be deparsed. The options are comma-separated and follow normal backend option conventions. The possible options are:

-*l* Adds #line declarations to the output based on line and file locations of the original code.

-*p* Prints parentheses wherever they are legal, not just where they are required. Useful for seeing how Perl is parsing your expressions.

−*sletters*
Provides style options for the output. In this initial release, the only style option provided is C, which "cuddles" else, elsif, and continue blocks so that, for example, you would get:

```
} else {
```

instead of:

```
}
   else {
```

The default is to not cuddle.

−*uPackage*
Deparses subroutines in package *Package* as well as the main program, subroutines called by the main program, and subroutines in the main program. Multiple −*u* arguments can be given, separated by commas.

B::Disassembler

Disassembles Perl bytecode.

B::Lint

Provides program checking for Perl programs, equivalent to running Perl with the −*w* option. Named after the Unix *lint* program for checking C programs. Invoked as:

```
perl -MO=Lint[,options] program
```

program is the name of the Perl program to be checked. The options are separated by commas and follow normal backend option conventions. Most of the options are *lint*-check options, where each option is a word specifying one *lint* check. Preceding an option with no− turns off that option. Options specified later override earlier options. There is also one non-lint-check option, −*u*. Here is the list of available options:

all Turns all warnings on.

context
Warns whenever an array is used in implicit scalar context.

dollar-underscore
Warns whenever $_ is explicitly used anywhere or whenever it is used as the implicit argument of a print statement.

implicit-read
Warns whenever an operation implicitly reads a Perl special variable.

implicit-write
> Warns whenever an operation implicitly writes to a Perl special variable.

none
> Turns off all warnings.

private-names
> Warns whenever any variable, subroutine, or method name lives in a non-current package but begins with an underscore (_); doesn't warn about an underscore as a single-character name, e.g., $_.

regexp-variables
> Warns whenever one of the regular-expression variables $', $&, or $` is used.

−u Package
> Normally checks only the main program code and all subroutines defined in package main; *−u* lets you specify other packages to be checked.

undefined-subs
> Warns whenever an undefined subroutine is invoked.

B::Showlex

Shows lexical variables used in functions or files. Invoke as:

```
perl -MO=Showlex[,sub] filename
```

If *sub* is provided and is the name of a subroutine in file *filename*, B::Showlex prints the lexical variables used in that subroutine. Otherwise, it prints the file-scope lexicals in *filename*.

B::Stackobj

Serves as a helper module for the CC backend.

B::Terse

Walks the Perl syntax tree, printing terse information about the ops. Invoke as:

```
perl -MO=Terse[,exec] filename
```

If exec is specified, walks the tree in execution order instead of syntax order.

B::Xref

Perl compiler backend that generates a cross-reference listing of variables, subroutines, and formats in a Perl program. Results are grouped by file, then subroutine, then package, then objects within the package with line numbers. The line numbers are given as a comma-separated list. A line number may be preceded by one of the following code letters:

Code	Meaning
%	Subroutine or method call
f	Format definition
i	Introduction, e.g., a lexical defined with my
s	Subroutine definition

Invoke B::Xref like this:

```
perl -MO=Xref[,options] program
```

program is the Perl program whose cross-reference you want. Options are separated by commas and follow normal backend option conventions. The possible options are:

−D Specifies internal debug options. Most useful if specified with *−r* option. Debug options are:

    0   Prints each operator as it's being processed, in the execution order of the program.

    t   Prints the object on the top of the stack as it is being tracked.

−ofilename
    Sends output to *filename* instead of STDOUT.

−r Produces raw output in machine-readable form for each definition or use of a variable, subroutine, or format.

base

Provides a shortcut for setting up @ISA. You can say:

```
use base qw(A B);
```

instead of:

```
BEGIN {
    require Foo;
    require Bar;
    push @ISA, qw(Foo Bar);
}
```

Benchmark

Provides routines for timing the execution of your code and formatting the results. Inherits only from the Exporter class. Its functions are:

new

new *Benchmark*

Returns the current time. By getting the current time before and after running the code, you can calculate the time it takes the code to run.

clearallcache

clearallcache

Clears the entire cache. Exported on request.

clearcache

clearcache *(count)*

Clears the cached time for *count* rounds of the null loop. Exported on request.

debug

*Benchmark->***debug***(flag)*

·Enables or disables debugging by setting the $Benchmark::Debug flag.

disablecache

disablecache

Disables use of the cache. Exported on request.

enablecache

enablecache

Resumes caching. Exported on request.

timediff

timediff *(t1, t2)*

Calculates the difference between two times and returns the difference as a Benchmark object suitable for passing to timestr. Always exported.

timeit

timeit *(count, code)*

Runs *code* and reports the time it took. Always exported. Takes the following arguments:

count
> The number of times to run the loop

code
> The code to run, specified as either a code reference or a string

timestr

timestr *(timediff[, style[, format]])*

Converts times to printable strings. Always exported. Takes the following arguments:

timediff
> The object containing the times to be formatted.

style
> The output format. The possible values of style are:

> `all` Shows all of the following times: wallclock, user, system, user time of children, and system time of children.

> `auto`
>> Like `all`, except that if the children times are both zero, it acts like `noc`.

> `noc` Shows all except the two children times.

> `nop` Shows only wallclock and the two children times.

format
> Indicates the `printf(3)`-style format specifier (without the leading %) to use for printing the times. The default is `"5.2f"`.

timethese

timethese *(count, \%codehashref[, style])*

Times each of several pieces of code and reports the results separately. Always exported. Takes the following arguments:

count
> The number of times to run the loop.

\%codehashref
> Reference to a hash where the keys are names and the values are either strings or code references; each key/value pair specifies a piece of code to run.

style
> Determines the format of the output. See `timestr` for the possible values of *style*.

timethis

timethis *(count, code[, title[, style]])*

Runs a chunk of code several times. Always exported. Takes the following arguments:

count
> The number of times to run the loop.

→

code

> The code to run, specified as either a code reference or a string.

title

> The title of the result; default is `"timethis COUNT"`.

style

> Determines the format of the output. See `timestr` for the possible values of *style*.

---

blib

Pragma for testing programs against a package before the package has been installed. Given a directory path, `blib` starts in that directory to look for a `blib` directory structure; if it doesn't find one there, it works its way back up five levels. If no path is specified, it starts looking in the current directory.

`blib` is meant to be used from the command line:

```
perl -Mblib script [args...]
perl -Mblib=dir script [args...]
```

However, you can also call it from a Perl program:

```
use blib;
use blib 'dir';
```

Carp

Provides routines for generating error messages. Its subroutines generally report errors from the perspective of the calling program. Its functions are:

---

carp

carp *msg*

Warns of an error; reports the error as having occurred in the calling routine, not in the routine that contains the `carp`.

```
Use Carp;
carp "text of error message";
```

cluck

cluck *msg*

Warns of errors and prints a stack backtrace; reports the error as having occurred in the calling routine. Not exported by default.

```
use Carp qw(cluck);
cluck "text of error message";
```

confess

confess *msg*

Dies and prints a stack backtrace. Reports the error as having occurred at the point where confess was called.

croak

croak *msg*

Dies, reporting error as having occurred in the calling routine.

CGI

The CGI (Common Gateway Interface) library permits object-oriented web form creation and processing. The CGI.pm module contains the bulk of functionality for CGI programming. Four subclasses provide interfaces to various server environments and additional features. They are described below. For complete information on how CGI works and a description of CGI.pm see Chapter 9, *CGI Overview*, and Chapter 10, *The CGI.pm Module*.

CGI::Apache

Sets up the environment for using CGI.pm with the Perl-Apache API. The new constructor for this class creates an Apache::CGI class object that interfaces to the API.

CGI::Carp

Creates Carp-like CGI routines for writing error messages to the HTTPD or other error log. Exports functions for warn, die, carp, confess, and croak. The functions write timestamped error messages to your server log or other output that you specify. See the section on the Carp module for details on the Carp functions.

Two other functions are provided by this module. Neither are automatically exported, so you must explicitly import them in use:

```
use CGI::Carp qw(carpout fatalsToBrowser);
```

carpout

carpout \ *fh*

Sends error messages to the filehandle *fh*. You should provide a reference to the filehandle *glob*, although you can also just use the filehandle's name for this function.

fatalsToBrowser

fatalsToBrowser

When this routine is imported via use, fatal errors, such as those produced by die and confess, send error messages to the browser as well as the error log. A simple HTTP response is created with the error message, followed by a request to send mail to the web administrator.

CGI::Cookie

Provides an interface to Netscape (HTTP/1.1) cookies that can be used in conjunction with CGI.pm or independently. To use CGI::Cookie, you create a new cookie object with the constructor new. You can then send the cookie to the browser in one of the following ways:

- From a CGI script, create a Set-Cookie field in the HTTP header for each cookie you want to send ($c is the cookie object):

  ```
  print "Set-Cookie: $c0";
  ```

- With CGI.pm (see Chapter 10), use the header method with a −cookie argument:

  ```
  print header(-cookie=>$c);
  ```

- Using *mod_perl* (see Chapter 11, *Web Server Programming with mod_perl*), use the request object's header_out method:

  ```
  $r->header_out('Set-Cookie',$c);
  ```

The following methods are provided for CGI::Cookie:

new

$c = new CGI::Cookie(*attribs*)

Constructor. Creates a new cookie. Attributes are:

-domain = *domain_name*
 Optional, points to domain name or fully qualified hostname to which cookie will be returned. If missing, browser will return cookie only to the server that set it.

$\rightarrow$

-expires = *date*

> Optional expiration date, in any of the date formats recognized by CGI.pm. If missing, cookie expires at the end of this browser session.

-name = *name*

> Required. Scalar value with the cookie name.

-path = *path*

> Optional, points to a partial URL on the current server; cookies will be returned to any URL beginning with this path. Defaults to /.

-secure = *boolean*

> Optional. If true, browser will only return cookie if a cryptographic protocol is in use.

-value = *value*

> Required. The value of the cookie; can be a scalar, an array reference, or a hash reference.

as_string

> *$c*->**as_string**

Turns internal representation of cookie into RFC-compliant text. Called internally by overloading the "" operator, or can be called directly.

domain

> *$c*->**domain***(val)*

Gets or sets the cookie's domain. With no parameter, gets the current value; otherwise sets the new value.

expires

> *$c*->**expires***(val)*

Gets or sets the cookie's expiration date. With no parameter, gets the current expiration date; otherwise sets the new value.

fetch

> *%cookies* = **fetch CGI::Cookie**

Returns a hash containing cookies returned by the browser, where the keys are the cookie names and the values are the cookie values. In a scalar context, fetch returns a hash reference.

name

> *$c*->**name***(val)*

Gets or sets the cookie's name. With no parameter, returns the current name; otherwise sets the new value.

Modules

parse

> *%cookies* = **parse** **CGI::Cookie***(stored_cookies)*

Retrieves cookies stored in an external form.

path

> *$c->***path***(val)*

Gets or sets the cookie's path. With no parameter, returns the current path; otherwise sets the new value.

raw_fetch

> *%cookies* = **raw_fetch** **CGI::Cookie**

Like `fetch`, but does no unescaping of reserved characters; useful for retrieving cookies set by a foreign server.

value

> *$c->***value***(val)*

Gets or sets the cookie's value. With no parameter, returns the current value; otherwise sets the new value. In array context, returns the current value as an array. In scalar context, returns the first value of a multivalued cookie.

CGI::Fast

CGI interface for FastCGI. FastCGI is a type of gateway for web servers that improves performance by loading scripts as persistently running processes. CGI::Fast provides a new constructor to create a CGI object that runs in this environment. FastCGI requires both a server and a version of Perl that are FastCGI enabled. See *www.fastcgi.com* for more information.

CGI::Push

Provides an interface to do server push operations, letting you rewrite pages whose content changes regularly. A server push operation automatically sends updates to a page on a push-capable browser. CGI::Push exports the function do_push to implement page redraws. This method can be used on a CGI::Push object or on its own:

```
$q = new CGI::Push;
$q->do_push(-next_page => \&sub);
 # or
do_push (-next_page => \&sub);
```

do_push requires one argument: a reference to a subroutine that will draw the next page. You may optionally specify a subroutine that draws the last page and the interval between page updates. Additional parameters to do_push are those that can be used with a CGI::headers object.

do_push

do_push *(params)*

Implements a server push operation, which updates a page at specific intervals. Parameters are:

-delay => *n*
> Specifies the number of seconds, *n*, to wait before the next call to the page-drawing subroutine.

-last_page => \&*sublast*
> Runs the subroutine *sublast* to draw the last page update of a server push operation. The -last_page routine is invoked when the -next_page routine returns false. A reference to a subroutine glob should be provided for this parameter, but the name of the subroutine is also acceptable.

-next_page => \&*sub*
> *sub* is the name of the subroutine responsible for redrawing the page and counting the number of iterations (if you want repeated updating). The do_push routine ends when *sub* returns false (or when the -last_page subroutine is invoked). A reference to a subroutine glob should be provided for this parameter, but the name of the subroutine is also acceptable.

-type = *string*
> Specifies the content type of the pushed data. The default value is text/html.

CGI::Switch

Provides a new method that tries to call new in each of the Apache::CGI, CGI::XA, and CGI classes, returning the first CGI object that it successfully gets.

Class::Struct

Formerly named Class::Template; exports a single function, struct. struct takes a list of element names and types, and optionally a class name, and creates a Perl class that implements a "struct-like" data structure. It also creates a constructor method, new, for creating objects of the class (so a class created this way must not itself define a new method).

Each element in the struct data has an accessor method, which is used to assign to the element and to fetch its value. The default accessor can be overridden by declaring a sub of the same name in the package. Each element's type can be scalar, array, hash, or class.

struct

struct *(paramlist)*

Creates a class, with object methods for each element of the class. The parameter list *paramlist* can take one of three forms:

```
struct( CLASS_NAME => [ ELEMENT_LIST ]); # object is array-based
struct( CLASS_NAME => { ELEMENT_LIST }); # object is hash-based
struct( ELEMENT_LIST );     # class name is current package name
                            # and object is array-based
```

The array-based element lists are faster and smaller, but the hash-based list is more flexible. The class that is created can be a subclass of the UNIVERSAL class, but not of any other class.

Element list

The items in the ELEMENT_LIST are of the form:

```
NAME => TYPE, ...
```

where each NAME=>TYPE pair declares one element of the struct. Each element name is defined as an accessor method, unless a method is explicitly defined with that name. (In that case, a warning is issued if the −w flag is set.)

Element types and accessor methods

There are four possible element types, each represented by a string. Each string may start with an asterisk (*), indicating that a reference to the element is to be returned. The type of an element determines the accessor method provided. The following list shows the element types, the strings that represent them, and the accessor:

*array (@ or *@)*
> The element is an array, initialized to ( ). With no argument, the accessor returns a reference to the element's whole array.

> With one or two arguments, the first argument is an index specifying one element of the array; the second argument, if present, is the value to be assigned to that array element.

*class (Class_Name or *Class_Name)*
> The element's value must be a reference blessed to the named class or to one of its subclasses. The element is initialized to the result of calling the new constructor of the named class.

> The accessor's argument, if any, is the value to be assigned to the element. The accessor croaks if it's not an appropriate object reference.

*hash (% or *%)*
> The element is a hash, initialized to ( ). With no argument, the accessor returns a reference to the element's whole hash.

> With one or two arguments, the first argument is a key specifying one element of the hash; the second argument, if present, is the value to be assigned to that hash element.

$\rightarrow$

*scalar ($ or *$)*
> The element is a scalar, initialized to undef. The accessor's argument, if any, is assigned to the element.

Config

Used to access configuration information. When Perl is built, the Configure script obtains and saves this information in a hash, %Config, in *Config.pm* itself. Config checks to be sure it's running with the same Perl version as the one that created the hash.

The index into the hash is the shell variable name. %Config is always exported; the following three functions are exported on request:

config_sh

config_sh

Returns all Perl configuration information.

```
use Config(qw(config_sh));
print config_sh();
```

returns:

```
archlibexp='sun4-solaris'
cc='cc'
ccflags='-I/usr/local/include/sfio -I/usr/local/include'
```

config_vars

config_vars *(names)*

Returns the name/value pairs for the requested configuration variables. Prints the results to STDOUT.

```
use Config(qw(config_vars));
print config_vars(qw(osname ccflags));
```

returns:

```
osname='solaris'
ccflags='-I/usr/local/include/sfio -I/usr/local/include'
```

myconfig

myconfig

Returns a summary of the major Perl configuration values.

constant

A Perl pragma that declares compile-time constants with a given scalar or list value. By default, the value is evaluated in list context, but you can override the default by specifying `scalar`.

```
use constant NAME1 => value1;
use constant NAME2 => scalar value2;
```

CPAN

Lets you access CPAN; search for a module, a bundle, an author, or a distribution; download a module or distribution; install it; and `make` it. The CPAN module can be used either interactively from the command line or programmatically:

```
perl -MCPAN -eshell;          #run from the command line
```

Or:

```
use CPAN;

my $obj = CPAN::Shell->install('ExtUtils::MakeMaker');
```

This section describes the use of the CPAN module from a program. See Chapter 2, *Installing Perl*, for information on using it interactively and for details of the available commands. These commands, available interactively from the shell, are methods of the class CPAN::Shell. From a program, they are available both as methods (e.g., `CPAN::Shell->install( . . . )`) and as functions in the calling package (e.g., `install( . . . )`).

Each of the commands that produce listings of modules (`r`, autobundle, and `u`) returns a list of the IDs of all modules within the list. The IDs of all objects available within a program are strings that can be expanded to the corresponding real objects with the `CPAN::Shell->expand("Module",@things)` method. expand returns a list of CPAN::Module objects according to the `@things` arguments. In scalar context, it returns only the first element of the list.

Session and Cache Managers

The CPAN module contains a session manager, which keeps track of objects that have been fetched, built, and installed in the current session. No status is retained between sessions.

There is also a cache manager, which keeps track of disk space used and deletes extra space. The cache manager keeps track of the build directory, `$CPAN::Config->{build_dir}`, and uses a simple FIFO mechanism to delete directories below `build_dir` when they grow bigger than `$CPAN::Config->{build_cache}`.

The original distribution files are kept in the directory `$CPAN::Config->{keep_source_where}`. This directory is not covered by the cache manager, but must be controlled by the user. If the same directory is used as both `build_dir` and `keep_source_where`, your sources are deleted with the same FIFO mechanism.

Bundles

The CPAN module recognizes a bundle as a Perl module in the namespace Bundle:: that does not define any functions or methods and usually contains only pod documentation. It starts like a Perl module with a package declaration and a $VERSION variable. After that the pod section looks like any other pod with the difference that it contains a special section that begins with:

```
=head1 CONTENTS
```

This section consists of lines like this:

```
Module_Name [Version_String] [- optional text]
```

where *Module_Name* is the name of a module (for example, Term::ReadLine), not the name of a distribution file, and the version and text are optional. If there is text, it is preceded by a –. The distribution of a bundle should follow the same convention as other distributions.

Bundles are treated specially in the CPAN package. When you tell CPAN to install a bundle, it installs all the modules in the CONTENTS section of the pod. You can install your own bundles locally by placing a conforming bundle file somewhere in your @INC path. The autobundle command available in the shell interface does that for you by including all currently installed modules in a snapshot bundle file (see Chapter 2).

Configuration

When the CPAN module is installed, a site-wide configuration file is created as *CPAN/Config.pm*. The default values defined there can be overridden locally in the file *CPAN/MyConfig.pm*. You can store this file in *$HOME/.cpan/CPAN/MyConfig.pm*, because *$HOME/.cpan* is added to the search path of the CPAN module before the use or require statements. Chapter 2 lists the keys defined in the hash reference $CPAN::Config and how to set and query them.

CD-ROM Support

The *urllist* parameter in the configuration table contains a list of URLs to be used for downloading. If the list contains any *file* URLs, CPAN looks there first for files (except index files). So if you are using a CD-ROM containing the CPAN contents, include the CD-ROM as a *file* URL at the end of *urllist* since it is likely to be out-of-date. You can do this with:

```
o conf urllist push file://localhost/CDROM/CPAN
```

CPAN::FirstTime

The CPAN::FirstTime module has one function, init, which is an initialization routine called automatically the first time a user uses the CPAN module. It asks the user a series of questions, and writes the answers into a CPAN::Config file.

CPAN::Nox

A wrapper for *CPAN.pm* that prevents the use of any compiled extensions while it's executing. Run it in interactive mode if you have upgraded Perl and now your extensions aren't working:

```
perl -MCPAN::Nox -eshell;
```

Cwd

The Cwd module provides three functions that get the pathname of the current working directory. Using these functions instead of the *pwd* command will make your code more portable, because not all systems have *pwd*.

cwd

cwd

Gets the current working directory. This is the safest way to get it.

getcwd

getcwd

Does the same thing as cwd by reimplementing the C library functions getcwd(3) or getwd(3) in Perl.

fastcwd

fastcwd

A faster way to get the directory, but somewhat more dangerous because of the way it works internally.

Data::Dumper

Converts Perl data structures into strings that can be printed or used with eval to reconstruct the original structures. Takes a list of scalars or reference variables and writes out their contents in Perl syntax. Several interfaces to Data::Dumper are provided:

- Simple procedural interface:

  ```
  print Dumper($foo, $bar);
  ```

- Extended usage with names:

  ```
  print Data::Dumper->Dump([$foo, $bar], [qw(foo *ary)]);
  ```

- Object-oriented interface:

```
$d = Data::Dumper->new([$foo, $bar], [qw(foo *ary)]);
...
print $d->Dump;
```

By default, references are identified as $VARn$, where n is a numeric suffix. References to substructures within $VARn$ are labeled using arrow notation. In the extended usage form, references can be given user-specified names. See the Data::Dumper manpage for examples of the module's use.

Several configuration variables can be used to control the output generated using the procedural interface. These variables control the default state of the object created by the new method. Each variable has a corresponding method that can be used later to query or modify the object. In the following list, each variable is followed by the corresponding method:

`$Data::Dumper::Bless`
`$obj->Bless([newval])`

> Can be set to a string that specifies an alternative to the bless builtin operator used to create objects. A function with the specified name should exist and should accept the same arguments as the builtin. Default is bless.

`$Data::Dumper::Deepcopy`
`$obj->Deepcopy([newval])`

> If set to Boolean value, enables deep copies of structures; cross-referencing is then only done when absolutely essential. Default is 0.

`$Data::Dumper::Indent`
`$obj->Indent([newval])`

> Controls the style of indentation for the output. Can be set to:

> 0   No newlines, indentation, or spaces between list items
> 1   Newlines, but each level in the structure is indented a fixed amount
> 2   Default. Takes into account the length of hash keys so the hash values line up.
> 3   Like 2, but also annotates array elements with their index, with each annotation on its own line

`$Data::Dumper::Freezer`
`$obj->Freezer([newval])`

> If set to a method name, Data::Dumper invokes that method via the object before attempting to turn it into a string. Set to an empty string to disable. Default is empty string.

`$Data::Dumper::Pad`
`$obj->Pad([newval])`

> Specifies the string that is prefixed to every output line. Default is an empty string.

`$Data::Dumper::Purity`

`$obj->Purity([`*`newval`*`])`

Controls degree to which `eval` can recreate the original reference structures. Setting the value to 1 outputs additional Perl statements to correctly recreate nested references. Default is 0.

`$Data::Dumper::Quotekeys`

`$obj->Quotekeys([`*`newval`*`])`

If set to a Boolean value, controls whether hash keys are quoted. If false, avoids quoting hash keys that look like a simple string. Default is 1, which always quotes hash keys.

`$Data::Dumper::Terse`

`$obj->Terse([`*`newval`*`])`

When set, Data::Dumper outputs single, non–self-referential values as atoms or terms rather than as statements. `$VAR`*`n`* names are avoided as much as possible. Such output may not be parsable by `eval`.

`$Data::Dumper::Toaster`

`$obj->Toaster([`*`newval`*`])`

If set to a method name, Data::Dumper issues a method call for any objects that are to be dumped using the syntax `bless(data, class)->method()`. Set to an empty string to disable. Default is empty string.

`$Data::Dumper::Useqq`

`$obj->Useqq([`*`newval`*`])`

When set, enables the use of double quotes to represent string values. In addition, `\n`, `\t`, and `\r` are used to represent non-space whitespace; "unsafe" characters are backslashed; and unprintable characters are output as quoted octal integers. Default is 0. Currently, the `Dumpxs` method does not honor this flag.

`$Data::Dumper::Varnam`

`$obj->Varname([`*`newval`*`])`

Specifies the prefix to use for tagging variable names in the output. Default is VAR.

The following methods and functions are provided:

---

new

$obj = Data::Dumper->new *(arrayref[, arrayref])*

Constructor. Creates a new Data::Dumper object. The first argument is an anonymous array of values to be dumped. The optional second argument is an anonymous array of names for the values. The names don't need a leading $ and must be comprised of alphanumeric characters. You can begin a name with a * to specify that the dereferenced type must be dumped instead of the reference itself for array and hash references.

Dump

$obj->Dump
Data::Dumper->Dump(arrayref[, arrayref])

Returns stringified form of values stored in the object, with their order preserved, subject to the configuration options. In array context, returns a list of strings corresponding to the supplied values.

Dumper

Dumper (list)

Function that returns the stringified form of the values in the list, subject to the configuration options. The values are named $VARn in the output. Returns a list of strings in array context.

DumperX

DumperX (list)

Identical to Dumper, except that it calls the xsub implementation. Only available if the xsub extension to Data::Dumper is installed.

Dumpxs

$obj->Dumpxs
Data::Dumper->Dumpxs(arrayref[, arrayref])

Identical to Dump, but is written in C and therefore is much faster. Available only if the xsub extension to Data::Dumper is installed.

Reset

$obj->Reset

Clears the internal table of "seen" references, returning the object itself.

Seen

$obj->Seen([hashref])

Queries or adds to the internal table of references that have been encountered. The references aren't dumped, but their names are inserted when they are encountered subsequently. With no argument, returns the "seen" list of name => value pairs, in array context. Otherwise, returns the object itself.

Values

$obj->Values([arrayref])

Queries or replaces the internal array of values to be dumped. With no arguments, returns the names. Otherwise, returns the object itself.

DB_File

Ties a Perl hash to one of the Berkeley DB database types and lets you use functions provided in the DB API:

```
[$X =] tie %hash,  "DB_File", $filename [, $flags, $mode, $DB_HASH];
[$X =] tie %hash,  "DB_File", $filename, $flags, $mode, $DB_BTREE;
[$X =] tie @array, "DB_File", $filename, $flags, $mode, $DB_RECNO;
```

The types are:

$DB_HASH
 Stores key/data pairs in data files; equivalent to other hashing packages like DBM, NDBM, ODBM, GDBM, and SDBM.

$DB_BTREE
 Stores key/data pairs in a binary tree.

$DB_RECNO
 Uses a record (line) number to access fixed-length and variable-length flat text files through the same key/value-pair interface as in $DB_HASH and $DB_BTREE.

After you've tied a hash to a database:

```
$db = tie %hash, "DB_File", "filename";
```

you can access the Berkeley DB API functions:

```
$db->put($key, $value, R_NOOVERWRITE);  # invoke the DB "put" function
```

All the functions defined in the *dbopen(3)* manpage are available except close and dbopen itself. The constants defined in the *dbopen* manpage are also available.

Here are the functions available (the comments note only the differences from the equivalent C function):

del

$X->del(key[, flags])

Removes key/value pairs from the database. *flags* is optional.

fd

*$X->*fd

Returns a file descriptor that represents the underlying database. No difference from the equivalent C function.

get

*$X->*get*(key, value[, flags])*

Retrieves data from the database by key. *flags* is optional. The value associated with *key* is returned in *value.*

put

*$X->*put*(key, value[, flags])*

Stores a key/value pair in the database. *flags* is optional. If R_IAFTER or R_IBEFORE is set, then *key* is set to the record number of the inserted key/value pair.

seq

*$X->*seq*(key, value[, flags])*

Returns the next sequential key/value pair from the database. *flags* is optional. Both *key* and *value* are set.

sync

*$X->*sync*([flags])*

Synchronizes the database by flushing any cached data to disk. *flags* is optional.

Devel::SelfStubber

Generates stubs in a module that uses the SelfLoader, either printing the necessary stubs or generating the whole module with the stubs inserted in the correct location before the _ _DATA_ _ token. The default is to just print the stubs.

stub

stub *(module[, dir])*

Generates the stubs. Takes the following arguments:

→

module

> Name of the module, in the form Devel::SelfStubber (with no *.pm* at the end).

dir Library directory that contains the module; defaults to the current directory.

To just print the stubs:

```
use Devel::SelfStubber;
Devel::SelfStubber->stub(module, dir);
```

To generate the whole module, with the stubs inserted correctly, set the variable $Devel::SelfStubber::JUST_STUBS to 0:

```
use Devel::SelfStubber;
$Devel::SelfStubber::JUST_STUBS = 0;
Devel::SelfStubber->stub(module, dir);
```

diagnostics

Provides more descriptive diagnostics than those generated by the Perl compiler and interpreter. Uses the longer, more explanatory error messages found in the *perldiag* manpage. Can be used as a pragma or as a standalone program, *splain*. When used as a pragma, diagnostics affects the compilation phase of your program as well as the execution phase. As a standalone module, it is used to postprocess errors after execution has completed.

The *splain* program links to *diagnostics.pm* to act on the standard error output of a Perl program. The program's output can be sent to a file, which is then used as input to *splain*, or it can be piped directly to *splain*. Output from *splain* is directed to STDOUT.

Options

> −*p* Sets the variable $diagnostics::PRETTY to true.

> −*v* Prints the *perldiag* manpage introduction, then any diagnostic messages.

As a pragma:

```
use diagnostics [-verbose]
```

enables the use of diagnostics in your program (and enables Perl's −*w* flag). Compilation is then subject to the enhanced diagnostics, which are issued to STDERR. Set the diagnostics::PRETTY variable in a BEGIN block to provide nicer escape sequences for pagers, so your output looks better. The -verbose option prints the *perldiag* manpage introduction, then any diagnostic messages. Functions are:

```
enable
```

> Turns diagnostics on at runtime.

`disable`
> Turns diagnostics off at runtime.

DirHandle

Provides methods for accessing Perl's directory functions, avoiding namespace pollution. Creates anonymous glob to hold a directory handle and closes the dirhandle automatically when the last reference goes out of scope. The methods provided are:

new

> *$dh* = new DirHandle *[dirname]*

> Constructor. Creates a new directory handle. The optional directory name, *dirname*, defaults to the current directory.

close

> *$dh*->close()

> Closes a directory handle; equivalent to the `closedir` function.

open

> *$dh*->open*(dirname)*

> Opens directory *dirname*; equivalent to the `opendir` function.

read

> *$dh*->read()

> Reads directory entries. Equivalent to the `readdir` function. In scalar context, reads the next directory entry; in list context, reads all entries.

rewind

> *$dh*->rewind()

> Sets current position to beginning of directory; equivalent to the `rewinddir` function.

DynaLoader

The standard Perl interface to the dynamic linking mechanisms available on many platforms.

Using DynaLoader

Use DynaLoader like this:

```
package Module;
require DynaLoader;
@ISA = qw(... DynaLoader ...);

bootstrap Module;
```

The bootstrap method calls your module's bootstrap routine directly if the module is statically linked into Perl. Otherwise the module inherits the bootstrap method from DynaLoader, which loads in your module and calls its bootstrap method.

Extending to New Architectures

If you want to extend DynaLoader to a new architecture, you need to know about its internal interface. The variables it uses are:

$dl_debug

Enables internal debugging messages on the Perl side of the DynaLoader; by default, is set to $ENV{'PERL_DL_DEBUG'} if that is defined.

A similar debugging variable is added to the C code (see *dlutils.c*) and enabled if Perl was built with the *-DDEBUGGING* flag, or it can be set via the PERL_DL_DEBUG environment variable. Set to 1 for minimal information or higher for more detail.

@dl_library_path

Default list of directories to search for libraries; initialized to hold the list of directories in $Config{'libpth'}. Should also be initialized with other directories that can be determined from the environment at runtime.

@dl_resolve_using

List of additional libraries or other shared objects for resolving undefined symbols. Required only on platforms without automatic handling for dependent libraries.

@dl_require_symbols

List of one or more symbol names in the library/object file to be dynamically loaded. Only required on some platforms.

Of the following subroutines, bootstrap and dl_findfile are standard across all platforms and are defined in *DynaLoader.pm*. The others are defined in the *.xs* file that supplies the implementation for the platform.

bootstrap

bootstrap *(modulename)*

Normal entry point for automatic dynamic loading in Perl.

dl_error

dl_error

Gets error message text from the last failed DynaLoader function:

```
$message = dl_error();
```

dl_expandspec

dl_expandspec *(spec)*

Used for systems that require special filename handling to deal with symbolic names for files. *spec* specifies the filenames that need the special handling.

dl_findfile

dl_findfile *(names)*

Determines the full paths to one or more loadable files, given their generic names and optionally one or more directories. Searches directories in @dl_library_path by default and returns an empty list if no files are found.

dl_find_symbol

dl_find_symbol *(libref, symbol)*

Looks in *libref* for the address of symbol *symbol*. Returns the address, or undef if not found.

dl_install_xsub

dl_install_xsub *(perl_name, symref[, filename])*

Creates a new Perl external subroutine. Takes the following arguments:

perl_name
    Name of the new subroutine.

symref
    Pointer to the function that implements the routine.

filename
    The source file for the function. If not defined, DynaLoader is used.

dl_load_file

dl_load_file *(filename)*

Dynamically loads *filename*, which must be the path to a shared object or library; returns undef on error.

dl_undef_symbols

dl_undef_symbols

Returns list of symbol names that remain undefined after dl_load_file, or ( ) if the names are unknown.

English

Provides aliases for the Perl built-in special variables. Everything else about the variables and their use remains the same. Be aware, though, that using the English module significantly slows down a program for regular expressions.

Some of the Perl variables match some *awk* built-in variables. For those cases, you'll find two English names: a short version (which is the *awk* name) and a longer version. For example, you can use either $ERRNO (the *awk* name) or $OS_ERROR to refer to the Perl variable $!.

Here is the list of variables, and their English alternatives:

Perl	English	Perl	English
@_	@ARG	$?	$CHILD_ERROR
$_	$ARG	$!	$OS_ERROR
$%	$MATCH	$!	$ERRNO
$`	$PREMATCH	$@	$EVAL_ERROR
$'	$POSTMATCH	$$	$PROCESS_ID
$+	$LAST_PAREN_MATCH	$$	$PID
$.	$INPUT_LINE_NUMBER	$<	$REAL_USER_ID
$.	$NR	$<	$UID
$/	$INPUT_RECORD_SEPARATOR	$>	$EFFECTIVE_USER_ID
$/	$RS	$>	$EUID
$|	$OUTPUT_AUTOFLUSH	$(	$REAL_GROUP_ID
$,	$OUTPUT_FIELD_SEPARATOR	$(	$GID
$,	$OFS	$)	$EFFECTIVE_GROUP_ID
$\	$OUTPUT_RECORD_SEPARATOR	$)	$EGID
$\	$ORS	$0	$PROGRAM_NAME
$"	$LIST_SEPARATOR	$]	$PERL_VERSION
$;	$SUBSCRIPT_SEPARATOR	$^A	$ACCUMULATOR
$;	$SUBSEP	$^D	$DEBUGGING
$%	$FORMAT_PAGE_NUMBER	$^F	$SYSTEM_FD_MAX
$=	$FORMAT_LINES_PER_PAGE	$^I	$INPLACE_EDIT

Perl	English	Perl	English
$-	$FORMAT_LINES_LEFT	$^P	$PERLDB
$~	$FORMAT_NAME	$^T	$BASETIME
$^	$FORMAT_TOP_NAME	$^W	$WARNING
$:	$FORMAT_LINE_BREAK_CHAR- ACTERS	$^X	$EXECUTABLE_NAME
$^L	$FORMAT_LINEFEED	$^O	$OSNAME

Env

Lets your program treat environment variables as simple variables instead of having to access them from the %ENV pseudo-hash where they are kept.

```
use Env;

use Env qw(var1 var2 ...);
```

Internally, Env uses an import function that ties suitably named environment variables to global Perl variables with the same names. By default, it ties all variables yielded by keys %ENV. A "suitable" environment has a name that begins with an alphabetic character and contains only alphanumeric characters or underscores.

When use Env is invoked with arguments, the arguments are interpreted as a list of environment variables to tie, but the variables don't have to exist yet. After a variable has been tied, you can use it like a normal variable, accessing or changing its value.

You untie a variable by setting its value to undef.

Errno

Provides system errno constants from *errno.h* include file. Defines and conditionally exports all the error constants defined in *errno.h*. There is one export tag, :POSIX, which exports all POSIX-defined error numbers.

The file *Errno.pm* is automatically generated and shouldn't be updated. Any changes made to the file will be lost.

Exporter

Implements a default import method for other modules to inherit if they don't want to define their own. If you are writing a module, you can do the following:

```
package Module;
use Exporter ();
@ISA = qw(Exporter);

@EXPORT = qw(...);
@EXPORT_OK = qw(...);
%EXPORT_TAGS = (tag => [...]);
```

where @EXPORT is a list of symbols to export by default, @EXPORT_OK is a list of symbols to export on request, and %EXPORT_TAGS is a hash that defines names for sets of symbols. Names in %EXPORT_TAGS must also appear in @EXPORT or @EXPORT_OK.

Then Perl programs that want to use your module just say:

```
use Module;              # Import default symbols
use Module qw(...);      # Import listed symbols
use Module ();           # Do not import any symbols
```

The Exporter can handle specialized import lists. An import list is the list of arguments passed to the import method. If the first entry begins with !, :, or /, the list is treated as a series of specifications that add to or delete from the list. A leading ! means delete, rather than add.

Symbol	Meaning
[!]name	This name only
[!]:DEFAULT	All names in @EXPORT
[!]:tag	All names in $EXPORT_TAGS{tag} anonymous list
[!]/pattern/	All names in @EXPORT and @EXPORT_OK that match pattern

Exporter methods are:

export_to_level

> *package*->**export_to_level**(*n, what_to_export*)

Used when you can't use Exporter's import method directly. Takes the following arguments:

n   An integer specifying how far up the calling stack to export your symbols.

what_to_export
   Array of symbols to export, usually @_.

import

import

The default import method.

require_version

> *module_name*->**require_version**(*value*)

Validates the version of module *module_name*, checking that it is at least *value*.

export_fail

*module_name->***export_fail***(failed_symbols)*

Returns a list of symbols that couldn't be imported. The default method provided by Exporter returns the list unchanged.

export_tags

export_tags*(taglist)*

Adds tagged sets of symbols to @EXPORT.

export_ok_tags

export_ok_tags*(taglist)*

Adds tagged sets of symbols to @EXPORT_OK.

ExtUtils::Command

Provided with the standard Win32 port to replace common Unix commands in MakeFiles. Includes subroutines for the following commands:

cat

cat *file . . . [> destination]*

Concatenates all specified files into *destination* file or to STDOUT.

chmod

chmod *mode files . . .*

Sets Unix-like permissions on all files specified, where *mode* gives the permissions to set.

cp

cp *source . . . destination*

Copies a single source file *source* to *destination*. Multiple source files can be specified if *destination* is an existing directory.

eqtime

eqtime *source destination*

Sets the "modified time" of *destination* to that of *source*.

mkpath

mkpath *directory . . .*

Creates *directory*, including any parent directories.

mv

mv *source . . . destination*

Moves sourcefile *source* to *destination*. Multiple sourcefiles are allowed if *destination* is an existing directory.

rm_f

rm_f *files . . . .*

Removes *files*, even if they are read-only.

rm_rf

rm_rf *directories . . . .*

Removes *directories* recursively, even if they are read-only.

test_f

test_f *file*

Tests for the existence of *file*.

touch

touch *file . . .*

Makes sure *file* exists and sets the current timestamp.

ExtUtils::Embed

Generally called from the Makefile that builds your application to provide initialization functions for embedding Perl code in C or C++ applications. For example:

```
perl -MExtUtils::Embed -e xsinit
perl -MExtUtils::Embed -e ldopts
```

Uses the configuration information kept in *Config.pm* (see the Config module, above). Exports the following functions:

ccdlflags

ccdlflags

Prints `$Config{ccdlflags}`.

ccflags

ccflags

Prints `$Config{ccflags}`.

ccopts

ccopts

Combines `perl_inc`, `ccflags`, and `ccdlflags`.

ldopts

ldopts

Outputs arguments for linking the Perl library and extensions to your application. When invoked as:

```
perl -MExtUtils::Embed -e ldopts --
```

the following options are recognized:

–std
> Output arguments for linking the Perl library and any extensions linked with the current Perl.

–I <path1:path2>
> Search path for *ModuleName.a* archives. Default is `@INC`.

–– <list of linker args>
> Additional linker arguments to be considered.

Any additional arguments found before the `––` token are taken as the names of modules to generate code for.

Can also be called with parameters:

```
'ldopts($std,[@modules],[@link_args],$path)'
```

When called this way, returns the argument string rather than printing it to STDOUT. The optional parameters are:

$std
> Boolean, equivalent to the *–std* option.

[@modules]
> Array reference, equivalent to adding module names before the `––` token.

→

[@link_args]
>   Array reference, equivalent to adding linker arguments after the -- token.

$path
>   Equivalent to the −*I* option.

perl_inc

perl_inc

For including Perl header files. For example, if you say:

```
perl -MExtUtils::Embed -eperl_inc
```

the module prints the following:

```
-I$Config{archlibexp}/CORE
```

xsinit

xsinit

Generates C/C++ code for the XS initializer function. When invoked as:

```
perl -MExtUtils::Embed -e xsinit --
```

the following options are recognized:

−o [filename]
>   Prints to the filename specified. Defaults to *perlxsi.c*. If *filename* is STD-OUT, prints to standard output.

−std
>   Writes code for extensions that are linked with the current Perl.

>   Any additional arguments are expected to be names of modules to generate code for.

>   Can also be called with parameters:

```
'xsinit($filename,$std,[@modules])'
```

When called this way, the following optional parameters are accepted:

$filename
>   Equivalent to the −*o* option.

$std
>   Boolean, equivalent to the −*std* option.

[@modules]
>   An array reference, equivalent to adding module names after the -- token.

xsi_header

xsi_header

Returns a string defining the same EXTERN_C macro as *perlmain.c*; also #includes *perl.h* and *EXTERN.h*.

xsi_protos

xsi_protos *(modules)*

Returns string of *boot_$ModuleName* prototypes for each module in *modules*.

xsi_body

xsi_body *(modules)*

Returns string of calls to newXS that glue the module bootstrap function to *boot_ModuleName* for each module in *modules*.

ExtUtils::Install

Used by MakeMaker for handling the platform-dependent installation and deinstallation of modules; not meant to provide general-purpose tools. Exports the following functions:

install

install *(\hashref, verbose, nonono)*

Installs files. Takes the following arguments:

\hashref
> Reference to a hash, where each key is a directory to copy from and the value is the directory to copy into. The whole tree below the "from" directory is copied, with timestamps and permissions preserved.
>
> The hash has two additional keys: read and write. After copying everything, install writes the list of target files to the file named by $hashref->{write}. If there is another file named by $hashref->{read}, its contents are merged into the written file.

verbose
> Verbose switch.

nonono
> Don't-really-do-it switch.

install_default

install_default *([fullext])*

Calls `install` with the same arguments as the MakeMaker defaults. Takes zero or one argument. With no argument, it treats `$ARGV[0]` as the argument. If present, the argument contains the value of MakeMaker's FULLEXT key.

pm_to_blib

pm_to_blib *(\hashref[, dir])*

Takes a hash reference as the first argument and copies all the keys of the hash to the corresponding values. Filenames with the *.pm* extension are autosplit. The optional second argument is the autosplit directory.

uninstall

uninstall *(packlistfile, verbose, nonono)*

Uninstalls files. Takes the following arguments:

packlistfile
> Name of file containing filenames to be unlinked.

verbose
> Verbose switch.

nonono
> No-don't-really-do-it-now switch.

ExtUtils::Installed

Provides inventory management for installed modules, based on the contents of the *.packlist* files that are created during installation. It also permits classifying the installed files and extracting directory information from the *.packlist* files.

new

$inst = ExtUtils::Installed->new()

Searches for all installed *.packlists* on the system and stores their contents. Takes no parameters, uses ExtUtils::Packlist to read the *.packlist* files.

directories

$inst->directories*(module[, string[, dir[, . . .]]])*

Returns list of directories. Only returns directories that contain files from the specified module. Parameters are:

$\rightarrow$

module

> Required. The name of a module; returns a list of all directories in the package.

string

> Optional. Possible values are prog, man, or all to return program directories, manual directories, or all directories, respectively.

dir   Optional. One or more directories. If specified, only directories under the specified directories are returned.

directory_tree

*$inst->***directory_tree***(module[, string[, dir[, . . .]]])*

Like directories, but includes all intermediate directories.

files

*$inst->***files***(module[, string[, dir[, . . .]]])*

Returns list of filenames. Parameters are:

module

> Required. The name of a module; returns a list of all filenames in the package. For a list of core files, use the special module name Perl.

string

> Optional. Possible values are prog, man, or all to return program files, manual files, or all files, respectively.

dir   Optional. One or more directories. If specified, only filenames under the specified directories are returned.

modules

*$inst->***modules***()*

Returns list of names of all the installed modules. Calls the Perl "core" by the special name Perl.

packlist

*$inst->***packlist***(module)*

Returns the ExtUtils::Packlist object for the specified module.

validate

*$inst->***validate***(module[, arg])*

Takes the name of a module as a required parameter and validates that all files listed in the packlist for the module actually exist. Returns list of any missing files. With an optional second argument that evaluates to true, removes missing files from *.packlist*.

version

*$inst->**version**(module)*

Returns the version number of the specified module.

ExtUtils::Liblist

Used for building a Makefile for a Perl module. Takes a list of libraries and returns platform-appropriate lines that can be included in the Makefile.

```
require ExtUtils::Liblist;
ExtUtils::Liblist::ext($potential_libs[, $verbose]);
```

The input list *$potential_libs* is in the form *-llib1 -llib2 -llib3*. Additional library paths may be included in the form *-L/another/path*, which affects searches for all subsequent libraries. If the Boolean *$verbose* is specified, verbose output messages are provided. Returns a list of four scalar values:

EXTRALIBS
> List of libraries that need to be linked with *ld* when linking a Perl binary that includes a static extension.

LDLOADLIBS
> List of static or dynamic libraries that can or must be linked when creating a shared library using *ld*.

LD_RUN_PATH
> Colon-separated list of the directories in LDLOADLIBS.

BSLOADLIBS
> List of libraries that are needed but can be linked in dynamically with the DynaLoader at runtime.

The Win32 version (in the standard Perl distribution) has several differences from the Unix-OS/2 version:

- *-l* and *-L* are not required on the library and path specifications.

- Entries must be libraries, not plain object files.

- If *$potential_libs* is empty, the return value is also empty.

- The specified libraries can include both static and import libraries.

- LDLOADLIBS and EXTRALIBS are always identical; BSLOADLIBS and LD_RUN_PATH are always empty.

ExtUtils::MakeMaker

Writes a Makefile for use during module installation. Provides a function, WriteMakefile, which creates an object whose attributes are set from various sources and which actually writes the Makefile. See Chapter 2 for information about the use of the Makefile and MakeMaker during module installation. This section explains the details of actually creating the Makefile with MakeMaker. It assumes an understanding of *make* and Makefiles.

If you are a Perl programmer writing a module, you should run *h2xs* to generate the template for your module. Among other things, *h2xs* creates a file called *Makefile.PL*, and it's *Makefile.PL* that runs MakeMaker. On the other hand, if you are installing a module, you can usually just run the *Makefile.PL* that came with the module, perhaps adding a PREFIX argument if you are installing the module locally (see Chapter 2). In either case, you shouldn't need to run ExtUtils::Make-Maker directly unless you have special requirements.

A typical call to MakeMaker might look like this example from the CGI distribution:

```
use ExtUtils::MakeMaker;
WriteMakefile(
        NAME => "CGI",
        DISTNAME => "CGI-modules",
        VERSION => "2.76",
        linkext => { LINKTYPE => '' },
        dist => {COMPRESS=>'gzip -9f', SUFFIX => 'gz'},
);
```

MakeMaker attributes can be passed as arguments to WriteMakefile, as in the example, or they can be passed as *name=value* pairs on the command line:

```
perl Makefile.PL PREFIX=/home/mydir/Perl/Modules
```

To see what MakeMaker is doing, you can say:

```
perl Makefile.PL verbose
```

The following attributes can be specified:

C   Reference to array of *.c* filenames. Initialized from a directory scan and the values portion of the XS attribute hash. Not currently used by MakeMaker but may be handy in *Makefile.PLs*.

CCFLAGS
String to be included in the compiler call command line between the INC and OPTIMIZE arguments.

CONFIG
An array reference containing a list of attributes to get from %Config. The following values are always added to CONFIG:

ar	cc	cccdlflags	ccdlflags
dlext	dlsrc	ld	lddlflags
ldflags	libc	lib_ext	obj_ext
ranlib	sitelibexp	sitearchexp	so

CONFIGURE

Reference to a subroutine that should return a hash reference. The hash may contain further attributes that need to be determined by some evaluation method.

DEFINE

An attribute containing additional defines.

DIR

Reference to array of subdirectories containing *Makefile.PL* files.

DISTNAME

Your name for distributing the package (by *tar* file). Defaults to NAME, below.

DL_FUNCS

Reference to a hash of symbol names for routines to be made available as universal symbols. Each key/value pair consists of the package name and an array of routine names in that package. Used only under AIX (export lists) and VMS (linker options) at present. Defaults to "$PKG" => ["boot_$PKG"].

DL_VARS

Array of symbol names for variables to be made available as universal symbols. Used only under AIX (export lists) and VMS (linker options) at present. Defaults to [].

EXCLUDE_EXT

Array of module names to exclude when doing a static build. Ignored if INCLUDE_EXT is present.

EXE_FILES

Reference to array of executable files to be copied to the INST_SCRIPT directory. *make realclean* deletes them from there.

NO_VC

If set, the Makefile does not check the current version of MakeMaker against the version the Makefile was built under. Should be used interactively, not written into your *Makefile.PL* file.

FIRST_MAKEFILE

Name of the Makefile to be produced. Defaults to the contents of MAKEFILE, but can be overridden.

FULLPERL

Perl binary that can run this module.

H

Reference to array of *.h* filenames. Similar to C attribute.

IMPORTS

Used only on OS/2.

INC

Directories containing include files, in −*I* form. For example:

```
INC => "-I/usr/5include -I/path/to/inc"
```

INCLUDE_EXT

> Array of module names to be included when doing a static build. If present, only those modules that are explicitly mentioned are used for the build (instead of all installed extensions). It is not necessary to mention DynaLoader or the current module when filling in INCLUDE_EXT—they are always included.

INSTALLARCHLIB

> Used by *make install*, which copies files from INST_ARCHLIB to this directory if INSTALLDIRS is set to *perl*.

INSTALLBIN

> Directory to install binary files into.

INSTALLDIRS

> Determines which of the two sets of installation directories to choose. There are two possible values:
>
> `perl`
> > Uses INSTALLLPRIVLIB and INSTALLARCHLIB directories.
>
> `site`
> > The default. Uses INSTALLSITELIB and INSTALLSITEARCH directories.

INSTALLMAN1DIR

> Directory where command man pages are put during *make install*. Defaults to `$Config{installman1dir}`.

INSTALLMAN3DIR

> Directory where library man pages are put during *make install*. Defaults to `$Config{installman3dir}`.

INSTALLPRIVLIB

> Used by *make install*, which copies files from INST_LIB to this directory if INSTALLDIRS is set to `perl`.

INSTALLSCRIPT

> Used by *make install*, which copies files from INST_SCRIPT to this directory.

INSTALLSITELIB

> Used by *make install*, which copies files from INST_LIB to this directory if INSTALLDIRS is set to `site` (the default).

INSTALLSITEARCH

> Used by *make install*, which copies files from INST_ARCHLIB to this directory if INSTALLDIRS is set to `site` (the default).

INST_ARCHLIB

> Same as INST_LIB for architecture-dependent files.

INST_BIN

> Directory where real binary files are put during *make*, for later copying to INSTALLBIN during *make install*.

INST_EXE

> Deprecated. Old name for INST_SCRIPT, which you should use instead.

INST_LIB

Directory to hold library files for this module while it is being built.

INST_MAN1DIR

Directory to hold the command manpages at *make* time.

INST_MAN3DIR

Directory to hold the library manpages at *make* time.

INST_SCRIPT

Directory where executable files should be installed during *make*. Defaults to *./blib/bin*, to have a dummy location during testing. *make install* copies the files in INST_SCRIPT to INSTALLSCRIPT.

LDFROM

Used by the *ld* command to specify the files to link/load from. Defaults to $(OBJECT).

LIBPERL_A

Filename of the Perl library that will be used with this module. Defaults to *libperl.a.*

LIB Can only be set at when *Makefile.PL* is run; both INSTALLPRIVLIB and INSTALLSITELIB are set to the value of LIB.

LIBS

Anonymous array of alternative library specifications to be searched for (in order) until at least one library is found. Note that any element of the array contains a complete set of arguments for the *ld* command.

LINKTYPE

Should be used only to force static linking (see linkext below). Possible values are static or dynamic. Default is dynamic unless usedl=undef in *config.sh*.

MAKEAPERL

Boolean. Tells MakeMaker to include the rules for making a Perl binary. Normally handled automatically by MakeMaker and not needed by the user.

MAKEFILE

Name of the Makefile to be produced.

MAN1PODS

Reference to a hash of pod-containing files to be converted to manpages and installed as requested at configure time. Default is all EXE_FILES files that include pod directives.

MAN3PODS

Reference to a hash of *.pm* and *.pod* files to be converted to manpages and installed as requested at configure time. Default is all *.pod* and any *.pm* files that include pod directives.

MAP_TARGET

Name for new Perl binary if one is to be produced. Default is `perl`.

MYEXTLIB

Name of library that the module builds and links to.

NAME

Perl module name for this module (e.g., DBD::Oracle). Defaults to the directory name but should be explicitly defined in the *Makefile.PL*.

NEEDS_LINKING

Boolean. Can be set to speed up MakeMaker processing a very little bit, but not needed since MakeMaker will figure out if linking is needed.

NOECHO

Controls *make*'s echo (@) feature. Defaults to @. By setting it to an empty string, you can generate a Makefile that echos all commands. Used mainly in debugging MakeMaker itself.

NORECURS

Boolean. If set, inhibits descending into subdirectories.

OBJECT

List of object files. Defaults to `$(BASEEXT)$(OBJ_EXT)`; can be set to a long string containing all object files.

OPTIMIZE

If set to `-g`, turns debugging on. Defaults to `-O`. Passed to subdirectory *make*s.

PERL

Perl binary for tasks that can be done by miniperl.

PERLMAINCC

The call to the program that can compile *perlmain.c*. Defaults to `$(CC)`.

PERL_LIB

Directory containing the Perl library to use.

PERL_ARCHLIB

Same as PERL_LIB for architecture-dependent files.

PERL_SRC

Directory containing the Perl source code. Avoid using this attribute, since it may be undefined.

PL_FILES

Reference to hash of files to be processed as Perl programs. By default, MakeMaker turns any **.PL* file it finds (except the *Makefile.PL*) into a key and the basename of the file into the value. The **.PL* files are expected to produce output to the target files themselves.

PM Reference to hash of *.pm* and **.pl* files to be installed.

PMLIBDIRS
> Reference to array of subdirectories containing library files. Defaults to `['lib', $(BASEEXT)]`. The directories are scanned and any files they contain are installed in the corresponding location in the library. A `libscan` method can be used to alter the behavior. Defining PM in the *Makefile.PL* overrides PMLIBDIRS.

PREFIX
> Can be used to set the three INSTALL* attributes at once so that they have PREFIX as a common directory node.

PREREQ_PM
> Reference to a hash of modules that need to be available to run this module (e.g., Fcntl for SDBM_File). The name of each required module is the key and the desired version is the value. If the required version is 0, MakeMaker just checks to see if any version is installed.

SKIP
> Reference to an array specifying sections of the Makefile that shouldn't be written. Do not use the SKIP attribute for the negligible speedup, which may seriously damage the resulting Makefile.

TYPEMAPS
> Reference to array of typemap filenames. Use when the typemaps are in a directory other than the current directory or when they are not named typemap. The last typemap in the list takes precedence, but a typemap in the current directory has highest precedence even if it isn't listed in TYPEMAPS. The default system typemap has lowest precedence.

VERSION
> Your version number for the package. Defaults to 0.1.

VERSION_FROM
> Names a file for MakeMaker to parse to find the version number for the package, so you don't need to specify VERSION. The file must contain a single line to compute the version number. The first line in the file that contains the regular expression:

> `/([\$*])(([\w:\']*)\bVERSION)\b.*\=/`

> is evaluated with `eval` and the result assigned to VERSION.

XS Reference to a hash of *.xs* files. MakeMaker defaults this. For example:

> `{'name_of_file.xs' => 'name_of_file.c'}`

> The *.c* files are automatically deleted by a *make clean*.

XSOPT
> String of options to pass to *xsubpp*, which might include −C++ or −extern but not typemaps, which go in TYPEMAPS.

XSPROTOARG

May be set to an empty string, which is identical to –prototypes or –noprototypes. Defaults to the empty string.

XS_VERSION

Your version number for the package's *.xs* file. Defaults to the value of VERSION.

The following lowercase attributes can be used to pass parameters to the methods that implement the corresponding part of the Makefile:

clean

Extra files to clean.

depend

Extra dependencies.

dist

Distribution options.

dynamic_lib

Options for dynamic library support.

installpm

Installation options related to AutoSplit. Deprecated as of MakeMaker 5.23. See the *pm_to_blib* entry for ExtUtils::Install.

linkext

Linking style.

macro

Extra macros to define.

realclean

Extra files to *make realclean.*

tool_autosplit

Attributes for the tool_autosplit method.

If specifying attributes isn't sufficient to accomplish what you want, you can define your own subroutines in the *Makefile.PL* that returns the text to be written to the Makefile. You can also override MakeMaker's subroutines (described in the section on ExtUtils::MM_Unix) this way.

ExtUtils::Manifest

Provides utilities for maintaining and using a MANIFEST file. The MANIFEST file is essentially a packing list, included with a module, so the user who installs the module can be sure that all the files are actually present. The file created by ExtUtils::Manifest is a list of filenames, one per line, with an optional comment on each line.

ExtUtils::Manifest optionally uses a file called MANIFEST.SKIP, which contains regular expressions specifying files that are not to be included in MANIFEST. Manifest also defines two global variables that are used by several of the functions:

$ExtUtils::Manifest::MANIFEST
> The name of the MANIFEST file. Changing the value results in different MANIFEST and different MANIFEST.SKIP files. Default is MANIFEST.

$ExtUtils::Manifest::Quiet
> If true, the functions work silently. Default is 0.

Provides six functions, which are exportable on request:

---

filecheck

filecheck

Finds files below the current directory that are not mentioned in the MANIFEST file. Consults MANIFEST.SKIP for files that shouldn't be included.

---

fullcheck

fullcheck

Does both manicheck and filecheck.

---

manicheck

manicheck

Checks whether all files in current directory's MANIFEST file really exist.

---

manicopy

manicopy *(read, target, how)*

Copies files to a target directory. Takes the following arguments:

read
> Hash whose keys are the names of the files to be copied, typically returned by maniread.

target
> Target directory into which files are to be copied.

how
> Can be used to specify a different method of "copying." Values are:
>
> cp Copy the files.
>
> ln Create hard links.
>
> best
>> Link the files, but copy any symbolic link to make a tree with no symbolic links. (The default.)

---

mkmanifest

mkmanifest

Writes the names of all files in and below the current directory to the file in the current directory that is named in the $ExtUtils::Manifest::MANIFEST variable. Skips files in MANIFEST.SKIP.

manifind

manifind

Returns a hash reference whose keys are the files found below the current directory. The values are null strings, representing the MANIFEST comments that aren't there.

maniread

maniread *([file])*

Reads the MANIFEST file specified in *$file* (the default is MANIFEST). Returns a hash reference whose keys are the filenames and whose values are the comments. Discards blank lines and lines starting with #.

skipcheck

skipcheck

Lists files that were skipped because they were found in MANIFEST.SKIP.

ExtUtils::Miniperl

Generates a file, *perlmain.c*, that contains the bootstrap code to make the modules associated with the libraries available from within Perl. ExtUtils::Miniperl itself is generated automatically from a script called *minimod.PL* when Perl is built; typically, it is used from within a Makefile generated by ExtUtils::MakeMaker rather than being called directly. The module exports one subroutine:

writemain

writemain *(dirs)*

Takes an argument list of directories that contain archive libraries needed by Perl modules and writes the file to be compiled as *perlmain.c* to STDOUT.

ExtUtils::Mkbootstrap

Typically called from a module's *Makefile*. It writes a *.bs* file that is needed by some architectures to do dynamic loading.

```
use ExtUtils::Mkbootstrap;
mkbootstrap();
```

ExtUtils::Mksymlists

Produces option files used by some operating systems' linkers during creation of shared libraries for dynamic extensions. Normally called from a *Makefile* when a module is built; it exports one function:

Mksymlists

Mksymlists *(varlist)*

Creates the linker option file. The *varlist* argument is a list of key/value pairs; for example:

```
use ExtUtils::Mksymlists;
Mksymlists({ NAME    => $name,
             DL_VARS  => [$var1, $var2, $var3],
             DL_FUNCS => [$pkg1 => [$func1, $func2],
                          $pkg2 => [$func3]]});
```

Valid keys are:

DLBASE
> The name by which the linker knows the module. If not specified, it is derived from the NAME attribute. Currently used only by OS/2.

DL_FUNCS
> Identical to the MakeMaker DL_FUNCS attribute and usually taken from it. Its value is a reference to a hash, where each key is a package name and each value is a reference to an array of function names to be exported by the module.

DL_VARS
> Identical to the MakeMaker DL_VARS attribute, and usually taken from it. Its value is a reference to an array of variable names to be exported by the extension.

FILE
> The name of the linker option file (minus the OS-specific extension) if you don't want to use the default value (the last word of the NAME attribute).

FUNCLIST
> An alternate way of specifying function names to be exported from the module. Its value is a reference to an array of function names to be exported, which are passed unaltered to the linker options file.

$\rightarrow$

NAME

The name of the module for which the linker option file is to be produced. Should always be specified.

ExtUtils::MM_OS2

Provides methods for use with MakeMaker for OS2 systems. Used internally by MakeMaker if needed. See ExtUtils::MM_Unix for documentation of the methods provided there. Overrides the implementation of the methods, not the interface.

ExtUtils::MM_Unix

Provides methods for MakeMaker to handle portability issues. You never need to require this module, but you might want to if you are working on improving MakeMaker's portability

Provides methods for both Unix and non-Unix systems; on non-Unix systems, they can be overridden by methods defined in other MM_* modules. The methods are listed here:

catdir

catdir *list*

Concatenates a list of directory names to form a complete path ending with a directory. On Unix, joins the names with /.

catfile

catfile *list*

Concatenates one or more directory names and a filename to form a complete path ending with a filename. On Unix, joins the names with /.

dir_target

dir_target *array*

Takes an array of required directory names and returns a *Makefile* entry to create an *.exists* file in the directories. Returns nothing if the entry has already been processed.

file_name_is_absolute

file_name_is_absolute *filename*

Takes a path as argument and returns true if it is an absolute path.

find_perl

find_perl *version,* *names,* *dirs, trace*

Searches for an executable Perl. Takes the following arguments:

version
> The executable must be at least the version given by *version.*

names
> Array reference. The name of the executable must be an entry in the array.

dirs
> Array reference. The executable must be in a directory that is one of the entries in the array.

trace
> If *trace* is true, prints debugging information.

guess_name

guess_name

Guesses the name of the package based on the working directory's name. Called only if the NAME attribute is missing.

has_link_code

has_link_code

Returns true if there are C, XS, MYEXTLIB, or similar objects in this object that need a compiler. Does not descend into subdirectories.

libscan

libscan *filename*

Uses `init_dirscan` to find a file; returns false if the file should not be included in the library. Used primarily to keep revision-control directories from being installed.

lsdir

lsdir *dir, regexp*

Returns all entries in the specified directory that match the regular expression Takes the following arguments:

dir Name of the directory.

regexp
> Regular expression to match the entries against.

maybe_command_in_dirs

maybe_command_in_dirs

For future use.

maybe_command

maybe_command *filename*

Returns true if *filename* is likely to be a command.

needs_linking

needs_linking

Returns true if the module needs linking. Searches subdirectories.

nicetext

nicetext *target*

The MM_Unix version returns the argument with no processing.

path

path

Returns PATH environment variable as an array.

perl_script

perl_script *filename*

Returns true if *filename* is likely to be a Perl script. With MM_Unix, this is true for any ordinary, readable file.

prefixify

prefixify *attrname, oldprefix, newprefix*

Processes a path attribute in `$self->{` *attrname* `}`. Looks the attribute up in `%Config` if it doesn't have a value. Takes the following arguments:

attrname
> Name of the attribute to be processed.

oldprefix
> Prefix to be replaced.

newprefix
> New prefix, replaced in-place.

replace_manpage_separator

> replace_manpage_separator *filename*

Takes the filename of a package and replaces the subdirectory delimiter (/ in Unix) with ::. Returns the altered name.

Methods to Produce the Makefile

ExtUtils::MM_Unix has some additional methods that are called in sequence to produce a Makefile. The list of methods is specified in the array @ExtUtils::Make-Maker::MM_Sections, one method per section. The routines are all called the same way and so are just listed here. Each method returns the string to be put into its section of the *Makefile*.

The methods are called in the order that they are listed in the following table, reading down the columns:

post_initialize	top_targets	realclean
const_config	linkext	dist_basics
constants	dlsyms	dist_core
const_loadlibs	dynamic	dist_dir
const_cccmd	dynamic_bs	dist_test
tool_autosplit	dynamic_lib	dist_ci
tool_xsubpp	static	install
tools_other	static_lib	force
dist	installpm	perldepend
macro	installpm_x	makefile
depend	manifypods	staticmake
post_constants	processPL	test
pasthru	installbin	test_via_harness
c_o	subdirs	test_via_script
xs_c	subdir_x	postamble
xs_o	clean	

Finally, there are two special methods: post_initialize and postamble. They each return an empty string by default and can be defined in *Makefile.PL* to insert customized text near the beginning or end of the *Makefile*.

ExtUtils::MM_VMS

Provides methods for use with MakeMaker for VMS systems. Used internally by MakeMaker if needed. See ExtUtils::MM_Unix for documentation of the methods provided there. Overrides the implementation of the methods, not the interface.

ExtUtils::MM_Win32

Provides methods for use with MakeMaker for Win32 systems. Used internally by MakeMaker in the standard Win32 Perl distribution if needed. See ExtUtils::MM_Unix for a documentation of the methods provided there. Overrides the implementation of these methods, not the interface.

catfile

catfile

Concatenates one or more directory names and a filename to form a complete path, ending with a filename.

constants

constants

Initializes constants, .SUFFIXES, and .PHONY.

static_lib

static_lib

Defines how to produce the *.a (or equivalent) files.

dynamic_bs

dynamic_bs

Defines targets for bootstrap files.

dynamic_lib

dynamic_lib

Defines how to produce the *.so (or equivalent) files.

canonpath

canonpath

Performs a logical cleanup of a path.

perl_script

perl_script *filename*

Takes one argument, a filename, and returns the filename if the argument is likely to be a Perl script.

pm_to_blib

pm_to_blib

Defines a target that copies all files in the hash PM to their destination and autosplits them. See ExtUtils::Install.

test_via_harness

test_via_harness

Helper method to write the test targets.

tool_autosplit

tool_autosplit

Use Win32-style quoting on command line.

tools_other

tools_other

Win32 overrides. Defines SHELL, LD, TOUCH, CP, MV, RM_F, RM_RF, CHMOD, and UMASK_NULL in the Makefile. Also defines the Perl programs MKPATH, WARN_IF_OLD_PACKLIST, MOD_INSTALL, DOC_INSTALL, and UNINSTALL.

xs_o

xs_o

Defines suffix rules to go from XS to object files directly.

top_targets

top_targets

Defines the targets `all`, `subdirs`, `config`, and `O_FILES`.

manifypods

manifypods

We don't want manpage process.

dist_ci

dist_ci

Changes command-line quoting. (Same as MM_Unix version.)

dist_core

dist_core

Changes command-line quoting. (Same as MM_Unix version.)

pasthru

pasthru

Defines the string that is passed to recursive *make* calls in subdirectories.

ExtUtils::Packlist

Manages *.packlist* files. Supports an extended *.packlist* format. The original format is a list of absolute pathnames, one pathname per line. In the extended format, each line can also contain a list of attributes as key/value pairs, which are used by the *installperl* script. For example:

```
/usr/local/bin/perl from=/usr/local/pbeta/bin/perl5.005 type=link
/usr/local/bin/perl5.005 type=file
/usr/local/lib/perl5/5.005/AnyDBM_File.pm type=file
```

Also see ExtUtils::Installed.

new

$pl = ExtUtils::Packlist->new *([plfile])*

Constructor. Takes the name of a *.packlist* as the optional parameter and returns a reference to a hash that has an entry for each line in the oldstyle *.packlist*s. For files in the extended format, the value for each key is a hash containing the key/value pairs on the line associated with that key.

packlist_file

$pl->packlist_file *()*

Returns the name of the associated *.packlist* file.

read

$pl->read *([plfile])*

Reads the *.packlist* specified by the *plfile* parameter if given; otherwise reads the file associated with *$pl*. Calls `Carp::croak` if the file doesn't exist.

validate

$pl->validate ([arg])

Checks that each file in the *.packlist* exists. An optional argument can be specified; if the argument is present and evaluates to true, missing files are removed from the internal hash. Returns a list of missing files, or an empty list if the files all exist.

write

$pl->write ([plfile])

Writes to a *.packlist*. Optionally takes the name of the *.packlist* to be written; otherwise overwrites the *.packlist* associated with *$pl*. If the value associated with a hash key is a scalar, the entry written to the *.packlist* is a simple file-name. If the value is a hash, the entry written is the filename followed by the key/value pairs from the hash.

ExtUtils::testlib

Used for testing a module after it's been built and before it's been installed, when you don't want to (or can't) run *make test*. Adding:

```
use ExtUtils::testlib;
```

to your test program causes the intermediate directories used by *make* to be added to @INC, allowing you to run the test.

Fatal

Provides a way to replace functions that return false on failure with equivalents that die instead, so you can use the functions without having to test the return values explicitly. Fatal reports errors via die; you can trap them with $SIG{__DIE__} if you want to take some action before the program exits. You can use Fatal for both user-defined functions and Perl core operators except exec and system.

import

import Fatal *function*

Wraps *function* in an equivalent function that will die on failure.

Fcntl

A translation of the C *fcntl.h* program that uses *h2xs* (which builds a Perl extension from a C header file) and the C compiler to translate #define symbols and make them available as functions. Exports the following routines by default; each routine returns the value of the #define that is the same as the routine name:

FD_CLOEXEC	F_DUPFD	F_GETFD	F_GETFL	F_GETLK
F_RDLCK	F_SETFD	F_SETFL	F_SETLK	F_SETLKW
F_UNLCK	F_WRLCK	O_APPEND	O_CREAT	O_EXCL
O_NDELAY	O_NOCTTY	O_NONBLOCK	O_RDONLY	O_RDWR
O_TRUNC	O_WRONLY			

fields

Pragma that provides the ability to define class fields at compile time, by updating the %FIELDS hash in the calling package. The %FIELDS hash is set up at compile time as well; use the base pragma to copy fields from base classes, and then fields to add new fields. Lets you have objects with named fields that are as compact and fast as arrays to access. For more details, see the *fields* manpage and the pseudo-hash section of the *perlref* manpage.

File::Basename

Parses a file's path, returning its three component pieces: the path to the file, the file's basename, and the file's extension. For example, for:

```
/usr/local/lib/perl5/SelectSaver.pm
```

the path is */usr/local/lib/perl5*, the basename is *SelectSaver*, and the extension is *.pm*. File::Basename exports the following functions:

basename

basename *(fullname[, suffixlist])*

Returns the first element of the list that would be produced if you called fileparse with the same arguments. Provides compatibility with the Unix *basename* command. Takes the following arguments:

fullname
> Input file specification

suffixlist
> Optional list containing patterns to be matched against the end of *fullname* to find the suffix

dirname

dirname *(fullname)*

Returns the directory portion of the input file specification. *fullname* is the input file specification.

fileparse

fileparse *(fullname[, suffixlist])*

Divides a file specification into its three parts, returning them in the order: filename, path, suffix.

```
($name, $path, $suffix) = fileparse($fullname, @suffixlist)
```

The arguments are the same as for basename.

fileparse_set_fstype

fileparse_set_fstype *(os-string)*

Called before the other routines to select the appropriate file specification syntax for your operating system, to be used in future File::Basename calls. Currently valid values for *$os-string* (the operating system) are VMS, MSWin32, MSDOS, AmigaOS, os2, RISCOS, and MacOS. Uses Unix syntax by default.

File::CheckTree

Runs file tests on a set of files. Exports one function, validate, which takes a single multi-line string as input. Each line of the string contains a filename plus a test to run on the file. The test can be followed with || die to make it a fatal error if it fails. The default is || warn. Prepending ! to the test reverses the sense of the test. You can group tests (e.g., -rwx); only the first failed test of the group produces a warning. For example:

```
use File::CheckTree;

$warnings += validate( q{
    /vmunix             -e || die
    /bin                cd
        csh             !-ug
        sh              -ex
    /usr                -d || warn "What happened to $file?\n"
});
```

Available tests include all the standard Perl file-test operators except $-t$, $-M$, $-A$, and $-C$. Unless it dies, validate returns the number of warnings issued.

File::Compare

Compares the contents of two sources, each of which can be a file or a filehandle. Returns 0 if the sources are equal, 1 if they are unequal, and −1 on error. File::Compare provides two functions:

compare

> **compare** *(file1, file2[, buffsize])*

> Compares *file1* to *file2*. Exported by default. If present, *buffsize* specifies the size of the buffer to use for the comparison.

cmp

> **cmp** *(file1, file2[, buffsize])*

> cmp is a synonym for compare. Exported on request.

Modules

File::Copy

Copies or moves files or filehandles from one location to another. Returns 1 on success, 0 on failure, or sets $! on error.

copy

> **copy** *(source, dest[, buffsize])*

> Copies *source* to *dest*. Takes the following arguments:

> *source*
>> The source string, FileHandle reference, or FileHandle glob. If *source* is a filehandle, it is read from; if it's a filename, the filehandle is opened for reading.

> *dest*
>> The destination string, FileHandle reference, or FileHandle glob. *dest* is created if necessary and written to.

> *buffsize*
>> Specifies the size of the buffer to be used for copying. Optional.

cp

> **cp** *(source, dest[, buffsize])*

> Like copy, but exported only on request.

> ```
> use File::Copy "cp"
> ```

move

move *(source, dest)*

Moves *source* to *dest*. If the destination exists and is a directory, and the source is not a directory, then the source file is renamed into the directory specified by *dest*.

Return values are the same as for copy.

mv

mv *(source, dest)*

Like move, but exported only on request.

```
use File::Copy "mv"
```

File::DosGlob

Provides a portable enhanced DOS-like globbing for the standard Perl distribution. DosGlob lets you use wildcards in directory paths, is case-insensitive, and accepts both backslashes and forward slashes (although you may have to double the backslashes). Can be run three ways:

- From a Perl script:

```
require 5.004
use File::DosGlob 'glob';

@perlfiles = glob  "..\pe?l/*.p?";
print <..\pe?l/*.p?>;
```

- With the *perl* command, on the command line:

```
# from the command line (overrides only in main::)
% perl -MFile::DosGlob=glob -e "print <../pe*/*p?>"
```

- With the *perlglob.bat* program on the DOS command line:

```
% perlglob ../pe*/*p?
```

When invoked as a program from the command line, File::DosGlob prints null-separated filenames to STDOUT.

File::Find

Looks for files that match a particular expression. Exports two functions:

find

find (\&wanted, dir1[, dir2 ...])

Works like the Unix *find* command; traverses the specified directories, looking for files that match the expressions or actions you specify in a subroutine called wanted, which you must define. For example, to print out the names of all executable files, you could define wanted this way:

```
sub wanted {
    print "$File::Find::name\n" if -x;
}
```

Provides the following variables:

$File::Find::dir
: Current directory name ($_ has the current filename in that directory).

$File::Find::name
: Contains "$File::Find::dir/$_". You are *chdir*ed to $File::Find::dir when find is called.

$File::Find::prune
: If true, find does not descend into any directories.

$File::Find::dont_use_nlink
: Set this variable if you're using the Andrew File System (AFS).

finddepth

finddepth (\&wanted, dir1[, dir2 ...])

Like find, but does a depth-first search.

The standard Perl distribution comes with a Perl script, *find2perl*, which takes a Unix *find* command and turns it into a wanted subroutine.

File::Path

Creates and deletes multiple directories with specified permissions. Exports two methods:

mkpath

mkpath (*path, bool, perm*)

Creates a directory path and returns a list of all directories created. Takes the following arguments:

path
: Name of the path or reference to a list of paths to create.

$\rightarrow$

bool

> Boolean. If true, `mkpath` prints the name of each directory as it is created. Default is false.

perm

> Numeric mode indicating the permissions to use when creating the directories. Default is 0777.

---

rmtree

rmtree *(root, prt, skip)*

Deletes subtrees from the directory structure, returning the number of files successfully deleted. Symbolic links are treated as ordinary files. Takes the following arguments:

root

> Root of the subtree to delete or reference to a list of roots. The roots, and all files and directories below each root, are deleted.

prt Boolean. If true, `rmtree` prints a message for each file, with the name of the file and whether it's using `rmdir` or `unlink` to remove it (or if it's skipping the file). Default is false.

skip

> Boolean. If true, `rmtree` skips any files to which you do not have delete access (under VMS) or write access (under other operating systems). Default is false.

File::Spec

Performs common operations on file specifications in a portable way. To do that, it automatically loads the appropriate operating-system-specific module, which is one of File::Spec::Mac, File::Spec::OS2, File::Spec::Unix, File::Spec::VMS, or File::Spec::Win32. The complete reference of available functions is given in File::Spec::Unix; the functions are inherited by the other modules and overridden as necessary. Subroutines should be called as class methods, rather than directly.

File::Spec::Mac

File::Spec for MacOS.

---

canonpath

File::Spec->canonpath

Nothing to do; returns what it's given.

---

catdir

File::Spec->catdir(*dir[, dir . . .]*)

Concatenates two or more directory names to form a complete path. Ends with a directory name and appends a trailing : if there isn't one. You can get a relative path by either beginning the first argument with : or putting " " as the first argument.

catfile

File::Spec->catfile(*dir[, dir . . .], file*)

Concatenates one or more directory names and a filename to form a complete path that ends with a filename. Uses `catdir`.

curdir

File::Spec->curdir

Returns string representing the current directory.

file_name_is_absolute

File::Spec->file_name_is_absolute(*path*)

Takes a path as argument and returns true if it is an absolute path.

path

File::Spec->path

Returns null list for MacPerl applications, or `$ENV{Commands}`, suitably split, for the MacPerl tool under MPW.

rootdir

File::Spec->rootdir

Returns string representing the root directory. Under MacPerl, returns the name of the startup volume.

updir

File::Spec->updir

Returns string representing the parent directory.

File::Spec::OS2

File::Spec for OS/2. Overrides the implementation of the File::Spec::Unix methods, but not the interface.

File::Spec::Unix

File::Spec for Unix. Provides methods for File::Spec to use in manipulating file specifications.

---

canonpath

File::Spec->canonpath

Does logical cleanup of path.

---

catdir

File::Spec->catdir(*dir[, dir . . .]*)

Concatenates two or more directory names to form a complete path. Ends with a directory name.

---

catfile

File::Spec->catfile(*dir[, dir . . .], file*)

Concatenates one or more directory names and a filename to form a complete path that ends with a filename.

---

curdir

File::Spec->curdir

Returns ., representing the current directory.

---

file_name_is_absolute

File::Spec->file_name_is_absolute(*path*)

Takes a path as argument and returns true if it is an absolute path.

---

join

File::Spec->join(*dir[, dir . . .], file*)

Same as catfile.

---

no_upwards

File::Spec->no_upwards(*files*)

Strips names of files referring to a parent directory from a list of filenames. Doesn't strip symbolic links.

path

File::Spec->path

Returns the PATH environment variable as an array.

rootdir

File::Spec->rootdir

Returns /, representing the root directory.

updir

File::Spec->updir

Returns .., representing the parent directory.

File::Spec::VMS

File::Spec for VMS. Overrides the implementation of the File::Spec::Unix methods, but not the interface.

catdir

File::Spec->catdir(*dirspecs*)

Concatenates a list of directories and returns the result as a VMS-syntax directory specification.

catfile

File::Spec->catfile(*filespecs*)

Concatenates a list of file specifications and returns the result as a path.

curdir

File::Spec->curdir

Returns string representing the current directory.

file_name_is_absolute

File::Spec->file_name_is_absolute(*path*)

Takes a path as argument and returns true if it is an absolute path. Checks for VMS directory specification as well as Unix separators.

path

File::Spec->path

Translates the logical name DCL$PATH as a searchlist.

rootdir

File::Spec->rootdir

Returns string representing the root directory.

updir

File::Spec->updir

Returns string representing the parent directory.

File::Spec::Win32

File::Spec for Win32. Overrides the implementation of the File::Spec::Unix methods, but not the interface.

canonpath

File::Spec->canonpath

Performs logical cleanup of a path, doesn't physically check the filesystem.

catfile

File::Spec->catfile(*dir[, dir . . .], file*)

Concatenates one or more directory names and a filename to form a complete path that ends with a filename.

File::stat

Provides the same file status information as the Perl functions `stat` and `lstat`. Exports two functions that return File::stat objects. The objects have methods that return the equivalent fields from the Unix *stat(2)* call:

Field	Meaning
dev	Device number of filesystem
ino	Inode number
mode	File mode
nlink	Number of links to the file
uid	Numeric user ID of owner
gid	Numeric group ID of owner
rdev	Device identifier
size	Size of file, in bytes
atime	Last access time
mtime	Last modified time
ctime	Inode change time
blksize	Preferred blocksize for filesystem I/O
blocks	Number of blocks allocated

You can access the status fields either with the methods or by importing the fields into your namespace with the :FIELDS import tag and then accessing them by prepending st_ to the field name (e.g., `$st_mode`). Here are examples of doing it both ways:

```
use File::stat;

$stats = stat($file);
print $stats->uid;
print $st_uid;
```

stat

> stat *(file)*

Returns status information for the file or filehandle pointed to by *file*. If *file* is a symbolic link, returns the information for the file that the link points to.

lstat

> lstat *(file)*

Returns the same information as `stat`, but if *file* is a symbolic link, returns the status information for the link.

FileCache

Closes and re-opens files as necessary so you can always write to a file even if you already have the maximum number of files open. Exports one function:

cacheout

cacheout *(path)*

Makes sure the file at *path* is created and accessible through the filehandle also named *path*. You don't need to invoke cacheout between successive accesses to the same file.

FileHandle

Provides object methods for working with filehandles. Provides the following methods:

new

$fh = new FileHandle *[filename[, mode]]*

Constructor. Creates a FileHandle, which is a reference to a newly created symbol. The optional parameters, *filename* and *mode*, are passed to open. The FileHandle object is returned if the open succeeds, otherwise it is destroyed.

new_from_fd

$fh = new_from_fd *FileHandle fd, mode*

Constructor. Creates a FileHandle, but it takes the file descriptor, *fd*, instead of *filename* as a parameter, along with *mode*; the parameters are required.

fdopen

*$fh->*fdopen *fdname [openmode]*

Like open, except that its first parameter is not a filename but a filehandle name, a FileHandle object, or a file descriptor number.

getpos

$pos = *$fh->*getpos

If the C functions fgetpos(3) and fsetpos(3) are available, getpos returns the current position, *$pos*, of the FileHandle.

open

$fh->open *filename [openmode]*

Takes *filename* and, optionally, the open mode, and opens a file. If the mode is present, it can be either in Perl form (e.g., >, +<) or in POSIX form (e.g., w, r+).

setpos

$fh->setpos *pos*

Uses the value (*pos*) returned by getpos to restore a previous position of the FileHandle.

setvbuf

$fh->setvbuf(params)

Takes the same parameters as the C function setvbuf(3) and uses the C function to set the buffering policy for the FileHandle.

Modules

The following additional FileHandle methods act as front-ends for the corresponding built-in Perl functions (see the O'Reilly book *Programming Perl* or the *perlfunc* manpage for more detail):

```
clearerr        getc
close           gets
eof             seek
fileno          tell
```

The next group of FileHandle methods correspond to Perl special variables (see *Programming Perl* or the *perlvar* manpage):

```
autoflush                        format_page_number
format_formfeed                  format_top_name
format_line_break_characters     input_line_number
format_lines_left                input_record_separator
format_lines_per_page            output_field_separator
format_name                      output_record_separator
```

Finally, the following methods are useful:

$fh->print
See Perl's built-in print function.

$fh->printf
See Perl's built-in printf function.

$fh->getline
Works like Perl's <FILEHANDLE> construct, except that it can be safely called in an array context (but it still returns just one line).

$fh->getlines

Works like Perl's <FILEHANDLE> construct when called in an array context to read all remaining lines in a file.

FindBin

Finds the full path to a script's *bin* directory, letting you use relative paths to that directory without needing to know the actual location:

```
use FindBin;
use lib "$FindBin::Bin/../lib";
```

or:

```
use FindBin qw($Bin);
use lib "$Bin/../lib";
```

FindBin exports the following variables:

$Bin

Path to *bin* directory from which script was invoked.

$Script

Basename of script from which Perl was invoked.

$RealBin

$Bin with all links resolved.

$RealScript

$Script with all links resolved.

If you invoke Perl with the −*e* option or read the Perl script from STDIN, then FindBin sets both $Bin and $RealBin to the current directory.

GDBM_File

Allows Perl programs to make use of the facilities provided by the GNU gdbm library. Most of the *libgdbm.a* functions are available as methods of the GDBM_File interface. See the *gdbm(3)* manpage and the description of DB_File in this chapter. The following is an example of the use of GDBM_File:

```
use GDBM_File;

tie %hash, "GDBM_File", $filename, &GDBM_WRCREAT, 0644);
# read/writes of %hash are now read/writes of $filename
untie %hash;
```

Getopt::Long

Lets your program accept command-line options with long names, introduced by −−. Standard single-character options are also accepted. Options that start with −− may have an argument appended, following a space or an equals sign (=):

```
--foo=bar
--foo bar
```

Provides two functions: GetOptions and config.

GetOptions

$result = **GetOptions(***option-descriptions***)**

Uses descriptions from *option-descriptions* to retrieve and process the command-line options with which your Perl program was invoked. The options are taken from @ARGV. After GetOptions has processed the options, @ARGV contains only command-line arguments that were not options. Returns 0 if errors are detected. Each option description consists of two elements:

Option specifier
Defines the option name and optionally a value as an argument specifier.

Option linkage
A reference to a variable that is set when the option is present.

GetOptions can also take as a first argument a reference to a hash that describes the linkage for the options. The linkage specified in the argument list takes precedence over the one specified in the hash. Thus the following are equivalent:

```
%optctl = (size => \$offset);
&GetOptions(\%optctl, "size=i");
```

and:

```
&GetOptions("size=i" => \$offset);
```

Option specifiers

Each option specifier consists of an option name and possibly an argument specifier. The name can be a name, or a list of names separated by |; the first name in the list is the true name of the option and the others are treated as aliases. Option names may be invoked with the shortest unique abbreviation.

Values for argument specifiers are:

<none>
Option takes no argument. The option variable is set to 1.

!

Option does not take an argument and may be negated, that is, prefixed by "no".

=s

Option takes a mandatory argument that is a string to be assigned to the option variable. Even if the argument starts with - or --, it is assigned to the option variable rather than treated as another option.

:s

Option takes an optional string argument. If the option is invoked with no argument, an empty string ("") is assigned to the option variable. If

→

the argument starts with − or −−, it is treated as another option rather than assigned to the option variable.

=i

Option takes a mandatory integer argument, which may start with − to indicate a negative value.

:i

Option takes an optional integer argument that may start with − to indicate a negative value. With no argument, the value 0 is assigned to the option variable.

=f

Option takes a mandatory floating-point argument that may start with − to indicate a negative value.

:f

Option takes an optional floating-point argument that may start with − to indicate a negative value. With no argument, the value 0 is assigned to the option variable.

A hyphen (−) by itself is considered an option whose name is the empty string. A double hyphen (−−) by itself terminates option processing. Any options following the double hyphen remain in @ARGV when GetOptions returns. If an argument specifier ends with @ (e.g., =s@), then the option is treated as an array.

The special option specifier <> can be used to designate a subroutine to handle non-option arguments. For this specifier to be used, the variable $Getopt::Long::order must have the value of the predefined and exported variable, $PERMUTE. See the description of Getopt::Long::config below.

Linkage specification

The linkage specifier can be a reference to a:

Scalar
The new value is stored in the referenced variable. If the option occurs more than once, the previous value is overwritten.

Array
The new value is appended (pushed) onto the referenced array.

Subroutine
The referenced subroutine is called with two arguments: the option name, which is always the true name, and the option value.

If no linkage is explicitly specified, but a hash reference is passed, GetOptions puts the value in the hash. For array options, a reference to an anonymous array is generated.

If no linkage is explicitly specified and no hash reference is passed, GetOptions puts the value into a global variable named after the option, prefixed by opt_. Characters that are not part of the variable syntax are translated to underscores. For example, −−fpp-struct-return sets the variable $opt_fpp_struct_return.

config

Getopt::Long::config(*optionlist*)

Sets the variables in *optionlist* to change the default behavior of `GetOptions`. The following options are available:

`$Getopt::Long::autoabbrev`
> If true, option names can be invoked with unique abbreviations. Default is 1 (true) unless the environment variable `POSIXLY_CORRECT` has been set.

`$Getopt::Long::getopt_compat`
> If true, options can start with "+". Default is 1 unless the environment variable `POSIXLY_CORRECT` has been set.

`$Getopt::Long::order`
> Value indicates whether options and non-options may be mixed on the command line:
>
> `$PERMUTE`
>> Non-options may be mixed with options. The default if `POSIXLY_CORRECT` is not set.
>
> `$REQUIRE_ORDER`
>> Mixing is not allowed. The default if `POSIXLY_CORRECT` is set.

`$Getopt::Long::ignorecase`
> If true, ignore case when matching options. Default is 1.

`$Getopt::Long::VERSION`
> The version number of this Getopt::Long implementation in the format *major.minor*.

`$Getopt::Long::error`
> Internal error flag. May be incremented from a callback routine to cause options-parsing to fail.

`$Getopt::Long::debug`
> If true, enables debugging output. Default is 0 (false).

Getopt::Std

Processes single-character command-line options with option clustering. Exports two functions, which analyze `@ARGV`, extract information about the options, and return this information to your program in a set of variables. Processing of `@ARGV` stops when an argument without a leading – is encountered, if that argument is not associated with a preceding option. Otherwise, `@ARGV` is processed to the end and left empty.

getopt

getopt (*'switches'[,* \%opts])

switches is a string of the command-line options that take arguments. For each option, getopt sets $opt_x (where *x* is the switch) to the value entered as an argument. If \%opts is specified, it is a reference to a hash in which getopt sets the key to the name of the switch and the value to the argument (and the $opt_ variables are not set).

getopts

getopts (*'switches'[,* \%opts])

Like getopt, except that all valid options are included in *switches* and options that take an argument are followed by a colon (:), e.g.:

```
getopt('oDI')    # -o, -D, & -I take arguments; there may be other options
getopts('o:DI')  # -o, -D, and -I are the only valid options; only -o
                 # takes an argument
```

\%opts means the same as with getopt.

I18N::Collate

The use of I18N::Collate is now deprecated, although it is still provided for compatibility with older programs. Don't use it in new programs, as its functionality was integrated into the core Perl in Perl 5.004. See the locale pragma.

integer

Pragma that tells the compiler to use integer operations from here to the end of the enclosing block. Improves processing time on systems without floating-point hardware support.

```
use integer;

$x = 10/3;   # $x is now 3, not 3.33333333333333333
```

Use the no integer directive to turn off integer inside an inner block.

IO

Loads all of the following IO modules with a single use statement: IO::Handle, IO::Seekable, IO::File, IO::Pipe, and IO::Socket.

IO::File

Inherits from IO::Handle and IO::Seekable, extending them with methods specific to filehandles. Provides three such methods:

new

$fb = new ([*params*])

Constructor. Creates an IO::File object, passing any parameters to the method open. If the open fails, the object is destroyed. Otherwise, it is returned to the caller.

new_tmpfile

$fb = new_tmpfile

Constructor. Creates an IO::File object opened for read/write on a newly created temporary file. If the system permits, the temporary file is anonymous; if the temporary file cannot be created or opened, the object is destroyed. Otherwise, it is returned to the caller.

open

$fb->open(*filename[, mode[, perms]]*)

Opens the newly-created filehandle. Accepts one, two, or three parameters. With one parameter, it acts as a front-end for Perl's built-in open function. With two parameters, the first parameter is a filename and the second is the open mode, optionally followed by a third parameter, the file permission value.

IO::Handle

The base class for all other IO handle classes. Its main purpose is for the other IO classes to inherit from it; programs should not create IO::Handle objects directly. Provides the following methods:

new

new

Constructor. Creates a new IO::Handle object.

Modules

new_from_fd

new_from_fd *(fd, mode)*

Constructor. Like new, creates an IO::Handle object. It requires two parameters, which are passed to the method fdopen; if the fdopen fails, the object is destroyed. Otherwise, it is returned to the caller.

clearerr

$fh->clearerr

Clears the given handle's error indicator.

error

$fh->error

Returns a true value if the given handle has experienced any errors since it was opened or since the last call to clearerr.

fdopen

$fh->fdopen *(fd, mode)*

Like an ordinary open except that the first parameter is a filehandle name, an IO::Handle object, or a file descriptor number.

flush

$fh->flush

Flushes the given handle's buffer.

getline

$fh->getline

Works like <*$fh*>, described in the section on "I/O Operators" in the *perlop* manpage, but is more readable and can be safely called in an array context, while still returning one line.

getlines

$fh->getlines

Works like <*$fh*> when called in an array context to read all the remaining lines in a file, but is more readable. croaks if called in scalar context.

opened

$fh->opened

Returns true if the object is currently a valid file descriptor.

ungetc

$fh->ungetc (*ord*)

Pushes a character with the ordinal value *ord* back onto the given handle's input stream.

untaint

$fh->untaint

Special method for working under −*T* and setuid/gid scripts. Marks the object as taint-clean, and as such, data read from it is also considered taint-clean.

write

$fh->write (*buf, len*[, *offset*])

Like write found in C; that is, the opposite of read. The wrapper for the Perl write function is format_write.

IO::Handle also provides the following methods, which are not described in detail here because they are simply front-ends for the corresponding built-in functions. See Chapter 5, *Function Reference*, for more information.

Method	Description
close	Closes file or pipe
eof	Returns 1 if next read will return end-of-file
fileno	Returns file descriptor for a filehandle
getc	Returns next character from input file
print	Prints a string or comma-separated list of strings
printf	Prints a formatted string
read	Reads data from a filehandle
stat	Returns an array of status information for a file
sysread	Reads data from a filehandle with system call read(2)
syswrite	Writes data to a filehandle with system call write(2)
truncate	Truncates a file to a specified length

Finally, the following methods act on the equivalent Perl variables. See Chapter 4 for more information.

Method	Description
autoflush	If nonzero, forces a flush now and after each write or print (default 0)
format_page_number	Current page number
format_lines_per_page	Current page length (default 60)
format_lines_left	Number of lines left on page
format_name	Name of current report format
format_top_name	Name of current top-of-page format
format_line_break_characters	Current set of linebreak chars for a format
format_formfeed	Formfeed char used by formats (default \f)
format_write	Wrapper for write function
input_record_separator	Input record separator (default newline)
input_line_number	Current input line number for last filehandle accessed
output_field_separator	Output field separator for print
output_record_separator	Output record separator for print

IO::Pipe

Provides an interface for creating pipes between processes.

new

$pipe = new IO::Pipe([readfh, writefh])

Constructor. Creates an IO::Pipe object, which is a reference to a newly created symbol. The two optional arguments should be objects blessed into IO::Handle or one of its subclasses. These objects are used for the system call to pipe. With no arguments, the method handles is called on the new IO::Pipe object.

reader

$pipe->reader([args])

Object is reblessed into a subclass of IO::Handle and becomes a handle at the reading end of the pipe. If there are any args, then fork is called and the arguments are passed to exec.

writer

$pipe->writer([args])

The object is reblessed into a subclass of IO::Handle and becomes a handle at the writing end of the pipe. If there are any args, then fork is called and the arguments are passed to exec.

handles

$pipe->handles()

Called during construction by IO::Pipe::new on the newly created IO::Pipe object. Returns an array of two objects blessed into IO::Pipe::End, or a subclass.

IO::Seekable

Intended to be inherited by other IO::Handle-based objects to provide methods that allow seeking of the file descriptors. Has no constructor.

```
use IO::Seekable;
package IO::XXX;
@ISA = qw(IO::Seekable);
```

Provides two methods:

seek

$fh->seek(offset, whence)

Front-end for the corresponding built-in seek function, which sets a filehandle's position in the file. Takes the following arguments:

offset
> The offset where you want to set the position.

whence
> The position in the file that the offset is relative to. Possible values are: 0 for the beginning of the file, 1 for the current position, or 2 for end of file. May also be expressed as the following constants, which are exported:

SEEK_SET
> Beginning of file

SEEK_CUR
> Current position

SEEK_END
> End of file

tell

$fh->tell()

Front-end for the corresponding built-in tell function, which returns the current file position in bytes (starting from 0).

IO::Select

Implements an object-oriented approach to the system `select` function call. Allows the user to see what IO handles are ready for reading, writing, or have an error condition pending.

---

new

> $s = IO::Select->new([*handles*])

Constructor. Creates a new object and optionally initializes it with a set of handles.

---

add

> $s->add(*handles*)

Adds list of handles to the IO::Select object, to be returned when an event occurs. IO::Select keeps the list of handles in a cache, which is indexed by the handle's file number. Each handle can be an IO::Handle object, an integer, or a reference to an array, where the first element is an IO::Handle object or an integer.

---

bits

> $s->bits()

Returns the bit string that is suitable for use as argument to the core `select` call.

---

can_read

> $s->can_read([*timeout*])

Returns array of handles that are ready for reading. *timeout* is the maximum amount of time to wait before returning an empty list. If *timeout* is not given, and any handles are registered, then the call blocks.

---

can_write

> $s->can_write([*timeout*])

Same as can_read, but checks for handles that can be written to.

---

count

> $s->count()

Returns the number of handles that the object checks for when one of the can_ methods is called or the object is passed to the `select` static method.

---

exists

$s->exists(*handle*)

Returns the handle if it is present, otherwise returns undef.

handles

$s->handles

Returns an array of all registered handles.

has_error

$s->has_error([*timeout*])

Same as can_read, but checks for handles that have an error condition.

remove

$s->remove(*handles*)

Removes all the given handles from the object, locating them by file number.

select

$s->select(*read, write, error*[, *timeout*])

Static method; call it with the package name like new. read, write, and error
are either undef or IO::Select objects. The optional argument *timeout* has the
same effect as for the core select call.

Returns an array of three elements, each a reference to an array, or an empty
array on error. The arrays hold the handles that are ready for reading, ready
for writing, and have error conditions, respectively.

IO::Socket

Provides an object interface to creating and using sockets. It is built on the
IO::Handle interface and inherits all the methods defined by IO::Handle.

IO::Socket defines methods for only those operations that are common to all types
of socket. IO::Socket exports all functions (and constants) defined by Socket. See
Chapter 13, *Sockets*, for detailed information.

IPC::Msg

System V Msg IPC object class. Uses constants defined in IPC::SysV.

---

new

$msg = new IPC::Msg(*key, flags*)

Creates a new message queue associated with *key* and uses *flags* to set the permissions. Creates the new message queue if the following are true:

- *key* is equal to IPC_PRIVATE.

- *key* doesn't already have an associated message queue and FLAGS & IPC_CREAT is true.

---

id

$msg->id

Returns the system identifier for the message queue.

---

rcv

$msg->rcv(*buf, len*[, *type*[, *flags*]])

Reads a message from the queue, returning the type of the message.

---

remove

$msg->remove

Removes and destroys the message queue.

---

set

$msg->set(*stat*)
$msg->set(*name=>value*[,*name=>value* . . .])

Accepts either a stat object as returned by the stat method or a list of name/value pairs and sets the following values of the stat structure associated with the message queue:

```
uid
gid
mode (the permission bits)
qbytes
```

snd

$msg->snd(*type, msg*[, *flags*])

Puts a message of type *type* on the queue with the data from *msg*. See the
msgsnd function.

stat

$ds = $msg->stat

Returns an object of type IPC::Msg::stat (which is a subclass of Class::Struct)
that provides the following fields:

```
uid    gid    cuid    cgid
mode   qnum   qbytes  lspid
lrpid  stime  rtime   ctime
```

See the stat function and your system documentation for more information.

IPC::Open2

Opens a child process that allows two-way communication between your program
and the child. Returns the process ID of the child process or reports a fatal error
on failure. Exports one function:

open2

open2 (*rdr, *wtr, cmd_with_args)

Forks a child process to execute the specified command. Takes the following
arguments:

*rdr
> Represents a read filehandle that your program can use to read from the
> command $cmd's standard output. Can be a FileHandle object or a refer-
> ence to a typeglob.

*wtr
> Represents a write filehandle that your program can use to write to the
> command $cmd's standard input. Can be a FileHandle object or a refer-
> ence to a typeglob.

cmd_with_arguments
> The command to be executed by the child process, and its arguments.
> Can be specified two ways:

```
$cmd_with_args
$cmd, "arg1", "arg2", ...
```

IPC::Open3

IPC::Open3 works like IPC::Open2.

```
use IPC::Open3;

$pid = open3($wtr, $rdr, $err, $cmd_with_args);
$pid = open3($wtr, $rdr, $err, $cmd, "arg1", "arg2", ...);
```

The following differences apply:

- The first two arguments ($wtr and $rdr) are passed in the opposite order.

- A third filehandle can be passed, for standard error. If this argument is given as "", then STDERR and STDOUT for $cmd are on the same filehandle.

- If $wtr begins with <, then the leading < is stripped from the name and the remainder is assumed to be a regular filehandle for an open file, rather than a reference to a typeglob. open3 opens this file as STDIN for $cmd and closes it in the parent. Likewise, if $rdr or $err begins with >, then $cmd directs STDOUT or STDERR directly to that file rather than to the parent.

IPC::Semaphore

System V Semaphore IPC object class. Uses constants defined in IPC::SysV.

---

new

$sem = new IPC::Semaphore(*key, nsems, flags*)

Creates a new semaphore set associated with *key* and containing *nsems* semaphores. Uses *flags* to set the permissions. Creates the new set if the following are true:

- *key* is equal to IPC_PRIVATE.

- *key* doesn't already have an associated semaphore identifier and FLAGS & IPC_CREAT is true.

---

getall

$sem->getall

Returns the values of the semaphore set as an array.

---

getncnt

$sem->getncnt(*sem*)

Returns the number of processes waiting for the semaphore *sem* to become greater than its current value.

---

getpid

> *$sem->getpid(sem)*

Returns the process ID of the last process that operated on semaphore *sem*.

getval

> *$sem->getval(sem)*

Returns the current value of semaphore *sem*.

getzcnt

> *$sem->getzcnt(sem)*

Returns the number of processes waiting for the semaphore *sem* to become zero.

id

> *$sem->id*

Returns the system identifier for the semaphore set.

op

> *$sem->op(oplist)*

Passes a list of operations to the semop function. *oplist* is the list of operations, consisting of a concatenation of smaller lists. Each of the smaller lists has three values: the semaphore number, the operation, and a flag. See the semop function in Chapter 5 for more information.

remove

> *$sem->remove*

Removes and destroys the semaphore set.

set

> *$sem->set(stat)*
> *$sem->set(name=>value[, name=>value . . .])*

Accepts either a stat object as returned by the stat method or a list of name/value pairs and sets the following values of the stat structure associated with the semaphore set:

```
uid
gid
mode (the permission bits)
```

setall

> $sem->setall(*values*)

Sets the values of all the semaphores in the set to those given by the *values* list. The number of values on the list must match the number of semaphores in the set.

setval

> $sem->setval(*n, value*)

Sets the *n*th value in the semaphore set to *value*.

stat

> $ds = $sem->stat

Returns an object of type `IPC::Semaphore::stat` (which is a subclass of Class::Struct) that provides the following fields:

```
uid     gid     cuid    cgid
mode    ctime   otime   nsems
```

IPC::SysV

Defines and conditionally exports all the constants defined in your system include files that are needed by the System V IPC calls.

ftok

> **ftok** *(path, id)*

Returns a key based on *path* and *id* for use by `msgget`, `semget`, and `shmget`.

less

Pragma, currently unimplemented, that may someday be a compiler directive to make certain trade-offs, such as:

```
use less 'memory';
```

lib

Permits adding additional directories to Perl's default search path at compile time. The directories are added at the front of the search path.

```
use lib list;
```

adds the directories specified in *list* to @INC.

For each directory *$dir* in *list*, lib looks for an architecture-specific subdirectory that has an *auto* subdirectory under it—that is, it looks for *$dir/$archname/auto*. If it finds that directory, then *$dir/$archname* is also added to the front of @INC, preceding *$dir*.

Normally, you should only *add* directories to @INC. However, you can also delete directories. The statement:

```
no lib list
```

deletes the first instance of each named directory from @INC. To delete all instances of all the specified names from @INC, specify :ALL as the first parameter of *list*.

As with adding directories, lib checks for a directory called *$dir/$archname/auto* and deletes the *$dir/$archname* directory from @INC. You can restore @INC to its original value with:

```
@INC = @lib::ORIG_INC;
```

locale

Pragma that tells the compiler to disable (or enable) the use of POSIX locales for built-in operations (LC_CTYPE for regular expressions and LC_COLLATE for string comparison). Each no locale or use locale affects statements to the end of the enclosing block.

Math::BigFloat

Provides methods that permit use of floating-point numbers of arbitrary length. The following apply to all methods, except as noted:

- The object $f remains unchanged.

- All methods except fcmp return a number string (*nstr*) of the form /[+-]\d+E[+-]\d+/, with embedded whitespace ignored.

- A return value of NaN indicates either that an input parameter was "Not a Number" or that an illegal operation was attempted.

- A similar default scale value is computed for square roots.

new

> *$f* = Math::BigFloat->new(*string*)

Creates a new object, *$f*.

fabs

> *$f*->fabs()

Returns absolute value of *$f*.

fadd

> *$f*->fadd(*nstr*)

Returns sum of *nstr* and *$f*.

fcmp

> *$f*->fcmp(*nstr*).

Compares *$f* to *nstr*. Returns -1, 0, or 1 depending on whether *$f* is less than, equal to, or greater than *nstr*, or undef if *nstr* is not a number.

fdiv

> *$f*->fdiv(*nstr*[,*n*])

Returns *$f* divided by *nstr* to *n* places. If *scale* (the number of digits) is unspecified, division is computed to the number of digits given by:

```
max($div_scale, length(dividend)+length(divisor))
```

ffround

> *$f*->ffround(*n*)

Returns *$f* rounded at *n*th place.

fmul

> *$f*->fmul(*nstr*)

Returns *$f* multiplied by *nstr*.

fneg

> *$f*->fneg()

Returns negative of *$f*.

fnorm

> *$f*->fnorm()

Returns normalization of *$f.*

fround

> *$f*->fround(*n*)

Returns value of *$f* rounded to *n* digits.

fsqrt

> *$f*->fsqrt([*n*])

Returns square root of *$f* to *n* places.

fsub

> *$f*->fsub(*nstr*)

Returns *$f* minus *nstr.*

Math::BigInt

Allows use of arbitrary length integers, where the following apply to all methods, except as noted:

- The object *$i* remains unchanged.

- Big integer strings (*bints*) have the form /^\s*[+-]?[\d\s]+$/.

- All methods except bcmp return a big integer string or strings.

- Embedded whitespace is ignored.

- Output values are always in the canonical form: /^[+-]\d+$/.

- The return value NaN results when an input argument is not a number, or when a divide by zero is attempted.

new

> *$i* = Math::BigInt->new(*string*)

Creates a new object, *$i.*

babs

> *$i->babs*

Returns absolute value of *$i*.

badd

> *$i->badd(bint)*

Returns sum of *bint* and *$i*.

bcmp

> *$i->bcmp(bint)*

Compares *$i* to *bint*. The bcmp method returns -1, 0, or 1 depending on whether *$f* is less than, equal to, or greater than the number string given as an argument. If the number string is undefined or null, undef is returned.

bdiv

> *$i->bdiv(bint)*

Returns *$i* divided by *bint*. In list context, returns a two-element array containing the quotient of the division and the remainder; in scalar context, returns only the quotient.

bgcd

> *$i->bgcd(bint)*

Returns greatest common divisor of *$i* and *bint*.

bmod

> *$i->bmod(bint)*

Returns *$i* modulus *bint*.

bmul

> *$i->bmul(bint)*

Returns *$i* multiplied by *bint*.

bneg

> *$i->bneg*

Returns negative of *$i*.

bnorm

> $i->bnorm

Returns normalization of $i.

bsub

> $i->bsub(*bint*)

Returns $i minus *bint*.

Math::Complex

Provides support for complex numbers, including a full set of mathematical functions; permits creation and manipulation of complex numbers. Numerous overload and other operations are provided for working with complex numbers. See the documentation for the module for the complete list and also for a discussion of complex numbers. The following methods are provided:

emake

> $z = Math::Complex->emake(*args*)
> cplxe $z = cplxe(*args*)

Creates a complex number using the polar form.

display_format

> display_format (*[format]*)

When called as a method, sets display format for current object. If *format* is not specified, returns the current setting. Possible settings are:

c   Cartesian format

p   Polar format

When called as a function, overrides the default display format, which is Cartesian.

make

> $z = Math::Complex->make(*args*)
> cplx $z = cplx(*args*)

Creates a complex number using the Cartesian form.

Math::Trig

Defines many trigonometric functions not defined by the core Perl, plus the constant pi and some additional functions for converting angles. For example:

```
use Math::Trig;

$x = tan(0.9);
$halfpi = pi/2;
```

The following functions are defined. A slash (/) between two functions means the values are aliases.

acsc/acosec, asec, acot/acotan
: Arcus cofunctions of sine, cosine, and tangent

acsch/acosech, asech, acoth/acotanh
: Arcus cofunctions of hyperbolic sine, cosine, and tangent

asin, acos, atan
: Arcus (inverse) functions of sine, cosine, and tangent

asinh, acosh, atanh
: Arcus functions of hyperbolic sine, cosine, and tangent

atan2(y, x)
: Principal value of arc tangent of y/x

csc/cosec, sec, cot/cotan
: Cofunctions of sine, cosine, and tangent

csch/cosech, sech, coth/cotanh
: Cofunctions of hyperbolic sine, cosine, and tangent

deg2rad
: Degrees to radians

deg2grad
: Degrees to gradians

grad2deg
: Gradians to degrees

grad2rad
: Gradians to radians

pi   The trigonometric constant pi

rad2deg
: Radians to degrees

rad2grad
: Radians to gradians

`sinh, cosh, tanh`
    Hyperbolic sine, cosine, and tangent

`tan` Tangent

NDBM_File

Provides Perl programs with tied access to NDBM database files. See Perl's built-in `tie` function and the DB_File module.

Net::hostent

Overrides the core `gethostbyname` and `gethostbyaddr` functions with object-oriented versions that return Net::hostent objects. The objects have methods that return the fields of the same name from the *hostent* structure in *netdb.h*:

Field	Description
addr	Address of host, for backwards compatibility
addr_list	List of addresses returned from name server
addrtype	Host address type
aliases	List of aliases
length	Length of address
name	Name of host

You can access the structure fields either with the methods or by importing the fields into your namespace with the :FIELDS import tag and then accessing them by prepending h_ to the field name:

```
$host_obj->name()
$h_name
```

Net::hostent exports the following:

---

gethost

gethost *(host)*

Front-end for `gethostbyaddr` and `gethostbyname`. If *host* is numeric, calls `gethostbyaddr`, otherwise calls `gethostbyname`.

---

gethostbyaddr

gethostbyaddr *(addr, addrtype)*

Returns information about the host with address *addr* of type *addrtype*.

---

gethostbyname

gethostbyname *(hostname)*

Returns information about the host with name *hostname*.

Net::netent

Returns information for a network. Overrides the core getnetbyname and getnet-byaddr functions with object-oriented versions that return Net::netent objects. The objects have methods that return the fields of the same name from the *netent* structure in *netdb.h*:

Field	Description
addrtype	Net address type
aliases	Array of aliases
name	Name of net
net	Network number

You can access the structure fields either with the methods or by importing the fields into your namespace with the :FIELDS import tag and then accessing them by prepending n_ to the field name:

```
$net_obj->name()
$n_name
```

Net::netent exports the following:

---

getnet

> **getnet** *(net)*
>
> Front-end for getnetbyaddr and getnetbyname. If *net* is numeric, calls get-netbyaddr, otherwise calls getnetbyname.

---

getnetbyaddr

> **getnetbyaddr** *(addr, addrtype)*
>
> Returns information about the net with address *addr* of type *addrtype*.

---

getnetbyname

> **getnetbyname** *(netname)*
>
> Returns information about the net with name *netname*.

Net::Ping

Provides methods to create ping objects and test the reachability of remote hosts on the network. After the object has been created, a variable number of hosts can be pinged multiple times before closing the connection. The methods are:

new

$p = Net::Ping->new([*proto*[, *def_timeout*[, *bytes*]]])

Creates a new ping object. All arguments are optional. Takes the following arguments:

proto

> The protocol to use when doing a *ping*. Default is udp. The possible protocols are:

> i cmp

>> Sends an icmp echo message to the remote host. If the echoed message is received correctly back from the remote host, that host is considered reachable. Requires the program to be run as root or setuid to root.

> tcp Attempts to establish connection to remote host's *echo* port. If successful, remote host is considered reachable. No data is actually echoed. No special privileges are required, but overhead is higher than for the others.

> udp Sends a udp packet to remote host's *echo* port. If the echoed packet is received back from the remote host and contains the same data as was sent, the remote host is considered reachable. Requires no special privileges.

def_timeout

> Default timeout in seconds to be used if timeout not passed to the ping method. Must be greater than zero; defaults to 5 seconds.

bytes

> Number of bytes included in the ping packet sent to the remote host. Ignored if protocol is tcp. Default is 1 if protocol is udp, otherwise 0. These are also the minimum number of bytes; the maximum is 1024.

close

$p->close()

Closes network connection for this ping object. The connection can also be closed by undef $p and is automatically closed if the ping object goes out of scope.

ping

$p->ping(*host*[, *timeout*])

Pings remote host and waits for a response. Takes the following arguments:

host

> Specified as either the hostname or the IP number of the remote host.

→

timeout

> Optional, must be greater than 0 seconds if specified. Defaults to whatever was specified when the ping object was created.

If *host* cannot be found or there is a problem with the IP number, returns undef. Otherwise, returns 1 if the host is reachable and 0 if it is not.

pingecho

pingecho (*host*[, *timeout*])

Provides backward compatibility with the previous version of Net::Ping. Uses the tcp protocol, with return values and parameters the same as described for ping.

Net::protoent

Returns information for an Internet protocol. Overrides the core getprotoent, getprotobyname, and getprotobynumber functions with object-oriented versions that return Net::protoent objects. The functions take a default second argument of tcp. The objects have methods that return the fields of the same name from the *protoent* structure in *netdb.h*:

Field	Description
aliases	List of aliases
name	Name of host
proto	Protocol

You can access the structure fields either with the methods or by importing the fields into your namespace with the :FIELDS import tag and then accessing them by prepending p_ to the field name:

```
$proto_obj->name()
$p_name
```

getproto

getproto (*protocol*)

Front-end for getprotobynumber and getprotobyname. If *protocol* is numeric, calls getprotobynumber, otherwise calls getprotobyname.

getprotoent

getprotoent (*protocol*)

Front-end for getprotobynumber and getprotobyname. If *protocol* is numeric, calls getprotobynumber, otherwise calls getprotobyname.

getprotobyname

getprotobyname *(addr, addrtype)*

Returns information about the host with address *addr* of type *addrtype*.

getprotobynumber

getprotobynumber *(hostname)*

Returns information about the host with name *hostname*.

Net::servent

Returns information for an Internet service. Overrides the core getservent, getservbyname, and getservbyport functions, replacing them with versions that return Net::servent objects. The functions take a default second argument of tcp. The objects have methods that return the fields of the same name from the *servent* structure in *netdb.h*:

Field	Description
aliases	List of aliases
name	Name of service
port	Port
proto	Protocol to use

You can access the structure fields either with the methods or by importing the fields into your namespace with the :FIELDS import tag and then accessing them by prepending s_ to the field name:

```
$serv_obj->name()
$s_name
```

getserv

getserv *(service)*

Front-end for getservbyport and getservbyname. If *service* is numeric, calls getservbyport, otherwise calls getservbyname.

getservbyname

getservbyname *(name)*

Returns information for the Internet service with protocol name *name*.

getservbyport

getservbyport(*port*)

Returns information for the Internet service with port number *port*.

getservent

getservent

Returns entries from the database of Internet services.

O

Generic interface to the Perl compiler backends. Also see the B module.

```
perl -MO=backend[,options] perlscript
```

ODBM_File

Provides Perl programs with tied access to ODBM database files. See Perl's built-in `tie` function and the DB_File module.

Opcode

Permits defining an *operator mask* so that any code containing a masked opcode will not compile or execute when Perl next compiles any code. Not usually used directly; for examples of Opcode's use, see the `ops` pragma and the Safe module.

Valid opcodes are listed in the array `op_name` in the file *opcode.h*. Many Opcode functions and methods take lists of operators, which are composed of elements. Each element can be a:

name (opname) or negated name
> Name of operator, usually lowercase. Prefixing the name with an exclamation mark (!) removes it from the accumulated set of operations.

set (opset)
> Operator set. Binary string holding a set of zero or more operators.

tag name (optag) or negated tag
> Operator tag name; refers to groups (or sets) of operators. Begins with a colon (:). Negated by prefixing with an exclamation mark (!). Several *optags* are predefined, including the following. See the manpage for the Opcode module for the opcodes included in each tag.

```
:base_core    :base_io     :base_loop
:base_math    :base_mem    :base_orig
:browse       :dangerous   :default
```

```
:filesys_open    :filesys_read    :filesys_write
:others          :ownprocess      :still_to_be_decided
:subprocess      :sys_db
```

Functions

All the following functions can be exported:

define_optag

define_optag *(optag, opset)*

Defines *optag* as symbolic name for the set *opset*.

empty_opset

empty_opset

Returns an empty opset.

full_opset

full_opset

Returns an opset that includes all operators.

invert_opset

invert_opset *(opset)*

Returns an opset that is the inverse of *opset*.

opcodes

opcodes

In scalar context, returns the number of opcodes in this version of Perl.

opdesc

opdesc *(op, ...)*

Takes list of operator names and returns the corresponding list descriptions.

opdump

opdump *([pat])*

Writes two-column list of operator names and descriptions to STDOUT. If *pat* is specified, only lines matching the (case-insensitive) pattern are output.

opmask

opmask

Returns an opset corresponding to the current opmask.

opmask_add

opmask_add *(opset)*

Adds *opset* to the current opmask.

opset

opset *(op, . . .)*

Returns an opset containing the listed operators.

opset_to_hex

opset_to_hex *(opset)*

Returns string representation of *opset*.

opset_to_ops

opset_to_ops *(opset)*

Returns list of operator names corresponding to the operators in the set *opset*.

verify_opset

verify_opset *(opset[, . . .])*

Returns true if *opset* appears to be a valid opset, else returns false. croaks instead of returning false if optional second parameter is true.

ops

Pragma that disables unsafe opcodes during compilation. Can also be used to specify opcodes to be disabled. Generally used with the *−M* option on the command line:

```
perl -Mops=:default ...    # only allow reasonably safe operations
perl -M-ops=system ...     # disable system opcode
```

See the Opcode module for more information.

overload

Lets you substitute class methods or your own subroutines for standard Perl operators. For example, the code:

```
package Number;
use overload
    "+"  => \&add,
    "*=" => "muas";
```

declares function add for addition and method muas in the Number class (or one of its base classes) for the assignment form *= of multiplication.

Arguments to use overload are key/value pairs, where the key is the operation being overloaded, and the value is the function or method that is to be substituted. Legal values are values permitted inside a &{ ... } call, so a subroutine name, a subroutine reference, or an anonymous subroutine are all legal. Legal keys (overloadable operations) are:

Type	Operations
Arithmetic	+ - * / % ** << >> x . += -= *= /= %= **= <<= >>= x= .=
Comparison	< <= > >= == != <=> lt le gt ge eq ne cmp
Bit and unary	% ^ | neg ! ~
Increment, decrement	++ --
Transcendental	atan2 cos sin exp abs log sqrt
Boolean, string, numeric conversion	bool "" 0+
Special	nomethod fallback =

The functions specified with the use overload directive are typically called with three arguments. If the corresponding operation is binary, then the first two arguments are the two arguments of the operation. However, the first argument should always be an object in the package, so in some cases, the order of the arguments will be interchanged before the method is called. The third argument provides information on the order and can have these values:

false (0)
> The order of arguments is as in the current operation.

true (1)
> The arguments are reversed.

undefined
> The current operation is an assignment variant, but the usual function is called instead.

Unary operations are considered binary operations with the second argument undefined.

The special nomethod key should be followed by a reference to a function of four parameters and called when the overloading mechanism cannot find a method for some operation. The first three arguments are the arguments for the corresponding method if it were found; the fourth argument is the symbol corresponding to the missing method. If several methods are tried, the last one is used.

For example, 1-$a can be equivalent to:

```
&nomethodMethod($a, 1, 1, "-")
```

if the pair "nomethod" => "nomethodMethod" was specified in the use overload directive.

The special fallback key governs what to do if a method for a particular operation is not found. There are three possible cases, depending on the value associated with the fallback key:

undefined
> Tries to use a substituted method. If that fails, it tries to call the method specified for nomethod; if that also fails, an exception is raised.

true
> The same as undefined, but no exception is raised. Instead, Perl silently reverts to non-overloaded operation.

defined, but false
> Tries to call the method specified for nomethod; if that fails, an exception is raised.

The overload module provides the following public functions:

StrVal

overload::StrVal(*arg*)

Gives string value of *arg* if stringify overloading is absent.

Overloaded

overload::Overloaded(*arg*)

Returns true if *arg* is subject to overloading of some operations.

Method

overload::Method(*obj, op*)

Returns the undefined value or a reference to the method that implements *op*.

Pod::Functions

Used internally by Pod::Html for use in converting from pod to HTML.

Pod::Html

Converts files from pod to HTML format. Not generally used directly, but via the *pod2html* script (see Chapter 4), which is included in the standard distribution.

Pod::Text

Converts files from pod format to formatted ASCII text. Not generally used directly, but via the *pod2text* script (see Chapter 4). Termcap is optionally supported for boldface and underlining and can be enabled with:

```
$Pod::Text::termcap=1
```

Otherwise, backspaces are used to simulate bold and underlined text. Exports one function:

pod2text

pod2text *(filename[, filehandle])*

Converts from pod to text format. Takes the following arguments:

filename
    File to convert, or <&STDIN to read from STDIN.

filehandle
    Optional. Filehandle glob to which output should be sent (*STDOUT to write to STDOUT).

POSIX

Provides access to standard POSIX 1003.1 identifiers: functions, classes, and constants. Can be used to import one or multiple symbols:

```
use POSIX;                      # import all symbols
use POSIX qw(setsid);           # import one symbol
use POSIX qw(:errno_h :fcntl_h); # import sets of symbols
```

Functions listed as C-specific are not implemented.

_exit	Identical to C function _exit(2)
abort	Identical to C function abort(3)
abs	Identical to Perl's abs function
access	Determines accessibility of a file; returns undef on failure
acos	Identical to C function acos(3)
alarm	Identical to Perl's alarm function

asctime	Identical to C function asctime(3)
asin	Identical to C function asin(3)
assert	Similar to C macro assert(3)
atan	Identical to C function atan(3)
atan2	Identical to Perl's atan2 function
atexit	C-specific; use END {}
atof	C-specific
atoi	C-specific
atol	C-specific
bsearch	Not supplied
calloc	C-specific
ceil	Identical to C function ceil(3)
chdir	Identical to Perl's chdir function
chmod	Identical to Perl's chmod function
chown	Identical to Perl's chown function
clearerr	Uses method FileHandle::clearerr
clock	Identical to C function clock(3)
close	Closes a file; returns undef on failure
closedir	Identical to Perl's closedir function
cos	Identical to Perl's cos function
cosh	Identical to C function cosh(3)
creat	Creates a new file
ctermid	Generates path name for the controlling terminal
ctime	Identical to C function ctime(3)
cuserid	Gets user's login name
difftime	Identical to C function difftime(3)
div	C-specific
dup	Similar to C function dup(2); returns undef on failure
dup2	Similar to C function dup2(2); returns undef on failure
errno	Returns the value of errno
execl	C-specific; use Perl's exec
execle	C-specific; use Perl's exec
execlp	C-specific; use Perl's exec
execv	C-specific; use Perl's exec
execve	C-specific; use Perl's exec
execvp	C-specific; use Perl's exec
exit	Identical to Perl's exit function
exp	Identical to Perl's exp function
fabs	Identical to Perl's abs function
fclose	Uses method FileHandle::close
fcntl	Identical to Perl's fcntl function
fdopen	Uses method FileHandle::new_from_fd
feof	Uses method FileHandle::eof
ferror	Uses method FileHandle::error
fflush	Uses method FileHandle::flush
fgetc	Uses method FileHandle::getc
fgetpos	Uses method FileHandle::getpos
fgets	Uses method FileHandle::gets
fileno	Uses method FileHandle::fileno

floor	Identical to C function `floor(3)`
fmod	Identical to C function `fmod(3)`
fopen	Uses method `FileHandle::open`
fork	Identical to Perl's `fork` function
fpathconf	Returns value of a configurable limit on a file or directory, or `undef` on failure
fprintf	C-specific; use Perl's `printf` function
fputc	C-specific; use Perl's `print` function
fputs	C-specific; use Perl's `print` function
fread	C-specific; use Perl's `read` function
free	C-specific
freopen	C-specific; use Perl's `open` function
frexp	Returns mantissa and exponent of a floating-point number
fscanf	C-specific; use <> and regular expressions
fseek	Uses method `FileHandle::seek`
fsetpos	Uses method `FileHandle::setpos`
fstat	Gets file status
ftell	Uses method `FileHandle::tell`
fwrite	C-specific; use Perl's `print` function
getc	Identical to Perl's `etc` function
getchar	Returns one character from STDIN
getcwd	Returns name of current working directory
getegid	Returns effective group ID (*gid*)
getenv	Returns value of the specified environment variable
geteuid	Returns the effective user ID (*uid*)
getgid	Returns the user's real group ID (*gid*)
getgrgid	Identical to Perl's `getgrgid` function
getgrnam	Identical to Perl's `getgrnam` function
getgroups	Returns ids of the user's supplementary groups
getlogin	Identical to Perl's `getlogin` function
getpgrp	Identical to Perl's `getpgrp` function
getpid	Returns ID of the process (*pid*)
getppid	Identical to Perl's `getppid` function
getpwnam	Identical to Perl's `getpwnam` function
getpwuid	Identical to Perl's `getpwuid` function
gets	Returns one line from STDIN
getuid	Returns user's ID (*uid*)
gmtime	Identical to Perl's `gmtime` function
isalnum	Identical to C function, but can apply to one character or a whole string
isalpha	Identical to C function, but can apply to one character or a whole string
isatty	Returns Boolean indicating whether the specified filehandle is connected to a TTY
iscntrl	Identical to C function, but can apply to one character or a whole string
isdigit	Identical to C function, but can apply to one character or a whole string

isgraph	Identical to C function, but can apply to one character or a whole string
islower	Identical to C function, but can apply to one character or a whole string
isprint	Identical to C function, but can apply to one character or a whole string
ispunct	Identical to C function, but can apply to one character or a whole string
isspace	Identical to C function, but can apply to one character or a whole string
isupper	Identical to C function, but can apply to one character or a whole string
isxdigit	Identical to C function, but can apply to one character or a whole string
kill	Identical to Perl's kill function
labs	C-specific; use Perl's abs function
ldexp	Identical to C function ldexp(3)
ldiv	C-specific; use division operator (/) and Perl's int function
link	Identical to Perl's link function
localeconv	Gets numeric formatting information. Returns reference to a hash containing the current locale formatting values.
localtime	Identical to Perl's localtime function
log	Identical to Perl's log function
log10	Identical to C function log10(3)
longjmp	C-specific; use Perl's die function
lseek	Moves the read/write file pointer; returns undef on failure
malloc	C-specific
mblen	Identical to C function mblen(3)
mbstowcs	Identical to C function mbstowcs(3)
mbtowc	Identical to C function mbtowc(3)
memchr	C-specific; use Perl's index
memcmp	C-specific; use eq
memcpy	C-specific; use =
memmove	C-specific; use =
memset	C-specific; use x
mkdir	Identical to Perl's mkdir function
mkfifo	Similar to C function mkfifo(2); returns undef on failure
mktime	Converts date/time information to a calendar time; returns undef on failure
modf	Returns integral and fractional parts of a floating-point number
nice	Similar to C function nice(3); returns undef on failure
offsetof	C-specific
open	Opens file for reading or writing; returns undef on failure
opendir	Opens directory for reading; returns undef on failure
pathconf	Retrieves value of a configurable limit on a file or directory; returns undef on failure
pause	Similar to C function pause(3); returns undef on failure

---

perror	Identical to C function `perror(3)`
pipe	Creates an interprocess channel
pow	Computes `$x` raised to the power `$exponent`
printf	Prints specified arguments to STDOUT
putc	C-specific; use Perl's `print` function
putchar	C-specific; use Perl's `print` function
puts	C-specific; use Perl's `print` function
qsort	C-specific; use Perl's `sort` function
raise	Sends specified signal to current process
rand	Non-portable; use Perl's `rand` function
read	Reads from a file; returns `undef` on failure
readdir	Identical to Perl's `readdir` function
realloc	C-specific
remove	Identical to Perl's `unlink` function
rename	Identical to Perl's `rename` function
rewind	Seeks to beginning of file
rewinddir	Identical to Perl's `rewinddir` function
rmdir	Identical to Perl's `rmdir` function
scanf	C-specific; use <> and regular expressions
setgid	Sets real group id for this process
setjmp	C-specific; use `eval {}`
setlocale	Modifies and queries program's locale
setpgid	Similar to C function `setpgid(2)`; returns `undef` on failure
setsid	Identical to C function `setsid(8)`
setuid	Sets real user ID for this process
sigaction	Detailed signal management; returns `undef` on failure
siglongjmp	C-specific; use Perl's `die` function
sigpending	Examines blocked, pending signals and returns `undef` on failure
sigprocmask	Changes and/or examines this process's signal mask; returns `undef` on failure
sigsetjmp	C-specific; use `eval {}`
sigsuspend	Installs signal mask and suspends process until signal arrives; returns `undef` on failure
sin	Identical to Perl's `sin` function
sinh	Identical to C function `sinh(3)`
sleep	Identical to Perl's `sleep` function
sprintf	Identical to Perl's `sprintf` function
sqrt	Identical to Perl's `sqrt` function
srand	Identical to Perl's `srand` function
sscanf	C-specific; use regular expressions
stat	Identical to Perl's `stat` function
strcat	C-specific; use `.=`
strchr	C-specific; use `index`
strcmp	C-specific; use `eq`
strcoll	Identical to C function `strcoll(3)`
strcpy	C-specific; use `=`
strcspn	C-specific; use regular expressions
strerror	Returns error string for the specified `errno`

strftime	Converts date and time to string and returns the string
strlen	C-specific; use length
strncat	C-specific; use .= and/or substr
strncmp	C-specific; use eq and/or substr
strncpy	C-specific; use = and/or substr
stroul	C-specific
strpbrk	C-specific
strrchr	C-specific; use rindex and/or substr
strspn	C-specific
strstr	Identical to Perl's index function
strtod	C-specific
strtok	C-specific
strtol	C-specific
strtoul	C-specific
strxfrm	String transformation; returns the transformed string
sysconf	Retrieves values of system configurable variables; returns undef on failure
system	Identical to Perl's system function
tan	Identical to C function tan(3)
tanh	Identical to C function tanh(3)
tcdrain	Similar to C function tcdrain(3); returns undef on failure
tcflow	Similar to C function tcflow(3); returns undef on failure
tcflush	Similar to C function tcflush(3); returns undef on failure
tcgetpgrp	Identical to C function tcgetpgrp(3)
tcsendbreak	Similar to C function tcsendbreak(3); returns undef on failure
tcsetpgrp	Similar to C function tcsetpgrp(3); returns undef on failure
time	Identical to Perl's time function
times	Returns, in clock ticks, elapsed realtime since some point in the past, user and system times for this process, and user and system times for child processes
tmpfile	Uses method FileHandle::new_tmpfile
tmpnam	Returns a name for a temporary file
tolower	Identical to Perl's lc function
toupper	Identical to Perl's uc function
ttyname	Identical to C function ttyname(3)
tzname	Retrieves time conversion information from the tzname variable
tzset	Identical to C function tzset(3)
umask	Identical to Perl's umask function
uname	Gets name of current operating system
ungetc	Uses method FileHandle::ungetc
unlink	Identical to Perl's unlink function
utime	Identical to Perl's utime function
vfprintf	C-specific
vprintf	C-specific
vsprintf	C-specific
wait	Identical to Perl's wait function

waitpid	Waits for child process to change state; identical to Perl's waitpid function
wcstombs	Identical to C function wcstombs(3)
wctomb	Identical to C function wctomb(3)
write	Writes to file; returns undef on failure

The following sections show the classes that are defined and their methods:

POSIX::SigAction

new

$sigaction = **POSIX::SigAction->new**(*sigsub, sigset, flags*)

Constructor. Creates a new POSIX::SigAction object. Takes the following arguments:

sigsub
> The fully qualified name of a signal-handler subroutine.

sigset
> A POSIX::SigSet object.

flags
> The sa_flags.

POSIX::SigSet

new

$sigset = **POSIX::SigSet->new** [(*args*)]

Constructor. Creates new SigSet object. Optional arguments are used to initialize the set.

addset

$sigset->**addset**(*sig*)

Adds signal *sig* to SigSet object; returns undef on failure.

delset

$sigset->**delset**(*sig*)

Removes signal *sig* from SigSet object; returns undef on failure.

emptyset

> *$sigset*->emptyset()

Initializes SigSet object to empty; returns undef on failure.

fillset

> *$sigset*->fillset()

Initializes SigSet object to include all signals; returns undef on failure.

ismember

> *$sigset*->ismember(*sig*)

Tests SigSet object for a specific signal *sig*.

POSIX::Termios

new

> *$termios* = POSIX::Termios->new

Constructor. Creates new Termios object.

getattr

> *$termios*->getattr([*fd*])

Gets terminal control attributes for a given *fd* (default is 0 for STDIN); returns undef on failure.

getcc

> *$c_cc[ind]* = *$termios*->getcc(*ind*)

Retrieves value from the *c_cc* field of a Termios object. Takes index *ind* since @*c_cc* is an array.

getcflag

> *$c_cflag* = *$termios*->getcflag

Retrieves *c_cflag* field of a Termios object.

getiflag

> *$c_iflag* = *$termios*->**getiflag**

Retrieves *c_iflag* field of a Termios object.

getispeed

> *$ispeed* = *$termios*->**getispeed**

Retrieves input baud rate.

getlflag

> *$c_lflag* = *$termios*->**getlflag**

Retrieves *c_lflag* field of a Termios object.

getoflag

> *$c_oflag* = *$termios*->**getoflag**

Retrieves *c_oflag* field of a Termios object.

getospeed

> *$ospeed* = *$termios*->**getospeed**

Retrieves output baud rate.

setattr

> *$termios*->**setattr**(*fd, option*)

Sets terminal control attributes for a given *fd*; returns undef on failure. *option*
tells when to set the attributes and is one of TCSADRAIN, TCSAFLUSH, or
TCSANOW.

setcc

> *$termios*->**setcc**(*ind, value*)

Sets *value* in the *c_cc* field, indexed by *ind*, of a Termios object.

setcflag

> *$termios*->**setcflag**(*flag*)

Sets *flag* in the *c_cflag* field of a Termios object.

setiflag

$termios->**setiflag(***flag***)**

Sets *flag* in the *c_iflag* field of a Termios object.

setispeed

$termios->**setispeed(***value***)**

Sets input baud rate to *value*; returns undef on failure.

setlflag

$termios->**setlflag(***flag***)**

Sets *flag* in the *c_lflag* field of a Termios object.

setoflag

$termios->**setoflag(***flag***)**

Sets *flag* in the *c_oflag* field of a Termios object.

setospeed

$termios->**setospeed(***value***)**

Sets the output baud rate to *value*. Returns undef on failure.

Constants

The following constants are associated with the Termios class:

Baud rate values

```
B0   B75  B134 B200 B600  B1800 B4800 B19200
B50  B110 B150 B300 B1200 B2400 B9600 B38400
```

c_cc index values

```
VEOF VERASE VKILL VSUSP  VSTOP VTIME
VEOL VINTR  VQUIT VSTART VMIN  NCCS
```

c_cflag field values

```
CLOCAL CSIZE CS6 CS8    HUPCL  PARODD
CREAD  CS5   CS7 CSTOPS PARENB
```

c_iflag field values

```
BRKINT IGNBRK IGNPAR INPCK  IXOFF PARMRK
ICRNL  IGNCR  INLCR  ISTRIP IXON
```

c_lflag field values

```
ECHO   ECHONL ISIG
ECHOE  ICANON NOFLSH
ECHOK  IEXTEN TOSTOP
```

c_oflag field values

```
OPOST
```

Terminal interface values

```
TCSADRAIN TCIOFLUSH TCIFLUSH
TCSANOW   TCOFLUSH  TCSAFLUSH
TCOON     TCION     TCIOFF
```

The following are other constants defined in the POSIX module:

Pathname constants

```
_PC_CHOWN_RESTRICTED  _PC_LINK_MAX   _PC_MAX_CANON
_PC_MAX_INPUT         _PC_NAME_MAX   _PC_NO_TRUNC
_PC_PATH_MAX          _PC_PIPE_BUF   _PC_VDISABLE
```

POSIX constants

```
_POSIX_ARG_MAX       _POSIX_CHILD_MAX    _POSIX_CHOWN_RESTRICTED
_POSIX_JOB_CONTROL   _POSIX_LINK_MAX     _POSIX_MAX_CANON
_POSIX_MAX_INPUT     _POSIX_NAME_MAX     _POSIX_NGROUPS_MAX
_POSIX_NO_TRUNC      _POSIX_OPEN_MAX     _POSIX_PATH_MAX
_POSIX_PIPE_BUF      _POSIX_SAVED_IDS    _POSIX_SSIZE_MAX
_POSIX_STREAM_MAX    _POSIX_TZNAME_MAX   _POSIX_VDISABLE
_POSIX_VERSION
```

System configuration

```
_SC_ARG_MAX       _SC_CHILD_MAX    _SC_CLK_TCK     _SC_JOB_CONTROL
_SC_NGROUPS_MAX   _SC_OPEN_MAX     _SC_SAVED_IDS   _SC_STREAM_MAX
_SC_TZNAME_MAX    _SC_VERSION
```

Error constants

```
E2BIG   EACCES  EAGAIN    EBADF    EBUSY        ECHILD  EDEADLK
EDOM    EEXIST  EFAUL     EFBIG    EINTR        EINVAL
EIO     EISDIR  EMFILE    EMLINK   ENAMETOOLONG         ENFILE
ENODE   ENOENT  ENOEXEC   ENOLCK   ENOMEM       ENOSPC
ENOSYS  ENOTDIR ENOTEMPTY ENOTTY   ENXIO        EPERM
EPIPE   ERANGE  EROFS     ESPIPE   ESRCH        EXDEV
```

File control constants

```
FD_CLOEXEC  F_DUPFD     F_GETFD    F_GETFL   F_GETLK   F_OK
F_RDLCK     F_SETFD     F_SETFL    F_SETLK   F_SETLKW  F_UNLCK
F_WRLCK     O_ACCMODE   O_APPEND   O_CREAT   O_EXCL    O_NOCTTY
O_NONBLOCK  O_RDONLY    O_RDWR     O_TRUNC   O_WRONLY
```

Floating-point constants

```
DBL_DIG         DBL_EPSILON     DBL_MANT_DIG   DBL_MAX
DBL_MAX_10_EXP  DBL_MAX_EXP     DBL_MIN        DBL_MIN_10_EXP
DBL_MIN_EXP     FLT_DIG         FLT_EPSILON    FLT_MANT_DIG
FLT_MAX         FLT_MAX_10_EXP  FLT_MAX_EXP    FLT_MIN
```

```
FLT_MIN_10_EXP  FLT_MIN_EXP     FLT_RADIX      FLT_ROUNDS
LDBL_DIG        LDBL_EPSILON    LDBL_MANT_DIG LDBL_MAX
LDBL_MAX_10_EXP LDBL_MAX_EXP    LDBL_MIN       LDBL_MIN_10_EXP
LDBL_MIN_EXP
```

Limit constants

```
ARG_MAX     CHAR_BIT   CHAR_MAX    CHAR_MIN    CHILD_MAX
INT_MAX     INT_MIN    LINK_MAX    LONG_MAX    LONG_MIN
MAX_CANON   MAX_INPUT  MB_LEN_MAX  NAME_MAX    NGROUPS_MAX
OPEN_MAX    PATH_MAX   PIPE_BUF    SCHAR_MAX   SCHAR_MIN
SHRT_MAX    SHRT_MIN   SSIZE_MAX   STREAM_MAX  TZNAME_MAX
UCHAR_MAX   UINT_MAX   ULONG_MAX   USHRT_MAX
```

Locale constants

```
LC_ALL  LC_COLLATE  LC_CTYPE  LC_MONETARY  LC_NUMERIC  LC_TIME
```

Math constants

```
HUGE_VAL
```

Signal constants

```
SA_NOCLDSTOP SIGABRT    SIGALRM    SIGCHLD   SIGCONT  SIGFPE
SIGHUP       SIGILL     SIGINT     SIGKILL   SIGPIPE  SIGQUIT
SIGSEGV      SIGSTOP    SIGTERM    SIGTSTP   SIGTTIN  SIGTTOU
SIGUSR1      SIGUSR2    SIG_BLOCK  SIG_DFL   SIG_ERR  SIG_IGN
SIG_SETMASK  SIG_UNBLOCK
```

Stat constants

```
S_IRGRP  S_IROTH  S_IRUSR  S_IRWXG  S_IRWXO  S_IRWXU  S_ISGID
S_ISUID  S_IWGRP  S_IWOTH  S_IWUSR  S_IXGRP  S_IXOTH  S_IXUSR
```

Stat macros

```
S_ISBLK  S_ISCHR  S_ISDIR  S_ISFIFO  S_ISREG
```

Stdlib constants

```
EXIT_FAILURE  EXIT_SUCCESS  MB_CUR_MAX  RAND_MAX
```

Stdio constants

```
BUFSIZ  EOF  FILENAME_MAX  L_ctermid  L_cuserid  L_tmpname  TMP_MAX
```

Time constants

```
CLK_TCK  CLOCKS_PER_SEC
```

Unistd constants

```
R_OK    SEEK_CUR  SEEK_END     SEEK_SET  STDIN_FILENO
STDOUT_FILENO     STRERR_FILENO  W_OK     X_OK
```

Wait constants

```
WNOHANG  WUNTRACED
```

WIFEXITED WEXITSTATUS WIFSIGNALED WTERMSIG WIFSTOPPED WSTOPSIG

re

Pragma that lets you alter the behavior of regular expressions. Permits the following alterations:

use re 'debug'
> Causes Perl to produce debugging messages when compiling and at run time when using regular expressions. See the *re* manpage and the section on "Debugging regular expressions" in the *perldebug* manpage for details.

use re 'eval'
> Permits a regular expression to contain (?{ . . . }) zero-width assertion even if the regular expression contains variable interpolation, which normally isn't permitted for security reasons. The pragma is ignored if the regular expression comes from tainted data.

use re 'taint'
> When a tainted string is the target of a regular expression, causes the regular expression memories (or the values returned by the m// operator in list context) to be tainted.

Safe

Creates compartments for evaluating untrusted Perl code. Each compartment has an associated operator mask for excluding particular Perl operators from the compartment. See the Opcode module for more information on operators and operator masks. The default mask is applied during compilation to prevent all operations that give access to the system. Safe provides the following methods:

new

> *$cpt* = **new Safe** [(*namespace, mask*)]

Constructor. Creates a new compartment. Takes the following arguments:

namespace
> Optional. Root namespace to use for the compartment. Default is "Safe::Root0", which auto-increments for each new compartment.

mask
> Optional. Operator mask to use; defaults to a restrictive set.

mask

> *$cpt*->**mask** ([*mask*])

Sets operator mask for the compartment if *mask* is specified, otherwise it gets the current mask.

rdo

> *$cpt->rdo (filename)*

Evaluates the contents of file *filename* inside the compartment.

reval

> *$cpt->reval (string)*

Evaluates *string* as Perl code inside the compartment.

root

> *$cpt->root ([namespace])*

If *namespace* is specified, sets the root namespace for the compartment, otherwise gets the current namespace.

share

> *$cpt->share (varname[, . . .])*

Shares the variable(s) in the argument list with the compartment.

trap

> *$cpt->trap (op[, . . .])*

For each operator specified in the argument list, sets the corresponding bit in the compartment's operator mask.

untrap

> *$cpt->untrap (op[, . . .])*

For each operator specified in the argument list, resets the corresponding bit in the compartment's operator mask.

varglob

> *$cpt->varglob (varname)*

Returns a glob for the symbol table entry of *varname* in the compartment's package.

The following subroutines are available for export by Safe. The operator names can be found in the array op_name in the file *opcode.h* in the Perl distribution.

emptymask

emptymask

Returns a mask with all operators unmasked.

fullmask

fullmask

Returns a mask with all operators masked.

mask_to_ops

mask_to_ops *(mask)*

Takes an operator mask *mask* and returns a list of the names of operators masked in *mask*.

MAXO

MAXO

Returns the number of operators in a mask (and hence its length).

opcode

opcode *(op[, . . .])*

Takes a list of operator names and returns the corresponding list of opcodes.

op_mask

op_mask

Returns the operator mask in effect at the time the invocation to the subroutine was compiled.

opname

opname *(op[, . . .])*

Takes a list of opcodes and returns the corresponding list of operator names.

ops_to_mask

ops_to_mask *(op[, . . .])*

Takes a list of operator names and returns an operator mask with those operators masked.

SDBM_File

Provides Perl programs with tied access to SDBM database files. See Perl's built-in
tie function and the DB_File module.

Search::Dict

Searches for a key in an ordered text file and sets the file position. Exports one
function:

---

look

> **look** *fh, key, dict, fold*
>
> Performs string search and sets the position in filehandle *fh* to the first line
> with a key equal to or greater than *key*. Returns the new file position, or −1 in
> case of error. Takes the following arguments:
>
> *fh* Filehandle of the dictionary file.
>
> *key* Key to search for.
>
> *dict*
> > If true, searches in dictionary order, considering only word characters and
> > whitespace.
>
> *fold*
> > If true, ignore case.

SelectSaver

Provides a way to save and restore filehandles so you can temporarily use a different filehandle.

---

new

> **$saver = new SelectSaver [(*fh*)]**
>
> Constructor. Creates a new SelectSaver object, *$saver*, which saves the current
> filehandle. The optional parameter *fh* is the filehandle that is to temporarily
> replace the current filehandle. If *fh* is present, the current filehandle is saved
> in *$saver* and the new one becomes the current filehandle. With no parame-
> ter, the current filehandle is saved in the object *$saver*, and it also remains
> current.
>
> You can use the newly selected filehandle within the current block. When
> you exit the block, the previous filehandle is again made the current one, and
> the SelectSaver object in which it was stored is destroyed.

SelfLoader

Used when you want to include functions in your program, but you want to load them only if necessary. Functions to be self-loaded are placed after the line:

```
__DATA__
```

in your program. When the code is compiled, compilation stops at the `__DATA__` token. The SelfLoader exports the AUTOLOAD subroutine to the package; this subroutine loads the subroutines after `__DATA__` when they are required.

Shell

Allows you to invoke Unix shell utilities as if they were Perl subroutines. Arguments (including switches) are passed to the utilities as strings:

```
use Shell qw(date cp ps);  # list shell commands you want to use

$date = date();   # put the output of the date(1) command into $date
cp("-p" "/etc/passwd", "/tmp/passwd"); # copy password file to a tmp file
print ps("-ww"); # print the results of a "ps -ww" command
```

sigtrap

Pragma to enable simple signal handling. Provides two signal handlers that can be installed, or you can install your own handler; also provides options to specify which signals to trap. Ignores requests to trap signals not used in your system's architecture.

```
use sigtrap;                 # initialize default signal handlers
use sigtrap qw(die normal-signals);
use sigtrap 'handler' => \&handlername, 'normal-signals';
use sigtrap qw(handler handlername normal-signals
               stack-trace error-signals);
```

Signal Handler Options

Used to specify which handler is to be installed and used for signals installed after the handler:

die Installs handler that dies with a message indicating what signal was trapped.

handler *handlername*
    Installs your handler *handlername*.

stack-trace
    Default signal handler. Outputs stack trace to STDERR and tries to dump core.

Signal List Options

You can specify your own list of options:

```
use sigtrap qw(BUS SEGV PIPE ABRT);
```

or use one of the following built-in option lists:

error-signals
> Signals that indicate a serious problem: ABRT, BUS, EMT, FPE, ILL, QUIT, SEGV, SYS, and TRAP.

normal-signals
> Signals a program is most likely to encounter: HUP, INT, PIPE, and TERM.

old-interface-signals
> Default. Signals trapped by default in older versions of sigtrap: ABRT, BUS, EMT, FPE, ILL, PIPE, QUIT, SEGV, SYS, TERM, and TRAP.

Other Options

any Installs handlers only for subsequently listed signals that aren't already taken care of.

number
> Requires that the version of sigtrap being used must be at least number.

signal
> Installs a handler for any argument that looks like a signal name.

untrapped
> Installs handlers only for subsequently listed signals not already trapped or ignored.

Socket

Translation of the C *socket.h* file that uses *h2xs* and your C compiler. See Chapter 13 for the details.

strict

Pragma for doing strict error checking within the current block. Can be turned off by prefixing with no:

```
use strict 'vars';
no strict 'vars';
```

Provides three kinds of restriction:

strict 'refs'
> Generates runtime error if you use any symbolic references.

```
strict 'subs'
```
Generates compile-time error if you use a bareword identifier that's not a pre-declared subroutine.

```
strict 'vars'
```
Generates compile-time error if you access a variable that wasn't declared via `my`, isn't fully qualified, or wasn't imported.

`use strict` by itself (with no import list) is the most restrictive, causing all possible restrictions to be imposed.

subs

Pragma that predeclares subroutines whose names are given in a list:

```
use subs qw(sub[, ...]);
sub $arg[, ...];
```

This lets you use the subroutines without parentheses even before they're defined, and lets you override built-in functions.

Symbol

Provides functions for creating anonymous globs and qualifying variable names. Exports the following:

gensym

gensym

Creates an anonymous glob and returns a reference to it that can be used as a filehandle or directory handle.

ungensym

ungensym

For backward compatibility only; does nothing.

qualify

qualify *(symname[, pkg])*

Turns unqualified symbol names into qualified variable names (e.g., turns `myvar` into `MyPackage::myvar`).

qualify_to_ref

qualify_to_ref *(symname[, pkg])*

Like `qualify`, but returns a glob ref that can be used even if `use strict 'refs'` is in effect.

Sys::Hostname

Provides one function, hostname, which attempts to get the system hostname by doing checks appropriate to the operating system. Removes nulls, returns, and newlines from the result, which it then caches. croaks on failure.

```
use Sys::Hostname;
$host = hostname();
```

Sys::Syslog

Interfaces to Unix syslog(3) program. Requires the file *syslog.ph*, which must be created with *h2ph* by your system administrator. Provides the following four functions:

---

closelog

closelog

Closes the log file.

---

openlog

openlog *ident, logopt, facility*

Opens the log file. Takes the following arguments:

ident
> Prepended to every message.

logopt
> Logging options, containing one or more of:

> cons
>> Write messages to system console if they can't be sent to *syslogd*.

> ndelay
>> Open the connection immediately.

> nowait
>> Don't wait for child processes before logging messages to the console.

> pid Log process id.

facility
> Specifies the part of the system making the log entry.

---

setlogmask

setlogmask *mask_priority*

Sets log mask to *mask_priority* and returns the old mask.

---

syslog

> **syslog** *priority, mask, format, args*

If *priority* and *mask* permit, logs message formed as if by `sprintf` (*format, args*), with the addition that %m is replaced with the current error message from $!.

Term::Cap

Provides low-level functions to extract and use capabilities from a terminal capability (termcap) database. For general information about the use of this database, see the *termcap(5)* manpage. Provides the following functions:

Tgetent

> *$terminal* = **Tgetent** Term::Cap { TERM => *termtype*, OSPEED => *ospeed* }

Acts as the constructor for Term::Cap. Extracts the termcap entry for terminal type *termtype* and returns a reference to a terminal object. The termcap entry itself is `$terminal->{TERMCAP}`. Calls `Carp::croak` on failure. Takes the following arguments:

TERM => *termtype*
> Terminal type. Defaults to the value of the environment variable TERM if *termtype* is false or undefined.

OSPEED => *ospeed*
> The terminal output bit rate, specified as either a POSIX termios/SYSV termio speed or an old BSD-style speed. You can use the POSIX module to get your terminal's output speed (in *ospeed* here).

Tgoto

> *$terminal*->**Tgoto**('cm', *col, row*[, *fh*])

Produces control string to move the cursor relative to the screen. Doesn't cache output strings, but does % expansion as needed on control string. Takes the following arguments:

'cm'
> Required first argument ("cursor move").

col, row
> Column and row to move cursor to.

fh   Filehandle to receive the control string.

Tpad

$terminal->Tpad(*string, count, fh*)

Specifies padding required to create delay needed by terminal. Takes the following arguments:

string
> The string to pad with.

count
> The number of pad characters.

fh   The filehandle to pad.

Tputs

$terminal->Tputs(*'cap', count*[, *fh*])

Produces control string for capabilities other than cursor movement. Does not do % expansion, but does cache output strings if $count = 1. Takes the following arguments:

cap
> Capability to produce control string for.

count
> Should be 1 unless padding is required (see Tpad); if greater than 1, specifies amount of padding.

fh   Filehandle to receive the control string.

Trequire

$terminal->Trequire(*caps*)

Checks to see whether the named capabilities, *caps*, are defined in the terminal's termcap entry. For example:

```
$terminal->Trequire(qw/ce ku kd/);
```

Any undefined capabilities are listed and Carp::croak is called.

Term::Complete

Provides word completion on list of words in a specified array. Exports one function:

Complete

Complete (*'prompt_string', array*)

Sends string to the currently selected filehandle, reads the user's response, and returns the response. Takes the following arguments:

→

prompt_string

> The prompt for user input.

array

> The array of words against which the user's input is matched.

If any of the following characters are included in the user's response to *prompt_string*, they are treated as special characters:

TAB

> Does word completion, matching what the user has typed so far against the list of strings in *completion_list*. On a unique match, outputs the rest of the matched string and waits for the user to press the return key. Otherwise, leaves partial input unchanged and sounds the bell.

CTRL-D

> Prints all possible completions of the user's partial input, or the entire completion list if the partial input string is null, and reissues the prompt string and the partial input. Redefine by setting the variable `$Term::Complete::complete`.

CTRL-U

> Erases any partial input. Redefine by setting the variable `$Term::Complete::kill`.

DEL, BS

> Delete and backspace characters; both erase one character from the partial input string. Redefine by setting the variables `$Term::Complete::erase1` and `$Term::Complete::erase2`.

Term::ReadLine

Front-end to other ReadLine packages. Currently interfaces to Term-ReadLine, which is available on CPAN. Defines the variables `$IN` and `$OUT`, which return the filehandles for input and output, respectively, or `undef` if Readline input and output cannot be used for Perl. Provides the following methods:

new

> *$term* = new **Term::ReadLine** *'name'*

Constructor. Returns the handle for subsequent calls to other ReadLine methods. Argument *name* is the name of the application. Optionally can be followed by two arguments that are globs specifying input and output filehandles.

addhistory

> *$term*->**addhistory(***line***)**

Adds *line* to the input history.

Features

$term->Features

Returns a reference to a hash whose keys are features present in the current implementation and whose values are those assigned to each feature. Several optional features are used in the minimal interface: *appname* should be present if the first argument to new is recognized, and *minline* should be present if MinLine method is not a dummy. *autohistory* should be present if lines are put into history automatically (maybe subject to *MinLine*), and *addhistory* if the addhistory method is not a dummy.

findConsole

$term->findConsole

Returns array of two strings containing the most appropriate names for input and output files, using the conventions "<$in" and ">$out".

MinLine

$term->MinLine([*size*])

With *size* argument, serves as an advice on minimal size of line to be added to history. Without an argument, does not add anything to the history. Returns the old value.

ReadLine

$term->ReadLine

Returns the actual package that executes the commands. Some possible values are Term::ReadLine::Gnu, Term::ReadLine::Perl, or Term::ReadLine::Stub.

readline

$term->readline(*prompt*)

Prompts for input line and gets the result. Removes trailing newline and returns undef at end-of-file.

Test

Provides a framework for writing test scripts so you don't need to know the particular output that Test::Harness expects to see. Useful if you are writing modules and writing tests for those modules. Provides the following test types:

Normal
Tests that are expected to succeed.

Skip

Tests that need a platform-specific feature. They work like normal tests except that the first argument should evaluate to true if the required feature is *not* present.

Todo

Tests that are designed for maintaining an executable todo list; the tests aren't expected to succeed.

Test also provides an *onfail* hook that can trigger additional diagnostics for failures at the end of the test run. To use *onfail*, pass it an array reference of hash references where each hash contains at least these fields: package, repetition, and result, as well as any expected value or diagnostic string.

See the *Test* manpage for details and examples.

Test::Harness

Used by MakeMaker; runs Perl test scripts and prints some statistics. You can use the Test module to write test scripts without knowing the exact output Test::Harness expects. Exports one function:

runtests

runtests *(tests)*

Runs all test scripts named in *tests* and checks standard output for the expected okn strings. Prints performance statistics after all tests have been run.

Text::Abbrev

Given a list of strings, creates a hash of unambiguous abbreviations. Exports one function:

abbrev

abbrev *(\%hashref, list)*

Takes each string in *list* and constructs the hash referenced by *\%hashref.* Each key is an unambiguous truncation of one of the strings, and the value is the full string (where unambiguous means that there is only one possible expansion that matches one of the strings in the list).

For example, if *list* contains "file" and "find", then the key/value pairs created include:

```
fil  => file
file => file
fin  => find
find => find
```

Both "f" and "fi" are ambiguous, since they start both words, and therefore they don't appear as keys.

Text::ParseWords

Parses lines of text and returns an array of words. Provides three functions:

quotewords

quotewords *(delim, keep, lines)*

Accepts delimiter and list of lines and breaks the lines up at occurrences of the delimiter into a list of words. Exported by default. Takes the following arguments:

delim

> Delimiter, which can be a regular expression. Occurrences inside quotes are ignored.

keep

> Boolean. If false, quotes and single backslashes are removed from the list of words returned, and a double backslash is returned as a single backslash. If true, quotes and backslashes are retained.

lines

> The list of lines to be parsed.

old_shellwords

old_shellwords *(lines)*

Splits an array of lines into words. Exported on request. Same as the pre-Perl 5 program *shellwords.pl*.

shellwords

shellwords *(lines)*

Works like `old_shellwords`, but does not default to using `$_` if there is no argument. Exported by default.

Text::Soundex

Implements the soundex algorithm, which hashes a word (in particular, a surname) into a compressed form that approximates the sound of the word when spoken by an English speaker.

```
use Text::Soundex;

$code = soundex $string;   # get soundex code for a string
@codes = soundex @list;    # get list of codes for list of strings
```

Returns the value of the variable $soundex_nocode if there is no soundex code representation for a string. $soundex_nocode is initially set to undef, but can be reset to another value, e.g.:

```
$soundex_nocode = 'Z000';
```

Text::Tabs

Provides subroutines that expand tabs into spaces and compress ("unexpand") spaces into tabs. The appearance of the text is unchanged. Defines the tabstop variable, which defines the number of spaces equivalent to a tab. Default is 8. Exports the following functions:

expand

expand *(text)*

Given an array of strings *(text)* containing tabs, replaces each tab character with the equivalent number of spaces.

unexpand

unexpand *(text)*

Give an array of strings *(text)*, that may or may not contain tabs, replaces each *$tabstop* consecutive spaces with a tab character.

Text::Wrap

Wraps text into a paragraph. Defines the $columns variable, which specifies the output line length. Default is 76. Exported on request. Provides the following function:

wrap

wrap *(init_str, other_str, text)*

Breaks lines of array *text* at the word boundary closest to the size of a line. Prepends *init_str* to the first output line and *other_str* to subsequent lines, for indentation. Exported by default.

Thread

Provides Perl multithreading support. Distributed as a beta feature with Perl 5.005 and runs only on versions of Perl that were built with thread support. Has the following functions and methods:

new

> t = new Thread \&sub[, *params*]

Constructor. Starts a new thread in the referenced subroutine, \&sub, returning a thread object that represents the new thread. The optional parameter list is passed to the subroutine. Execution continues in both the new thread and the code.

async

> t = async {*block*};

Creates a new thread to execute the block that follows it. The block is treated as an anonymous subroutine (and therefore has a semicolon after the closing bracket). Returns a thread object. async isn't exported by default, so you can either specify use Thread qw(async); or fully qualify the name (Thread::async).

cond_broadcast

> cond_broadcast *var*

Like cond_wait, but unblocks all threads blocked in a cond_wait on the locked variable, not just one thread.

cond_signal

> cond_signal *var*

Takes the locked variable *var* and unblocks one thread that's cond_waiting on that variable. If multiple threads are so blocked, the one that will be unblocked can't be determined.

cond_wait

> cond_wait *var*

Takes the locked variable *var*, unlocks it, and blocks until another thread does a cond_signal or cond_broadcast for that variable. The variable is relocked after the cond_wait has been satisfied. If multiple threads are cond_waiting, all but one will reblock waiting to reacquire the lock.

eval

eval { $t->join}

Wraps an eval around a join. Waits for a thread to exit and passes any return values from the thread, putting errors into $@.

join

$t->join

Waits for a thread to end and when it does, returns any exit values from the thread. Blocks until the thread has ended, unless the thread has already terminated.

lock

lock *var*
lock *sub*

Locks a variable or a subroutine. A lock on a variable is maintained until the lock goes out of scope. If the variable is already locked by another thread, the lock call blocks until the variable is available. You can recursively lock the variable, which stays locked until the outermost lock goes out of scope.

Note that locks on variables only affect other lock calls; they don't prevent normal access to a variable. Also, locking a container object (e.g., an array) doesn't lock each element of the container.

Locking a subroutine blocks any calls to the subroutine until the lock goes out of scope; no other thread can access the subroutine while the lock is in effect.

list

Thread->list

Returns list of thread objects for all running and finished, but not joined, threads.

self

Thread->self

Returns an object representing the thread that made the call.

tid

*$id = $t->*tid

Returns an object representing the *tid* (thread id) of a thread. The ID is simply an integer that is incremented each time a new thread is created, starting with zero for the main thread of a program.

Thread::Queue

Provides a thread-safe queue. Any number of threads can add elements to the end of the queue or remove elements from the head.

new

$q = new Thread::Queue

Creates a new empty queue. Returns an object representing the queue.

dequeue

*$q->*dequeue

Removes and returns a scalar from the head of the queue. If the queue is empty, dequeue blocks the thread until another thread enqueues a scalar on the queue.

dequeue_nb

*$q->*dequeue_nb

Like dequeue but returns undef if the queue is empty, instead of blocking.

enqueue

*$q->*enqueue *list*

Adds the list of scalars, *list*, to the end of the queue.

pending

*$q->*pending

Returns the number of items remaining in the queue.

Thread::Semaphore

Provides a mechanism to regulate access to resources. Semaphores are more general than locks because they aren't tied to a particular scalar. They can have values other than zero or one, and they can be incremented or decremented by some specified number.

new

$sem = new Thread::Semaphore([*val*])

Constructor. Creates a new semaphore object, with an optional initial count of *val*, or 1 if *val* isn't specified.

down

down *[number]*

Decrements the semaphore's count by the specified number, which defaults to 1. If the resulting count would be negative, blocks until the semaphore's count has been increased to be equal to or larger than the amount you want to decrease it.

up

up *[number]*

Increments the semaphore's count by the specified number, which defaults to 1. If a thread is blocked waiting to decrement the count, and the increment brings the count high enough, the blocked thread is unblocked.

Thread::Signal

Starts a special signal handler thread to reliably run signal handlers. All signals are handed to this thread, which runs the associated $SIG{*signal*} handlers for them.

```
use Thread::Signal;

$SIG{HUP} = handler;
```

Thread::Specific

Provides thread-specific keys.

key_create

$k = key_create Thread::Specific

Constructor. Creates a Thread::Specific key object.

Tie::Array, Tie::StdArray

Provides methods for array-tying classes. See the *perltie* manpage for the functions needed for tying an array to a package. The basic Tie::Array package provides stub DELETE and EXTEND methods, and it implements PUSH, POP, SHIFT, UNSHIFT, SPLICE, and CLEAR in terms of basic FETCH, STORE, FETCHSIZE, and STORESIZE.

Tie::StdArray inherits from Tie::Array and provides the methods needed for tied arrays that are implemented as blessed references to an "inner" Perl array. It causes tied arrays to behave like standard arrays, allowing for selective method overloading.

See the *perltie* manpage for more detailed information and for examples. To write your own tied arrays, use the following required methods:

TIEARRAY

TIEARRAY *classname, list*

Constructor. This method is invoked by the command tie @*array, classname*. Associates an array instance with the specified class. *list* represents additional arguments needed to complete the association. Should return an object of a class that provides the remaining methods.

CLEAR

CLEAR *this*

Clears all values from the tied array associated with object *this*.

DESTROY

DESTROY *this*

Normal object destructor.

EXTEND

EXTEND *this, count*

Doesn't need to do anything. Provides information that the array is likely to grow to have *count* entries.

FETCH

FETCH *this, index*

Retrieves the data item in *index* for the tied array associated with object *this*.

FETCHSIZE

FETCHSIZE *this*

Returns the number of items in the tied array associated with object *this*.

POP

POP *this*

Removes the last element from the array and returns it.

PUSH

PUSH *this, list*

Appends elements of *list* to the array.

SHIFT

SHIFT *this*

Removes and returns the first element of the array, shifting the remaining elements down.

SPLICE

SPLICE *this, offset, length, list*

Performs the equivalent of a *splice* on the array. Returns a list of the original *length* elements at the specified offset. The arguments are:

offset
Optional. Defaults to zero; if negative, counts back from the end of the array.

length
Optional. Defaults to the rest of the array.

list May be empty.

STORE

STORE *this, index, value*

Stores value of a data item into *index* for the tied array associated with object *this*. If the resulting array is larger than the class's mapping for the array, undef should be returned for new positions.

STORESIZE

STORESIZE *this, count*

Sets the total number of items in the tied array associated with object *this* to *count*. If this makes the array larger than the class's mapping for the array, then undef should be returned for new positions. If it makes the array smaller than the mapping, then entries beyond *count* should be deleted.

UNSHIFT

UNSHIFT *this, list*

Inserts *list* elements at the beginning of the array, moving existing elements up to make room.

Tie::Handle

Provides skeletal methods for handle-tying classes. Tie::Handle provides a new method as backup in case a class has no TIEHANDLE method. See the *perltie* manpage for more detailed information and for examples. To write your own tied-handle classes, use the following methods:

TIEHANDLE

TIEHANDLE *classname, list*

Constructor. This method is invoked by the command tie *glob, *classname*. Associates new glob instance with class *classname*. *list* represents any additional arguments needed to complete the association.

DESTROY

DESTROY *this*

Frees storage associated with the tied handle *this*. Permits class to take some action when an instance is destroyed. Rarely needed.

GETC

GETC *this*

Gets one character from tied handle *this*.

PRINT

PRINT *this, list*

Prints the values in *list*.

PRINTF

PRINTF *this, format, list*

Prints the values in *list* using *format*.

READ

READ *this, scalar, length, offset*

Reads *length* bytes from *scalar* starting at *offset*.

READLINE

READLINE *this*

Reads one line from *this*.

WRITE

WRITE *this, scalar, length, offset*

Writes *length* bytes of data from *scalar* starting at *offset*.

Modules

Tie::Hash, Tie::StdHash

Provides skeletal methods for hash-tying classes. Tie::Hash provides a new method, as well as the methods TIEHASH, EXISTS, and CLEAR. The Tie::StdHash package inherits from Tie::Hash and causes tied hashes to behave like standard hashes, allowing for selective method overloading. It provides most methods required for hashes. The new method is provided as backup in case a class has no TIEHASH method.

To write your own tied hashes, the methods listed here are required. See the *perltie* manpage for more detailed information and for examples.

TIEHASH

TIEHASH *ClassName, list*

Constructor. Associates a new hash instance with class *ClassName*. *list* is a list of additional arguments needed to complete the association.

```
tie %hash, ClassName, list
```

CLEAR

CLEAR *this*

Clears all values from tied hash *this*.

DELETE

> **DELETE** *this, key*

> Deletes *key* from tied hash *this*.

EXISTS

> **EXISTS** *this, key*

> Verifies that *key* exists for tied hash *this*.

FETCH

> **FETCH** *this, key*

> Retrieves value associated with *key* for tied hash *this*.

FIRSTKEY

> **FIRSTKEY** *this*

> Returns key/value pair for the first key in tied hash *this*.

NEXTKEY

> **NEXTKEY** *this, lastkey*

> Returns next key/value pair after *lastkey* for tied hash *this*.

STORE

> **STORE** *this, key, value*

> Stores *value* into tied hash *this* with key *key*.

Tie::RefHash

Provides the ability to use references as hash keys after you've tied a hash variable to the module:

```
use Tie::RefHash;
tie hashvariable, 'Tie::RefHash', list;

untie hashvariable;
```

Uses the TIEHASH interface and provides the same methods.

Tie::Scalar, Tie::StdScalar

Provides some skeletal methods for scalar-tying classes. The basic Tie::Scalar package provides a new method, as well as methods TIESCALAR, FETCH, and STORE. The Tie::StdScalar package inherits from Tie::Scalar and causes scalars tied to it to behave like the built-in scalars, allowing for selective overloading of methods. The new method is provided as backup in case a class has no TIESCALAR method.

To write your own tied hashes, the methods listed here are required. See the *perltie* manpage for more detailed information and for examples.

TIESCALAR

TIESCALAR *ClassName, list*

Constructor. Associates new scalar instance with class *ClassName. list* represents any additional arguments needed to complete the association.

```
tie $scalar, ClassName, list
```

DESTROY

DESTROY *this*

Frees storage associated with the tied scalar referenced by *this*. Permits a class to perform specific actions when an instance is destroyed. Rarely needed.

FETCH

FETCH *this*

Retrieves value of the tied scalar referenced by *this*.

STORE

STORE *this, value*

Stores *value* in the tied scalar referenced by *this*.

Tie::SubstrHash

Provides a hash-table–like interface to a fixed-sized array that has a constant key size and record size.

```
require Tie::SubstrHash;
tie %myhash, "Tie::SubstrHash", key_len, value_len, table_size;
```

To tie a new hash to this package, specify the following:

key_len
> Length of each key

value_len
> Length of each value

table_size
> Size of the table given as the number of key/value pairs

An attempt to store a key/value pair where either the key or the value is the wrong length, or where the resulting table would be greater than *table_size*, results in a fatal error.

Time::gmtime

Replaces Perl's core gmtime function with a version that returns Time::tm objects. Exports two functions:

---

gmtime

$gm = gmtime()

Overrides the core gmtime function. The Time::tm object returned has methods with the same names as the structure fields they return. That is, to return the field mon, use the mon method:

```
use Time::gmtime;
$gm = gmtime();
print $gm->mon;
```

The field names (and therefore the method names) are the same as the names of the fields in the *tm* structure in the C file *time.h*: sec, min, hour, mday, mon, year, wday, yday, and isdst.

You can access the fields either with the methods or by importing the fields into your namespace with the :FIELDS import tag and prepending tm_ to the method name (for example, $tm_mon).

---

gmctime

$gmc = gmctime()

Overrides the core gmtime function in scalar context; returns a string with the date and time:

```
use Time::gmtime;
$gmc = gmctime();
print $gmc;
```

Then the output of the print command looks like:

```
Thu Apr 9 18:15:06 1998
```

Time::Local

Provides routines that take the time and return the number of seconds elapsed between January 1, 1970 and the specified time. The arguments are defined like the corresponding arguments returned by Perl's gmtime and localtime functions and the results agree with the results of those functions. Exports two functions; both return −1 if the integer limit is hit. On most machines this applies to dates after January 1, 2038.

timegm

> $time = **timegm**(*sec, min, hours, mday, mon, year*)

Converts from Greenwich time.

timelocal

> $time = **timelocal**(*sec, min, hours, mday, mon, year*)

Converts from local time.

Modules

Time::localtime

Replaces Perl's core localtime function with a version that returns Time::tm objects. Exports two functions:

localtime

> $lt = **localtime**()

Overrides the core localtime function. The Time::tm object returned has methods with the same names as the structure fields they return. That is, to return the field *mon*, use the mon method:

```
use Time::localtime;
$lt = localtime();
print $lt->mon;
```

The field names (and therefore the method names) are the same as the names of the fields in the *tm* structure in the C file *time.h*: sec, min, hour, mday, mon, year, wday, yday, and isdst. You can access the fields either with the methods or by importing the fields into your namespace with the :FIELDS import tag and prepending tm_ to the method name (for example, $tm_mon).

ctime

> ct = ctime()

Overrides the core localtime function in scalar context; returns a string with the date and time:

```
use Time::gmtime;
$ct = ctime();
print $ct
```

Then the output of the print command looks like:

```
Thu Apr  9 16:50:10 1998
```

Time::tm

Used internally by Time::localtime and Time::gmtime. Don't use it directly. Creates addressable Time::tm struct object.

UNIVERSAL

Base class; all blessed references inherit from it.

```
$sub = $obj->can('print');
```

```
$yes = UNIVERSAL::isa($ref, "HASH");
```

Provides the following methods:

can

> $sub = $obj->can(*method*)

Checks if object $obj has a method *method*. If so, returns a reference to the subroutine, otherwise returns undef. Can be called as either a static or object method call, or as a subroutine:

```
$ref = UNIVERSAL::can(val, method)
```

Returns a reference to the subroutine if *val* is a blessed reference with a method *method*, and undef if *val* is not blessed or does not have *method*.

isa

> io = $fd->isa(*type*)

Returns true if the reference is blessed into package *type* or inherits from that package. Can be called as a static or object method call, or as a subroutine:

```
UNIVERSAL::isa(val, type)
```

$\rightarrow$

Returns true if the first argument is a reference and either of the following is true:

- *val* is a blessed reference and is blessed into package *type* or inherits from package *type*

- *val* is a reference to a *type* of Perl variable (e.g., 'HASH')

VERSION

VERSION([*require*])

Returns the value of the variable $VERSION in the package the object is blessed into. With *require* specified, VERSION dies if the version of the package is not equal to or greater than the version specified in *require*. Can be called as either a static or object method call.

User::grent

Overrides core getgrent, getgruid, and getgrnam functions with versions that return User::grent objects. The object returned has methods with the same names as the structure fields they return. That is, to return the field *name*, use the name method:

```
use User::grent;
$gr = getgrgid(0) or die "No group zero";
if ( $gr->name eq 'wheel' && @{$gr->members} > 1 ) {
    print "gid zero name wheel, with other members";
}
```

The field names (and therefore the method names) are the same as the names of the fields in the *group* structure from the C file *grp.h*: *name, passwd, gid,* and *members* (not *mem*). The first three return scalars, the last an array reference. You can access the fields either with the methods or by importing the fields into your namespace with the :FIELDS import tag and prepending gr_ to the method name (for example, gr_name).

Exports four functions:

getgr

*$gr->*getgr(*arg*)

Front-end that forwards a numeric *arg* to getgrid and other *args* to getgrname.

getgrent

$gr = getgrent()

Successive calls to getgrent return objects representing successive entries from the group file.

getgrgid

> *$gr* = **getgrgid**(*gid*)

Accesses the group file by group id *gid*.

getgrnam

> *$gr* = **getgrnam**(*gname*)

Accesses the group file by group name *gname*.

User::pwent

Overrides core `getpwent`, `getpwuid`, and `getpwnam` functions with versions that return User::pwent objects. The object returned has methods with the same names as the structure fields they return. That is, to return the field *name*, use the name method:

```
use User::pwent;
$pw = getpwnam('daemon') or die "No daemon user";
if ( $pw->uid == 1 && $pw->dir =~ m#^/(bin|tmp)?$# ) {
    print "gid 1 on root dir";
}
```

The field names (and therefore the method names) are the same as the names of the fields in the *passwd* structure from the C file *pwd.h*: *name, passwd, uid, gid, quota, comment, gecos, dir,* and *shell*. You can access the fields either with the methods or by importing the fields into your namespace with the :FIELDS import tag and prepending pw_ to the method name (for example, pw_name).

Exports four functions:

getpw

> *$pw*->**getpw**(*arg*)

Front-end that forwards a numeric *arg* to `getpwuid` and other *args* to `getpwnam`.

getpwent

> *$pw*->**getpwent**()

Successive calls to `getpwent` return objects representing successive entries from the password table.

getpwnam

> *$pw->*get**pwnam**(*name*)

Accesses the password table by user's *name*.

getpwuid

> *$pw->*get**pwuid**(*uid*)

Accesses the password table by user's id number, *uid*.

vars

Pragma that, given a list of variable names, predeclares all variables in the list, making sure they are available to routines whose loading is delayed (e.g., routines that are loaded by the AutoLoader or SelfLoader). This allows you to use the variables under use strict. The vars pragma also disables warnings about typographical errors.

```
use vars qw($var1 @var2 %var3);
```

vmsish

Pragma that currently supports three VMS-specific language features:

status
> Makes $? and system return VMS status values instead of emulating POSIX.

exit
> Makes exit take a VMS status value instead of assuming that exit 1 is an error.

time
> Makes all times relative to the local time zone.

PART IV

CGI

CHAPTER 9

CGI Overview

Perl is the most commonly used language for CGI programming on the World Wide Web. The Common Gateway Interface (CGI) is an essential tool for creating and managing comprehensive web sites. With CGI, you can write scripts that create interactive, user-driven applications.

CGI allows the web server to communicate with other programs that are running on the same machine. For example, with CGI, the web server can invoke an external program, while passing user-specific data to the program (such as what host the user is connecting from, or input the user has supplied through an HTML form). The program then processes that data, and the server passes the program's response back to the web browser.

Rather than limiting the Web to documents written ahead of time, CGI enables web pages to be created on the fly, based upon the input of users. You can use CGI scripts to create a wide range of applications, from surveys to search tools, from Internet service gateways to quizzes and games. You can increment the number of users who access a document or let them sign an electronic guestbook. You can provide users with all types of information, collect their comments, and respond to them.

For Perl programmers, there are two approaches you can take to CGI. They are:

- Programs that handle all CGI interaction directly, without the use of a module such as CGI.pm. While often frowned upon by Perl programmers because it's more likely to introduce bugs, bypassing the modules has the advantage of avoiding the overhead of CGI.pm for quick, dirty tasks. This chapter explains the concepts of CGI necessary if you intend to write CGI programs from scratch.

- CGI.pm is a Perl module designed to facilitate CGI programming. For nontrivial CGI programs, especially ones that need to maintain state over multiple transactions, CGI.pm is indispensable, and is included in the standard Perl distribution as of Perl 5.004. Rather than discuss it in Chapter 8, *Standard Modules*, with the rest of the standard libraries, however, its complexity and importance made it a candidate for its own chapter, Chapter 10, *The CGI.pm Module*.

One performance hit for CGI programs is that the Perl interpreter needs to be started up each and every time a CGI script is called. For improving performance on Apache systems, the *mod_perl* Apache module embeds the Perl interpreter directly into the server, avoiding the startup overhead. Chapter 11, *Web Server Programming with mod_perl*, talks about installing and using *mod_perl*.

A Typical CGI Interaction

For an example of a CGI application, suppose you create a guestbook for your website. The guestbook page asks users to submit their first name and last name using a fill-in form composed of two input text fields. Figure 9-1 shows the form you might see in your browser window.

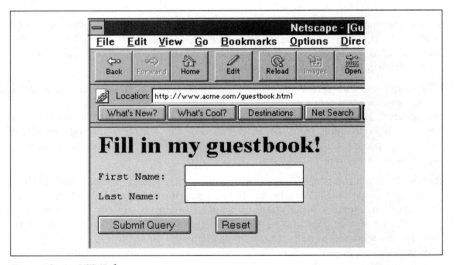

Figure 9-1: HTML form

The HTML that produces this form might read as follows:

```
<HTML><HEAD><TITLE>Guestbook</TITLE></HEAD>
<BODY>
<H1>Fill in my guestbook!</H1>
<FORM METHOD="GET" ACTION="/cgi-bin/guestbook.pl">
<PRE>
First Name:    <INPUT TYPE="TEXT" NAME="firstname">
Last Name:     <INPUT TYPE="TEXT" NAME="lastname">

<INPUT TYPE="SUBMIT">    <INPUT TYPE="RESET">
</FORM>
```

The form is written using special "form" tags, as follows:

- The <form> tag defines the method used for the form (either GET or POST) and the action to take when the form is submitted—that is, the URL of the CGI program to pass the parameters to.

- The <input> tag can be used in many different ways. In its first two invocations, it creates a text input field and defines the variable name to associate with the field's contents when the form is submitted. The first field is given the variable name firstname and the second field is given the name lastname.

- In its last two invocations, the <input> tag creates a "submit" button and a "reset" button.

- The </form> tag indicates the end of the form.

When the user presses the "submit" button, data entered into the <input> text fields is passed to the CGI program specified by the action attribute of the <form> tag (in this case, the */cgi-bin/guestbook.pl* program).

Transferring the Form Data

Parameters to a CGI program are transferred either in the URL or in the body text of the request. The method used to pass parameters is determined by the method attribute to the <form> tag. The GET method says to transfer the data within the URL itself; for example, under the GET method, the browser might initiate the HTTP transaction as follows:

```
GET /cgi-bin/guestbook.pl?firstname=Joe&lastname=Schmoe HTTP/1.0
```

The POST method says to use the body portion of the HTTP request to pass parameters. The same transaction with the POST method would read as follows:

```
POST /cgi-bin/guestbook.pl HTTP/1.0
     ... [More headers here]

firstname=Joe&lastname=Schmoe
```

In both of these examples, you should recognize the firstname and lastname variable names that were defined in the HTML form, coupled with the values entered by the user. An ampersand (&) is used to separate the variable=value pairs.

The server now passes the variable=value pairs to the CGI program. It does this either through Unix environment variables or in standard input (STDIN). If the CGI program is called with the GET method, then parameters are expected to be embedded into the URL of the request, and the server transfers them to the program by assigning them to the QUERY_STRING environment variable. The CGI program can then retrieve the parameters from QUERY_STRING as it would read any environment variable (for example, from the %ENV hash in Perl). If the CGI program is called with the POST method, parameters are expected to be embedded into the body of the request, and the server passes the body text to the program as standard input (STDIN).

Other environment variables defined by the server for CGI store such information as the format and length of the input, the remote host, the user, and various client information. They also store the server name, the communication protocol, and the name of the software running the server. (We provide a list of the most common CGI environment variables later in this chapter.)

The CGI program needs to retrieve the information as appropriate and then process it. The sky's the limit on what the CGI program actually does with the information it retrieves. It might return an anagram of the user's name, or tell her how many times her name uses the letter "t," or it might just compile the name into a list that the programmer regularly sells to telemarketers. Only the programmer knows for sure.

Creating Virtual Documents

Regardless of what the CGI program does with its input, it's responsible for giving the browser something to display when it's done. It must either create a new document to be served to the browser or point to an existing document. On Unix, programs send their output to standard output (STDOUT) as a data stream that consists of two parts. The first part is either a full or partial HTTP header that (at minimum) describes the format of the returned data (e.g., HTML, ASCII text, GIF, etc.). A blank line signifies the end of the header section. The second part is the body of the output, which contains the data conforming to the format type reflected in the header. For example:

```
Content-type: text/html

<HTML>
<HEAD><TITLE>Thanks!</TITLE></HEAD>
<BODY><H1>Thanks for signing my guest book!</H1>
        ...
</BODY></HTML>
```

In this case, the only header line generated is Content-type, which gives the media format of the output as HTML (text/html). This line is essential for every CGI program, since it tells the browser what kind of format to expect. The blank line separates the header from the body text (which, in this case, is in HTML format as advertised).

The server transfers the results of the CGI program back to the browser. The body text is not modified or interpreted by the server in any way, but the server generally supplies additional headers with information such as the date, the name and version of the server, etc.

CGI programs can also supply a complete HTTP header itself, in which case the server does not add any additional headers but instead transfers the response verbatim as returned by the CGI program. The server needs to be configured to allow this behavior; see your server documentation on NPH (no-parsed headers) scripts for more information.

Here is the sample output of a program generating an HTML virtual document, with a complete HTTP header:

```
HTTP/1.0 200 OK
Date:  Thursday, 28-June-96 11:12:21 GMT
Server: NCSA/1.4.2
Content-type: text/html
Content-length: 2041

<HTML>
<HEAD><TITLE>Thanks!</TITLE></HEAD>
<BODY>
<H1>Thanks for signing my guestbook!</H1>
     ...
</BODY>
</HTML>
```

The header contains the communication protocol, the date and time of the response, and the server name and version. (200 OK is a status code generated by the HTTP protocol to communicate the status of a request, in this case successful.) Most importantly, the header also contains the content type and the number of characters (equivalent to the number of bytes) of the enclosed data.

The result is that after users click the "submit" button, they see the message contained in the HTML section of the response thanking them for signing the guestbook.

URL Encoding

Before data supplied on a form can be sent to a CGI program, each form element's name (specified by the name attribute) is equated with the value entered by the user to create a key/value pair. For example, if the user entered "30" when asked for his or her age, the key/value pair would be "age=30". In the transferred data, key/value pairs are separated by the ampersand (&) character.

Since under the GET method the form information is sent as part of the URL, form information can't include any spaces or other special characters that are not allowed in URLs, and also can't include characters that have other meanings in URLs, like slashes (/). (For the sake of consistency, this constraint also exists when the POST method is being used.) Therefore, the web browser performs some special encoding on user-supplied information.

Encoding involves replacing spaces and other special characters in the query strings with their hexadecimal equivalents. (Thus, URL encoding is also sometimes called *hexadecimal encoding.*) Suppose a user fills out and submits a form containing his or her birthday in the syntax mm/dd/yy (e.g., 11/05/73). The forward slashes in the birthday are among the special characters that can't appear in the client's request for the CGI program. Thus, when the browser issues the request, it encodes the data. The following sample request shows the resulting encoding:

```
POST /cgi-bin/birthday.pl HTTP/1.0
Content-length: 21

birthday=11%2F05%2F73
```

The sequence %2F is actually the hexadecimal equivalent of the slash character.

CGI scripts have to provide some way to "decode" the form data that the client has encoded. The best way to do this is to use CGI.pm (covered in Chapter 10) and let someone else do the work for you.

Extra Path Information

In addition to passing query strings, you can pass additional data, known as *extra path information*, as part of the URL. The server gauges where the CGI program name ends; anything following is deemed "extra" and is stored in the environment variable PATH_INFO. The following line calls a script with extra path information:

```
http://some.machine/cgi-bin/display.pl/cgi/cgi_doc.txt
```

In this example, we use a script with a *.pl* suffix to make it clear where the CGI program's path ends and the extra path information begins. Everything after *display.pl* is the extra path and is placed in the PATH_INFO environment variable. The PATH_TRANSLATED variable is also set, mapping the PATH_INFO to the DOCUMENT_ROOT directory (e.g., */usr/local/etc/httpd/public/cgi/cgi_doc.txt*).

CGI Environment Variables

Most of the information needed by CGI programs is made available via Unix environment variables. Programs can access this information as they would any environment variable (via the %ENV hash in Perl). The table below lists environment variables commonly available through CGI. However, since servers occasionally vary on the names of environment variables they assign, check with your own server documentation for more information.

Environment Variable	Content Returned
AUTH_TYPE	The authentication method used to validate a user. See REMOTE_IDENT and REMOTE_USER.
CONTENT_LENGTH	The length of the query data (in bytes or the number of characters) passed to the CGI program through standard input.
CONTENT_TYPE	The media type of the query data, such as text/html.
DOCUMENT_ROOT	The directory from which web documents are served.
GATEWAY_INTERFACE	The revision of the Common Gateway Interface that the server uses.
HTTP_ACCEPT	A list of the media types that the client can accept.
HTTP_COOKIE	A list of cookies defined for that URL.
HTTP_FROM	The email address of the user making the query (many browsers do not support this variable).
HTTP_REFERER	The URL of the document the client read before accessing the CGI program.
HTTP_USER_AGENT	The browser the client is using to issue the request.

Environment Variable	Content Returned
PATH_INFO	Extra path information passed to a CGI program.
PATH_TRANSLATED	The translated version of the path given by the variable PATH_INFO.
QUERY_STRING	The query information passed to the program. It is appended to the URL following a question mark (?).
REMOTE_ADDR	The remote IP address from which the user is making the request.
REMOTE_HOST	The remote hostname from which the user is making the request.
REMOTE_IDENT	The user making the request.
REMOTE_USER	The authenticated name of the user making the query.
REQUEST_METHOD	The method with which the information request was issued (e.g., GET, POST, HEAD).
SCRIPT_NAME	The virtual path (e.g., /cgi-bin/program.pl) of the script being executed.
SERVER_NAME	The server's hostname or IP address.
SERVER_PORT	The port number of the host on which the server is running.
SERVER_PROTOCOL	The name and revision number of the server protocol.
SERVER_SOFTWARE	The name and version of the server software that is answering the client request.

Here's a simple Perl CGI script that uses environment variables to display various information about the server:

```
#!/usr/local/bin/perl

print << EOF
Content-type: text/html

<HTML>
<HEAD><TITLE>About this Server</TITLE></HEAD>
<BODY><H1>About this Server</H1>
<HR><PRE>
Server Name:        $ENV{'SERVER_NAME'}<BR>
Running on Port:    $ENV{'SERVER_PORT'}<BR>
Server Software:    $ENV{'SERVER_SOFTWARE'}<BR>
Server Protocol:    $ENV{'SERVER_PROTOCOL'}<BR>
CGI Revision:       $ENV{'GATEWAY_INTERFACE'}<BR>
<HR></PRE>
</BODY></HTML>
```

The preceding program outputs five environments as an HTML document. In Perl, you can access the environment variables with the %ENV hash. Here's typical output of the program:

```
<HTML>
<HEAD><TITLE>About this Server</TITLE></HEAD>
<BODY><H1>About this Server</H1>
<HR><PRE>
Server Name:          www.whatever.com
Running on Port:      80
Server Software:      NCSA/1.4.2
Server Protocol:      HTTP/1.0
CGI Revision:         CGI/1.1
<HR></PRE>
</BODY></HTML>
```

CHAPTER 10

The CGI.pm Module

CGI.pm is a Perl module for creating and parsing CGI forms. It is distributed with core Perl as of Perl 5.004, but you can also retrieve CGI.pm from CPAN, and you can get the very latest version at any time from *ftp://ftp-genome.wi.mit.edu/ pub/software/WWW/*.

CGI is an object-oriented module. Don't let the object-oriented nature scare you off, though; CGI.pm is very easy to use, as evidenced by its overwhelming popularity among all levels of Perl programmers. To give you an idea of how easy it is to use CGI.pm, let's take a scenario in which a user fills out and submits a form containing her birthday. Without CGI.pm, the script would have to translate the URL-encoded input by hand (probably using a series of regular expressions) and assign it to a variable. For example, you might try something like this:

```perl
#!/usr/bin/perl
# cgi script without CGI.pm

$size_of_form_info = $ENV{'CONTENT_LENGTH'};
read ($STDIN, $form_info, $size_of_form_info);

# Split up each pair of key=value pairs
foreach $pair (split (/&/, $form_info)) {

        # For each pair, split into $key and $value variables
        ($key, $value) = split (/=/, $pair);

        # Get rid of the pesky %xx encodings
        $key =~ s/%([\dA-Fa-f][\dA-Fa-f])/pack ("C", hex ($1))/eg;
        $value =~ s/%([\dA-Fa-f][\dA-Fa-f])/pack ("C", hex ($1))/eg;

        # Use $key as index for $parameters hash, $value as value
        $parameters{$key} = $value;
}

# Print out the obligatory content-type line
print "Content-type: text/plain\n\n";
```

329

```
# Tell the user what they said
print "Your birthday is on " . $parameters{birthday} . ".\n";
```

Regardless of whether this code actually works, you must admit it's ugly. With CGI.pm, the script could be written:

```
#!/usr/bin/perl -w
# cgi script with CGI.pm

use CGI;

$query = CGI::new();
$bday = $query->param("birthday");
print $query->header();
print $query->p("Your birthday is $bday.");
```

Even for this tiny program, you can see that CGI.pm can alleviate many of the headaches associated with CGI programming.

As with any Perl module, the first thing you do is call the module with use. You then call the constructor (new( )), creating a new CGI object called $query. Next, get the value of the birthday parameter from the CGI program using the param method. Note that CGI.pm does all the work of determining whether the CGI program is being called by the GET or POST methods, and it also does all the URL decoding for you. To generate output, use the header method to return the content type header, and the p method to generate a paragraph marker <P> tag.

However, this is only the tip of the iceberg as far as what CGI.pm can do for you. There are three basic categories of CGI.pm methods: CGI handling, creating forms, and retrieving environment variables. (A fourth category is creating HTML tags, but we don't cover those in detail.) Table 10-1 lists most of these methods. They are also covered in more detail later in this chapter.

Table 10-1: CGI.pm Methods

CGI Handling

keywords	Gets keywords from an <ISINDEX> search.
param	Gets (or sets) the value of parameters.
append	Appends to a parameter.
import_names	Imports variables into a namespace.
delete	Deletes a parameter.
delete_all	Deletes all parameters.
save	Saves all parameters to a file.
self_url	Creates self-referencing URL.
url	Gets URL of current script without query information.
header	Creates HTTP header.
redirect	Creates redirection header.
cookie	Gets (or sets) a cookie.
nph	Declares this to be a NPH script.
dump	Prints all name/value pairs.

Table 10-1: CGI.pm Methods (continued)

Form Generation

start_html	Generates an <HTML> tag.
end_html	Generates an </HTML> tag.
autoEscape	Sets whether to use automatic escaping.
isindex	Generates an <ISINDEX> tag.
startform	Generates a <FORM> tag.
start_multipart_form	Generates a <FORM> tag for multipart/form-data encoding.
textfield	Generates an <INPUT TYPE=TEXT> tag.
textarea	Generates an <TEXTAREA> tag.
password_field	Generates an <INPUT TYPE=PASSWORD> tag.
filefield	Generates an <INPUT TYPE=FILE> tag.
popup_menu	Generates a popup menu via <SELECT SIZE=1> and <OPTION> tags.
scrolling_list	Generates a scrolling list via <SELECT> and <OPTION> tags.
checkbox_group	Generates a group of checkboxes via multiple <INPUT TYPE=CHECKBOX> tags.
checkbox	Generates a single checkbox via a <INPUT TYPE=CHECKBOX> tag.
radio_group	Generates a group of radio buttons via <INPUT TYPE=RADIO> tags.
submit	Generates a <SUBMIT> tag.
reset	Generates a <RESET> tag.
defaults	Generates a <DEFAULTS> tag.
hidden	Generates an <INPUT TYPE=HIDDEN> tag.
image_button	Generates a clickable image button via a <SELECT> tag.
button	Generates a JavaScript button.

Handling Environment Variables

accept	Gets accept types from ACCEPT header.
user_agent	Gets value of USER_AGENT header.
path_info	Gets value of EXTRA_PATH_INFO header.
path_translated	Gets value of PATH_TRANSLATED header.
remote_host	Gets value of REMOTE_HOST header.
raw_cookie	Gets value of HTTP_COOKIE header.
script_name	Gets value of SCRIPT_NAME header.
referer	Gets value of REFERER header.
auth_type	Gets value of AUTH_TYPE header.
remote_user	Gets value of REMOTE_USER header.

Table 10-1: CGI.pm Methods (continued)

Handling Environment Variables

user_name	Gets user name (not via headers).
request_method	Gets value of REQUEST_METHOD header.

Each of these methods is covered later in this chapter, in alphabetical order.

HTML Tag Generation

In addition to the form-generation methods, CGI.pm also includes a group of methods for creating HTML tags. The names of the HTML tag methods generally follow the HTML tag name (e.g., p for <P>) and take named parameters that are assumed to be valid attributes for the tag (e.g., img(src=>'camel.gif') becomes <IMG SRC="camel.gif">). We do not list all tags in this book; see the CGI.pm man-page for more information, or the book *Official Guide to Programming with CGI.pm* by Lincoln Stein (John Wiley & Sons, 1998).

Importing Method Groups

The syntax for calling CGI methods can be unwieldy. However, you can import individual methods and then call the methods without explicit object calls. The "birthday" example shown earlier could be written even more simply as follows:

```
#!/usr/bin/perl

use CGI param,header,p;

$bday = param("birthday");
print header();
print p("Your birthday is $bday.");
```

By importing the param, header, and p methods into your namespace, you no longer have to use the new constructor (since it is called automatically now), and you don't need to specify a CGI object with every method call.

CGI.pm also lets you import groups of methods, which can make your programs much simpler and more elegant. For example, to import all form-creation methods and all CGI-handling methods:

```
use CGI qw/:form :cgi/;
```

The method groups supported by CGI.pm are:

:cgi
> All CGI-handling methods

:cgi-lib
> All methods supplied for backwards compatibility with *cgi-lib*

:form
> All form-generation methods

`:html`

    All HTML methods

`:html2`

    All HTML 2.0 methods

`:html3`

    All HTML 3.0 methods

`:netscape`

    All methods generating Netscape extensions

`:ssl`

    All SSL methods

`:standard`

    All HTML 2.0, form-generation, and CGI methods

`:all`

    All available methods

You can also define new methods for HTML tag generation by simply listing them on the import line and then letting CGI.pm make some educated guesses. For example:

```
use CGI shortcuts,smell;

print smell {type=>'garlic',
         intensity=>'strong'}, "Scratch here!";
```

This will cause the following tag to be generated:

```
<SMELL TYPE="garlic" INTENSITY="strong">Scratch here!</SMELL>
```

Maintaining State

One of the first complications for any nontrivial CGI script is how to "maintain state." Since HTTP is a stateless protocol, there's no built-in mechanism for keeping track of requests from the server end. A CGI transaction involving multiple forms, therefore, needs to find a way to remember information supplied on previous forms. One way to deal with this issue is to use *cookies*, which allow the CGI program to save information on the browser's end; but not all browsers support cookies, and some users are uncomfortable with the perceived privacy infringement associated with cookies.

CGI.pm simplifies maintaining state without cookies. When a CGI.pm script is called multiple times, the input fields are given default values from the previous invocation.

Named Parameters

For most CGI.pm methods, there are two syntax styles. In the "standard" style, the position of the parameters determines how they will be interpreted—for example, parameter 1 is the name that the script should assign, parameter 2 is the initial value, etc. For example:

```
print $query=textfield('username', 'anonymous');
```

In the "named parameters" style, the parameters can be assigned like a hash, and the order doesn't matter. For example:

```
print $query->textfield(-name=>'name',
                        -default=>'value');
```

If you want to use named parameters, just call the use_named_parameters method early in the script.

Which syntax style should you use? It depends on how lazy you are and much control you need. Generally, "standard" syntax is faster to type. However, it is also harder to read, and there are many features that are simply not available using standard syntax (such as JavaScript support). In general, we recommend using the "named parameters" syntax for all but the most trivial scripts.

Using JavaScript Features

CGI.pm supports JavaScript scripting by allowing you to embed a JavaScript script into the HTML form within <SCRIPT> tags, and then calling the script using the -script parameter to the start_html method. You can then call the JavaScript functions as appropriate to the form elements.

Debugging

A complication of writing CGI scripts is that when debugging the script, you have to wrestle with the web server environment. CGI.pm provides support for debugging the script on the command line.

If you run the script on the command line without arguments, you will be placed into an "offline" mode, in which name-value pairs can be entered one-by-one. When you press CTRL-D, the script runs. For example:

```
% birthday
(offline mode: enter name=value pairs on standard input)
birthday=6/4/65
^D
Content-type: text/html

<P>Your birthday is 6/4/65.</P>
```

You can also supply the name/value parameters directly on the command line. For example:

```
% test birthday=6/4/65
Content-type: text/html

<P>Your birthday is 6/4/65.</P>
```

Multiple values can be separated by spaces (as separate arguments on the command line) or by ampersands (as in URL-encoded syntax). In fact, you can use URL-encoded syntax on the command line. This makes it easy to supply raw CGI input to the script for testing purposes. Just remember to protect the ampersand from the shell.

```
% test 'birthday=6%2f4%2f65&name=Fred%20Flintstone'
Content-type: text/html

<P>Fred Flintstone, your birthday is 6/4/65.</P>
```

CGI.pm Reference

The following methods are supported by CGI.pm:

accept

$query->**accept**([*'content_type'*])

Returns a list of media types that the browser accepts.

content_type
> If specified, returns instead the browser's preference for the specified content type, between 0.0 and 1.0.

append

$query->**append**(–name=>*'name'*,–values=>*'value'*)

Appends a value or list of values to the named parameter.

–name=>*'name'*
> The parameter to be appended.

–values=>*'value'*
> The value to append. Multiple values can be specified as a reference to an anonymous array.

auth_type

auth_type()

Returns the authorization method.

autoEscape

$query->**autoEscape**(undef)

Turns off autoescaping of form elements.

button

> **print** *$query*->**button(**' *name*';*function*'**)**

Generates a JavaScript button.

name
> The name of the button.

function
> The function to execute when the button is clicked.

> Using named parameters, the syntax is:

```
print $query->button(-name=>'name',
                     -value=>'label',
                     -onClick=>"function");
```

−value=>'label'
> The label to display for the button.

checkbox

> **print** *$query*->**checkbox(**' *name*' [';*checked*';*value*';*label*'**])**

Generates a single checkbox.

name
> The name to assign the input to (required).

'checked'
> Checkbox should be checked initially.

value
> The value to return when checked (default is on).

label
> The label to use for the checkbox (default is the name of the checkbox).

> Using named parameters, the syntax is:

```
print $query->checkbox(-name=>'name',
                       -checked=>'checked',
                       -value=>'value',
                       -label=>'label',
                       -onClick=>function);
```

−onClick=>function
> Browser should execute *function* when the user clicks on any checkbox in the group.

checkbox_group

> **print** *$query*->**checkbox_group(**' *name*', \@*list* [, *selected*';*true*',\%*label-hash*]**)**

Generates a list of checkbox elements.

name

The name to assign the input to (required).

\@list

An array reference with the list items. You can also use an anonymous array reference.

selected

The menu item(s) to be initially selected (default is that nothing is selected). This can be a single value or a reference to an array of values.

'true'

Insert newlines between the checkboxes.

\%labelhash

A hash reference listing labels for each list item. Default is the list text itself. See popup_menu for an example.

Using named parameters, the syntax is:

```
print $query->checkbox_group(-name=>'name',
                             -values=>\@list,
                             -default=>selected,
                             -linebreak=>'true',
                             -labels=>\%labelhash,
                             -columns=>n,
                             -columnheader=>'string',
                             -rows=>m,
                             -rowheader=>'string',
                             -onClick=>function);
```

-columns=>n

The number of columns to use.

-columnheader=>'string'

A header for the column.

-rows=m

The number of rows to use. If omitted and -columns is specified, the rows will be calculated for you.

-rowheader=>'string'

A header for the row.

-onClick=>function

Browser should execute *function* when the user clicks on any checkbox in the group.

---

cookie

$cookie=$query->cookie('name')

Defines or retrieves a cookie. See also header.

name

Name of the cookie (required).

→

Using named parameters, the syntax is:

```
$cookie = $query->cookie(-name=>'name',
                         -value=>'value',
                         -expires=>'expcode',
                         -path=>'partial_url',
                         -domain=>'domain_name',
                         -secure=>1);
   print $query->header(-cookie=>$cookie);
```

−value=>'*value*'
> A value to assign to the cookie. You can supply a scalar value, or a reference to an array or hash. If omitted, a cookie will be retrieved rather than defined.

−expires=>*expcode*
> Specify an expiration timestamp (such as +3d for 3 days). Values for *expcode* are:

> *n*s   *n* seconds

> *n*m   *n* minutes

> *n*h   *n* hours

> *n*d   *n* days

> *n*M   *n* months

> *n*Y   *n* years

> *day_of_week, dd-MMM-YY hh:mm:ss* GMT
>> At the specified time

> now   Expire immediately.

−path=>'*partial_url*'
> The partial URL for which the cookie is valid. Default is the current URL.

−domain=>'*domain_name*'
> The domain for which the cookie is valid.

−secure=>1
> Only use this cookie for a secure session.

---

defaults

print *$query*->**defaults**('*label*')

Generates a button that resets the form to its defaults. See also reset.

'*label*'
> The label to use for the button. If omitted, the label is "Defaults".

delete

> *$query->*delete(*'parameter'*)

Deletes a parameter.

'parameter'
> The parameter to delete.

delete_all

> *$query->*delete_all()

Deletes the entire CGI object.

dump

> print *$query->*dump([true])

Dumps all name/value pairs as an HTML list.

true
> If specified, print as plain text.

end_html

> *print $query->*end_html()

Ends an HTML document.

filefield

> print *$query->*filefield(*'name'* [,*'default'*,*size*,*maxlength*])

Generates a file upload field for Netscape browsers.

name
> The filename to assign the supplied file contents to (required).

default
> The initial value (filename) to place in the text field.

size
> The size of the text field (in characters).

maxlength
> The maximum length of the text field (in characters).

Using named parameters, the syntax is:

```
print $query->textfield(-name=>'name',
                        -default=>'value',
                        -size=>size,
                        -maxlength=>maxlength,
                        -override=>1,
                        -onChange=>function,
                        -onFocus=>function,
```

→

```
                          -onBlur=>function,
                          -onSelect=>function);
```

−override=>1

Text field should not inherit its value from a previous invocation of the script.

−onChange=>*function*

Browser should execute *function* when the user changes the text field.

−onFocus=>*function*

Browser should execute *function* when the focus is on the text field.

−onBlur=>*function*

Browser should execute *function* when the focus leaves the text field.

−onSelect=>*function*

Browser should execute *function* when the user changes a selected portion of the text field.

header

print *$query*->**header(**[*content_type* , *status* , *headers*]**)**

Generates the HTTP header for the document.

content_type

The content type to return. Default is text/html.

status

The HTTP status code and description to return. Default is 200 OK.

headers

Additional headers to include, such as Content-Length: 123.

Using named parameters, the syntax is:

```
print $query->header(-type=>'content_type',
                     -nph=>1,
                     -status=>'status_code',
                     -expires=>'expcode',
                     -cookie=>'cookie',
                     -target=>'frame',
                     -header=>'value');
```

−type=>*content_type*

Specify the content type.

−nph=>1

Use headers for a no-parse-header script.

−status=>*status_code*

Specify the status code.

−expires=>*expcode*

Specify an expiration timestamp (such as +3d for 3 days). Values for *expcode* are:

→

ns	n seconds
nm	n minutes
nh	n hours
nd	n days
nM	n months
nY	n years

day_of_week, *dd-MMM-YY hh:mm:ss* GMT
  At the specified time

now Expire immediately.

−cookie=>*cookie*
  Specify a cookie. The cookie may be a scalar value or an array reference.

−header=>*value*
  Specify any HTTP header.

−target=>*frame*
  Write to specified frame.

hidden

print *$query*->hidden(*'name'*, *'value'* [,*'value'* ...])

Generates a hidden text field.

name
  The name to give the value (required).

value
  The value to assign to *name*. Multiple values can be specified.

  Using named parameters, the syntax is:

```
print $query->hidden(-name=>'name',
                     -default=>'value');
```

  With named parameters, the value can also be represented as a reference to an array, such as:

```
print $query->hidden(-name=>'name',
                     -default=>['value1', 'value2', ...  ]);
```

image_button

print *$query*->image_button(*'name'*,*'url'* [,*'align'*])

Generates a clickable image map.

name
  The name to use. When clicked, the *x,y* position is returned as *name*.x and *name*.y, respectively.

→

url The URL of the image for the image map.

align
> The alignment type. May be TOP, BOTTOM, or MIDDLE.

Using named parameters, the syntax is:

```
print $query->image_button(-name=>'name',
                           -src=>'url',
                           -align=>'align',
                           -onClick=>function);
```

—onClick=>function
> Browser should execute *function* when the user clicks on the image.

---

import_names

> *$query->import_names('package')*

Creates variables in the specified package. Called import in older versions of CGI.pm.

package
> The package to import names into.

---

isindex

> **print *$query->isindex([action])***

Generates an <ISINDEX> tag.

action
> The URL of the index script. Default is the current URL.

Using named parameters, the syntax is:

```
print $query->isindex(-action=>$action);
```

---

keywords

> *@keyarray = $query->keywords()*

Retrieves keywords from an <ISINDEX> search.

@keyarray
> The array to contain the retrieved keywords.

---

nph

> **nph(1)**

Treats a CGI script as a no-parsed-header (NPH) script.

param

@name = *$query*->**param**([*parameter* [*newvalue1, newvalue2, . . .*]])

Gets or sets parameter names.

@name
> The array to contain the parameter names.

parameter
> An optional single parameter to fetch. When used with no arguments, param returns a list of all known parameter names.

newvalue1, newvalue2, . . .
> The optional new values to assign to the parameter.

> Using named parameters, the syntax is:

```
$query->param(-name=>'parameter',
              -value=>'newvalue');
```

or:

```
$query->param(-name=>'parameter',
              -values=>'newvalue1', 'newvalue2', ...);
```

password_field

print *$query*->**password_field**('*name*' [,'*value*',*size*,*maxlength*])

Generates a password input field.

name
> The name to assign the input to (required).

value
> The default password to place in the password field.

size
> The size of the password field (in characters).

maxlength
> The maximum length of the password field (in characters).

> Using named parameters, the syntax is:

```
print $query->password_field(-name=>'name',
                             -default=>'value',
                             -size=>size,
                             -maxlength=>maxlength,
                             -override=>1,
                             -onChange=>function,
                             -onFocus=>function,
                             -onBlur=>function,
                             -onSelect=>function);
```

-override=>1
> Text field should not inherit its value from a previous invocation of the script.

→

—onChange=>*function*
>Browser should execute *function* when the user changes the text field.

—onFocus=>*function*
>Browser should execute *function* when the focus is on on the text field.

—onBlur=>*function*
>Browser should execute *function* when the focus leaves the text field.

—onSelect=>*function*
>Browser should execute *function* when the user changes a selected portion of the text field.

path_info

path_info()

Returns extra path information.

path_translated

path_translated()

Returns translated extra path information.

popup_menu

print $*query*->popup_menu('*name*', \@*array* ['*selected*', \%*labelhash*])

Generates a popup menu.

name
>The name to assign the input to (required).

\@*array*
>An array reference listing the menu items. You can also use an anonymous array reference (see example below).

selected
>The menu item to be initially selected (default is first menu item or the item selected in previous queries).

\%*labelhash*
>A hash reference listing labels for each menu item. Default is menu item text. For example:

```
%labels = ('UPS'=>'United Parcel Service (UPS)',
           'FedExO'=>'Federal Express Overnight - 10AM delivery',
           'FedExS'=>'Federal Express Standard - 2PM delivery',
           'FedEx2'=>'Federal Express 2nd Day Delivery');

print $query->popup_menu('delivery_method',
```

→

```
                       ['UPS', 'FedExO', 'FedExS', 'FedEx2'],
                       'FedExO',
                       \%labels);
```

Using named parameters, the syntax is:

```
print $query->popup_menu(-name=>'name',
                         -values=>\@array,
                         -default=>'selected',
                         -labels=>\%labelhash,
                         -onChange=>function,
                         -onFocus=>function,
                         -onBlur=>function);
```

–onChange=>*function*

> Browser should execute *function* when the user changes the text field.

–onFocus=>*function*

> Browser should execute *function* when the focus is on on the text field.

–onBlur=>*function*

> Browser should execute *function* when the focus leaves the text field.

radio_group

print *$query*->**radio_group**(*'name'*, \@*list* [, *selected*, 'true', \%*label*])

Generates a set of radio buttons.

name

> The name to assign the input to (required).

\@*list*

> An array reference with the list items. You can also use an anonymous array reference.

selected

> The menu item to be initially selected.

'true'

> Insert newlines between radio buttons.

\%*label*

> A hash reference listing labels for each list item. Default is the list text itself. See popup_menu for an example.

Using named parameters, the syntax is:

```
print $query->radio_group(-name=>'name',
                          -values=>\@list,
                          -default=>'selected',
                          -linebreak=>'true',
                          -labels=>\%labelhash,
                          -columns=>n,
                          -columnheader=>'string',
```

→

```
                                            -rows=>m,
                                            -rowheader=>'string');
```

   −columns=>n
   > The number of columns to use.

   −columnheader=>'string'
   > A header for the column.

   −rows=m
   > The number of rows to use. If omitted and −columns is specified, the
   > rows will be calculated for you.

   −rowheader=>'string'
   > A header for the row.

raw_cookie

raw_cookie()

Returns the value of the HTTP_COOKIE header.

ReadParse

ReadParse()

Creates a hash named %in containing query information. Used for backwards
compatibility with the Perl4 *cgi-lib.pl.*

redirect

print $query->redirect('url')

Generates a header for redirecting the browser.

url The absolute URL to redirect to.

   > Using named parameters, the syntax is:

```
print $query->redirect(-uri=>'url',
                       -nph=>1);
```

referer

referer()

Returns the referring URL.

remote_host

remote_host()

Returns the remote host name or IP address, depending on the configuration
of the server.

remote_user

remote_user()

Returns the username supplied for authorization.

request_method

request_method()

Returns the request method.

reset

print *$query*->reset

Generates a button that resets the form to its initial values. See also `defaults`.

save

$query->save(*filehandle*)

Saves the form to the specified filehandle, to be read back with the new constructor.

filehandle
: The filehandle to save the file to.

script_name

script_name()

Returns the current partial URL.

scrolling_list

print *$query*->scrolling_list(' *name* ',\@*list*[,*selected*,*size*,'true',\%*label-hash*]);

Generates a scrolling list.

name
: The name to assign the input to (required).

\@*list*
: An array reference with the list items. You can also use an anonymous array reference.

selected
: The menu item(s) to be initially selected (default is that nothing is selected). This can be a single value or a reference to a list of values.

size
: The number of elements to display in the list box.

→

'true'
> Allow multiple selections.

\\%*labelhash*
> A hash reference listing labels for each list item. Default is the list text itself. See `popup_menu` for an example.

> Using named parameters, the syntax is:

```
print $query->scrolling_list(-name=>'name',
                             -values=>\@listarray,
                             -default=>selected,
                             -size=>size,
                             -multiple=>'true',
                             -labels=>\%labelhash,
                             -onChange=>function,
                             -onFocus=>function,
                             -onBlur=>function);
```

−onChange=>*function*
> Browser should execute *function* when the user changes the text field.

−onFocus=>*function*
> Browser should execute *function* when the focus is on on the text field.

−onBlur=>*function*
> Browser should execute *function* when the focus leaves the text field.

---

self_url

> *$url* = *$query*->**self_url**

Returns the URL of the current script with all its state information intact.

---

start_html

> print *$query*->**start_html**(['*title*', '*email*', '*base*', '*attribute='value'*])

Generates <HTML> and <BODY> tags.

title
> The title of the page.

email
> The author's email address.

base
> Whether to use a <BASE> tag in the header.

attribute='value'
> Specifies an attribute to the <BODY> tag.

> Using named parameters, the syntax is:

```
print $query->start_html(-title=>'title',
                         -author=>'email_address',
```

$\rightarrow$

```
                         -base=>'true',
                         -xbase=>'url',
                         -meta=>{'metatag1'=>'value1',
                                 'metatag2'=>'value2'},
                         -script=>'$script',
                         -onLoad=>'$function',
                         -onUnload=>'$function',
                         -attribute=>'value');
```

-title=>'title'
: Specifies the title of the page.

-author=>'email_address'
: Specifies the author's email address.

-xbase=>'url'
: Provides an HREF for the <BASE> tag. Default is the current location.

-meta=>{'metatag1'=>'value1', ... }
: Adds arbitrary meta information to the header as a reference to a hash. Valid tags are:

keywords
: Keywords for this document.

copyright
: Description for this document.

attribute=>'value'
: Specify an attribute to the <BODY> tag.

-script=>'$script'
: Specify a JavaScript script to be embedded within a <SCRIPT> block.

-onLoad=>'$function'
: Browser should execute the specified function upon entering the page.

-onUnload=>'$function'
: Browser should execute the specified function upon leaving the page.

---

startform

print *$query*->**startform**([*method, action, encoding*])

Generates a <FORM> tag.

method
: The request method for the form. Values are:

POST
: Use the POST method (default).

GET
: Use the GET method.

action
: The URL of the CGI script. Default is the current URL.

→

encoding
> The encoding scheme. Possible values are `application/x-www-form-urlencoded` and `multipart/form-data`.

Using named parameters, the syntax is:

```
print $query->startform(-method=>$method,
                        -action=>$action,
                        -encoding=>$encoding,
                        -name=>$name,
                        -target=>frame,
                        -onSubmit=>function);
```

`-name=>`*name*
> Names the form for identification by JavaScript functions.

`-target=>`*frame*
> Writes to the specified frame.

`-onSubmit=>`*function*
> A JavaScript function that the browser should execute upon submitting the form.

---

start_multipart_form

print *$query*->**start_multipart_form([** *method, action***])**

Generates <HTML> and <BODY> tags. Same as `startform`, but assumes `multipart/form-data` encoding as the default.

---

submit

print *$query*->**submit([** *'label'*, *value* **])**

Generates a submit button.

label
> The label to use for the button.

value
> The value to return when the form is submitted.

Using named parameters, the syntax is:

```
print $query->submit(-name=>'name',
                     -value=>'value',
                     -onClick=>function);
```

`-onClick=>`*function*
> Browser should execute *function* when the user clicks on the submit button.

---

textarea

print *$query*->**textarea(***'name'* **[,***'value'*,*rows*,*columns* **])**

Generates a large multiline text input box.

$\rightarrow$

name

The name to assign the input to (required).

value

The initial value to place into the text input box.

rows

The number of rows to display.

columns

The number of columns to display.

Using named parameters, the syntax is:

```
print $query->textarea(-name=>'name',
                       -default=>'value',
                       -rows=>rows,
                       -columns=>columns,
                       -override=>1,
                       -onChange=>function,
                       -onFocus=>function,
                       -onBlur=>function,
                       -onSelect=>function);
```

−override=>1

Text field should not inherit its value from a previous invocation of the script.

−onChange=>*function*

Browser should execute *function* when the user changes the text field.

−onFocus=>*function*

Browser should execute *function* when the focus is on on the text field.

−onBlur=>*function*

Browser should execute *function* when the focus leaves the text field.

−onSelect=>*function*

Browser should execute *function* when the user changes a selected portion of the text field.

textfield

print *$query*->**textfield**('*name*' [,'*value*', *size*, *maxlength*])

Generates a text input field.

name

The name to assign the input to (required).

value

The initial value to place in the text field.

size

The size of the text field (in characters).

→

maxlength
> The maximum length of the text field (in characters).

Using named parameters, the syntax is:

```
print $query->textfield(-name=>'name',
                        -default=>'value',
                        -size=>size,
                        -maxlength=>maxlength,
                        -override=>1,
                        -onChange=>function,
                        -onFocus=>function,
                        -onBlur=>function,
                        -onSelect=>function);
```

`-override=>1`
> Text field should not inherit its value from a previous invocation of the script.

`-onChange=>function`
> Browser should execute *function* when the user changes the text field.

`-onFocus=>function`
> Browser should execute *function* when the focus is on on the text field.

`-onBlur=>function`
> Browser should execute *function* when the focus leaves the text field.

`-onSelect=>function`
> Browser should execute *function* when the user changes a selected portion of the text field.

---

url

$url = $query->url

Returns a URL of the current script without query information.

---

use_named_parameters

use_named_parameters()

Specifies that functions should take named parameters.

---

user_agent

$query->user_agent([string])

Returns the value of the HTTP_USER_AGENT header.

string
> If specified, only returns headers matching the specified string.

---

user_name

user_name()

Returns the remote user's login name; unreliable.

CHAPTER 11

Web Server Programming with mod_perl

A common criticism of CGI is that it requires forking extra processes each time a script is executed. If you only have a few hits an hour, or even a few hits a minute, this isn't a big deal. But for a high-traffic site, lots of CGI scripts repeatedly spawning can have an unfortunate effect on the machine running the web server. The CGI scripts will be slow, the web server will be slow, and other processes on the machine will come to a crawl.

The solution to this problem is *mod_perl*. *mod_perl*, written by Doug MacEachern and distributed under CPAN, embeds the Perl interpreter directly into the web server. The effect is that your CGI scripts are precompiled by the server and executed without forking, thus running much more quickly and efficiently. Furthermore, CGI efficiency is only one facet of *mod_perl*. Since *mod_perl* is a complete Apache/Perl hybrid, other benefits to *mod_perl* include:

- Writing server-side includes in Perl

- Embedding Perl code into the Apache configuration files

- Writing complete Apache modules in Perl

Design of mod_perl

mod_perl is not a Perl module. It is a module of the Apache server, which is currently the most commonly used web server. With *mod_perl*, you can use Apache configuration directives not only to process CGI scripts much more efficiently, but also to handle all stages in processing a server request.

mod_perl embeds a copy of the Perl interpreter into the Apache *httpd* executable, providing complete access to Perl functionality within Apache. This enables a set of *mod_perl*-specific configuration directives, all of which start with the string Perl*. Most of these directives are used to specify handlers for various stages of the request, but not all. In addition, *mod_perl* lets you embed Perl code into your

Apache configuration files (within <Perl> ... </Perl> directives) and allows you to use Perl for server-side includes.

It might occur to you that sticking a large program into another large program makes a very, very large program. *mod_perl* certainly makes *httpd* significantly bigger. If you have limited memory capacity, *mod_perl* may not be for you. There are several ways to minimize the size of Apache with *mod_perl* (which you can find in the *mod_perl* manpage or the FAQs), ranging from fiddling with Apache configuration directives to building Perl with reduced memory consumption.

Installing mod_perl

If you already have Apache installed on your machine, you will have to rebuild it with *mod_perl*. You can get the source for both Apache and *mod_perl* from *http://www.apache.org/*. (You can also get *mod_perl* from CPAN.) If there isn't already an Apache *httpd* in the Apache source tree, you must build one. Then build *mod_perl* as directed in the *INSTALL* file for the *mod_perl* distribution.

As we've mentioned, *mod_perl* allows you to hook in Perl modules as handlers for various stages of a request. By default, however, the only callback hook that is enabled is PerlHandler, which is the one used to process content (i.e., a CGI document). If you want to use other hooks, for example to extend Apache's logging facilities via the PerlLogHandler directive, you'll need to specify it at build time as directed in the *INSTALL* file. For example:

```
% perl Makefile.PL PERL_LOG=1
```

The *mod_perl* Makefile replaces the *httpd* in the Apache source tree with a Perl-enabled one. When you install *mod_perl*, it not only installs the new *httpd* into your system area, it also installs several Perl modules including Apache::Registry.

At the time of this writing, both Apache and *mod_perl* are being ported to Win32. However, *mod_perl* will only run with the standard Perl Win32 port (not Active-State's). The *INSTALL.win32* file contains the instructions for installing *mod_perl* under Win32.

mod_perl Handlers

To understand *mod_perl*, you should understand how the Apache server works. When Apache receives a request, it processes it in several stages. First, it translates the URL to the associated resource (i.e., filename, CGI script, etc.) on the server machine. Then it checks to see if the user is authorized to access that resource, perhaps by requesting and checking an ID and password. Once the user has passed inspection, the server figures out what kind of data it's sending back (e.g., it decides a file ending in *.html* is probably a text/html file), creates some headers, and sends those headers back to the client with the resource itself. When all is said and done, the server makes a log entry.

At each stage of this process, Apache looks for routines to "handle" the request. Apache supplies its own handlers; for example, one of the default handlers is cgi-script, often seen applied to */cgi-bin*:

```
<Location /cgi-bin>
 ...
SetHandler cgi-script
 ...
</Location>
```

mod_perl allows you to write your own handlers in Perl, by embedding the Perl runtime library directly into the Apache *httpd* server executable. To use *mod_perl* for CGI (which is all that most people want to do with it), you assign the SetHandler directive to perl-script, and then assign the *mod_perl*-specific PerlHandler directive to a special Perl module called Apache::Registry.

```
SetHandler perl-script
PerlHandler Apache::Registry
```

PerlHandler is the *mod_perl* handler for the content retrieval stage of the transaction.

To use other handlers, you don't need to reassign SetHandler. For example, to identify a handler for the logging stage of the request:

```
<Location /snoop/>
PerlLogHandler Apache::DumpHeaders
</Location>
```

In order for this to work, *mod_perl* must have been built with the logging hooks enabled (as described in the previous section), and the Apache::DumpHeaders module must have been installed. *mod_perl* looks in Apache::DumpHeaders for a routine called handler() and executes it as the logging handler for that resource.

The following is a list of each of the handler directives that can be enabled by *mod_perl*, and the stages that each is used for. Only PerlHandler is enabled by default.

Handler	Purpose
PerlAccessHandler	Access stage
PerlAuthenHandler	Authentication stage
PerlAuthzHandler	Authorization stage
PerlChildInitHandler	Child initialization stage
PerlChildExitHandler	Child termination stage
PerlCleanupHandler	Cleanup stage
PerlFixupHandler	Fixup stage
PerlHandler	Response stage
PerlHeaderParserHandler	Header-parsing stage
PerlInitHandler	Initialization
PerlLogHandler	Logging stage
PerlPostReadRequestHandler	Post-request stage
PerlTransHandler	Translation stage
PerlTypeHandler	Type-handling stage

You can write your own handlers for each of these stages. But there are also dozens of modules that you can download from CPAN, some of which are listed at the end of this chapter.

Running CGI Scripts with mod_perl

What most people want to do with *mod_perl* is improve CGI performance. The *mod_perl* installation assumes this request by enabling the `PerlHandler` callback hook by default, and by installing the Apache::Registry module. `PerlHandler` is the handler used for the content retrieval stage of the server transaction. Apache::Registry is the Perl module that emulates the CGI environment so you can use "standard" Perl CGI scripts with *mod_perl* without having to rewrite them (much). This is by far the cheapest way to get improved CGI performance.

With Apache::Registry, each individual CGI program is compiled and cached the first time it is called (or whenever it is changed), and then remains available for all subsequent instances of that CGI script. This process avoids the costs of startup time.

Whereas most CGI scripts are kept in */cgi-bin/*, scripts that use Apache::Registry are placed in a separate directory, e.g., */perl-bin/*. The *access.conf* Apache configuration file needs to point to this directory by setting an alias and defining a handler for this new location.

```
Alias /perl-bin/ /usr/local/apache/perl-bin/

<Location /perl-bin>
SetHandler perl-script
PerlHandler Apache::Registry
PerlSendHeader On
Options ExecCGI
</Location>
```

Instead of using the `cgi-script` handler, we use the `perl-script` handler to give control to *mod_perl*. Next, the `PerlHandler` directive tells *mod_perl* that the Apache::Registry module should be used for serving all files in that directory. `PerlSendHeader` is another *mod_perl*-specific directive; in this case, it tells *mod_perl* to send response lines and common headers—by default, none are sent. (For NPH scripts, you'll want to turn this feature off again.) `Options ExecCGI` is a standard Apache header needed to tell Apache to treat the script as a CGI script.

If you want to load Perl modules in addition to Apache::Registry, you can use the PerlModule directive:

```
PerlModule CGI
```

If you include this line, you shouldn't need to explicitly use CGI in each Perl CGI script anymore, as CGI.pm will be loaded directly from the Apache server. Up to ten modules can be listed with the `PerlModule` directive.

CGI scripts in the new directory should work now. However, if you have problems, the *mod_perl* manpage offers some words of wisdom:

- Always use strict.

  "Standard" CGI scripts start with a clean slate every time. When switching to *mod_perl*, CGI programmers are often surprised to learn how often they take advantage of this fact. `use strict` tells you when your variables haven't been properly declared and might inherit values from previous invocations of the script.

- Don't call `exit()`.

  Calling `exit()` at the end of every program is a habit of many programmers. While often totally unnecessary, it usually doesn't hurt...except with *mod_perl*. If you're using *mod_perl* without Apache::Registry, `exit()` kills the server process. If `exit()` is the last function call, you can just remove it. If the structure of your program is such that it is called from the middle of the script, you can just put a label at the end of the script and use `goto()`. There's also an `Apache->exit()` call you can use if you're really attached to `exit()`s.

  If you're using Apache::Registry, you don't have to worry about this problem. Apache::Registry is smart enough to override all `exit()` calls with `Apache->exit()`.

In addition, it is recommended that you should use a recent version of Perl and of CGI.pm. You should scan the *mod_perl* documentation for the very latest compatibility news.

Server-Side Includes with mod_perl

Server-side includes (SSI) are tags embedded directly into an HTML file that perform special functions. They are most commonly used for running CGI scripts and displaying the result; most web page counters are performed using SSI.

If you use *mod_perl* with *mod_include* (another Apache server module), you can embed Perl subroutines into SSI directives. For example:

```
<!--#perl sub="sub {print ++Count}" -->
```

The Apache::Include module lets you include entire Apache::Registry scripts:

```
<!--#perl sub="Apache::Include" arg="/perl-bin/counter.pl" -->
```

You could have used standard SSI to include a CGI script for the same purpose, but this way is faster. To use *mod_include* with *mod_perl*, you need to configure *mod_perl* to do so at compile time.

<Perl> Sections

With *mod_perl*, you can use Perl in Apache configuration files. What this means is that you can make your Apache configuration much more flexible by using conditionals.

Any Perl code in Apache configuration files should be placed between `<Perl>` and `</Perl>` directives. This code can define variables and lists that are used by *mod_perl* to assign the associated Apache configuration directives; for example, assigning the `$ServerAdmin` variable will redefine the `ServerAdmin` Apache configuration directive.

Suppose you share the same Apache configuration files across multiple servers, and you only want to allow personal directories on one of them. You can use Perl directives like this:

```
<Perl>
if (`hostname` =~ /public/) {
        $UserDir = "public.html";
} else {
        $UserDir = "DISABLED";
}
1;
</Perl>
```

Directive blocks (such as <Location>...</Location>) can be represented as a hash. For example:

```
<Perl>
$Location{"/design_dept/"} = {
        DefaultType   => 'image/gif',
        FancyIndexing => 'On'
}
</Perl>
```

Apache:: Modules

Apache::Registry is the most commonly used *mod_perl* module. But there are many more, all available on CPAN. The following table lists the Apache::* modules and which handler they're designed to be used with, but you should also check the *apache-modlist.html* file on CPAN for the very latest listing.

PerlHandler

Apache::CallHandler	Maps filenames to subroutine calls
Apache::Dir	Controls directory indexing
Apache::Embperl	Embeds Perl code in HTML files
Apache::ePerl	Embedded Perl (ePerl) emulation
Apache::FTP	Emulates an FTP proxy
Apache::GzipChain	Compresses output from another handler
Apache::JavaScript	Generates JavaScript code
Apache::OutputChain	Chains multiple handlers via "filter" modules
Apache::PassFile	Sends files via OutputChain
Apache::Registry	Runs unaltered CGI scripts
Apache::RobotRules	Enforces *robots.txt* rules
Apache::Sandwich	Adds per-directory headers and footers
Apache::VhostSandwich	Adds headers and footers for virtual hosts
Apache::SSI	Implements server-side includes in Perl
Apache::Stage	Manages a document staging directory
Apache::WDB	Queries databases via DBI

PerlHeaderParserHandler

Apache::AgentDeny	Denies abusive clients

PerlAuthenHandler

Apache::Authen	Authenticates users

Apache::AuthCookie	Authenticates and authorizes users via cookies
Apache::AuthenDBI	Authenticates via Perl's DBI
Apache::AuthExpire	Expires authentication credentials
Apache::AuthenGSS	Authenticates users with Generic Security Service
Apache::AuthenLDAP	Authenticates users with LDAP
Apache::AuthNIS	Authenticates users with NIS
Apache::BasicCookieAuth	Accepts cookie or basic authentication credentials
Apache::DBILogin	Authenticates using a backend database
Apache::DCELogin	Authenticates within a DCE login context
Apache::AuthAny	Authenticates with any username/password

PerlAuthzHandler

Apache::AuthCookie	Authenticates and authorizes via cookies
Apache::AuthzAge	Authorizes based on age
Apache::AuthzDCE	Authorizes based on DFS/DCE ACL
Apache::AuthzDBI	Authorizes groups via DBI
Apache::AuthNIS	Authenticates and authorizes via NIS
Apache::RoleAuthz	Role-based authorization

PerlAccessHandler

Apache::AccessLimitNum	Limits user access by the number of requests
Apache::DayLimit	Limits access based on the day of the week
Apache::RobotLimit	Limits access of robots

PerlTypeHandler

Apache::AcceptLanguage	Sends file types based on user's language preference

PerlTransHandler

Apache::DynaRPC	Translates URIs into RPCs
Apache::Junction	Mounts remote web server namespace
Apache::LowerCaseGETs	Translates to lowercase URIs as needed
Apache::MsqlProxy	Translates URIs into mSQL queries
Apache::ProxyPassThru	Skeleton for vanilla proxy
Apache::ProxyCache	Caching proxy

PerlFixupHandler

Apache::HttpEquiv	Converts HTML HTTP-EQUIV tags to HTTP headers
Apache::Timeit	Benchmarks Perl handlers

PerlLogHandler

Apache::DumpHeaders	Displays HTTP transaction headers
Apache::Traffic	Logs the number of bytes transferred on a per-user basis
Apache::WatchDog	Looks for problematic URIs

PerlChildInitHandler

Apache::Resource	Limits resources used by *httpd* children

Server Configuration

Apache::ConfigLDAP	Configures server via LDAP and <Perl> sections

Apache::ConfigDBI	Configures server via DBI and <Perl> sections
Apache::ModuleConfig	Interfaces to configuration API
Apache::PerlSections	Utilities for <Perl> sections
Apache::httpd_conf	Methods to configure and run an *httpd*
Apache::src	Methods for finding and reading bits of source

Database

Apache::DBI	Manages persistent DBI connections.
Apache::Sybase	Manages persistent DBlib connections.
Apache::Mysql	Manages persistent mysql connections.

Interfaces and Integration with Various Apache C Modules

Apache::Constants	Constants defined in *httpd.h*
Apache::Include	Enables use of Apache::Registry scripts within SSI with *mod_include*
Apache::Global	Gives access to server global variables
Apache::LogError	Gives an interface to *aplog_error*
Apache::LogFile	Gives an interface to Apache's piped logs, etc.
Apache::Mime	Gives an interface to *mod_mime* functionality
Apache::Module	Gives an interface to Apache C module structures
Apache::Options	Imports Apache::Constants "options"
Apache::Scoreboard	Gives an interface to scoreboard API
Apache::Servlet	Gives an interface to the Java Servlet engine
Apache::Sfio	Gives an interface to `r->connection->client->sf*`

Development and Debug Tools

Apache::Debug	Provides debugging utilities to *mod_perl*
Apache::DProf	Hooks Devel::DProf into *mod_perl*
Apache::FakeRequest	Implements Apache methods offline
Apache::Peek	Emulates Devel::Peek for *mod_perl*
Apache::SawAmpersand	Makes sure no one is using $&, $', or $`
Apache::StatINC	Reloads files that are used or required files when updated
Apache::Status	Gets information about loaded modules
Apache::Symbol	Supports symbols
Apache::test	Defines handy routines for *make test* scripts

Miscellaneous

Apache::Byterun	Runs Perl bytecode modules
Apache::Mmap	Shares data via Mmap module
Apache::Persistent	Stores data via IPC::, DBI, or disk
Apache::PUT	Handler for the HTTP PUT method
Apache::RegistryLoader	Apache::Registry startup script loader
Apache::Safe	Adaptation of *safecgiperl*
Apache::Session	Maintains client <-> *httpd* session/state
Apache::SIG	Signal handlers for *mod_perl*
Apache::State	Powerful state engine

PART V

Databases

CHAPTER 12

Databases and Perl

Since one of Perl's greatest strengths is working with text, a genuine concern is how to store data. Flat files are one possibility, but don't scale very well, to say the least. Instead, you'll need to use a database.

There are two general solutions to using databases with Perl. For simple database purposes, DBM (Database Management) will serve your needs. DBM is a library supported by many (if not all) Unix systems and many non-Unix systems as well. If you use DBM with Perl, you can manipulate databases just like any hash.

For more elaborate databases with SQL interfaces, you can get a complete database product or shareware equivalent (depending on your needs) and use DBI and DBD. DBI is a module that provides a consistent interface for database solutions. A DBD is a database-specific driver that translates DBI calls as needed for that database.

In this chapter, we'll quickly cover DBM and then talk more at length about DBI/DBD.

DBM Databases and DBM Hashes

DBM is a simple database management facility for Unix systems. It allows programs to store a collection of key-value pairs in binary form, thus providing rudimentary database support for Perl. Practically all Unix systems support DBM, and for those that don't, you can get Berkeley DB from *http://www.sleepycat.com/db*.

To use DBM databases in Perl, you can associate a hash with a DBM database through a process similar to opening a file. This hash (called a DBM array) is then used to access and modify the DBM database. To associate a DBM database with a

DBM array, you can use either the dbmopen function or the tie function with a DBM-style module. (dbmopen is actually just a front-end to tie.) For example, with dbmopen:

```
dbmopen(%ARRAYNAME, "dbmfilename", $mode);
```

or (using tie with the DB_File module):

```
use DB_File;
tie(%ARRAYNAME, "DB_File", "dbmfilename");
```

The %ARRAYNAME parameter is a Perl hash. (If it already has values, the values are discarded.) This hash becomes connected to the DBM database called dbmfilename. This database may be stored on disk as a single file, or as two files called *dbmfilename.dir* and *dbmfilename.pag*, depending on the DBM implementation.

The $mode parameter is a number that controls the permissions of the pair of files if the files need to be created. The number is typically specified in octal. If the files already exist, this parameter has no effect. For example:

```
dbmopen(%BOOKS, "bookdb", 0666); # open %BOOKS onto bookdb
```

This invocation associates the hash %BOOKS with the disk files *bookdb.dir* and *bookdb.pag* in the current directory. If the files don't already exist, they are created with a mode of 0666, modified by the current *umask*.

The return value from dbmopen is true if the database could be opened or created, and false otherwise, just like the open function. If you don't want the files created, use a $mode value of undef.

Once the database is opened, anything you do to the DBM hash is immediately written to the database. See Chapter 4, *The Perl Language*, for more information on hashes.

```
dbmopen(%BOOKS, "bookdb", 0666) || die "Can't open database bookdb!";
$BOOKS{"1-56592-286-7"} = "Perl in a Nutshell";
```

The DBM array stays open throughout the program. When the program terminates, the association is terminated. You can also break the association in a manner similar to closing a filehandle, by using the dbmclose function (or untie if you used tie). See Chapter 5, *Function Reference*, for more information on dbmclose, dbmopen, and tie.

Design of DBI

If DBM is too primitive for your database requirements, you'll have to use a more sophisticated database package. Options include the commercial products Oracle, Sybase, and Informix, and the publically-available *msql* and *mysql*.

Prior to Perl Version 5 and DBI, the problem was that with all the database packages to choose from, there was no way to universalize database support for Perl. You'd have to rebuild the Perl executable itself against libraries that included subroutines for direct access to the database package. For example, *sybperl* and *oraperl* are both packages for building Perl Version 4 with Sybase and Oracle calls embedded, respectively. An application written for *sybperl* would not be portable to Oracle, or vice-versa. However, since current versions of Perl support binary extension loading at runtime, database support can now be added at runtime, which simplifies adding database interfaces to Perl programs while keeping the size of the Perl binary to a minimum.

Support for binary extensions doesn't mean that database access has been standardized. There are still many database extensions to Perl, each with a different API. However, they all share a strikingly similar set of commands: connect to the database, issue queries, fetch results, and disconnect. This consistency has made it possible to develop a standard set of methods to work with any database. DBI defines a set of functions, variables, and conventions that provide a consistent database programming interface for Perl.

Although DBI itself is language-independent, most DBI drivers require applications to use a dialect of SQL (structured query language) to interact with the database engine. SQL is a standard that was developed to allow programmers to manipulate relational databases. There are many implementations of SQL, and each database server adds nuances that deviate from the standard.

Database Drivers (DBDs)

The success of DBI is that it is only half of the story. The other half is a DBD, or a database driver. DBI provides the interface and framework for the drivers, but it's the database drivers that do the real work. Drivers implement the DBI methods for the private interface functions of the corresponding database engine.

Unless you're developing a sophisticated database application, you probably don't care about the drivers except that you want to install the correct one. Table 12–1 lists database servers, where you can find them, and the DBD driver designed for it. (The freeware or shareware database servers are available for download, and some of the commercial servers offer evaluation copies for download.)

Table 12–1: Database Servers

Server	URL	DBD
DB2	*http://www.software.ibm.com/data/db2/*	DBD::DB2
Empress	*http://www.empress.com/*	DBD::Empress
Fulcrum	*http://www.fulcrum.com*	DBD::Fulcrum
Informix	*http://www.informix.com/*	DBD::Informix
Ingres	*http://www.cai.com/products/ingres.htm*	
	http://epoch.cs.berkeley.edu:8000/postgres/index.html	DBD::Ingres
miniSQL	*http://www.hughes.com.au/*	DBD::mSQL
MySQL	*http://www.tcx.se/*	DBD::mysql
Oracle	*http://www.oracle.com/*	DBD::Oracle
PostgreSQL	*http://www.postgresql.com/*	DBD::Pg
QuickBase	*http://www.openbase.com/*	DBD::QBase
Solid	*http://www.solidtech.com/*	DBD::Solid
Sybase	*http://www.sybase.com/*	DBD::Sybase

Creating a Database

Before you can open a connection to a database with DBI, you must create the database. DBI isn't able to do this step for you, although your DBD might allow you to. For example, DBD:mSQL provides a `msqladmin` function. Your DBD might also support the `func` method, which is used to call private (and often nonportable) methods in the driver. You could use a one-liner like this to create the database from the command line:

```
perl -MDBI -e '$db_name = q[database_name_here]; \
    $result = DBD::mysql::dr->func($db_name, '_CreateDB');'
```

If your DBD allows to you to create databases via the API, it's likely that it will allow you to drop them, too.

```
perl -MDBI -e '$db_name = q[database_name_here]; \
    $result = DBD::mysql::dr->func($db_name, '_DropDB');'
```

Database Handles and Statement Handles

DBI methods work on two different types of handles: database handles and statement handles. A database handle is like a filehandle: `connect` is a DBI class method that opens a connection to a database and returns a database handle object.

```
$db_handle = DBI->connect(dbi:mSQL:bookdb, undef, undef)
    || die("Connect error: $DBI::errstr");
```

Statement handles are another thing entirely. DBI makes a distinction between the preparation of SQL statements and their execution, by allowing you to pre-format a statement into a statement handle. You can prepare a statement with the `prepare` method, which returns a statement handle. You can then assign a SQL statement to the statement handle via various statement handle methods, and execute it with the `execute` method when you're done. (You can also prepare and execute in the same command with the `do` method.)

Changes to the database are written to the database automatically if the Auto-Commit attribute is turned on. If AutoCommit is off, then use the `commit` method when you're ready to write the changes to the database.

AutoCommit is only one of many attributes that can be set for both database and statement handles. For example, if `$st_handle` is a statement handle, then you can set `$st_handle->{NULLABLE}` to determine if the fields can contain null characters. Table 12–2 is a listing of all the attributes supported by database handles, statement handles, or both.

Table 12–2: Attributes for Database and Statement Handles

Attributes for database handles

AutoCommit	Commit any changes to the database immediately, instead of waiting for an explicit call to commit. Default is true.

Attributes for statement handles

CursorName	The name of the cursor associated with the statement handle.
NAME	A reference to an array of field names.
NULLABLE	A reference to an array describing whether each field can contain a null character.
NUM_OF_FIELDS	Number of fields the prepared statement will return.
NUM_OF_PARAMS	Number of placeholders in the prepared statement.

Attributes common to all handles

Warn	Enables warnings.
CompatMode	Enables compatible behavior for a specific driver.
InactiveDestroy	Destroying a handle does not close prepared statements or disconnect from the database.
PrintError	Errors generate warnings.
RaiseError	Errors raise exceptions.
ChopBlanks	Truncate trailing space characters in fixed-width character fields.
LongReadLen	Controls the maximum length of long data.
LongTruncOk	Controls whether fetching long data that has been truncated should fail.

Databases

Placeholders

Many database drivers allow you to use question marks as placeholders in SQL statements, and then bind values to the placeholders before executing them. This enables you to prepare a single statement with placeholders and then reuse it for each row of the database. For example, the prepare statement might read:

```
$st_handle = $db_handle->prepare(q{
        insert into books (isbn, title) values (?, ?)
}) || die db_handle->errstr;
```

And a subsequent execute statement might read:

```
$st_handle->execute("1-56592-286-7", "Perl in a Nutshell")
        || die $db_handle->errstr;
```

DBI Methods

The following methods are available under DBI:

available_drivers

@drivers = DBI->available_drivers(*[nowarn]*)

Returns a list of available drivers by searching @INC for the presence of DBD::*
modules.

nowarn
> A boolean value specifying whether to suppress warnings if some drivers
> are hidden by others of the same name in earlier directories. Default is
> false (don't suppress).

bind_param

$result = *$st_handle*->bind_param(*n, value [, type]*)

Binds a value with a placeholder in a prepared statement.

n　The parameter number to bind.

value
> The value to associate with parameter *n*.

type
> The data type for the placeholder. The type can also be specified as an
> anonymous list ({TYPE => *type*}).

commit

$result = *$db_handle*->commit

Commits the most recent changes. See also the AutoCommit attribute.

connect

$db_handle = DBI->connect(*data_source, user, passwd, [\ %attr]*)

Connects to the specified database, returning a database handle object. The
connect method automatically installs the driver if it has not already been
installed.

data_source
> A string identifying the driver to connect to, and any other additional
> driver-specific information needed to identify the driver (e.g., a port num-
> ber.) The driver name is written in the form dbi:*driver_name*, e.g.,
> dbi:mSQL. (Default value is taken from the DBI_DSN environment vari-
> able.)

→

For example, a connection string for the mSQL driver always starts with dbi:mSQL:. The second colon should be followed by any information required by the driver to make the database connection. In the case of mSQL, you must supply a database name (bookdb in the following example), a hostname (localhost), and the port number of the database server (1114):

```
dbi:mSQL:bookdb:localhost:1114
```

user
> The user name for the database connection. (Default value is taken from the DBI_USER environment variable.)

passwd
> The password for the database connection. (Default value is taken from the DBI_PASS environment variable. Set this value at your own risk.)

\%attr
> A hash reference defining attributes for the database handle.

data_sources

> *@drivers* = **DBI->data_sources**(*driver*)

Returns a list of all databases available to the named driver. (The database server must be running for data_sources to return any results.)

driver
> The driver to list. If unspecified, the value of DBI_DRIVER is used.

disconnect

> *$result* = *$db_handle*->**disconnect**

Disconnects the database.

do

> *$rows* = *$db_handle*->**do**(*statement* [, *\%attr*, *@bind_values*])

Prepares and executes a statement, returning the number of rows affected.

statement
> The statement to execute.

\%attr
> Attributes to set for the new statement.

@bind_values
> Bind values for placeholder substitution.

dump_results

$rows = DBI::dump_results(*st_handle, maxlen, ldelim, fdelim, fileh*)

Runs DBI::neat() on all the rows of a statement handle and prints them for testing purposes.

st_handle
> The statement handle to retrieve.

maxlen
> The length at which to truncate with "..." (default is 35).

ldelim
> The delimiter between rows (default is "\n").

fdelim
> The delimiter between individual fields (default is ", ").

fileh
> The filehandle to print to (default is STDOUT).

err

$handle->err

Returns the error code from the last driver function called.

errstr

$handle->errstr

Returns the error message from the last driver function called.

func

$handle->func(*@arguments, function*)

Calls a private nonportable method on the specific handle.

@arguments
> The arguments to the function.

function
> The function name. Note that the function name is specified last.

execute

$result = $st_handle->execute([*@bind_values*])

Executes a prepared statement.

@bind_values
> Binds values for placeholder substitution.

fetch

*$arrayref = $st_handle->*fetch

Fetches the next row of data, returning an array reference with the field values.

fetchall_arrayref

*$arrayref = $st_handle->*fetchall_arrayref

Fetches all data from a prepared statement and returns a reference to an array of references.

fetchrow_array

*$array = $st_handle->*fetchrow_array

Fetches the next row of data, returning an array with the field values.

fetchrow_arrayref

*$arrayref = $st_handle->*fetchrow_arrayref

Fetches the next row of data, returning an array reference with the field values. Synonym for `fetch`.

fetchrow_hashref

*$hashref = $st_handle->*fetchrow_hashref

Fetches the next row of data, returning a hash reference containing the field values. The keys of the hash are the same as `$st_handle->{NAME}`.

finish

*$result = $st_handle->*finish

Disables further fetching from a statement.

neat

$newstring = DBI::neat*(string, maxlength)*

Converts a string to one with quoted strings, null values shown as undef, and unprintable characters shown as ".".

string
> The string to convert.

maxlength
> The length at which to truncate the string with " . . . ".

neat_list

$newstring = **DBI::neat_list**(*\@list, maxlength, delim*)

Converts each element of a list with `DBI::neat` and returns it as a string.

\@list
> A reference to the list to convert.

maxlength
> The length at which to truncate the string with " ... ".

delim
> The delimiter to use between list elements in the new string. The default is ", ".

ping

$result = *$db_handle*->**ping**

Determines if the database is still connected.

prepare

$st_handle = *$db_handle*->**prepare**(*statement [, \%attr]*)

Prepares a statement for execution and returns a reference to a statement handle object.

statement
> The statement to prepare.

\%attr
> Attributes to set for the assigned statement handle.

quote

$sql = *$db_handle*->**quote**(*string*)

Escapes special characters in a string for use in an SQL statement.

string
> The string to convert.

rollback

$result = *$db_handle*->**rollback**

Undoes the most recent database changes if not yet committed.

rows

$rows = *$st_handle*->**rows**

Returns the number of rows affected by the last change to the database.

bind_col

*$result = $st_handle->**bind_col***(col, \variable [, \ %attr])*

Binds a field of a select statement to a variable, to be updated whenever the row is fetched.

col The column number to bind.

\variable
> A reference to the variable to bind.

\ %attr
> Attributes to set for the statement handle.

bind_columns

*$result = $st_handle->**bind_columns***(\ %attr, @reflist)*

Runs bind_col on each column of the statement.

\ %attr
> Attributes to set for the statement handle.

@reflist
> A list of references to the variables to bind.

state

*$handle->**state***

Returns an error code in a five-character format.

trace

DBI->trace*(n, filename)*

Traces the execution of DBI.

n An integer indicating the level of trace/debugging information, as follows:

> 0   Disable the trace.
>
> 1   Trace the execution of the DBI.
>
> 2   Output detailed call trace information including parameters and return values.

filename
> The file to append trace information to.

trace

*$handle->*trace*(n, filename)*

Same as the class method DBI->trace, but for a specific database, statement, or driver handle.

DBI Environment Variables

The following environment variables are defined for use with DBI:

DBI_DSN
The data source value to use if none is specified with the connect method.

DBI_DRIVER
The driver to use if none is specified with the connect method.

DBI_USER
The username to use if none is specified with the connect method.

DBI_PASS
The password to use if none is specified with the connect method. (For security purposes, this environment variable should not be set except for testing.)

DBI_TRACE
Enables tracing behavior as with the trace method. DBI_TRACE can be set to any of the following values:

0   Disables the trace.

1   Traces the execution of the DBI.

2   Outputs detailed call trace information including parameters and return values.

filename
Appends trace information to the specified file; the trace level is set to 2.

PART VI

Network Programming

CHAPTER 13

Sockets

Why build networking functionality into your Perl scripts? You might want to access your email remotely, or write a simple script that updates files on a FTP site. You might want to check up on your employees with a program that searches for Usenet postings that came from your site. You might want to check a web site for any recent changes, or even write your own home-grown web server. The network is the computer these days, and Perl makes network applications easy.

Perl programmers have their choice of modules for doing common tasks with network protocols; Chapter 14, *Email Connectivity*, through Chapter 17, *The LWP Library*, cover the modules for writing email, news, FTP, and web applications in Perl. If you can do what you want with the available modules, you're encouraged to jump to those chapters and skip this one. However, there will be times that you'll have to wrestle with sockets directly, and that's where this chapter comes in.

Sockets are the underlying mechanism for networking on the Internet. With sockets, one application (a *server*) sits on a port waiting for connections. Another application (the *client*) connects to that port and says hello; then the client and server have a chat. Their actual conversation is done with whatever protocol they choose—for example, a web client and server would use HTTP, an email server would use POP3 and SMTP, etc. But at the most basic level, you might say that all network programming comes down to opening a socket, reading and writing data, and closing the socket again.

You can work with sockets in Perl at various levels. At the lowest level, Perl's built-in functions include socket routines similar to the system calls in C of the same name. To make these routines easier to use, the Socket module in the standard library imports common definitions and constants specific to your system's networking capabilities. Finally, the IO::Socket module provides an object interface to the socket functions through a standard set of methods and options for constructing both client and server communications programs.

Sockets provide a connection between systems or applications. They can be set up to handle streaming data or discrete data packets. Streaming data continually comes and goes over a connection. A transport protocol like TCP (Transmission Control Protocol) is used to process streaming data so that all of the data is properly received and ordered. Packet-oriented communication sends data across the network in discrete chunks. The message-oriented protocol UDP (User Datagram Protocol) works on this type of connection. Although streaming sockets using TCP are widely used for applications, UDP sockets also have their uses.

Sockets exist in one of two address domains: the Internet domain and the Unix domain. Sockets that are used for Internet connections require the careful binding and assignment of the proper type of address dictated by the Internet Protocol (IP). These sockets are referred to as Internet-domain sockets.

Sockets in the Unix domain create connections between applications either on the same machine or within a LAN. The addressing scheme is less complicated, often just providing the name of the target process.

In Perl, sockets are attached to a filehandle after they have been created. Communication over the connection is then handled by standard Perl I/O functions.

Built-in Socket Functions

Perl provides built-in support for sockets. The following functions are defined specifically for socket programming. For full descriptions and syntax, see Chapter 5, *Function Reference*.

socket
>Initializes a socket and assigns a filehandle to it.

bind
>For servers, associates a socket with a port and address. For clients, associates a socket with a specific source address.

listen
>(Server only.) Waits for incoming connection with a client.

accept
>(Server only.) Accepts incoming connection with a client.

connect
>(Client only.) Establishes a network connection on a socket.

recv
>Reads data from a socket filehandle.

send
>Writes data to a filehandle.

shutdown (or close)
>Terminates a network connection.

Regular functions that read and write filehandles can also be used for sockets, i.e., write, print, printf, and the diamond input operator, <>.

The socket functions tend to use hard-coded values for some parameters, which severely hurt portability. Perl solves this problem with a module called Socket, included in the standard library. Use this module for any socket applications that you build with the built-in functions (i.e., use Socket). The module loads the *socket.h* header file, which enables the built-in functions to use the constants and names specific to your system's network programming, as well as additional functions for dealing with address and protocol names.

The next few sections describe Perl socket programming using a combination of the built-in functions together with the Socket module. After that, we describe the use of the IO::Socket module.

Initializing a Socket

Both client and server use the socket call to create a socket and associate it with a filehandle. The socket function takes several arguments: the name of the filehandle, the network domain, an indication of whether the socket is stream-oriented or record-oriented, and the network protocol to be used. For example, HTTP (web) transactions require stream-oriented connections running TCP. The following line creates a socket for this case and associates it with the filehandle SH:

```
use Socket;
socket(SH, PF_INET, SOCK_STREAM, getprotobyname('tcp')) || die $!;
```

The PF_INET argument indicates that the socket will connect to addresses in the Internet domain (i.e., IP addresses). Sockets with a Unix domain address use PF_UNIX.

Because this is a streaming connection using TCP, we specify SOCK_STREAM for the second argument. The alternative would be to specify SOCK_DGRAM for a packet-based UDP connection.

The third argument indicates the protocol used for the connection. Each protocol has a number assigned to it by the system; that number is passed to socket as the third argument. In the scalar context, getprotobyname returns the protocol number.

Finally, if the socket call fails, the program will die, printing the error message found in $!.

Client Connections

On the client side, the next step is to make a connection with a server at a particular port and host. To do this, the client uses the connect call. connect requires the socket filehandle as its first argument. The second argument is a data structure containing the port and hostname that together specify the address. The Socket package provides the sockaddr_in function to create this structure for Internet addresses and the sockaddr_un function for Unix domain addresses.

The sockaddr_in function takes a port number for its first argument and a 32-bit IP address for the second argument. The 32-bit address is formed from the inet_aton function found in the Socket package. This function takes either a host-name (e.g., *www.oreilly.com*) or a dotted-decimal string (e.g., 207.54.2.25), and it returns the corresponding 32-bit structure.

Continuing with the previous example, a call to connect could look like this:

```
my $dest = sockaddr_in (80, inet_aton('www.oreilly.com'));
connect (SH, $dest) || die $!;
```

This call attempts to establish a network connection to the specified server and port. If successful, it returns true. Otherwise, it returns false and dies with the error in $!.

Assuming that the connect call has completed successfully and a connection has been established, there are a number of functions we can use to write to and read from the file handle. For example, the send function sends data to a socket:

```
$data = "Hello";
send (FH, $data);
```

The print function allows a wider variety of expressions for sending data to a file-handle.

```
select (FH);
print "$data";
```

To read incoming data from a socket, use either the recv function or the "dia-mond" input operator regularly used on filehandles. For example:

```
recv (FH, $buffer);
```

```
$input = <FH>;
```

After the conversation with the server is finished, use close or shutdown to close the connection and destroy the socket.

Server Connections

After creating a socket with the socket function as above, a server application must go through the following steps to receive network connections:

1. Bind a port number and machine address to the socket.

2. Listen for incoming connections from clients on the port.

3. Accept a client request and assign the connection to a specific filehandle.

We start out by creating a socket for the server:

```
my $proto = getprotobyname('tcp');
socket(FH, PF_INET, SOCK_STREAM, $proto) || die $!;
```

The filehandle $FH is the generic filehandle for the socket. This filehandle only receives requests from clients; each specific connection is passed to a different file-handle by accept, where the rest of the communication occurs.

A server-side socket must be bound to a port on the local machine by passing a port and an address data structure to the bind function via sockaddr_in. The

Socket module provides identifiers for common local addresses, such as localhost and the broadcast address. Here we use INADDR_ANY, which allows the system to pick the appropriate address for the machine:

```
my $sin = sockaddr_in (80, INADDR_ANY);
bind (FH, $sin) || die $!;
```

The listen function tells the operating system that the server is ready to accept incoming network connections on the port. The first argument is the socket file-handle. The second argument gives a queue length, in case multiple clients are connecting to the port at the same time. This number indicates how many clients can wait for an accept at one time.

```
listen (FH, $length);
```

The accept function completes a connection after a client requests and assigns a new filehandle specific to that connection. The new filehandle is given as the first argument to accept, and the generic socket filehandle is given as the second:

```
accept (NEW, FH) || die $!;
```

Now the server can read and write to the filehandle NEW for its communication with the client.

Socket Module Functions

The following functions are imported from the Socket module for use in socket applications:

inet_aton

inet_aton *(hostname)*

Translates a hostname such as *www.oreilly.com* or 18.181.0.24 into a data structure (a four-byte string) used for socket addresses. If the hostname cannot be resolved, the function returns the undefined value.

inet_ntoa

inet_ntoa *(addr_string)*

Translates a four-byte address string (as returned by inet_aton) into a string with the dotted-quad form of IP address.

sockaddr_in

sockaddr_in *(port, addr_string)*

pack_sockaddr_in *(port, addr_string)*

Takes a port number and a four-byte *addr_string* (as returned by inet_aton) and returns the socket address structure including those arguments packed

→

with the AF_INET argument. This structure is normally what you need for the arguments in `bind`, `connect`, and `send`, and is also returned by `getpeername`, `getsockname`, and `recv`.

sockaddr_un

sockaddr_un *(pathname)*

pack_sockaddr_un *(pathname)*

Takes one argument, a pathname, and returns the Unix domain socket address structure (the path packed in with AF_UNIX filled in). For Unix domain sockets, this structure is normally what you need for the arguments in `bind`, `connect`, and `send`, and is also returned by `getpeername`, `getsockname`, and `recv`.

unpack_sockaddr_in

unpack_sockaddr_in *(sockaddr)*

sockaddr_in *(sockaddr)*

Takes a socket address structure and returns an array of two elements (in list context): the port number and the four-byte IP address.

unpack_sockaddr_un

unpack_sockaddr_un *(sockaddr_un)*

sockaddr_un *(sockaddr_un)*

Takes a Unix domain socket address structure (as returned by `sockaddr_un`) and returns the pathname.

The following constants are defined in the Socket module:

INADDR_ANY
The four-byte packed string for the wildcard IP address that specifies any of the host's addresses (if the host has multiple addresses). This is equivalent to `inet_aton('0.0.0.0')`.

INADDR_BROADCAST
The four-byte packed string for the broadcast address. This is equivalent to `inet_aton('255.255.255.255')`.

INADDR_LOOPBACK
The four-byte packed string for the loopback address. This is equivalent to `inet_aton('localhost')`.

INADDR_NONE
The four-byte packed string for the "invalid" IP address (bitmask). Equivalent to `inet_aton('255.255.255.255')`.

The IO::Socket Module

The IO::Socket module included in the core Perl distribution provides an object-oriented approach to socket programming. This module provides a convenient way to handle the large number of options you have to deal with, and it handles the laborious task of forming addresses. IO::Socket is built upon the Socket module provided in the standard library. It inherits from IO::Handle, which supports a class of filehandle objects for much of the IO library. The following IO::Socket functions are simply frontends for the corresponding built-in functions and use the same syntax:

```
socket
socketpair
bind
listen
send
recv
peername (same as getpeername)
sockname (same as getsockname)
```

The accept function in IO::Socket is slightly different from the equivalent function, however, and is described later in the chapter.

IO:Socket contains two subclasses: INET and UNIX. The INET subclass is used to create and manipulate Internet-domain sockets, such as the ones used in the examples. The UNIX subclass creates Unix domain sockets.

Client-Side Sockets

IO::Socket greatly simplifies the implementation of a socket for client communications. The following example creates an Internet-domain socket (using the INET subclass) and attempts to connect to the specified server:

```
use IO::Socket;
$sock = new IO::Socket::INET (PeerAddr => 'www.ora.com',
                              PeerPort => 80,
                              Proto    => 'tcp');
die "$!" unless $sock;
```

IO::Socket::INET::new creates an object containing a socket filehandle and connects it to the host and port specified in PeerAddr and PeerPort. The object $sock can then be written to and read from like other socket filehandles.

Server-Side Sockets

On the server side, IO::Socket provides a nice wrapper for creating server sockets. The wrapper encompasses the socket, bind, and listen procedures, while creating a new IO::Socket object. For example, we can create an Internet-domain socket with IO::Socket::INET:

```
use IO::Socket;
$sock = new IO::Socket::INET (LocalAddr => 'maude.ora.com',
                              LocalPort => 8888,
```

```
                          Proto    => 'tcp',
                          Listen   => 5);
    die "$!" unless $sock;
```

The parameters for the new socket object determine whether it is a server or a client socket. Because we're creating a server socket, LocalAddr and LocalPort provide the address and port to bind to the socket. The Listen parameter gives the queue size for the number of client requests that can wait for an accept at any one time.

When the server receives a client request, it calls the accept method on the socket object. This creates a new socket object on which the rest of the communication can take place:

```
    $new_sock = $sock->accept();
```

When communication is finished on both client and server sockets, they should be destroyed with close. If a socket is not properly closed, the next time you attempt to use a socket with the same name, the system will complain that the socket is already in use.

IO::Socket Methods

The following methods are defined in IO::Socket and can be used on socket objects of either the INET or UNIX class:

---

accept

accept *([pkg])*

Performs the accept system call on a socket and returns a new object. The new object is created in the same class as the listen socket, unless *pkg* is specified. The object can be used to communicate with the client that was trying to connect. In a scalar context, the new socket is returned, or undef on failure. In an array context, a two-element array is returned containing the new socket and the peer address, or an empty list on failure.

---

timeout

timeout *([val])*

Sets or retrieves the timeout value associated with a socket. Without an argument, the current value is returned. If a timeout of *val* is given, the setting is changed to *val* and the previous value is returned.

---

sockopt

sockopt *(opt, [val])*

Sets and retrieves socket option *opt* in the SOL_SOCKET level. The value *val* is set for the option, if given. If no value is provided, the function returns the current setting for the option.

---

sockdomain

sockdomain

Returns the number representing the socket address domain. For example, an AF_INET socket has the value &AF_INET.

socktype

socktype

Returns the number representing the socket type. For example, a SOCK_STREAM socket has the value &SOCK_STREAM.

protocol

protocol

Returns the protocol number for the protocol being used on the socket, if known. If the protocol is unknown, as with an AF_UNIX socket, returns zero.

IO::Socket::INET Reference

An Internet-domain socket is created with the new method from the IO::Socket::INET subclass. The constructor can take the following options:

PeerAddr => *hostname*[:*port*]
> Specifies the remote host and optional port number for a client connection. *hostname* can be either a name, like *www.oreilly.com*, or an IP number of the form 207.44.21.2.

PeerPort => *port*
> Specifies the port number on the remote host for a client connection. The name of the service (such as http or nntp) may be used for the argument if the port number is not known.

LocalAddr => *hostname*[:*port*]
> Specifies the local address (and optional port number) to bind to a server-side socket.

LocalPort => *port*
> Specifies the local port number (or service name) to bind to a server-side socket.

Proto => *name*
> Specifies the protocol to be run on the socket, i.e., tcp or udp.

Type => SOCK_STREAM | SOCK_DGRAM
> Specifies the type of socket. SOCK_STREAM indicates a stream-based socket connection, and SOCK_DGRAM indicates a message-based (datagram) connection.

Network Programming

`Listen => ` *n*

Sets the listen-queue size to *n* number of client requests.

`Reuse => 1`

Given a non-zero number, this option allows the local bind address to be reused should the socket need to be reopened after an error.

`Timeout => ` *n*

Sets the timeout.

Whether a server (receiving) or client (requesting) socket is created depends on the parameters provided to the constructor. If `Listen` is defined, a server socket is automatically created. If no protocol is specified, it is derived from the service on the given port number. If no port number is given, `tcp` is used by default.

IO::Socket::INET methods

The following methods can be used on socket filehandle objects created by IO::Socket::INET:

---

sockaddr

sockaddr

Returns the address part (as a packed string) of the socket–address data structure for the socket.

---

sockport

sockport

Returns the local port number for the socket.

---

sockhost

sockhost

Returns the address part of the socket–address data structure in the dotted-quad string form, e.g., 207.44.27.2.

---

peeraddr

peeraddr

Returns the address part (packed string) of the socket–address data structure for the remote host to which a socket connects.

---

peerport

peerport

Returns the port number for the remote host to which a socket connects.

---

peerhost

peerhost

Returns the remote host address in the dotted-quad string form, i.e., 207.44.27.2.

IO::Socket::UNIX Reference

The IO::Socket::UNIX subclass creates a Unix-domain socket. Unix-domain sockets are local to the current host and are used internally to implement pipes, thus providing communication between unrelated processes. Using sockets provides finer control than using named pipes, also called FIFO (first-in, first-out) buffers. This is because receiving sockets can distinguish between different client connections, which can then be assigned to different sessions with the accept call.

The IO::Socket::UNIX constructor (new( )) creates the socket and returns an object containing a filehandle. The constructor can take the following options:

Type => SOCK_STREAM | SOCK_DGRAM
Indicates the type of socket: SOCK_STREAM for streaming, SOCK_DGRAM for packets or datagrams.

Local => *pathname*
Provides the pathname of the FIFO buffer to bind to the socket.

Peer => *pathname*
Provides the pathname to the destination FIFO buffer.

Listen => *n*
Creates a listen socket and sets the queue size to *n*.

The following methods can be used on an object created with IO::Socket::UNIX.

hostpath

hostpath

Returns the pathname to the local FIFO buffer.

peerpath

peerpath

Returns the pathname to the destination or peer FIFO.

CHAPTER 14

Email Connectivity

Electronic mail is arguably the most essential Internet application. In fact, for many people, it's their introduction to the Internet. Thus the Perl modules that deal with email are among the most useful modules. There are two major groups of modules that provide email capabilities. The first group is Graham Barr's *libnet* collection, which contains packages for developing client-side applications over the Internet in Perl. Table 14-1 lists some of the protocols implemented by the *libnet* modules.

Table 14–1: Protocols Implemented by the libnet Modules

Protocol	Module	Description
POP3	Net::POP3	Post Office Protocol, for reading email
SMTP	Net::SMTP	Simple Mail Transfer Protocol, for sending email
FTP	Net::FTP	File Transfer Protocol, for transferring files between hosts
NNTP	Net::NNTP	Network News Transfer Protocol, for reading Usenet news

In this chapter, we discuss Net::SMTP and Net::POP3. Chapter 15, *Usenet News*, talks about Net::NNTP, and Chapter 16, *FTP*, discusses Net::FTP. Other *libnet* modules, such as Net::SNPP and Net::Time, are not described here, but you can get information about them from CPAN or with the *perldoc* command if *libnet* is installed on your system.

The second group of mail-related modules are the Mail modules, many of which were also written by Graham Barr. They can be found on CPAN as the MailTools collection. The Mail modules also include Mail::Folder and its subclasses, written by Kevin Johnson, and Mail::POP3Client, by Sean Dowd. This chapter describes the following subset of the Mail modules:

Mail::Send
> Built on top of Mail::Mailer, providing better control of mail headers.

Mail::Mailer
> Interacts with external mail programs to send mail.

Mail::Folder
> Provides a base class and subclasses to work with mail folders.

Mail::Internet
> Provides functions to manipulate a mail message.

Mail::Address
> Extracts and manipulates RFC 822–compliant mail addresses.

Mail::POP3Client
> Provides an interface to a POP3 server, based on RFC 1081.

The rest of this chapter describes the modules; first the Net modules and then the Mail modules.

The Net Modules

Net::SMTP and Net::POP3 are the modules for sending and receiving email via the SMTP and POP3 protocols. When you use these modules, you are working at the socket level; they directly implement the Internet protocols for sending and receiving mail as defined in the relevant RFCs—RFC 821 for SMTP and RFC 1081 for POP3.

Send Email with Net::SMTP

The Simple Mail Transfer Protocol, or SMTP, is responsible for clients negotiating RCPT ("to") and FROM ("from") requests with an SMTP server, sending data to the SMTP server, and then sending an end-of-data indicator. Net::SMTP is a subclass of Net::Cmd and IO::Socket::INET that implements an interface to the SMTP and ESMTP protocols. These protocols send mail by talking to an SMTP server through a socket, as described in RFC 821.

When would you want to use Net::SMTP instead of sending mail with an external program? Since socket communications don't involve spawning an external program, your programs won't suffer from the overhead associated with running an extra process. Talking to SMTP is convenient for sending a volume of mail messages. Naturally, your server must have an SMTP server running or a remote mailhost must allow you to talk to it; otherwise you won't be able to use this module. That's when you can turn to Mail::Mailer or Mail::Send and let them provide an interface to an external mail program for you. This is the case, for example, with home computers, which don't generally run their own SMTP server.

The SMTP Protocol and the SMTP Session

The SMTP protocol defines the set of commands a client sends to an SMTP server, which is generally bound to port 25 of a mailhost. Requests and responses are negotiated between client and server.

When a client negotiates an SMTP session with a server, the server tells the client that it's listening. Once you're connected, you introduce yourself to the server by issuing a HELO command. The HELO command accepts one parameter—your hostname—and defaults to your remote hostname if you don't specify one. If the command is successful, the server sends a 250 response, as follows:

```
HELO
250 mail.somename.com Hello some-remote-host.com [127.0.0.1], pleased to meet
you
```

After you've been greeted by the server, send the MAIL command to tell the server who the message is from. The MAIL command takes the string From: user@hostname as an argument, and the server responds with a 250 message to indicate success:

```
MAIL From: <realuser@realhost.com>
250 realuser@realhost.com ... Sender ok
```

Then you send the RCPT command to tell the server who the recipient is:

```
RCPT To: <nospam@rid-spam-now.com>
250 nospam@rid-spam-now.com ... Recipient ok
```

Now you're ready to send the body of your message to the server. The DATA command tells the server that all data until a . on a line by itself is to be treated as the body of the mail message:

```
DATA
354 Enter mail, end with "." on a line by itself
Subject: Hi, just thought you'd be interested ...

Hi, this is the text of my mail message that I'm going to
send with Net::SMTP to show you how it works.
.
250 VAA09505 Message accepted for delivery
```

Once again you get a 250 response, indicating that the message has been accepted for delivery. At that point, you can exit the SMTP session with the QUIT command, which returns 221 on success:

```
QUIT
221 mail.somename.com closing connection
Connection closed by foreign host.
```

Net::SMTP Methods

The following methods are defined by Net:SMTP:

new

$smtp = Net::SMTP->new*(host[, options])*

Constructor. Takes the hostname of the remote mail server, *host*, and possibly some options, and creates a new SMTP object. Any options are passed to new as a hash, where the option is the key. The possible options are:

Debug

> Enables debug mode if set to 1. Provides information about your connection, requests, and responses.

Hello

> Sends a HELO command to the SMTP server. Takes a string that represents your domain; if not specified, Hello guesses your domain.

Timeout

> Time (in seconds) after which the client stops trying to establish a connection with the SMTP server. Defaults to 120 seconds. If the connection cannot be established, the constructor returns undef.

data

$smtp->data*([bodydata])*

Starts sending the body of the current message to the server. If specified, *bodydata* can be a list or a reference to a list; the contents of the list and the termination string .\r\n are sent to the server. Returns true if accepted.

If *bodydata* is not specified, then a true result means that the server is ready to receive data, which must be sent with the datasend and dataend methods (inherited from Net::Cmd).

dataend

$smtp->dataend*()*

Net::Cmd method issued after datasend to end the sending of data. Sends .\r\n to the server telling it that there's no more data coming and that it should send the message.

Here's an example that uses datasend and dataend:

```
@list_data = (1..10);

$smtp->data();
$smtp->datasend(@list_data);
$smtp->dataend();
```

datasend

$smtp->datasend*("data")*

Net::Cmd method that sends the body of the message to the remote server if the body wasn't specified with the data method.

domain

> *$smtp*->domain()

Returns the domain of the remote SMTP server, or undef.

expand

> *$smtp*->**expand**(*address*)

Requests the server to expand *address*. Returns an array containing the text from the server.

hello

> *$smtp*->**hello**(*domain*)

Identifies your domain to the mail server. Executes automatically when you create a Net::SMTP object, so you shouldn't have to do it manually.

help

> *$help_text* = *$smtp*->**help**(*[subject]*)

Returns help text from the server, or undef on failure. If *subject* is specified, returns help for that topic.

mail

> *$smtp*->**mail**(*address[, options]*)
> *$smtp*->**send**(*address*)
> **send_or_mail**(*address*)
> **send_and_mail**(*address*)

Takes the sender's address and sends the appropriate command (MAIL, SEND, SOML, or SAML) to the server to initiate the message-sending process.

mail can take some ESMTP options, passed as key/value pairs. See the Net::SMTP documentation for the details.

quit

> *$smtp*->**quit**

This method sends the QUIT command to the remote SMTP server and closes the socket connection.

recipient

> *$smtp->*recipient*(addr[, addr[, ...]])*

Tells the server to send the current message to all specified recipients. As defined in the RFC, each address is sent as a separate command to the server. If the sending of any address fails, the process aborts and returns false; you can then call `reset` to reset the server.

reset

> *$smtp->*reset*()*

Resets the server's status. Useful for cancelling a message after it has been initiated but before any data has been sent.

to

> *$smtp->*to*(address[, address[, ...]])*

Interchangeable with `recipient`.

verify

> *$smtp->*verify*(address)*

Verifies that the specified mail address is valid. However, many servers ignore `verify`, so it frequently doesn't work.

Retrieving Email with Net::POP3

You can use SMTP to send mail, but not to retrieve it. For retrieving messages, use the Post Office Protocol version 3 (POP3), described in RFC 1081. One way to do this is to use the Net::POP3 module. POP3 provides commands for interacting with the POP server, typically bound to port 110. Net::POP3 automates the transfer of email from a remote server to the local machine.

The POP server retrieves messages from a specified spooling directory on the remote system. The messages are stored in a file named for the username; anonymous logins are not permitted. Authentication is based on username and password and is done by sending the USER and PASS commands to the POP server. For example, identification of user `foo` with password `bar` looks like this:

```
USER foo
PASS bar
```

Net::POP3 has `user` and `pass` methods but may also authenticate users with `login`, which takes both username and password arguments. If authentication fails, the user cannot retrieve, delete, or alter any messages from the mail server. `login` returns the number of messages on the POP server for the user, or `undef` if authentication fails.

Authenticated users can retrieve information about their mailboxes, and they can get specific messages by message number.

A POP session to retrieve a mail message is negotiated with the server like this:

1. Connect to the POP server (the default port is 110).
2. Send USER command.
3. Send PASS command.
4. If authenticated, receive number of messages.
5. Send RETR *<message number>* command to retrieve a specific message.
6. Send QUIT command to end session.

The following methods are defined by Net:POP3:

new

$pop = Net::POP3->new *([host,] [options])*

Constructor. Creates a new Net::POP3 object. *host* is the name of the remote host to which you want to make a POP3 connection. If *host* is not specified, then the POP3_Host specified in Net::Config is used.

options are passed as key/value pairs, where the option is the key. The possible options are:

Debug
> Enables debugging information

Timeout
> Maximum time, in seconds, to wait for a response from the POP3 server. Default is 120 seconds.

apop

$pop->apop(user, pass)

Authenticates *user* with password *pass* with the server. The password is not sent in clear text. Requires the MD5 package, otherwise returns undef.

delete

$pop->delete(msgnum)

Marks message *msgnum* for deletion from the remote mailbox. All messages marked for deletion are removed when the connection to the server is closed.

get

$pop->get(msgnum)

Gets message *msgnum* from remote mailbox. Returns a reference to an array containing lines of text read from the server.

last

$pop->last()

Returns the highest message number.

list

$pop->list([msgnum])

If called with an argument, returns the size of message *msgnum*. If called without an argument, returns a hash reference, where the keys are the message numbers of all undeleted messages, and each corresponding value is the size of the message.

login

$pop->login([user[, pass]])

Sends both USER and PASS commands. If the password, *pass*, is not given, then Net::Netrc is used to look up the password based on the host and the username, *user*. If *user* is not specified, the current username is used. Returns the count of messages in the mailbox, or undef if the server can't authenticate the user.

pass

$pop->pass(pass)

Sends the PASS command with the password. Returns the number of messages in the mailbox.

popstat

$pop->popstat()

Returns a list with two elements: the number of undeleted elements and the size of the mailbox.

quit

$pop->quit()

Quits, closing the connection to the remote POP3 server and deleting all messages marked for deletion.

→

Network Programming

Note that if a Net::POP3 object goes out of scope before `quit` has been called, `reset` is called before the connection is closed, and any messages marked for deletion are not deleted.

reset

$pop->**reset**()

Resets status of the remote POP3 server. Clears the delete status on all messages that were marked for deletion.

top

$pop->**top**(*msgnum[, numlines]*)

Gets the header and the first *numlines* lines of body for message *msgnum*. Returns a reference to an array containing lines of text read from the server.

uidl

$pop->**uidl**(*[msgnum]*)

Returns a unique identifier for *msgnum* if specified. If *msgnum* is not specified, returns a reference to a hash where the keys are the message numbers and the values are the unique identifiers.

user

$pop->**user**(*user*)

Sends the USER command, identifying the user.

The Mail Modules

The Mail modules operate at a higher level than the Net modules, interacting with external mail packages such as *mail, mailx, sendmail,* or a POP3 server in the case of POP3Client. This section describes some of the MailTools modules, Mail::Folder, and Mail::POP3Client.

Send Email with Mail::Mailer

The Mail::Mailer module interacts with external mail programs. When you use Mail::Mailer or create a new Mail::Mailer object, you can specify which mail program you want your program to talk to:

```
use Mail::Mailer qw(mail);
```

Another way to specify the mailer is:

```
use Mail::Mailer;
$type = 'sendmail';
$mailprog = Mail::Mailer->new($type);
```

where $type is the mail program. Once you've created a new object, use the open function to send the message headers to the mail program as a hash of key/value pairs, where each key represents a header type, and where the value is the value of that header:

```
# mail headers to use in the message
%headers = (
    'To' => 'you@mail.somename.com',
    'From' => 'me@mail.somename.com',
    'Subject' => 'working?'
);
```

This code represents headers where the recipient of the mail message is *you@mail.somename.com,* the mail was sent from *me@mail.somename.com,* and the subject of the mail message is *"working?"*

Once %headers has been defined, it is passed to open:

```
$mailprog->open(\%headers);
```

You then send the body of the message to the mail program:

```
print $mailprog "This is the message body.\n";
```

Now, close the program when the message is finished:

```
$mailprog->close;
```

A practical example of using Mail::Mailer might be a command-line–driven application that works much like the Unix *mail* program, either reading STDIN until EOF or mailing a file specified on the command line.

Mail::Mailer uses the environment variable PERL_MAILERS to augment or modify the built-in mailer selection. PERL_MAILERS is specified in the following format:

```
"type1:mailbinary1;mailbinary2;...:type2:mailbinaryX;...:..."
```

The possible types are listed for the new method below.

The following methods are defined in Mail::Mailer:

___

new

$mailer = new Mail::Mailer [type, command]

Constructor. Creates a new Mailer object representing the message to be sent. If the optional arguments are specified, the value of *command* depends on *type,* which can be one of:

mail

> Use the Unix *mail* program. *command* is the path to *mail.* The module searches for *mailx, Mail,* and *mail,* in that order.

→

```
sendmail
```
Use the *sendmail* program. *command* is the path to *sendmail.*

```
test
```
Used for debugging. Calls */bin/echo* to display the data, but doesn't actually send any mail. *command* is ignored, if specified.

If no arguments are specified, the Mailer object searches for executables in the above order and uses the first one found as the default mailer.

---

close

*$mailer->*close

Closes the mail program.

---

open

*$mailer->*open(\ *%hashref)*

Sends message headers to the mail program. The headers are passed via a reference to a hash, where each key is the name of a header and the value is the contents of the header field. The value can be either a scalar or a reference to an array of scalars.

Better Header Control with Mail::Send

Mail::Send is built on top of Mail::Mailer, which means that you can also choose the mail program that sends the mail. Mail::Send has implemented the methods to, cc, bcc, and subject to replace the %headers hash used in Mail::Mailer.

Mail::Send uses the open method to open the mail program for output; it is built on Mail::Mailer's new method, so that:

```
# Start mailer and output headers
$fh = $msg->open('sendmail');
```

serves the same purpose as:

```
# use sendmail for mailing
$mailer = Mail::Mailer->new('sendmail)';
```

This code tells Mail::Send to use *sendmail* as the mail program.

Mail::Send also provides the set and add functions, which assign a value to a header tag and append a value to a header tag, respectively. The set function takes two arguments—a header tag and a value—and is used like this:

```
$msg->set($scalar, @array);
```

Therefore, to address a message to *you@mail.somename.com*:

```
$msg->set('To', 'you@mail.somename.com');
```

The above sets the To header to *you@mail.somename.com*; however, the following sets the To header to *postmaster@mail.somename.com* and *you@mail.somename.com*, because they represent an array of values.

```
$msg->set('To', ('you@mail.somename.com', 'postmaster@mail.somename.com'));
```

You might think that you could use the set function as follows to add multiple values to a header value:

```
$msg->set('To', 'you@mail.somename.com');
$msg->set('To', 'someone@their.mailaddress.com');
```

However, set doesn't append information from one call to another, and the example above would send the mail only to *someone@their.mailaddress.com*. To append a name to the To header, use the add method. For example:

```
$msg->add('To', 'you@mail.somename.com');
$msg->add('To', 'someone@their.mailaddress.com');
```

The following methods are defined for Mail::Send:

new

$msg = new Mail::Send *[header=>'value'[, . . .]]*

Constructor. Creates a new Mail::Send object that is the mail message you want to send. You can include values for headers when you create the object or later, by calling the appropriate methods.

add

$msg->add(header, values)

Adds a header to the message. *header* is the header to be added, and *values* is a list of values to be appended to that header.

bcc

$msg->bcc(values)

Adds a Bcc header containing the mail addresses specified in the list of *values* to the message. If there already is a Bcc, the new values replace any old values.

cancel

$msg->cancel

Not implemented yet, but will cancel the message.

cc

$msg->cc(values)

Adds a Cc header containing the mail addresses in the list of *values* to the message. If there already is a Cc, the new values replace any old values.

close

*$fh->*close

Closes the filehandle *$fh* (which was returned by open) and sends the message.

delete

$msg->delete*(header)*

Deletes the header *header* from the message.

open

*$fh = $msg->*open

Opens a filehandle for the message object. The filehandle is a Mail::Mailer object.

set

$msg->set(header, values)

Sets the header *header* to the contents of the array *values*.

subject

$msg->subject*('What this message is about')*

Sets the value of the Subject field.

to

$msg->to(values)

Sets the To field to the list of recipients in *values*.

Handle Folders with Mail::Folder

Once you've begun downloading and reading your mail from a POP server, you might want to save or categorize your messages into folders, which allow you to add, delete, save, and move messages easily. You can do this with Mail::Folder, which was written by Kevin Johnson as an object-oriented, folder-independent interface to mail folders. Mail::Folder supports a number of mailbox formats with the following interfaces:

Mail::Folder::Emaul
>A folder interface somewhat similar to MH.

Mail::Folder::Maildir
>An interface to *maildir* folders.

Mail::Folder::Mbox
>Standard Unix mailbox format.

Mail::Folder::NNTP
>The beginnings of an interface to NNTP; not all the methods are implemented yet.

If you are interested in writing a folder interface, see the documentation for the module. The documentation explains the concepts and issues involved, and describes some of the methods you may need to override.

The following methods are defined for Mail::Folder:

---

new

>*$folder* = **new**(*ftype[, foldername][, options]*)

Creates a new Mail::Folder object of the specified type. Arguments are:

ftype
>The type of folder. Possible values are mbox, maildir, emaul, or NNTP.

foldername
>The name of the folder. If present, the open method is called with *foldername* as the argument.

options
>A hash where the following options may be the keys:

>Content-Length
>>Content-length header is created or updated by append_message and update_message.

>Create
>>If set, the folder is created if it doesn't already exist.

>DefaultFolderType
>>Autodetects folder type if create option is set and AUTODETECT has been set.

>DotLock
>>Uses *.lock*-style folder locking with the proper folder interface (currently used only with the mbox interface).

>Flock
>>Uses flock-style folder locking with the proper folder interface (currently used only with the mbox interface).

→

NFSLock

> Deals with NFS-style file locking with the proper folder interface and the NFS server in question.

notMUA

> If set, makes updates but doesn't save message labels or the current message indicator. If not set (the default), saves labels and the current message indicator as appropriate for the folder interface.

Timeout

> Overrides the default timeout value. Specified in seconds. Particularly useful for folder interfaces that involve network communications.

add_label

> *$folder*->add_label(*msg_num, label*)

Associates the label *label* with the message *msg_num*. Returns 1 on success or 0 if the label has a length of 0. Possible values of *label* are:

deleted

> Used by delete_message and sync to process message deletion.

edited

> Added by update_message to indicate that the message has been edited.

filed, forwarded, printed, replied

> Not acted on.

seen

> Message has been viewed by the user. Set by get_message for any message it has retrieved.

append_message

> *$folder*->append_message(\ *$mi_ref*)

Adds message to a folder. Argument is a reference to a Mail::Internet object.

clear_label

> *$folder*->clear_label(*label*)

Deletes the association with *label* for all messages in the folder. Returns the number of messages for which there was an association.

close

> *$folder*->close

Does any necessary housekeeping and closes the folder.

current_message

*$folder->*current_message*([msg_num])*

With no argument, returns the message number of the current message in the folder. With an argument, sets the current message number for the folder to *msg_num*.

debug

*$folder->*debug*([value])*

Sets the level of debugging information for the object to *value*. With no argument, returns the current debugging level.

debug_print

*$folder->*debug_print*(text)*

Prints *text*, plus some additional information, to STDERR.

delete_label

*$folder->*delete_label*(msg_num, label)*

Deletes the association of *label* with *msg_num*. Returns 1 on success and 0 if there was no association.

delete_message

*$folder->*delete_message*(msgs)*

Takes a list of messages, *msgs*, to be marked for deletion. The messages aren't actually deleted until sync is called.

dup

*$folder->*dup*(msg_num, \$folder_ref)*

Copies the message specified by *msg_num* to the folder referenced by \$folder_ref. Like refile, but doesn't delete the original message. Generates a fatal error if no folder is currently open or if the folder doesn't contain message *msg_num*.

first_labeled_message

*$folder->*first_labeled_message*(label)*

Returns the message number of the first message in the folder that has *label* associated with it, or 0 if there are none.

first_message

*$folder->*first_message

Returns the message number of the first message in the folder.

foldername

*$folder->*foldername

Returns the name of the folder that the object has opened.

get_fields

*$folder->*get_fields*(msg_num, fields)*

Retrieves the fields specified in the list *fields* for message *msg_num*. If called in list context, returns a list; in scalar context, returns a reference to a list of the fields. Returns the fields in the same order as they were specified.

get_header

*$folder->*get_header*(msg_num)*

Extracts a message header; takes one argument—the message number. Returns a reference to a Mail::Header object.

get_message

*$folder->*get_message*(msg_num)*

Takes a message number as argument and returns a Mail::Internet object reference to that message, or 0 on failure.

get_message_file

*$folder->*get_message_file*(msg_num)*

Like `get_message`, but returns a filename instead of a Mail::Internet object reference.

get_mime_header

*$folder->*get_mime_header*(msg_num)*

This method works much like `get_header`, but returns a reference to a MIME::Head object instead. Takes one argument, the message number.

get_mime_message

*$folder->***get_mime_message** *(msg_num[, parserobject][, options])*

Returns a MIME::Entity object for the specified message. Calls
get_message_file to get a message to parse, creates a MIME::Parser object,
and uses that to create the MIME::Entity object. The arguments are:

msg_num
> The number of the message.

parserobject
> If specified, used instead of internally creating a parser object.

options
> Map onto the equivalent MIME::Parser methods. Specified as key/value
> pairs, with possible values of: output_dir, output_prefix, out-
> put_to_core. See the MIME::Parser documentation for details.

get_option

*$folder->***get_option***(option)*

Returns the setting for the specified option, or undef if the option doesn't
exist.

inverse_select

*$folder->***inverse_select***(\ $func_ref)*

Returns a list, in no specific order, of message numbers that do not match a
set of criteria. The argument, *\ $func_ref*, is a reference to a function used to
determine the criteria. The function is passed a reference to a Mail::Internet
object containing only a header.

is_readonly

*$folder->***is_readonly**

Returns 1 if the folder has the readonly attribute set, otherwise returns 0.

label_exists

*$folder->***label_exists***(msg_num, label)*

Returns 1 if *label* is associated with message *msg_num*, otherwise returns 0.

last_labeled_message

$folder->last_labeled_message*(label)*

Returns the message number of the last message in the folder with the label *label* associated with it, or 0 if there is no such message number.

last_message

$folder->last_message

Returns the message number of the last message in the folder.

list_all_labels

$folder->list_all_labels

Returns a list, in no specific order, of all labels associated with messages in the folder. If called in scalar context, returns the number of labels associated with the messages.

list_labels

$folder->list_labels*(msg_num)*

Returns a list, in no specific order, of all labels associated with *msg_num*. If called in scalar context, returns the number of labels associated with the message.

message_exists

$folder->message_exists*(msg_num)*

Returns 1 if a message with the number *msg_num* exists in the folder, otherwise returns 0.

message_list

$folder->message_list

Returns a list of the message numbers in the folder, in no specific order. The syntax is:

```
print $folder->message_list."\n"
```

next_labeled_message

$folder->next_labeled_message*(msg_num, label)*

Returns the message number of the next message in the folder relative to *msg_number* that has the label *label* associated with it, or 0 if there is no such message.

next_message

*$folder->*next_message*([msg_num])*

Returns the number of the next message in the folder relative to *msg_num* if it is specified, otherwise relative to the current message. Returns 0 if at end of folder.

open

*$folder->*open*(foldername)*

If you didn't specify a folder name in the constructor, you need to call the open method, which takes the folder name as an argument and opens the folder. Also sets readonly if the folder is determined to be read-only.

pack

*$folder->*pack

For formats that allow message number sequences to have gaps, renames the files in the folders to eliminate any such gaps. May result in some messages being renumbered.

prev_labeled_message

*$folder->*prev_labeled_message*(msg_num, label)*

Returns the message number of the previous message in the folder relative to *msg_num* that has the label *label* associated with it, or 0 if there is no such message.

prev_message

*$folder->*prev_message*([msg_num])*

Returns the number of the previous message in the folder relative to *msg_num* if it is specified, otherwise relative to the current message. Returns 0 if at the beginning of the folder.

qty

*$folder->*qty

Returns the number of messages in the folder. The syntax is:

```
print "There are ".$folder->qty." messages in your folder\n";
```

refile

$folder->**refile**(*msg_num, \$fldr_ref*)

Moves messages between folders. Takes a message number and folder reference as arguments.

select

$folder*->**select**(\ *$func_ref)

Returns a list of messages that meet a set of criteria. The argument, \ *$func_ref*, is a reference to a function used to determine the criteria. The function is passed a reference to a Mail::Internet object containing only a header. The list is returned in no specific order.

select_label

$folder->**select_label**(*label*)

Returns a list of messages with the label *label*. If called in scalar context, returns the number of messages that have the label.

set_option

$folder->**set_option**(*option, value*)

Sets the specified option to *value*.

set_readonly

$folder->**set_readonly**

Sets the `readonly` attribute for the folder. Once `readonly` has been set, `sync` won't perform any updates to the actual folder.

sort

$folder*->**sort**(\ *$func_ref)

Returns a sorted list of messages. \ *$func_ref* is a reference to a function that is passed two Mail::Header message references and returns an integer less than, equal to, or greater than 0 to indicate the sort order.

sync

$folder->**sync**

Synchronizes the folder with internal data structures and reads in any new messages since the last `open` or `sync`. Does not perform any updates if the `readonly` attribute has been set.

undelete_message

$folder->undelete_message(msgs)

Unmarks a list of messages, *msgs*, that have been marked for deletion.

update_message

$folder->update_message(msg_num, \$mref)

Replaces the message specified by *msg_num* with the contents of the message given by *\$mref*, which is a reference to a Mail::Internet object.

Handle Messages with Mail::Internet

Mail::Internet implements a number of helpful functions for manipulating a mail message. These include body, print_header, and head. Mail::Internet is built on top of Mail::Header, which parses the header of an email message, and it inherits the Mail::Header constructor style that requires a file descriptor or reference to an array be used. For example:

```
@lines = <STDIN>;
$mi_obj = new Mail::Internet([@lines]);
```

reads a mail message from STDIN (using a reference to an array). The following example reads a mail message from a filehandle, FILE.

```
open(FILE, "/home/nvp/Mail/nvp");
$mi_obj = new Mail::Internet(\*FILE);
close(FILE);
```

The print_header function outputs the header of a message to a file descriptor; the default is STDOUT.

```
open(FILE, "/home/nvp/Mail/nvp");
$mi_obj = new Mail::Internet(\*FILE);
close(FILE);
$mi_obj->print_header(\*STDOUT);
```

The above example might output:

```
From nvp Mon Jun  9 00:11:10 1997
Received: (from nvp@localhost) by mail.somename.com (8.8/8.8) id
    AAA03248 for nvp; Mon, 9 Jun 1997 00:11:09 -0500 (EST)
Date: Mon, 9 Jun 1997 00:11:09 -0500 (EST)
From: "Nathan V. Patwardhan" <nvp>
Message-Id: <199706090511.AAA03248@mail.somename.com>
To: nvp
Subject: pop test
X-Status:
X-Uid: 1
Status: RO
```

where print_body also takes a file descriptor as an argument, but only outputs the body of the message, whereas the print function outputs an entire message.

Network Programming

new

$mail = new Mail::Internet ([arg], [options])

Creates a new Mail::Internet object. *arg* is optional and may be either a file descriptor (a reference to a glob) or a reference to an array. If present, the new object is initialized with headers either from the array or read from the file descriptor. *options* is a list of options in the form of key/value pairs. Possible options are:

Header
> Mail::Internet should not attempt to read a mail header from *arg*, if it was specified. Value is a Mail::Header object.

Body
> Mail::Internet should attempt to read the body from *arg*, if it was specified. Value is a reference to an array that contains the lines of the message body.

Modify
> Reformats the headers if true. Mail::Header option.

MailFrom
> Specifies behavior for headers in the form "From ". Mail::Header option. Possible values are:

> IGNORE
>> Ignores and discards the headers.

> ERROR
>> Calls die.

> COERCE
>> Renames headers to Mail-From.

> KEEP
>> Keeps headers as they are.

FoldLength
> Value is default line length for folding headers. Mail::Header option.

add_signature

$mail->add_signature ([file])

Appends a signature to the message. *file* is a file that contains the signature; if not specified, the file $ENV{HOME}/.signature is checked for a signature.

body

$mail->body ()

Returns the body of the message as a reference to an array. Each entry in the array represents one line of the message.

escape_from

> *$mail->escape_from()*

Inserts a leading > on any line that starts with "From ", to avoid the problems that some applications have if a message contains a line starting with "From ".

head

> *$headobj = $mail->head()*

Returns the Mail::Header object that holds the headers for the current message.

nntppost

> *$mail->nntppost([options])*

Posts an article via NNTP; requires Net::NNTP. Options are passed as key/value pairs. Available options are:

Debug
> Debug value to pass to Net::NNTP.

Host
> Name of NNTP server to connect to.

Port
> Port number to connect to on remote host.

print_header

> *$mail->print_header([*fd])*
> *$mail->print_body([*fd])*
> *$mail->print([*fd])*

Prints the header, body, or whole message to file descriptor *fd, which should be a reference to a glob. If the file descriptor is not given, the output is sent to STDOUT:

```
$mail->print(\*STDOUT);  # Print message to STDOUT
```

remove_sig

> *$mail->remove_sig([nlines])*

Removes a user's signature from the body of a message. Looks for a line equal to "-- " within the last *nlines* lines of the message and removes that line and all lines after it. *nlines* defaults to 10.

reply

$reply = $mail->reply()

Creates a new object with headers initialized for a reply to the current object and with a body that is an indented copy of the current message.

smtpsend

$mail->smtpsend()

Sends the Mail::Internet message via SMTP to all addresses on the To, Cc, and Bcc lines. Finds the SMTP host by trying to connect first to hosts specified in $ENV{SMTPHOSTS}, then to mailhost, and then to localhost.

In a future release of Mail::Internet, smtpsend will be able to take the hostname as a parameter, as nntppost does.

tidy_body

$mail->tidy_body()

Removes all leading and trailing lines that contain only whitespace from the message body.

unescape_from

$mail->unescape_from()

Removes the escaping added by escape_from.

Parse Email Addresses with Mail::Address

Mail::Address parses RFC 822-compliant mail addresses of the form:

```
"Full Name or Phrase" <username@host> (Comment Area)
```

For example, under RFC 822, an address might be represented as:

```
"Nathan V. Patwardhan" <nvp@mail.somename.com> (No Comment)
```

or:

```
"Nathan V. Patwardhan" <nvp@mail.somename.com>
```

The Mail::Address constructor parses an email address into three parts based on the categories shown above:

```
$addr = Mail::Address->new("Full Name or Phrase",
                           "username@host",
                           "(Comment Area)");
```

Mail::Address also outputs portions of the mail address with the functions phrase, address, comment, format, name, host, and user. The phrase, address, and comment functions represent the first, second, and third entities that were passed to the Mail::Address constructor, where the `phrase` function:

```
print $addr->phrase();
```

outputs:

```
Nathan V. Patwardhan
```

The `address` function:

```
print $addr->address();
```

outputs:

```
nvp@mail.somename.com
```

And the `comment` function:

```
print $addr->comment();
```

outputs:

```
No Comment
```

A real mail address can be "unmangled," or parsed from its *user@somehost.com* format, with the `user` and `host` functions. The `user` function removes everything starting with the @ to the end of the address, and `host` removes everything up to and including the @. Using the previous example of *nvp@mail.somename.com*, the following line:

```
print $addr->user;
```

outputs:

```
nvp
```

And the following line using the `host` function:

```
print $addr->host;
```

outputs:

```
nvp@mail.somename.com
```

Mail::Address Reference

new

> *$addr* = **Mail::Address->new***(phrase, address[, comment])*

Constructor. Creates new Mail::Address object representing an address with the specified elements. In a message, these three elements show up as:

```
phrase <address> (comment)
address (comment)
```

parse

Mail::Address->parse(*line*)

Constructor. Parses the specified line, usually a To, Cc, or Bcc line, and returns a list of extracted Mail::Address objects.

address

$addr->**address**()

Returns the address part of the object.

canon

$addr->**canon**()

Unimplemented, but should return the UUCP canon for the message.

comment

$addr->**comment**()

Returns the comment part of the object.

format

$addr->**format**()

Returns a string representing the address in a form suitable for the To, Cc, or Bcc line of a message

host

$addr->**host**()

Returns the host portion of the address.

name

$addr->**name**()

Takes information contained in the object and uses various heuristics to try to identify the name of the person or group.

path

$addr->**path**()

Unimplemented, but should return the UUCP path for the message.

phrase

> *$addr->*phrase*()*

Returns the phrase part of the object.

user

> *$addr->*user*()*

Returns the user id portion of the address.

Reading Email with Mail::POP3Client

Many networks have machines dedicated to sending and receiving email. Since users might hold accounts on *foo.bar.com*, while mail is sent to *pop-server.bar.com*, there must be a means to transfer the mail from the "post office" machine to the host on which the user works. The Post Office Protocol, or POP, negotiates this mail transfer.

When a user wants to retrieve his or her mail, the user's mail client connects to the POP server and authenticates the user with a login name and password, as we described earlier. Once authenticated, the user can list, read, and delete messages from the POP server.

The Mail::POP3Client module simplifies the process of "talking POP" by implementing a number of functions to login, parse, and read mail messages held on the POP server. Information that the POP server needs, such as the user's login name and password, and possibly some optional information (the name of the POP host, the port, and a debugging flag) are passed to the constructor when a new POP3Client object is created. For example:

```
use Mail::POP3Client;

$pop = Mail::POP3Client->new("login",      # required
                     "password",  #required
                     "pophost.your.domain", # not required
                     port,        # default is 110
                     debug_flag); # any positive integer
```

POP3Client provides functions to perform the following:

Counting messages

The Count function returns the number of messages in the mailbox. Once they have been authenticated, users can list the headers of the messages in their mailbox using the Head function in conjunction with the Count function, as shown in the following example:

```
use strict;
use Mail::POP3Client;
```

```
my($pop, $num_mesg, $i);
$pop = Mail::POP3Client->new("nvp",
                            "xxxxxx");

$num_mesg = $pop->Count;              # How many messages are there?
print("You have ".$num_mesg." new message(s).\n");

for ($i = 1; $i <= $num_mesg; $i++) {
    print $pop->Head($i), "\n";    #print header for each message
}
```

You can also use a regular expression to parse the headers and display certain information, such as the sender and subject of each mail message:

```
my($pop, $num_mesg, $i);

$pop = Mail::POP3Client->new("nvp",
                            "xxxxxx");

for ($i = 1; $i <= $pop->Count; $i++) {
    foreach ($pop->Head($i)) {
                # output from and subject
        print $_." " if /^(From|Subject)/;
    }
      print "\n";
}
```

Getting and setting the host and port

The Host method returns or sets the current POP host. For example:

```
$obj->Host;
```

returns the current POP host. To set the new POP host to *new-pop.bar.com*, you could do this:

```
$new_host = 'new-pop.bar.com';
$obj->Host($new_host);
```

The Port method works like Host, returning or setting the current port that the POP server is bound to:

```
$obj->Port;              #return the current port for the POP server

$new_port = 7000;        #set the port to 7000
$obj->Port($new_port);
```

Retrieving the message body

Naturally, you'll want to read more than the headers of your mail messages, so you'll want to use the Body, HeadAndBody, and Retrieve methods. Body outputs the body of the message, while HeadAndBody and Retrieve are synonyms that output both the head and the body of the message.

Deleting and undeleting messages

Messages can be deleted from the POP mailbox with the `Delete` method. `Delete` marks messages on the server for deletion; they aren't permanently removed until a QUIT command is received. `Delete` takes one argument—the number of the message to delete:

```
$pop->Delete(1);        #delete the first message
```

Like most mail programs, Mail::POP3Client can undelete messages that have been marked for deletion. Use the `Reset` method to do this:

```
$pop->Reset(1);         #undelete the first message
```

Checking the connection

Most programs that require a user to log in will time out after a certain period of time for security and resource reasons. The `Alive` method checks to see if the connection to the POP server is still open; it returns true if the connection is good, and false otherwise.

Explicitly opening and closing connections

POP connections can be explicitly opened and closed with `Login` and `Close`. `Close` takes no arguments and closes the connection to the POP server.

Mail::POP3Client Methods

The following methods are defined by Mail::POP3Client:

---

new

> *$pop* = new Mail::POP3Client*("user", "pwd"[, "host"[, port[, debug]]])*

Constructor. Creates a new POP3 connection. The arguments are:

user
> The username.

pwd
> The password.

host
> Optional. The POP3 host; defaults to pop.

port
> Optional. The POP3 port number; defaults to 110.

debug
> Enables debugging (to STDERR) on the object if set to a positive integer. Defaults to 0.

Alive

> $pop->**Alive**()

Tests to see if the connection is alive and returns true or false.

Body

> $pop->**Body**(*msgnum*)

Gets the body of the specified message.

Close

> $pop->**Close**()

Closes the connection gracefully, performing any pending deletes on the server.

Connect

> $pop->**Connect**(*[host, port]*)

Starts the connection to the POP3 server. Optionally takes the POP3 host and port number as arguments.

Count

> $pop->**Count**(*[num]*)

With an argument, sets the number of remote messages to *num*. Otherwise returns the number of messages. Set during Login.

Delete

> $pop->**Delete**(*msgnum*)

Marks the specified message number for deletion. The message isn't actually deleted until you QUIT (i.e., when you Close the connection); before then, it can be "undeleted" with Reset.

Head

> $pop->**Head**(*msgnum*)

Gets the headers of the specified message.

HeadAndBody

> $pop->**HeadAndBody**(*msgnum*)

Gets both headers and body of the specified message.

Host

$pop->Host(["host"])

With an argument, sets the current host. Otherwise, returns the host.

Last

$pop->Last()

Returns the number of the message last retrieved from the server.

List

$pop->List()

Returns a list containing the size of each message.

Login

$pop->Login()

Attempts to log in to the server connection.

Message

$pop->Message()

Returns the last status message received from the server.

Pass

$pop->Pass(["pass"])

With an argument, sets the current password. Otherwise, returns the current password.

POPStat

$pop->POPStat()

Returns the results of a POP3 STAT command and sets the size of the mailbox.

Port

$pop->Port([port])

With an argument, sets the current port number. Otherwise, returns the port number.

Reset

*$pop->*__Reset__*()*

Tells the server to unmark any message marked for deletion.

Retrieve

*$pop->*__Retrieve__*(msgnum)*

Same as HeadAndBody.

Size

*$pop->*__Size__*([num])*

With an argument, sets the size of the remote mailbox to *num*. Otherwise returns the size of the mailbox. Set by POPStat.

Socket

*$pop->*__Socket__*()*

Returns the socket's file descriptor.

State

*$pop->*__State__*()*

Returns the internal state of the connection. Possible return values are DEAD, AUTHORIZATION, or TRANSACTION.

User

*$pop->*__User__*(["user"])*

With an argument, sets the current username. Otherwise, returns the current name.

CHAPTER 15

Usenet News

Usenet is a collection of bulletin-board–like newsgroups on the Internet, covering thousands of topics. Whatever your interest, chances are you'll find a newsgroup in which it is discussed.

Usenet has been around since late 1979. The current implementation is based on the Network News Transfer Protocol (NNTP), defined in RFC 977 and released in March 1986. Information is propagated through Usenet by a system of newsfeeds in which one site requests a newsfeed from another site, and a third site requests a newsfeed from the second site, etc. There is no central Usenet authority—like Perl, it runs on the spirit of cooperation and sharing. When you run a news reader, such as *tin* or the news reader in a web browser, your client software talks to the NNTP server on the news host. When you post a message to a newsgroup, this posting is received by your NNTP server and passed on to other servers throughout the distribution area you specified for the posting. Each server periodically receives updated newsgroup information and newly posted news articles.

This chapter explores NNTP commands and responses. It introduces Net::NNTP, which implements NNTP commands and simplifies the process of writing a Perl-based NNTP news client. It also describes News::Newsrc, a module that provides methods for managing a *.newsrc* file.

There are two kinds of NNTP commands—the official set of commands as defined in RFC 977 and a number of extensions that have been added since the RFC was written. The extensions are described in an IETF Internet Draft document, "Common NNTP Extensions" by Stan Barber, which can be found at *ftp://ftp.academ.com/pub/nntp/ietf/nntpext.txt*.

The NNTP Protocol

Before you write your own news client, you should have some idea of how the NNTP protocol works. Like other servers, an NNTP server is bound to a port (usually port 119). It listens for incoming connections, takes the appropriate action, and returns a response to the client. When a news client connects with an NNTP server, or to the port on which the NNTP server is running, a message like the following is produced:

```
Trying 0.0.0.0...
Connected to hostname.mydomain.com.
Escape character is '^]'.
200 newshost.mydomain.com InterNetNews NNRP server INN 1.5.1 17-Dec-1996 ready
(posting ok).
```

Many NNTP servers understand the *help* (or *HELP*) command. When a client issues a *help* command, many NNTP servers respond with a list of all available commands. For example:

```
200 news.mydomain.com InterNetNews NNRP server INN 1.5.1 17-Dec-1996 ready
(posting ok).
HELP
100 Legal commands
  authinfo user Name|pass Password|generic <prog> <args>
  article [MessageID|Number]
  body [MessageID|Number]
  date
  group newsgroup
  head [MessageID|Number]
  help
  ihave
  last
  list [active|active.times|newsgroups|distributions|distrib.pats|overview.fmt
|subscriptions]
  listgroup newsgroup
  mode reader
  newgroups yymmdd hhmmss ["GMT"] [<distributions>]
  newnews newsgroups yymmdd hhmmss ["GMT"] [<distributions>]
  next
  post
  slave
  stat [MessageID|Number]
  xgtitle [group_pattern]
  xhdr header [range|MessageID]
  xover [range]
  xpat header range|MessageID pat [morepat...]
  xpath MessageID
Report problems to <usenet@news.mydomain.com>
```

After connecting to the NNTP server, you can get a list of available newsgroups with the *list active* command, and you can then select a newsgroup. If you were to connect directly to *news.mydomain.com* and use the *group* command to select the newsgroup *local.test*, your session might look like this:

```
200 news.mydomain.com InterNetNews NNRP server INN 1.5.1 17-Dec-1996 ready
(posting ok).
group local.test
211 4 1 4 local.test
```

```
QUIT
205 .
```

The four numbers (in this example, 211 4 1 4) preceding the group name (*local.test*) represent the success code, total number of articles, and the first and last article numbers, respectively. So in this example, 211 is the success code. There are four articles in the *local.test* group, starting with article number 1 and ending with number 4.

Every article in a newsgroup has two identifiers associated with it. The first is the message number and the second is a message ID. The message number is the number of that article on the server to which you are connecting. The message ID is an identifier that is always associated with the article on every server that receives the article. An article that has the message number 4 on your server might be number 83 on someone else's server. The message ID, however, will be the same on both. So, for example, if you want to post an article that refers to another article, use the message ID.

Once the *group* command has successfully identified a newsgroup, the client can request a particular article by sending an *article* request to the server. The *article* command takes either a message ID or a message number as an argument. For example:

```
article 4
Path: newshost.mydomain.com!news-w.ans.net!newsfeeds.ans.net!philabs ...
From: user@mydomain.com (User Name)
Newsgroups: local.test
Subject: Is anybody there?
Date: 21 Apr 1997
```

If the *article* command is successful, the server returns the selected message.

The *xhdr* command returns the selected headers ("X-headers") from articles in a certain newsgroup. The X-headers contain all the information about the news article, including the poster's email address, the subject of the message, the date and time the message was posted, the newsgroup(s) the message appears in, and the message ID. For example, if you want to see the subjects of the articles in the *local.test* newsgroup, you can run xhdr subject 1-4, as follows:

```
xhdr subject 1-4
221 subject fields follow
1   Is anybody there?
2   Re: Is anybody there?
3   Re: Is anybody there?
4   Get a life!
```

The 221 status code indicates that the *xhdr* completed successfully and returned the requested headers. A Usenet client might display these headers to the user, who can then select the articles to read based on the subject lines.

A command similar to *xhdr* is *xpat*, which matches X-headers against a pattern string you give it. For example, executing xpat subject 1-9 *anybody* for *local.test* might look like this:

```
xpat subject 1-9 *anybody*
221 subject matches follow.
```

```
1   Is anybody there?
2   Re: Is anybody there?
3   Re: Is anybody there?
```

You can also post news articles with NNTP. When you issue the *post* command, the server returns a code of 340 if posting is permitted. If you get an error, like 501, you cannot post articles with this command. Most servers require that you include Newsgroups, Subject, and From headers. You will receive a 240 reply if your message has been successfully posted. Here's an example of posting to *local.test* using NNTP:

```
200 news.mydomain.com InterNetNews NNRP server INN 1.5.1 17-Dec-1996 ready
(posting ok).
post
340 Ok
Newsgroups: local.test
Subject: talking NNTP
From: user@mydomain.com

This is a test posting.
240 Article posted
QUIT
205 .
```

The server returns a code of 205 upon disconnecting. When the article arrives in *local.test*, it looks like this:

```
From news.mydomain.com!not-for-mail Sun Mar  9 19:18:37 1997
Path: news.mydomain.com!not-for-mail
From: user@mydomain.com
Newsgroups: local.test
Subject: talking NNTP
Date: 10 Mar 1997 00:09:33 GMT
Organization: Perl in a Nutshell
Lines: 2
Distribution: local
Message-ID: <5fvjft$k3$2@news.mydomain.com>
NNTP-Posting-Host: newshost.mydomain.com
Xref: newshost.mydomain.com local.test:6

This is a test posting.
```

Net::NNTP

Net::NNTP is one of the *libnet* modules. It provides methods for programming a news client to interface with an NNTP server. Net::NNTP implements the NNTP protocol as defined in RFC 977, as well as a number of extensions defined in the IETF Internet Draft document mentioned earlier.

For example, the following code:

```
$nntp->post(@message);
```

is equivalent to issuing the *post* command and associated X-headers directly to an NNTP server on port 119.

Initializing the NNTP Client

To use Net::NNTP, create a new Net::NNTP object:

```
use Net::NNTP;

$nntp = Net::NNTP->new;   # Use default port and options
```

Once you've created the object, you can use any of the Net::NNTP methods on that object. The Net::NNTP methods generally parallel the functionality of the raw NNTP commands. Your news client can be written to perform many functions, including:

- Authenticating a user to the server

- Listing available newsgroups

- Retrieving news headers and articles

- Extracting headers

- Checking for new articles

- Posting articles

- Listing information such as active messages in a newsgroup, new newsgroups, valid distribution areas, or message IDs of newly arrived messages

Net::NNTP Reference

Net::NNTP includes methods that implement many of the extensions to RFC 977; the description indicates if a method is an extension. Extensions that are not supported by Net::NNTP are AUTHINFO GENERIC, XINDEX, XSEARCH, and XTHREAD. In addition, some extensions supported by Net::NNTP may not be supported by a particular server.

Unless otherwise stated, all the methods return either true or false to indicate success or failure. If a method returns a value instead, then it returns undef or an empty list to indicate failure.

In this list, *message-spec* refers to a single message ID, a single message number, or a reference to a list of two message numbers. It can also be passed as a list of two message numbers, but this is for compatibility only and is now deprecated.

Where pattern-matching is indicated, the matching is done according to the NNTP specification. See the Net::NNTP documentation for details.

Network
Programming

---

new

> *$nntp* = **Net::NNTP->new** *([host[, options]])*

Constructor. Creates a new Net::NNTP object. Arguments are:

host
> The name of the remote host to which an NNTP connection is required. If not specified, the constructor checks the environment variables

$\rightarrow$

NNTPSERVER and NEWSHOST, in that order, then Net::Config. Defaults to news if nothing is found.

options

Options, passed as key/value pairs. Possible options are:

Timeout

Maximum time, in seconds, to wait for a response from the NNTP server. Default is 120 seconds. A value of 0 causes all I/O operations to block.

Debug

Enables printing of debugging information to STDERR.

active

*$nntp->***active***([pattern])*

Similar to list, but only returns active groups that match the pattern. (An extension.)

active_times

*$nntp->***active_times***()*

Returns a reference to a hash where the keys are the group names and the values are references to arrays containing the time the group was created and an identifier, possibly an email address, for the creator. (An extension.)

article

*$nntp->***article***([msgid | msgnum])*

Retrieves the header, a blank line, then the body (text) of the article, specified as either a message ID or a message number. With no arguments, returns the current article in the current newsgroup as a reference to an array containing the article.

authinfo

*$nntp->***authinfo***(user, pass)*

Authenticates the user to the server, passing the user's username and password.

body

*$nntp->***body***([msgid | msgnum])*

Retrieves the body (text) of the article specified by either a message id or a message number. Takes the same arguments as article. Returns a reference to an array containing the body of the article.

date

$nntp->date*()*

Returns the date on the remote server, in Unix time format (seconds since 1970).

distributions

$nntp->distributions*()*

Returns a reference to a hash where the keys are the valid distribution names and the values are the distribution descriptions. (An extension.)

group

$nntp->group*([group])*

Sets and/or gets the current group. With no argument, returns information about the current group, otherwise sets the current group to *group*.

In a scalar context, group returns the group name. In an array context, it returns a list containing the number of articles in the group, the first article number, the last article number, and the group name.

head

$nntp->head*([msgid | msgnum])*

Retrieves the header of the article specified by *msgid* or *msgnum*. Takes the same arguments as article and returns a reference to an array containing the article's header.

ihave

$nntp->ihave*(msgid[, message])*

Informs the server that the client has an article whose ID is *msgid*. The optional argument *message* can be either an array of lines or a reference to an array. If *message* is specified, and the server wants a copy, it is sent, returning true on successful completion.

If *message* is not specified, then the message must be sent using the Net::Cmd datasend and dataend methods.

last

$nntp->last*()*

Sets the current article pointer to the previous article in the current newsgroup. Returns the article's message ID.

list

$nntp$->list()

Returns information about all active newsgroups. The result is a reference to a hash where the key is a newsgroup name and each value is a reference to an array. The elements in the array are the first article number in the group, the last article number in the group, and any information flags.

listgroup

$nntp$->listgroup([group])

Returns a reference to a list of all active messages in newsgroup *group*, or the current newsgroup if *group* is not specified. (An extension.)

newgroups

$nntp$->newgroups(since[, distributions])

Like list, but returns groups created after a certain time and optionally in one of a set of distribution areas. Arguments are:

since
> Time value; only groups created after this time should be returned.

distributions
> Optional distribution pattern or reference to a list of distribution patterns. If present, only groups matching a specified distribution area should be returned.

newnews

$nntp$->newnews(since[, groups[, distributions]])

Returns a reference to a list containing the message-ids of all news posted after *since*, that are in newsgroups matching *groups*, with a distribution that matches *distributions*. Arguments are:

since
> Time value; only groups created after this time should be returned.

groups
> Optional group pattern or reference to a list of group patterns indicating which groups should be checked for new messages.

distributions
> Optional distribution pattern or reference to a list of distribution patterns. If present, only groups matching a specified distribution area should be returned.

newsgroups

*$nntp->*newsgroups*([pattern])*

Returns a reference to a hash where the keys are all newsgroup names that match *pattern*, or all newsgroups if no pattern is specified, and each value contains the description text for the group. (An extension.)

next

*$nntp->*next*()*

Sets the current article pointer to the next article in the current newsgroup. Returns the message ID of the article.

nntpstat

*$nntp->*nntpstat*([msgid | msgnum])*

Similar to article, except that no text is returned. When selecting by message number within a newsgroup, sets the current article pointer without sending text. Selecting by message ID is valid, but doesn't alter the current article pointer and therefore is of little use. Returns the message ID of the current article.

overview_fmt

*$nntp->*overview_fmt*()*

Returns a reference to an array containing the names of the fields returned by xover. (An extension.)

post

*$nntp->*post*([message])*

Posts a new article to the news server. If *message* is specified and posting is allowed, then the message is sent. If *message* is not specified, the message must be sent using the Net::Cmd datasend and dataend methods. *message* can be either an array of lines or a reference to an array.

postok

*$nntp->*postok*()*

Returns true if the server's initial response indicated that it allows posting.

quit

*$nntp->*quit*()*

Quits the remote server and closes the socket connection.

Network Programming

reader

$nntp->reader()

Tells the server that you are a reader and not another server; required by some servers. (An extension.)

slave

$nntp->slave()

Tells the remote server that this is not a user client, but is probably another news server.

subscriptions

$nntp->subscriptions()

Returns a reference to a default list of newsgroups recommended for new users to subscribe to. (An extension.)

xgtitle

$nntp->xgtitle(pattern)

Returns a reference to a hash where the keys are all the newsgroup names that match *pattern*, and each value is the text of the newsgroup's description. (An extension.)

xhdr

$nntp->xhdr(header, message-spec)

Gets the header field *header* for all the messages specified in *message-spec*. Returns a reference to a hash where the keys are the message numbers and each value contains the text of the requested header for that message. (An extension.)

xover

$nntp->xover(message-spec)

Returns a reference to a hash where the keys are the message numbers and each value contains a reference to an array of the overview fields for that message. (An extension.)

The names of the fields can be obtained by calling `overview_fmt`.

xpat

$nntp->**xpat***(header, pattern, message-spec)*

Like `xhdr`, but returns only headers where the text of the header matches *pattern*. (An extension.)

xpath

$nntp->**xpath***(message-id)*

Returns the path to the file on the server that contains the specified message. (An extension.)

xrover

$nntp->**xrover***(message-spec)*

Returns reference information for the article(s) specified. Returns a reference to a hash where the keys are the message numbers and the values are the `References:` lines from the articles. (An extension.)

The News::Newsrc Module

Most Unix-based newsreaders parse and extract your newsgroup information from a *.newsrc* file. This file contains an entry for each newsgroup, with the name of the group and a comma-separated list of article numbers from 1 to the current article. The first entry in the list shows articles that have been read; the remaining entries list unread articles. Each entry also has a colon (`:`) following the name if you are subscribed to that newsgroup or an exclamation point (`!`) if you are currently unsubscribed.

In order for you to read a newsgroup, your newsreader needs to be connected to an NNTP server. The newsreader then checks the *.newsrc* entry for that newsgroup to determine which articles you haven't yet read, and displays the first unread article. You can then read the articles sequentially or select which articles you want to read. When you "catch-up" a newsgroup by marking all the articles as "read," or when you exit from the newsreader program, your *.newsrc* file is updated to reflect your activity during that session.

The News::Newsrc module provides methods for managing your *.newsrc* file. Some of the functions it provides include letting you add, remove, or reorder newsgroups; subscribe to or unsubscribe from newsgroups; and mark articles as read or unmark them. Unless you tell it to rearrange the order of the newsgroups in *.newsrc*, News::Newsrc leaves the order unchanged.

Network Programming

new

$newsrc = **new** *News::Newsrc*

Constructor. Creates a new News::Newsrc object that contains no newsgroups.

add_group

$newsrc->**add_group***(groupname[, options])*

Adds newsgroup to *.newsrc*, as a subscribed group. Defaults to adding at the end. The arguments are:

groupname
Name of the newsgroup to add.

options
Hash with one entry, indicating where to put the newsgroup. Key is where, and possible values are:

after => *group*
Put immediately after newsgroup *group*, or last if *group* is not there.

alpha
Put in alphabetical order.

before => *group*
Put immediately before newsgroup *group*.

first
Put as first newsgroup.

last
Put as last newsgroup.

number => *n*
Put at position *n*, where the first position is 0. If position is negative, count from the end of the list backwards *n* positions.

del_group

$newsrc->**del_group***(groupname)*

Removes specified newsgroup *groupname* from *.newsrc*.

exists

$newsrc->**exists***(groupname)*

Returns true if newsgroup *groupname* is in *.newsrc*.

groups

*$newsrc->***groups***()*

Returns list of newsgroups in *.newsrc*. In scalar context, returns an array reference.

load

*$newsrc->***load***([filename])*

Loads newsgroups in *filename* into *$newsrc*, replacing any newsgroups that are already there. Defaults to *$HOME/.newsrc*.

mark

*$newsrc->***mark***(groupname, article_number[, options])*

Adds an article to the list for a specified newsgroup. Arguments are:

groupname
    Newsgroup to add an article to.

article_number
    Article number of the article to add.

options
    Hash. See description under `add_group`.

marked

*$newsrc->***marked***(groupname, article_number)*

Returns true if the newsgroup exists and contains the specified article. Arguments are:

groupname
    Group to report on.

article_number
    Number of the article to verify.

marked_articles

*$newsrc->***marked_articles***(groupname)*

Returns the list of articles in group *groupname*. In scalar context, returns an array reference.

mark_list

*$newsrc->**mark_list**(groupname, \@article_list[, options])*

Adds articles to the list for a specified group. Arguments are:

groupname
> Group to add articles to.

\@article_list
> Reference to list of articles to add.

options
> Hash. See description under add_group.

mark_range

*$newsrc->**mark_range**(groupname, n, m[, options])*

Adds articles in the specified range to the list. Arguments are:

groupname
> Newsgroup to add articles to.

n   Number of the first article in the range.

m   Number of the last article in the range.

options
> Hash. See description under add_group.

save

*$newsrc->**save**()*

Saves changes to *.newsrc* file.

save_as

*$newsrc->**save_as**(filename)*

Saves changes to specified file *filename*, rather than to *.newsrc* file.

sub_groups

*$newsrc->**sub_groups**()*

Returns list of subscribed groups in *.newsrc*.

subscribe

*$newsrc->**subscribe**(groupname)*

Subscribes to newsgroup *groupname*. If the group is not in *.newsrc*, it is added; its location may be given in *options*, as specified for add_group.

subscribed

*$newsrc->***subscribed***(groupname)*

Returns true if the group *groupname* exists and is subscribed to.

unmark

*$newsrc->***unmark***(groupname, article_number[, options])*

Removes specified article from the group list. Arguments are:

groupname
 Newsgroup to remove articles from.

article_number
 Article to remove.

options
 Hash. See description under add_group.

unmarked_articles

*$newsrc->***unmarked_articles***(groupname, n, m[, options])*

Returns the list of articles from *n* to *m*, inclusive, that are not in the article list for the newsgroup. Arguments are:

groupname
 Group to return articles from.

n Number of the first article in the range.

m Number of the last article in the range.

options
 Hash. See description under add_group.

unmark_list

*$newsrc->***unmark_list***(groupname, \@article_list[, options)*

Removes specified list of articles from the group list. Arguments are:

groupname
 Group to remove articles from.

\@article_list
 Reference to list of articles to remove.

options
 Hash. See description under add_group.

Network
Programming

unmark_range

*$newsrc->*__unmark_range__*(groupname, n, m[, options])*

Removes a range of articles from *n* to *m* from *.newsrc*. Arguments are:

groupname
> Group to remove articles from.

n   Number of the first article in the range.

m   Number of the last article in the range.

options
> Hash. See description under `add_group`.

unsub_groups

*$newsrc->*__unsub_groups__*()*

Returns list of unsubscribed groups in *.newsrc*. In scalar context, returns an array reference.

unsubscribe

*$newsrc->*__unsubscribe__*(groupname[, options])*

Unsubscribes from newsgroup in *.newsrc*. If the group is not in *.newsrc*, it is added. Arguments are:

groupname
> Group to unsubscribe from.

options
> Hash. See description under `add_group`.

CHAPTER 16

FTP

The File Transfer Protocol (FTP) is a popular means of transferring files between computers. FTP communication follows the client/server model: the client initiates a conversation by sending commands, and the server responds with messages and status codes, as well as by sending or receiving files. This chapter discusses two FTP-related modules included in the *libnet* distribution: Net::FTP, which provides a number of wrapper functions for implementing the client side of FTP, and Net::Netrc, which provides an interface for getting information from a *.netrc* file.

The FTP protocol permits two-way file transactions, in which files can be sent to or taken from an FTP server. These transactions involve the local filesystem (on the client side) and the remote filesystem (on the server side). When a file is transferred between the local and remote systems, its filename on the destination system is the same as on the source system unless you specify a new filename.

The FTP protocol also lists the types of files that can be transferred. These types define (among many other things) how end-of-line characters are handled for different types of files.

The FTP Protocol

When a server accepts FTP requests, it opens a port (generally port 21) for incoming connections and authenticates clients based on account or anonymous privileges. A user may log in with a legitimate account on that machine, provide her own password, and be given access to any file she normally has access to under the Unix shell. Many servers also allow "anonymous" FTP, in which users log in with the name "anonymous" and use their email address as the password. They are then granted restricted access to a limited portion of the filesystem.

Network Programming

The FTP commands defined in RFC 959 are listed in the following table:

Command	Meaning
ABOR	Abort previous FTP command
ACCT	Specify the user's account
ALLO	Tell server to allocate additional storage for new file
APPE	Tell server to append to an existing file
CDUP	Change to parent directory
CWD	Change directory
DELE	Delete a file
HELP	Get help
LIST	List files for display
MKD	Make a directory
MODE	Specify the data transfer mode
NLST	List files for additional processing
NOOP	No-op
PASS	Specify the user's password
PASV	Tell server to go into "passive" mode
PORT	Specify data port for connection
PWD	Print working directory
QUIT	Close connection
REIN	Reinitialize connection
REST	Restart a file transfer
RETR	Retrieve a file
RMD	Remove a directory
RNFR	Specify pathname of file to be renamed
RNTO	Specify new name of file being renamed
SITE	Provide additional site-specific services
SMNT	Mount a different file system
STAT	Get status
STOR	Tell server to accept a file for storage
STOU	Tell server to create unique name for new file
STRU	Specify the file structure
SYST	Tell server to declare its operating system
TYPE	Specify the data representation type
USER	Specify the username

Exactly which FTP commands are available depends on the server; some servers implement a subset, or possibly a superset, of the commands defined in the RFC. Net::FTP, which we'll discuss in this chapter, provides methods that implement all the commands except the following:

ALLO   HELP   MODE   REIN   SITE   SMNT   STAT   STRU   SYST

Net::FTP

Net::FTP is used to transfer files from remote hosts. Using Net::FTP, you can write simple FTP clients that transfer files from remote servers based on information passed on the command line or from hard-coded variables. Here is an example of a client that connects to a remote FTP server and gets a file from the server:

```
#!/usr/local/bin/perl -w

use Net::FTP;

$hostname = 'remotehost.com';
$username = 'anonymous';
$password = 'myname@mydomain.com';

# Hardcode the directory and filename to get
$home = '/pub';
$filename = 'TESTFILE';

# Open the connection to the host
$ftp = Net::FTP->new($hostname);              # construct object
$ftp->login($username, $password);            # log in

$ftp->cwd($home),"\n";                        # change directory
print $ftp->ls($home),"\n";

# Now get the file and leave
$ftp->get($filename);
$ftp->quit;
```

FTP clients have also been integrated with most World Wide Web browsers, using *ftp://* in place of *http://*. When the URL points to a directory, the browser displays a listing of the directory, where each filename is a link to that file. When the URL points directly to a file, the remote file is downloaded.

Here's an example that uses Net::FTP to list files from a remote FTP server on a web page, with a link from each file to the URL of the file on the remote site:

```
#!/usr/local/bin/perl -w

use Net::FTP;

$hostname = 'remotehost.com';                 # ftp host
$username = 'anonymous';                       # username
$password = 'myname@mydomain.com';             # password
$home = '/pub';

$ftp = Net::FTP->new($hostname);              # Net::FTP constructor
$ftp->login($username, $password);            # log in w/username and password

$pwd = $ftp->pwd;                             # get current directory

# Now, output HTML page.
print <<HTML;
Content-type: text/html
<HTML>

  <HEAD>
    <TITLE>Download Files</TITLE>
```

Network Programming

```
    </HEAD>
    <BODY>

        <B>Current working directory:</B> $pwd<BR>
        Files to download: <P>
HTML

    @entries = $ftp->ls($home);         # slurp all entries into an array
    foreach (@entries) { # now, output links for all files in the ftp area
                        # as links
        print "<INPUT TYPE=hidden NAME=\"files\" VALUE=\"$_\">\n";
        print "<A HREF=\"ftp://$hostname$_\">",
        "<IMG SRC=\"http://www/icons/f.gif\" border=0>\n";
        print " $_</A><BR>\n";
    }
    print <<HTML;
    </BODY>
</HTML>
HTML
$ftp->quit;                # end FTP session
```

The Net::FTP module implements a subset (as shown earlier in this chapter) of the FTP protocol as defined in RFC 959. In addition to providing the methods shown below, the module inherits from Net::Cmd. Some of the Net::FTP methods return an object derived from the *dataconn* class (which is in turn derived from the IO::Socket::INET class), as noted in the entries for those methods.

The following methods are defined by Net::FTP:

---

new

> $ftp = Net::FTP->new(*host[, options]*)

Constructs a new Net::FTP object. Arguments are:

host
> The name of the remote host.

options
> A hash specifying any of the following information:
>
> Firewall
>> Name of an FTP firewall.
>
> Port
>> Port number to use for the FTP connection. Defaults to 21.
>
> Timeout
>> Timeout value. Defaults to 120 seconds.
>
> Debug
>> Debug level.
>
> Passive
>> True or false, specifying whether to perform transfers in passive mode.

abort

*$ftp->*abort*()*

Aborts the current transaction.

appe

*$ftp->*appe*(file)*

Appends data to the end of the remote file *file*, which is created if it doesn't exist. If the user calls either pasv or port, returns true or false. Otherwise, returns a reference to a Net::FTP::dataconn object.

append

*$ftp->*append*(local[, remote])*

Appends the contents of a local file to an existing file on the remote system. Arguments are:

local
> Either the name of the file on the local system to transfer, or a filehandle.

remote
> The name of the file on the remote system. If *local* is a filehandle, *remote* must be specified.

authorize

*$ftp->*authorize*([auth[, resp]])*

Authorizes the user to send data outside the firewall, for use with FTP proxies. If authorization *auth* and response *resp* are not specified, authorize uses Net::Netrc to do a lookup.

Called with no arguments by login if the connection is through a firewall.

ascii

*$ftp->*ascii*([args])*

Changes the type of data transfer to ascii. Like type, without the need to specify the first argument.

binary

*$ftp->*binary*([args])*

Changes the type of data transfer to binary. Like type, without the need to specify the first argument.

Network
Programming

byte

$ftp->byte([args])

Changes the data transfer type to byte. Not supported. If specified, defaults to binary. Like type, without the need to specify the first argument.

cdup

$ftp->cdup()

Goes up one level in the directory hierarchy.

cwd

$ftp->cwd([dir])

Changes the working directory to *dir*. With no argument, changes the directory to root.

delete

$ftp->delete([filename])

Deletes the specified file from the server.

dir

$ftp->dir([dir])

Lists the specified server directory in long format. Returns a reference to the list. *dir* defaults to the current working directory.

ebcdic

$ftp->ebcdic([args])

Changes the data transfer type to ebcdic. Not supported. If specified, defaults to binary. Like type, without the need to specify the first argument.

get

$ftp->get(remote[, local])

Retrieves a file from the server. If specified, *local* is the name to give the file on the local system, otherwise the name stays the same. Arguments are:

remote
> Name of the file to retrieve from the remote system.

local
> Either the new filename on the local system, or a filehandle. If omitted, the same filename is used.

list

*$ftp->*list *([dir])*

Lists a directory, *dir*, for display. If the user calls either pasv or port, returns true or false. Otherwise, returns a reference to a Net::FTP::dataconn object. If directory is omitted, defaults to the current directory.

login

$ftp->([login[, passwd[, account]]])

Logs user into an FTP server. Arguments are:

login
> Login name. If not specified, defaults to anonymous or to the value in *$HOME/.netrc*.

passwd
> Password. If not specified, defaults to the user's email address or to the value in *$HOME/.netrc*.

account
> Additional account information, for files on the FTP server that have special access restrictions.

ls

*$ftp->*ls *([dir])*

Lists directory, *dir*, returning a reference to the list. Defaults to the current working directory.

mdtm

*$ftp->*mdtm *(file)*

Returns the modification time of remote file *file*.

mkdir

*$ftp->*mkdir *(dir[, recursive])*

Makes a new directory. Arguments are:

dir The new directory name.

recursive
> If true, creates all directories in the path as needed.

nlst

*$ftp->*nlst*([dir])*

Lists a directory, *dir*, for further processing. With no argument, defaults to the current directory. If the user calls either `pasv` or `port`, returns true or false. Otherwise, returns a reference to a Net::FTP::dataconn object.

pasv

*$ftp->*pasv*()*

Puts server in passive mode.

pasv_wait

*$ftp->*pasv_wait*(server)*

Waits for a transfer to complete between a passive and a non-passive server, where *server* is the Net::FTP object for the non-passive server.

pasv_xfer

*$ftp->*pasv_xfer*(file1, server, [file2])*

Transfers a file between two remote servers. Arguments are:

file1
> The file to transfer from the server represented by the Net::FTP object.

server
> Destination server.

file2
> New name of the file on the destination server. If omitted, the original name is used.

pasv_xfer_unique

*$ftp->*pasv_xfer_unique*(file1, server[, file2])*

Like `pasv_xfer`, but stores the file on the remote server with a new (unique) name.

port

*$ftp->*port*([port])*

Sends a PORT command telling the server to use port *port*. With no argument, a socket is created and its information is sent.

put

*$ftp->*put*(local[, remote])*

Puts a file onto the server. Arguments are:

local
> The name of the file to transfer from the local system, or a filehandle.

remote
> The new filename on the remote system. If omitted, the same filename is used. If *local* is a filehandle, the remote filename must be specified.

put_unique

*$ftp->*put_unique*(local[, remote])*

Puts a file with a unique name onto the server. Arguments are:

local
> The name of the file to transfer from the local system, or a filehandle.

remote
> The new filename on the remote system. If a file exists by that name, a new unique filename is created.

pwd

*$ftp->*pwd*()*

Returns the current directory path.

quit

*$ftp->*quit*()*

Closes the connection.

quot

*$ftp->*quot*(cmd[, args])*

Sends a literal FTP protocol command to the server and waits for a response. Returns the most significant digit of the response code.

rename

*$ftp->*rename*(file1, file2)*

Renames a file on the server. Arguments are:

file1
> The old name of the file.

$\rightarrow$

file2
> The new name of the file.

---

retr

*$ftp->*__retr__*(file)*

Retrieves file *file* from the remote server. If the user calls either pasv or port, returns true or false. Otherwise, returns a reference to a Net::FTP::dataconn object.

---

rmdir

*$ftp->*__rmdir__*(dir)*

Removes directory *dir*.

---

size

*$ftp->*__size__*(file)*

Returns the size of file *file* in bytes.

---

stor

*$ftp->*__stor__*(file)*

Tells the server to store a new file under the name *file*. If the user calls either pasv or port, returns true or false. Otherwise, returns a reference to a Net::FTP::dataconn object.

---

stou

*$ftp->*__stou__*(file)*

Like stor, but stores file on the remote server with a unique name, *file*. If the user calls either pasv or port, returns true or false. Otherwise, returns a reference to a Net::FTP::dataconn object.

---

supported

*$ftp->*__supported__*(cmd)*

Returns true if the server supports the command *cmd*.

---

type

ftp->type(type[, args])

Changes the type of data transfer. Possible types are ascii, ebcdic, byte, and binary. The value of *args* depends on the type.

unique_name

ftp->unique_name()

Returns the name of the last file stored with a unique name.

FTP Configuration with Net::Netrc

Unix-based FTP clients use a file called *.netrc*, which you can configure to automate FTP access to sites you frequently visit. With a properly defined *.netrc* file, you can simply execute the FTP command to a favorite FTP host and be automatically logged in to the FTP server. Your *.netrc* file contains one line for each connection you want to be able to make. The following tokens can be specified for each entry:

machine *name*

Specifies a remote machine to which you want to autologin:

    machine remotehost.com

Instead of machine *name*, you can specify the single word default to match any machine name. This is usually used for anonymous logins to machines not listed in *.netrc*.

login *name*

If present, identifies the user who logs in to the remote machine, where *name* is the login name.

password *passwd*

If present, gives the password for the user. The autologin process uses the specified password if the remote server requires one.

account *acctpw*

If present, gives an additional password for the user. The autologin process uses this password if the remote server requires one.

macdef *name*

If present, defines a macro with the specified name. Net::Netrc simply parses this field, in order to maintain compatibility with FTP.

Here's an example of a typical *.netrc* entry:

    machine remotehost.com login username password userpasswd

Entering your username and password for remote sites in unencrypted form has serious security implications. Many sites consider *.netrc* files a violation of security policy and do not allow them. In addition, most FTP clients require that the *.netrc* file be owned by you and readable only by you, with permissions set to 0400 or 0600. If the permissions aren't correctly set, the autologin process aborts. Net::Netrc follows this security convention—if the permissions and ownership are not correct, the *.netrc* file isn't read, and a warning message is issued.

Net::Netrc implements a simple interface to the *.netrc* file, telling you which hosts you can automatically connect to. It doesn't actually connect to any remote hosts; it's simply used to query your configuration file and return the value of the tokens.

The following methods are supplied by Net::Netrc:

lookup

> *$machine* = Net::Netrc->lookup*(host[, login])*

Constructor. Looks up and returns a reference to the entry for the specified host machine, *host*. Without the optional *login* argument, lookup returns the first entry in the *.netrc* file for the machine.

If there is no matching entry, lookup returns a reference to the default entry.

account

> *$machine*->account

Returns account information specified by the *.netrc* account entry, if there is any.

lpa

> *(@login_pass_account)* = *$machine*->lpa

Returns a list of login, password, and account information specified by the *.netrc* tokens.

login

> *$machine*->login

Returns the username (login id) specified by the *.netrc* login token.

password

> *$machine*->password

Returns the password specified by the *.netrc* password token.

CHAPTER 17

The LWP Library

LWP, the library for web access in Perl, is a bundle of modules that provide a consistent, object-oriented approach to creating web applications. The library, downloaded as the single file named *libwww-perl*, contains the following classes:

File
> Parses directory listings.

Font
> Handles Adobe Font Metrics.

HTML
> Parses HTML files and converts them to printable or other forms.

HTTP
> Provides client requests, server responses, and protocol implementation.

LWP
> The core of all web client programs. It creates network connections and manages the communication and transactions between client and server.

URI
> Creates, parses, and translates URLs.

WWW
> Implements standards used for robots (automatic client programs).

Each module provides different building blocks that make up a whole web transaction—from connection, to request, to response and returned data. Each part is encapsulated by an object to give a standard interface to every web program you write. The following section gives an overview of how LWP works to create a web client.

Network Programming

LWP Overview

Any web transaction requires an application that can establish a TCP/IP network connection and send and receive messages using the appropriate protocol (usually HTTP). TCP/IP connections are established using sockets, and messages are exchanged via socket filehandles. See Chapter 13, *Sockets*, for information on how to manually create socket applications. LWP provides an object for this application with LWP::UserAgent for clients; HTTP::Daemon provides a server object. The UserAgent object acts as the browser: it connects to a server, sends requests, receives responses, and manages the received data. This is how you create a User-Agent object:

```
use LWP::UserAgent;
$ua = new LWP::UserAgent;
```

The UserAgent now needs to send a message to a server requesting a URL (Universal Resource Locator) using the request method. request forms an HTTP request from the object given as its argument. This request object is created by HTTP::Request.

An HTTP request message contains three elements. The first line of a message always contains an HTTP command called a *method*, a Universal Resource Identifier (URI), which identifies the file or resource the client is querying, and the HTTP version number. The following lines of a client request contain header information, which provides information about the client and any data it is sending the server. The third part of a client request is the entity body, which is data being sent to the server (for the POST method). The following is a sample HTTP request:

```
GET /index.html HTTP/1.0
User-Agent: Mozilla/1.1N (Macintosh; I; 68K)
Accept: */*
Accept: image/gif
Accept: image/jpeg
```

LWP::UserAgent->request forms this message from an HTTP::Request object. A request object requires a method for the first argument. The GET method asks for a file, while the POST method supplies information such as form data to a server application. There are other methods, but these two are most commonly used.

The second argument is the URL for the request. The URL must contain the server name, for this is how the UserAgent knows where to connect. The URL argument can be represented as a string or as a URI::URL object, which allows more complex URLs to be formed and managed. Optional parameters for an HTTP::Request include your own headers, in the form of an HTTP::Headers object, and any POST data for the message. The following example creates a request object:

```
use HTTP::Request;

$req = new HTTP::Request(GET, $url, $hdrs);
```

The URL object is created like this:

```
use URI::URL;

$url = new URI::URL('www.ora.com/index.html');
```

And a header object can be created like this:

```
use HTTP::Headers;

$hdrs = new HTTP::Headers(Accept => 'text/plain',
                          User-Agent => 'MegaBrowser/1.0');
```

Then you can put them all together to make a request:

```
use LWP::UserAgent;  # This will cover all of them!

$hdrs = new HTTP::Headers(Accept => 'text/plain',
                          User-Agent => 'MegaBrowser/1.0');
$url = new URI::URL('www.ora.com/index.html');
$req = new HTTP::Request(GET, $url, $hdrs);
$ua = new LWP::UserAgent;
$resp = $ua->request($req);
if ($resp->is_success) {
        print $resp->content;}
else {
        print $resp->message;}
```

Once the request has been made by the user agent, the response from the server is returned as another object, described by HTTP::Response. This object contains the status code of the request, returned headers, and the content you requested, if successful. In the example, is_success checks to see if the request was fulfilled without problems, thus outputting the content. If unsuccessful, a message describing the server's response code is printed.

There are other modules and classes that create useful objects for web clients in LWP, but the above examples show the most basic ones. For server applications, many of the objects used above become pieces of a server transaction, which you either create yourself (such as response objects) or receive from a client (like request objects).

Additional functionality for both client and server applications is provided by the HTML module. This module provides many classes for both the creation and interpretation of HTML documents.

The rest of this chapter provides information for the LWP, HTTP, HTML, and URI modules.

The LWP Modules

The LWP modules provide the core of functionality for web programming in Perl. It contains the foundations for networking applications, protocol implementations, media type definitions, and debugging ability.

The modules LWP::Simple and LWP::UserAgent define client applications that implement network connections, send requests, and receive response data from servers. LWP::RobotUA is another client application that is used to build automated web searchers following a specified set of guidelines.

LWP::UserAgent is the primary module used in applications built with LWP. With it, you can build your own robust web client. It is also the base class for the Simple and RobotUA modules. These two modules provide a specialized set of functions for creating clients.

Additional LWP modules provide the building blocks required for web communications, but you often don't need to use them directly in your applications. LWP::Protocol implements the actual socket connections with the appropriate protocol. The most common protocol is HTTP, but mail protocols (like SMTP), FTP for file transfers, and others can be used across networks.

LWP::MediaTypes implements the MIME definitions for media type identification and mapping to file extensions. The LWP::Debug module provides functions to help you debug your LWP applications.

The following sections describe the RobotUA, Simple, and UserAgent modules of LWP.

LWP::RobotUA

The Robot User Agent (LWP::RobotUA) is a subclass of LWP::UserAgent, and is used to create robot client applications. A robot application requests resources in an automated fashion. Robots perform such activities as searching, mirroring, and surveying. Some robots collect statistics, while others wander the Web and summarize their findings for a search engine.

The LWP::RobotUA module defines methods to help program robot applications and observes the Robot Exclusion Standards, which web server administrators can define on their web site to keep robots away from certain (or all) areas of the site.

The constructor for an LWP::RobotUA object looks like this:

```
$rob = LWP::RobotUA->new(agent_name, email, [$rules]);
```

The first parameter, agent_name, is the user agent identifier that is used for the value of the User-Agent header in the request. The second parameter is the email address of the person using the robot, and the optional third parameter is a reference to a WWW::RobotRules object, which is used to store the robot rules for a server. If you omit the third parameter, the LWP::RobotUA module requests the robots.txt file from every server it contacts, and then generates its own WWW::RobotRules object.

Since LWP::RobotUA is a subclass of LWP::UserAgent, the LWP::UserAgent methods are used to perform the basic client activities. The following methods are defined by LWP::RobotUA for robot-related functionality:

as_string

> $rob->as_string()

Returns a human-readable string that describes the robot's status.

delay

$rob->delay ([time])

Sets or returns the specified *time* (in minutes) to wait between requests. The default value is 1.

host_wait

$rob->host_wait *(netloc)*

Returns the number of seconds the robot must wait before it can request another resource from the server identified by *netloc.*

no_visits

$rob->no_visits *(netloc)*

Returns the number of visits to a given server. *netloc* is of the form *user:password@host:port.* The user, password, and port are optional.

rules

$rob->rules *([$rules])*

Sets or returns the WWW:RobotRules object *$rules* to be used when determining if the module is allowed access to a particular resource.

LWP::Simple

LWP::Simple provides an easy-to-use interface for creating a web client, although it is only capable of performing basic retrieving functions. An object constructor is not used for this class; it defines functions to retrieve information from a specified URL and interpret the status codes from the requests.

This module isn't named Simple for nothing. The following lines show how to use it to get a web page and save it to a file:

```
use LWP::Simple;

$homepage = 'oreilly_com.html';
$status = getstore('http://www.oreilly.com/', $homepage);
print("hooray") if is_success($status);
```

The retrieving functions get and head return the URL's contents and header contents respectively. The other retrieving functions return the HTTP status code of the request. The status codes are returned as the constants from the HTTP::Status module, which is also where the is_success and is_failure methods are obtained. See the section on HTTP::Status later in this chapter for a listing of the response codes.

The user-agent identifier produced by LWP::Simple is LWP::Simple/n.nn, where n.nn is the version number of LWP being used.

The following list describes the functions exported by LWP::Simple:

get

get *(url)*

Returns the contents of the specified *url*. Upon failure, get returns undef. Other than returning undef, there is no way of accessing the HTTP status code or headers returned by the server.

getprint

getprint *(url)*

Prints the contents of the *url* on standard output and returns the HTTP status code given by the server.

getstore

getstore *(url, file)*

Stores the contents of the specified *url* into *file* and returns the HTTP status code given by the server.

head

head *(url)*

Returns header information about the specified *url* in the form of: ($content_type, $document_length, $modified_time, $expires, $server). Upon failure, head returns an empty list.

is_error

is_error *(code)*

Given a status *code* from getprint, getstore, or mirror, returns true if the request was not successful.

is_success

is_success *(code)*

Given a status *code* from getprint, getstore, or mirror, returns true if the request was successful.

mirror

mirror *(url, file)*

Copies the contents of the specified *url* into *file*, when the modification time or length of the online version is different from that of the named file.

LWP::UserAgent

Requests over the network are performed with LWP::UserAgent objects. To create an LWP::UserAgent object, use:

```
$ua = new LWP::UserAgent;
```

You give the object a request, which it uses to contact the server, and the information you requested is returned. The most often used method in this module is request, which contacts a server and returns the result of your query. Other methods in this module change the way request behaves. You can change the timeout value, customize the value of the User-Agent header, or use a proxy server.

The following methods are supplied by LWP::UserAgent:

request

**$ua->request**(*$request, [file | $sub, size]*)

Performs a request for the resource specified by *$request*, which is an HTTP::Request object. Returns the information received from the server as an HTTP::Response object. Normally, doing a $ua->request($request) is enough. You can also specify a subroutine to process the data as it comes in, or you can provide a filename in which to store the entity body of the response. The arguments are:

$request
 An HTTP::Request object. The object must contain the method and URL of the site to be queried. This object must exist before request is called.

file Name of the file in which to store the response's entity body. When this option is used on request, the entity body of the returned response object will be empty.

$sub
 A reference to a subroutine that will process the data of the response. If you use the optional third argument, *size*, the subroutine will be called any time that number of bytes is received as response data. The subroutine should expect each chunk of the entity-body data as a scalar in the first argument, an HTTP::Response object as the second argument, and an LWP::Protocol object as the third argument.

size
 Optional argument specifying the number of bytes of the entity body received before the *sub* callback is called to process response data.

Network Programming

agent

> $ua->agent([string])

When invoked with no arguments, this method returns the current value of the identifier used in the User-Agent HTTP header. If invoked with an argument, the User-Agent header will use *string* as its identifier in the future.

clone

> $ua->clone()

Returns a copy of the LWP::UserAgent object.

cookie_jar

> $ua->cookie_jar([$cjar])

Specifies the "cookie jar" object to use with the UserAgent object, or returns it if invoked with no argument. *$cjar* is a reference to an HTTP::Cookies object that contains client cookie data. See the HTTP::Cookies section for more information.

credentials

> $ua->credentials(netloc, realm, uname, pass)

Uses the given username and password for authentication at the given network location and realm. This method sets the parameters for either the WWW-Authenticate or Proxy-Authenticate headers in a request. The `get_basic_credentials` method is called by `request` to retrieve the username and passwords, if they exist. The arguments are:

netloc
> The network location (usually a URL string) to which the username and password apply.

realm
> The name of the server-defined range of URLs that this data applies to.

uname
> The username for authentication.

pass
> The password for authentication. By default, the password will be transmitted with MIME base-64 encoding.

env_proxy

> $ua->env_proxy()

Defines a scheme/proxy URL mapping by looking at environment variables. For example, to define the HTTP proxy, one would define the HTTP_PROXY environment variable with the proxy's URL. To define a domain to avoid the

$\rightarrow$

proxy, one would define the NO_PROXY environment variable with the domain that doesn't need a proxy.

from

$ua->from([email])

When invoked with no arguments, this method returns the current value of the email address used in the From header. If invoked with an argument, the From header will use that email address in the future. (The From header tells the web server the email address of the person running the client software.)

get_basic_credentials

$ua->get_basic_credentials(realm, url)

Returns the list containing the username and password for the given *realm* and *url* when authentication is required by the server. This function is usually called internally by request. This method becomes useful when creating a subclass of LWP::UserAgent with its own version of get_basic_credentials. From there, you can rewrite get_basic_credentials to do more flexible things, like asking the user for the account information, or referring to authentication information in a file. All you need to do is return a list, where the first element is a username and the second element is a password.

is_protocol_supported

$ua->is_protocol_supported(proto)

Given a scheme, this method returns a true or false (nonzero or zero) value. A true value means that LWP knows how to handle a URL with the specified protocol. If it returns a false value, LWP does not know how to handle the URL.

max_size

$ua->max_size([size])

Sets or returns the maximum *size* (in bytes) for response content. The default is undef, which means that there is no limit. If the returned content is partial because the size limit was exceeded, then an X-Content-Range header will be added to the response.

mirror

$ua->mirror(url, file)

Given a URL and file path, this method copies the contents of *url* into the file when the length or modification date headers are different from any previous retrieval. If the file does not exist, it is created. This method returns an HTTP::Response object, where the response code indicates what happened.

no_proxy

$ua->no_proxy*(domains)*

Do not use a proxy server for the specified *domains*.

parse_head

$ua->parse_head*([boolean])*

Sets or returns a true or false value indicating whether response headers from the <head> sections of HTML documents are initialized. The default is true.

proxy

$ua->proxy*(prot, proxy_url)*

Defines a URL (*proxy_url*) to use with the specified protocols, *prot*. The first parameter can be a reference to a list of protocol names or a scalar that contains a single protocol. The second argument defines a proxy URL to use with the protocol.

timeout

$ua->timeout*([secs])*

When invoked with no arguments, `timeout` returns the timeout value of a request. By default, this value is three minutes. Therefore, if the client software doesn't hear back from the server within three minutes, it will stop the transaction and indicate that a timeout occurred in the HTTP response code. If invoked with an argument, the timeout value is redefined to be that value.

use_alarm

$ua->use_alarm*([boolean])*

Retrieves or defines the ability to use `alarm` for timeouts. By default, timeouts with `alarm` are enabled. If you plan on using `alarm` for your own purposes, or it isn't supported on your system, it is recommended that you disable `alarm` by calling this method with a value of zero.

The HTTP Modules

The HTTP modules implement an interface to the HTTP messaging protocol used in web transactions. Its most useful modules are HTTP::Request and HTTP::Response, which create objects for client requests and server responses. Other modules provide means for manipulating headers, interpreting server response codes, managing cookies, converting date formats, and creating basic server applications.

Client applications created with LWP::UserAgent use HTTP::Request objects to create and send requests to servers. The information returned from a server is saved as an HTTP::Response object. Both of these objects are subclasses of HTTP::Message, which provides general methods of creating and modifying HTTP messages. The header information included in HTTP messages can be represented by objects of the HTTP::Headers class.

HTTP::Status includes functions to classify response codes into the categories of informational, successful, redirection, error, client error, or server error. It also exports symbolic aliases of HTTP response codes; one could refer to the status code of 200 as RC_OK and refer to 404 as RC_NOT_FOUND.

The HTTP::Date module converts date strings from and to machine time. The HTTP::Daemon module can be used to create webserver applications, utilizing the functionality of the rest of the LWP modules to communicate with clients.

HTTP::Request

This module summarizes a web client's request. For a simple GET request, you define an object with the GET method and assign a URL to apply it to. Basic headers would be filled in automatically by LWP. For a POST or PUT request, you might want to specify a custom HTTP::Headers object for the request, or use the contents of a file for an entity body. Since HTTP::Request inherits everything in HTTP::Message, you can use the header and entity body manipulation methods from HTTP::Message in HTTP::Request objects.

The constructor for HTTP::Request looks like this:

```
$req = http::Request->new (method, url, [$header, [content]]);
```

The method and URL values for the request are required parameters. The header and content arguments are not required, nor even necessary for all requests. The parameters are described as follows:

method
A string specifying the HTTP request method. GET, HEAD, and POST are the most commonly used. Other methods defined in the HTTP specification such as PUT and DELETE are not supported by most servers.

url The address and resource name of the information you are requesting. This argument may be either a string containing an absolute URL (the hostname is required), or a URI::URL object that stores all the information about the URL.

$header
A reference to an HTTP::Headers object.

content
A scalar that specifies the entity body of the request. If omitted, the entity body is empty.

The following methods can be used on HTTP::Request objects:

as_string

*$req->*as_string

Returns a text version of the request object as a string with \n placed after
each line. Information about the object reference is also included in the first
line. The returned string looks like this example:

```
--- HTTP::Request=HASH(0x68148) ---
PUT http://www.ora.com/example/hi.text
Content-Length: 2
Content-Type: text/plain

hi
-----------------------------------
```

method

*$req->*method *([method])*

Sets or retrieves the HTTP method for an HTTP::Request object. Without an
argument, method returns the object's current method.

url

*$req->*url *([url])*

Sets or retrieves the URL for the request object. Without an argument, this
method retrieves the current URL for the object. *url* is a string containing the
new URL to set for the request or a URI::URL object.

HTTP::Response

Responses from a web server are described by HTTP::Response objects. An HTTP
response message contains a status line, headers, and any content data that was
requested by the client (like an HTML file). The status line is the minimum
requirement for a response. It contains the version of HTTP that the server is running, a status code indicating the success, failure, or other condition the request
received from the server, and a short message describing the status code.

If LWP has problems fulfilling your request, it internally generates an
HTTP::Response object and fills in an appropriate response code. In the context of
web client programming, you'll usually get an HTTP::Response object from
LWP::UserAgent and LWP::RobotUA.

If you plan to write extensions to LWP or to a web server or proxy server, you
might use HTTP::Response to generate your own responses.

The constructor for HTTP::Response looks like this:

```
$resp = HTTP::Response->new (rc, [msg, [header, [content]]]);
```

In its simplest form, an HTTP::Response object can contain just a response code. If you would like to specify a more detailed message than "OK" or "Not found," you can specify a text description of the response code as the second parameter. As a third parameter, you can pass a reference to an HTTP::Headers object to specify the response headers. Finally, you can also include an entity body in the fourth parameter as a scalar.

For client applications, it is unlikely that you will build your own response object with the constructor for this class. You receive a client object when you use the request method on an LWP::UserAgent object, for example:

```
$ua = LWP::UserAgent->new;
$req = HTTP::Request->new(GET, $url);
$resp = $ua->request($req);
```

The server's response is contained in the object $resp. When you have this object, you can use the HTTP::Response methods to get the information about the response. Since HTTP::Response is a subclass of HTTP::Message, you can also use methods from that class on response objects. See the HTTP::Message section later in this chapter for a description of its methods.

The following methods can be used on objects created by HTTP::Response:

as_string

$resp->as_string()

Returns a string version of the response with lines separated by \n. For example, this method would return a response string that looks like this:

```
--- HTTP::Response=HASH(0xc8548) ---
RC: 200 (OK)
Message: all is fine

Content-Length: 2
Content-Type: text/plain

hi
------------------------------------
```

base

$resp->base()

Returns the base URL of the response. If the response was hypertext, any links from the hypertext should be relative to the location returned by this method. LWP looks for the BASE tag in HTML and Content-Base/Content-Location HTTP headers for a base specification. If a base was not explicitly defined by the server, LWP uses the requesting URL as the base.

Network Programming

code

$resp->**code** *([code])*

When invoked without any parameters, this method returns the object's response code. Sets the status code of the object when invoked with an argument.

current_age

$resp->**current_age**()

Returns the number of seconds since the response was generated by the original server.

error_as_HTML

$resp->**error_as_HTML** ()

When is_error is true, this method returns an HTML explanation of what happened.

freshness_lifetime

$resp->**freshness_lifetime**()

Returns the number of seconds until the response expires. If expiration was not specified by the server, LWP will make an informed guess based on the Last-Modified header of the response.

fresh_until

$resp->**fresh_until**()

Returns the time when the response expires. The time is based on the number of seconds since January 1, 1970, UTC.

is_error

$resp->**is_error**()

Returns true when the response code is 400 through 599. When an error occurs, you might want to use error_as_HTML to generate an HTML explanation of the error.

is_fresh

$resp->**is_fresh**()

Returns true if the response has not yet expired.

is_info

$resp->is_info()

Returns true when the response code is 100 through 199.

is_redirect

$resp->is_redirect()

Returns true when the response code is 300 through 399.

is_success

$resp->is_success()

Returns true when the response code is 200 through 299.

message

$resp->message ([msg])

When invoked without any parameters, message returns the object's status code message—the short string describing the response code. When invoked with a scalar *msg* argument, this method defines the object's message.

HTTP::Headers

This module deals with HTTP header definition and manipulation. You can use these methods on HTTP::Request and HTTP::Response objects to retrieve headers they contain, or to set new headers and values for new objects you are building.

The constructor for an HTTP::Headers object looks like this:

```
$h = HTTP::Headers->new([name => val],...);
```

This code creates a new headers object. You can set headers in the constructor by providing a header name and its value. Multiple *name=>val* pairs can be used to set multiple headers.

The following methods can be used by objects in the HTTP::Headers class. These methods can also be used on objects from HTTP::Request and HTTP::Response, since they inherit from HTTP::Headers. In fact, most header manipulation will occur on the request and response objects in LWP applications.

clone

$h->clone()

Creates a copy of the current object, $h, and returns a reference to it.

Network Programming

header

$b->header(field [=> $val], . . .)

When called with just an HTTP header as a parameter, this method returns the current value for the header. For example, $myobject->('content-type') would return the value for the object's Content-Type header. To define a new header value, invoke header with a hash of header=>value pairs, where the value is a scalar or reference to an array. For example, to define the Content-Type header, you would do this:

```
$h->header('content-type' => 'text/plain');
```

push_header

$b->push_header(field => val)

Adds a new header field and value to the object. Previous values of the field are not removed.

```
$h->push_header(Accept => 'image/jpeg');
```

remove_header

$b->remove_header(field, . . .)

Removes the header specified in the parameter(s) and the header's associated value.

scan

$b->scan($sub)

Invokes the subroutine referenced by *$sub* for each header field in the object. The subroutine is passed the name of the header and its value as a pair of arguments. For header fields with more than one value, the subroutine will be called once for each value.

The HTTP::Headers class allows you to use a number of convenience methods on header objects to set (or read) common field values. If you supply a value for an argument, that value will be set for the field. The previous value for the header is always returned. The following methods are available:

```
date
expires
if_modified_since
if_unmodified_since
last_modified
content_type
content_encoding
content_length
content_language
title
```

```
user_agent
server
from
referrer
www_authenticate
proxy_authenticate
authorization
proxy_authorization
authorization_basic
proxy_authorization_basic
```

HTTP::Status

This module provides methods to determine the type of a response code. It also exports a list of mnemonics that can be used by the programmer to refer to a status code.

The following methods are used on response objects:

is_info
> Returns true when the response code is 100 through 199.

is_success
> Returns true when the response code is 200 through 299.

is_redirect
> Returns true when the response code is 300 through 399.

is_client_error
> Returns true when the response code is 400 through 499.

is_server_error
> Returns true when the response code is 500 through 599.

is_error
> Returns true when the response code is 400 through 599. When an error occurs, you might want to use error_as_HTML to generate an HTML explanation of the error.

HTTP::Status exports the following constant functions for you to use as mnemonic substitutes for status codes. For example, you could do something like:

```
if ($rc = RC_OK) {....}
```

Here are the mnemonics, followed by the status codes they represent:

```
RC_CONTINUE (100)
RC_SWITCHING_PROTOCOLS (101)
RC_OK (200)
RC_CREATED (201)
RC_ACCEPTED (202)
RC_NON_AUTHORITATIVE_INFORMATION (203)
RC_NO_CONTENT (204)
RC_RESET_CONTENT (205)
RC_PARTIAL_CONTENT (206)
RC_MULTIPLE_CHOICES (300)
RC_MOVED_PERMANENTLY (301)
RC_MOVED_TEMPORARILY (302)
```

```
RC_SEE_OTHER (303)
RC_NOT_MODIFIED (304)
RC_USE_PROXY (305)
RC_BAD_REQUEST (400)
RC_UNAUTHORIZED (401)
RC_PAYMENT_REQUIRED (402)
RC_FORBIDDEN (403)
RC_NOT_FOUND (404)
RC_METHOD_NOT_ALLOWED (405)
RC_NOT_ACCEPTABLE (406)
RC_PROXY_AUTHENTICATION_REQUIRED (407)
RC_REQUEST_TIMEOUT (408)
RC_CONFLICT (409)
RC_GONE (410)
RC_LENGTH_REQUIRED (411)
RC_PRECONDITION_FAILED (412)
RC_REQUEST_ENTITY_TOO_LARGE (413)
RC_REQUEST_URI_TOO_LARGE (414)
RC_UNSUPPORTED_MEDIA_TYPE (415)
RC_REQUEST_RANGE_NOT_SATISFIABLE (416)
RC_INTERNAL_SERVER_ERROR (500)
RC_NOT_IMPLEMENTED (501)
RC_BAD_GATEWAY (502)
RC_SERVICE_UNAVAILABLE (503)
RC_GATEWAY_TIMEOUT (504)
RC_HTTP_VERSION_NOT_SUPPORTED (505)
```

HTTP::Date

The HTTP::Date module is useful when you want to process a date string. It exports two functions that convert date strings to and from standard time formats:

time2str

time2str *([time])*

Given the number of seconds since machine epoch, this function generates the equivalent time as specified in RFC 1123, which is the recommended time format used in HTTP. When invoked with no parameter, the current time is used.

str2time

str2time *(str [, zone])*

Converts the time specified as a string in the first parameter into the number of seconds since epoch. This function recognizes a wide variety of formats, including RFC 1123 (standard HTTP), RFC 850, ANSI C asctime, common log file format, Unix *ls -l*, and Windows *dir*, among others. When a time zone is not implicit in the first parameter, this function will use an optional time zone specified as the second parameter, such as "–0800" or "+0500" or "GMT". If the second parameter is omitted and the time zone is ambiguous, the local time zone is used.

HTTP::Cookies

HTTP cookies provide a mechanism for preserving information about a client or user across several different visits to a site or page. The "cookie" is a name-value pair sent to the client on its initial visit to a page. This cookie is stored by the client and sent back in the request upon revisit to the same page.

A server initializes a cookie with the Set-Cookie header. Set-Cookie sets the name and value of a cookie, as well as other parameters such as how long the cookie is valid and the range of URLs to which the cookie applies. Each cookie (a single name-value pair) is sent in its own Set-Cookie header, so if there is more than one cookie being sent to a client, multiple Set-Cookie headers are sent in the response. Two Set-Cookie headers may be used in server responses: Set-Cookie is defined in the original Netscape cookie specification, and Set-Cookie2 is the latest, IETF-defined header. Both header styles are supported by HTTP::Cookies. The latest browsers also support both styles.

If a client visits a page for which it has a valid cookie stored, the client sends the cookie in the request with the Cookie header. This header's value contains any name-value pairs that apply to the URL. Multiple cookies are separated by semicolons in the header.

The HTTP::Cookies module is used to retrieve, return, and manage the cookies used by an LWP::UserAgent client application. Setting cookies from LWP-created server requires only the coding of the proper response headers sent by an HTTP::Daemon server application. HTTP::Cookies is not designed to be used in setting cookies on the server side, although you may find use for it in managing sent cookies.

The new constructor for HTTP::Cookies creates an object called a cookie jar, which represents a collection of saved cookies usually read from a file. Methods on the cookie jar object allow you to add new cookies or to send cookie information in a client request to a specific URL. The constructor may take optional parameters, as shown in the following example:

```
$cjar = HTTP::Cookies->new( file => 'cookies.txt',
                            autosave => 1,
                            ignore_discard => 0 );
```

The cookie jar object $cjar created here contains any cookie information stored in the file *cookies.txt*. The autosave parameter takes a boolean value which determines if the state of the cookie jar is saved to the file upon destruction of the object. ignore_discard also takes a boolean value to determine if cookies marked to be discarded are still saved to the file.

Cookies received by a client are added to the cookie jar with the extract_cookies method. This method searches an HTTP::Response object for Set-Cookie and Set-Cookie2 headers and adds them to the cookie jar. Cookies are sent in a client request using the add-cookie-header method. This method takes an HTTP::Request object with the URL component already set, and if the URL matches any entries in the cookie jar, adds the appropriate Cookie headers to the request.

These methods can be used on a cookie jar object created by HTTP::Cookies:

add_cookie_header

$cjar->add_cookie_header($request)

Adds appropriate Cookie headers to an HTTP::Request object $request. $request must already be created with a valid URL address. This method will search the cookie jar for any cookies matching the request URL. If the cookies are valid (i.e., have not expired) they are used to create Cookie headers and are added to the request.

as_string

$cjar->as_string([discard])

Returns the current contents of the cookie jar as a string. Each cookie is output as a Set-Cookie3 header line followed by "0". If *discard* is given and is true, cookies marked to be discarded will not be output. Set-Cookie3 is a special LWP format used to store cookie information in the save file.

clear

$cjar->clear([domain, [path, [key]]])

Without arguments, this method clears the entire contents of the cookie jar. Given arguments, cookies belonging to a specific *domain*, *path*, or with a name, *key*, will be cleared. The arguments are ordered for increasing specificity. If only one argument is given, all cookies for that domain will be deleted. A second argument specifies a distinct *path* within the *domain*. To remove a cookie by keyname, you must use all three arguments.

extract_cookies

$cjar->extract_cookies($response)

Searches an HTTP::Response object $response for any Set-Cookie and Set-Cookie2 headers and stores the cookie information in the cookie jar.

load

$cjar->load([file])

Loads cookie information into the cookie jar from the file specified during construction (default) or from the named *file*. The file must be in the format produced by the save method.

revert

$cjar->revert

Restores the cookie jar to its state before the last save.

save

> *$cjar->save([file])*

Saves the state of the cookie jar to the file specified during construction (by default) or to the named *file*. The cookies are saved in a special LWP format as Set-Cookie3 header lines. This format is not compatible with the standard Set-Cookie and Set-Cookie2 headers, but you are not likely to use this file to set new cookies in response headers.

set_cookie

> *$cjar->set_cookie(version, key, val, path, domain, port, path_spec, secure, maxage, discard, \%misc)*

Sets a cookie in the cookie jar with the information given in the arguments. The number and order of arguments represent the structure of elements in the Set-Cookie3 header lines used to save the cookies in a file.

version
A string containing the cookie-spec version number.

key The name of the cookie.

val The value of the cookie.

path
The pathname of the URL for which the cookie is set.

domain
The domain name for which the cookie is set.

port
The port number of the URL for which the cookie is set.

path_spec
A Boolean value indicating if the cookie is valid for the specific URL path or all the URLs in the domain. The path is used if true; otherwise, the cookie is valid for the entire domain.

secure
A Boolean value indicating that the cookie should only be sent over a secure connection for true, or over any connection, if false.

maxage
The number of seconds that the cookie will be valid, from the time it was received. Adding the *maxage* to the current time will yield a value that can be used for an expiration date.

discard
A Boolean value indicating that the cookie should not be sent in any future requests and should be discarded upon saving the cookie jar, unless the ignore_discard parameter was set to true in the constructor.

$\rightarrow$

%misc

The final argument is a reference to a hash, *%misc*, that contains any additional parameters from the Set-Cookie headers such as Comment and URLComment, in key/value pairs.

scan

$cjar->scan(\&callback)

Invokes the *callback* subroutine for each cookie in the cookie jar. The subroutine is called with the same arguments that are given to the save method, described above. Any undefined arguments will be given the value undef.

HTTP::Cookies::Netscape

The HTTP::Cookies class contains one subclass that supports Netscape-style cookies within a cookie jar object. Netscape-style cookies were defined in the original cookie specification for Navigator 1.1, which outlined the syntax for the Cookie and Set-Cookie HTTP headers. Netscape cookie headers are different from the newer Set-Cookie2–style cookies in that they don't support as many additional parameters when a cookie is set. The Cookie header also does not use a version-number attribute. Many browsers and servers still use the original Netscape cookies, and the Netscape subclass of HTTP::Cookies can be used to support this style.

The new constructor for this subclass creates a Netscape-compatible cookie jar object like this:

```
$njar = HTTP::Cookies::Netscape->new(
           File    => "$ENV{HOME}/.netscape/cookies",
           AutoSave => 1 );
```

The methods described above can be used on this object, although many of the parameters used in Set-Cookie2 headers will simply be lost when cookies are saved to the cookie jar.

HTTP::Daemon

The HTTP::Daemon module creates HTTP server applications. The module provides objects based on the IO::Socket::INET class that can listen on a socket for client requests and send server responses. The objects implemented by the module are HTTP 1.1 servers. Client requests are stored as HTTP::Request objects, and all the methods for that class can be used to obtain information about the request. HTTP::Response objects can be used to send information back to the client.

An HTTP::Daemon object is created by using the new constructor. Since the base class for this object is IO::Socket::INET, the parameters used in that class's constructor are the same here. For example:

```
$d = HTTP::Daemon->new ( LocalAddr => 'maude.oreilly.com',
                         LocalPort => 8888,
                         Listen => 5 );
```

The HTTP::Daemon object is a server socket that automatically listens for requests on the specified port (or on the default port if none is given). When a client request is received, the object uses the accept method to create a connection with the client on the network.

```
$d = HTTP::Daemon->new;
while ( $c = $d->accept ) {
    $req = $c->get_request;
    # process request and send response here
    }
$c = undef;   # don't forget to close the socket
```

The accept method returns a reference to a new object of the HTTP::Daemon::ClientConn class. This class is also based on IO::Socket::INET and is used to extract the request message and send the response and any requested file content.

The sockets created by both HTTP::Daemon and HTTP::Daemon::ClientConn work the same way as those in IO::Socket::INET. The methods are also the same except for some slight variations in usage. The methods for the HTTP::Daemon classes are listed in the sections below and include the adjusted IO::Socket::INET methods. For more detailed information about sockets and the IO::Socket classes and methods, see Chapter 13.

The following methods can be used on HTTP::Daemon objects:

accept

$d->accept *([pkg])*

Accepts a client request on a socket object and creates a connection with the client. This method is the same as IO::Socket->accept, except it will return a reference to a new HTTP::Daemon::ClientConn object. If an argument is given, the connection object will be created in the package named by *pkg*. If no connection is made before a specified timeout, the method will return undef.

url

$d->url

Returns the URL string that gives access to the server root.

product_tokens

$d->product_tokens

Returns the string that the server uses to identify itself in the Server response header.

Network
Programming

HTTP::Daemon::ClientConn methods

The following methods can be used on HTTP::Daemon::ClientConn objects:

get_request

$c->get_request

Reads information from the client request and returns a reference to an HTTP::Request object. Returns undef if the request failed.

antique_client

$c->antique_client

Returns true if the client uses the HTTP/0.9 protocol (i.e., no status code or headers should be returned).

send_status_line

$c->send_status_line ([code, [msg, [proto]]])

Sends the status line composed of the given arguments back to the client. If the arguments are given, the default status line is sent as HTTP/1.1 200 OK. The arguments are:

code
> The numeric code indicating the status of the request, e.g., 200 for an OK request or 404 for a request for a resource that doesn't exist.

msg
> A short string describing the status code.

proto
> A string indicating the protocol and version number used by the server, e.g., HTTP/1.1.

send_basic_header

$c->send_basic_header ([code, [msg, [proto]]])

Sends status line composed of the specified parameters and the Date and Server headers to the client. If no arguments are given, the default status line HTTP/1.1 200 OK is used.

send_response

$c->send_response ([$resp | @resplist])

Sends a response to the client created from the HTTP::Response object, *$resp*, or the list of parameters, *@resplist*. The *resplist* parameters are the same as those used in the constructor for HTTP::Response and must at least contain a status code. If no argument is given, the default OK response is sent.

send_redirect

$c->send_redirect (*url, [code, [entity_body]]*)

Sends a redirect response to the client, with the location *url*, an absolute or a relative URL. The optional *code* argument should be one of the redirect status codes; the default is 301 Moved Permanently. An *entity_body* string can be sent as HTML that informs the user of the redirection.

send_error

$c->send_error (*[code, [msg]]*)

Returns an error response to the client. *code* can contain one of the error response codes; the default is 400 Bad Request. *msg* is a string describing the error displayed in the HTML entity body.

send_file_response

$c->send_file_response (*filename*)

Sends a response with the file *filename* as content. If *filename* is a directory, an index listing will be generated and sent as HTML.

send_file

$c->send_file (*filename*)

Copies contents of the file *filename* to the client as the response. *filename* can be a string that is interpreted as a filename, or a reference to a glob.

daemon

$c->daemon

Returns a reference to the HTTP::Daemon object from which the current ClientConn object was generated.

HTTP::Message

HTTP::Message is the generic base-class for HTTP::Request and HTTP::Response. It provides a couple of methods that are used on both classes. The constructor for this class is used internally by the Request and Response classes, so you will probably not need to use it. Methods defined by the HTTP::Headers class will also work on Message objects.

Network Programming

add_content

> *$r->add_content(data)*

Appends *data* to the end of the object's current entity body.

clone

> *$r->clone()*

Creates a copy of the current object, *$r*, and returns a reference to it.

content

> *$r->content ([content])*

Without an argument, content returns the entity body of the object. With a scalar argument, the entity body will be set to *content*.

content_ref

> *$r->content_ref()*

Returns a reference to the string containing the content body. This reference can be used to manage large content data.

headers

> *$r->headers()*

Returns the embedded HTTP::Headers object from the message object.

protocol

> *$r->protocol([string])*

Sets or retrieves the HTTP protocol *string* for the message object. This string looks like HTTP/1.1.

The HTML Module

The HTML modules provide an interface to parse HTML documents. After you parse the document, you can print or display it according to the markup tags, or you can extract specific information such as hyperlinks.

The HTML::Parser module provides the base class for the usable HTML modules. It provides methods for reading in HTML text from either a string or a file and then separating out the syntactic structures and data. As a base class, Parser does virtually nothing on its own. The other modules call it internally and override its empty methods for their own purposes. However, the HTML::Parser class is useful to you if you want to write your own classes for parsing and formatting HTML.

HTML::TreeBuilder is a class that parses HTML into a syntax tree. In a syntax tree, each element of the HTML, such as container elements with beginning and end tags, is stored relative to other elements. This preserves the nested structure and behavior of HTML and its hierarchy.

A syntax tree of the TreeBuilder class is formed of connected nodes that represent each element of the HTML document. These nodes are saved as objects from the HTML::Element class. An HTML::Element object stores all the information from an HTML tag: the start tag, end tag, attributes, plain text, and pointers to any nested elements.

The remaining classes of the HTML modules use the syntax trees and its nodes of element objects to output useful information from the HTML documents. The format classes, such as HTML::FormatText and HTML::FormatPS, allow you to produce text and PostScript from HTML. The HTML::LinkExtor class extracts all of the links from a document. Additional modules provide means for replacing HTML character entities and implementing HTML tags as subroutines.

HTML::Parser

This module implements the base class for the other HTML modules. A parser object is created with the new constructor:

```
$p = HTML::Parser->new();
```

The constructor takes no arguments.

The parser object takes methods that read in HTML either from a string or a file. The string-reading method can take data as several smaller chunks if the HTML is too big. Each chunk of HTML will be appended to the object, and the eof method indicates the end of the document. These basic methods are described below.

parse

$p->parse(string)

Reads HTML into the parser object from a given *string*. Performance problems occur if the string is too large, so the HTML can be broken up into smaller pieces, which will be appended to the data already contained in the object. The parse can be terminated with a call to the eof method.

parse_file

$p->parse_file(file)

Reads HTML into the parser object from the given *file*, which can be a filename or an open filehandle.

eof

$p->eof()

Indicates the end of a document and flushes any buffered text. Returns the parser object.

When the parse or parse_file method is called, it parses the incoming HTML with a few internal methods. In HTML::Parser, these methods are defined, but empty. Additional HTML parsing classes (included in the HTML modules or ones you write yourself) override these methods for their own purposes. For example:

```
package HTML::MyParser;
require HTML::Parser;
@ISA=qw(HTML::MyParser);

sub start {
    your subroutine defined here
    }
```

The following list shows the internal methods contained in HTML::Parser:

---

comment

comment*(comment)*

Invoked on comments from HTML—text between <!– and –>. The text of the comment (without the tags) is given to the method as the string *comment*.

---

declaration

declaration*(decl)*

Invoked on markup declaration tags—<!DOCTYPE ...>. The method is passed the text string contained in the tag without the <! and >.

---

end

end*(tag, origtext)*

Invoked on end tags—those with the </tag> form. The first argument, *tag*, is the tag name in lowercase, and the second argument, *origtext*, is the original HTML text of the tag.

---

start

start*(tag, $attr, attrseq, origtext)*

Invoked on start tags. The first argument, *tag*, is the name of the tag in lowercase. The second argument is a reference to a hash, *attr*. This hash contains all the attributes and their values in key/value pairs. The keys are the names of the attributes in lowercase. The third argument, *attrseq*, is a reference to an

$\rightarrow$

---

array that contains the names of all the attributes in the order they appeared in the tag. The fourth argument, *origtext*, is a string that contains the original text of the tag.

---

text

text(*text*)

Invoked on plain text in the document. The text is passed unmodified and may contain newlines. Character entities in the text are not expanded.

HTML::Element

The HTML::Element module provides methods for dealing with nodes in an HTML syntax tree. You can get or set the contents of each node, traverse the tree, and delete a node.

HTML::Element objects are used to represent elements of HTML. These elements include start and end tags, attributes, contained plain text, and other nested elements.

The constructor for this class requires the name of the tag for its first argument. You may optionally specify initial attributes and values as hash elements in the constructor. For example:

```
$h = HTML::Element->new('a', 'href' => 'http://www.oreilly.com');
```

The new element is created for the anchor tag, <a>, which links to the URL through its href attribute.

The following methods are provided for objects of the HTML::Element class:

---

as_HTML

$h->as_HTML()

Returns the HTML string that represents the element and its children.

---

attr

$h->attr(*name [,value]*)

Sets or retrieves the value of attribute *name* in the current element.

---

content

$h->content()

Returns the content contained in this element as a reference to an array that contains plain text segments and references to nested element objects.

---

delete

> *$h*->**delete**()

Deletes the current element and all of its child elements.

delete_content

> *$h*->**delete_content**()

Removes the content from the current element.

dump

> *$h*->**dump**()

Prints the tag name of the element and all its children to STDOUT. Useful for debugging. The structure of the document is shown by indentation.

endtag

> *$h*->**endtag**()

Returns the original text of the end tag, including the "</" and ">".

extract_links

> *$h*->**extract_links**(*[types]*)

Retrieves the links contained within an element and all of its child elements. This method returns a reference to an array in which each element is a reference to an array with two values: the value of the link and a reference to the element in which it was found. You may specify the tags from which you want to extract links by providing their names in a list of *types*.

implicit

> *$h*->**implicit**(*[boolean]*)

Indicates whether the element was contained in the original document (false) or whether it was assumed to be implicit (true) by the parser. Implicit tags are elements that the parser included appropriate to conform to proper HTML structure, such as an ending paragraph tag (</p>). You may also set this attribute by providing a *boolean* argument.

insert_element

> *$h*->**insert_element**(*$element, implicit*)

Inserts the object *$element* at the current position relative to the root object *$h* and updates the position (indicated by pos) to the inserted element.

→

Returns the new *$element*. The *implicit* argument is a boolean indicating whether the element is an implicit tag (true) or the original HTML (false).

is_empty

$h->is_empty*()*

Returns true if the current object has no content.

is_inside

$h->is_inside*(tag1 [,tag2, . . .])*

Returns true if the tag for this element is contained inside one of the tags listed as arguments.

parent

$h*->parent*([$new])

Without an argument, returns the parent object for this element. If given a reference to another element object, this element is set as the new parent object and is returned.

pos

$h*->pos*([$element])

Sets or retrieves the current position in the syntax tree of the current object. The returned value is a reference to the element object that holds the current position. The "position" object is an element contained within the tree that has the current object (*$h*) at its root.

push_content

$h->push_content*(content)*

Inserts the specified content into the current element. *content* can be either a scalar containing plain text or a reference to another element. Multiple arguments can be supplied.

starttag

$h->starttag*()*

Returns the original text of the start tag for the element. This includes the "<" and ">" and all attributes.

Network
Programming

tag

$h->tag([name])

Sets or retrieves the tag *name* for the element. Tag names are always converted to lowercase.

traverse

$h->traverse(sub, [ignoretext])

Traverses the current element and all of its children, invoking the callback routine *sub* for each element. The callback routine is called with a reference to the current element (the node), a startflag, and the depth as arguments. The start flag is 1 when entering a node and 0 when leaving (returning to a parent element). If the *ignoretext* parameter is true (the default), then the callback routine will not be invoked for text content. If the callback routine returns false, the method will not traverse any child elements of that node.

HTML::TreeBuilder

The HTML::TreeBuilder class provides a parser that creates an HTML syntax tree. Each node of the tree is an HTML::Element object. This class inherits both HTML::Parser and HTML::Elements, so methods from both of those classes can be used on its objects.

The methods provided by HTML::TreeBuilder control how the parsing is performed. Values for these methods are set by providing a boolean value for their arguments. Here are the methods:

implicit_tags

$p->implicit_tags(boolean)

If set to true, the parser will try to deduce implicit tags such as missing elements or end tags that are required to conform to proper HTML structure. If false, the parse tree will reflect the HTML as is.

ignore_unknown

$p->ignore_unknown(boolean)

If set to true, unknown tags in the HTML will be represented as elements in the parse tree.

ignore_text

> *$p*->ignore_text*(boolean)*

If set to true, text content of elements will not be included in elements of the parse tree. The default it false.

warn

> *$p*->warn*(boolean)*

If set to true, the parser will make calls to warn with messages describing syntax errors when they occur. Error messages are off by default.

HTML::FormatPS

The HTML::FormatPS module converts an HTML parse tree into PostScript. The formatter object is created with the new constructor, which can take parameters that assign PostScript attributes. For example:

```
$formatter = new HTML::FormatPS('papersize' => 'Letter');
```

You can now give parsed HTML to the formatter and produce PostScript output for printing. HTML::FormatPS does not handle table or form elements at this time.

The method for this class is format. format takes a reference to an HTML Tree-Builder object, representing a parsed HTML document. It returns a scalar containing the document formatted in PostScript. The following example shows how to use this module to print a file in PostScript:

```
use HTML::FormatPS;

$html = HTML::TreeBuilder->parse_file(somefile);
$formatter = new HTML::FormatPS;
print $formatter->format($html);
```

The following list describes the attributes that can be set in the constructor:

PaperSize
Possible values of 3, A4, A5, B4, B5, Letter, Legal, Executive, Tabloid, Statement, Folio, 10x14, and Quarto. The default is A4.

PaperWidth
Width of the paper in points.

PaperHeight
Height of the paper in points.

LeftMargin
Left margin in points.

RightMargin
Right margin in points.

Network Programming

HorizontalMargin
> Left and right margin. Default is 4 cm.

TopMargin
> Top margin in points.

BottomMargin
> Bottom margin in points.

VerticalMargin
> Top and bottom margin. Default is 2 cm.

PageNo
> Boolean value to display page numbers. Default is 0 (off).

FontFamily
> Font family to use on the page. Possible values are Courier, Helvetica, and Times. Default is Times.

FontScale
> Scale factor for the font.

Leading
> Space between lines, as a factor of the font size. Default is 0.1.

HTML::FormatText

The HTML::FormatText takes a parsed HTML file and outputs a plain text version of it. None of the character attributes will be usable, i.e., bold or italic fonts, font sizes, etc.

This module is similar to FormatPS in that the constructor takes attributes for formatting, and the `format` method produces the output. A formatter object can be constructed like this:

```
$formatter = new HTML::FormatText (leftmargin => 10, rightmargin => 80);
```

The constructor can take two parameters: `leftmargin` and `rightmargin`. The value for the margins is given in column numbers. The aliases `lm` and `rm` can also be used.

The `format` method takes an HTML::TreeBuilder object and returns a scalar containing the formatted text. You can print it with:

```
print $formatter->format($html);
```

The URI Module

The URI module contains functions and modules to specify and convert URIs. (URLs are a type of URI.) There are three URI modules: URL, Escape, and Heuristic. Of primary importance to many LWP applications is the URI::URL class, which creates the objects used by LWP::UserAgent to determine protocols, server locations, and resource names.

The URI::Escape module replaces unsafe characters in URL strings with their appropriate escape sequences. URI::Heuristic provides convenience methods for creating proper URLs out of short strings and incomplete addresses.

URI::Escape

This module escapes or unescapes "unsafe" characters within a URL string. Unsafe characters in URLs are described by RFC 1738. Before you form URI::URL objects and use that class's methods, you should make sure your strings are properly escaped. This module does not create its own objects; it exports the following functions:

uri_escape

> **uri_escape** *uri, [regexp]*
>
> Given a URI as the first parameter, returns the equivalent URI with certain characters replaced with % followed by two hexadecimal digits. The first parameter can be a text string, like "http://www.oreilly.com", or an object of type URI::URL. When invoked without a second parameter, uri_escape escapes characters specified by RFC 1738. Otherwise, you can pass in a regular expression (in the context of [ ]) of characters to escape as the second parameter. For example:
>
> ```
> $escaped_uri = uri_escape($uri, 'aeiou')
> ```
>
> This code escapes all lowercase vowels in $uri and returns the escaped version.

uri_unescape

> **uri_unescape** *uri*
>
> Substitutes any instance of % followed by two hexadecimal digits back into its original form and returns the entire URI in unescaped form.

URI::URL

This module creates URL objects that store all the elements of a URL. These objects are used by the request method of LWP::UserAgent for server addresses, port numbers, file names, protocol, and many of the other elements that can be loaded into a URL.

The new constructor is used to make a URI::URL object:

```
$url = new URI::URL($url_string [, $base_url])
```

This method creates a new URI::URL object with the URL given as the first parameter. An optional base URL can be specified as the second parameter and is useful for generating an absolute URL from a relative URL.

Network Programming

The following list describes the methods for the URI::URL class:

---

abs

$url->abs([base, [scheme]])

Returns the absolute URL, given a base. If invoked with no parameters, any previous definition of the base is used. The second parameter is a Boolean that modifies abs's behavior. When the second parameter is nonzero, abs will accept a relative URL with a scheme but no host, like "http:index.html".

---

as_string

$url->as_string()

Returns the URL as a scalar string. All defined components of the URL are included in the string.

---

base

$url->base([base])

Gets or sets the base URL associated with the URL in this URI::URL object. The base URL is useful for converting a relative URL into an absolute URL.

---

crack

$url->crack()

Returns an array with the following data:

```
(scheme, user, password, host, port, epath, eparams, equery, frag)
```

---

default_port

$url->default_port([port])

When invoked with no parameters, this method returns the default port for the URL defined in the object. The default port is based on the scheme used. Even if the port for the URL is explicitly changed by the user with the port method, the default port is always the same.

---

eparams

$url->eparams([param])

When invoked with no arguments, this method returns the escaped parameter of the URL defined in the object. When invoked with an argument, the object's escaped parameter is assigned to that value.

epath

$url->epath()

When invoked with no parameters, this method returns the escaped path of the URL defined in the object. When invoked with a parameter, the object's escaped path is assigned to that value.

eq

$url->eq(other_url)

Returns true when the object's URL is equal to the URL specified.

equery

$url->equery([string])

When invoked with no arguments, this method returns the escaped query string of the URL defined in the object. When invoked with an argument, the object's escaped query string is assigned to that value.

frag

$url->frag([frag])

When invoked with no arguments, this method returns the fragment of the URL defined in the object. When invoked with an argument, the object's fragment is assigned to that value.

full_path

$url->full_path()

Returns a string consisting of the escaped path, escaped parameters, and escaped query string.

host

$url->host([hostname])

When invoked with no parameters, this method returns the hostname in the URL defined in the object. When invoked with a parameter, the object's hostname is assigned to that value.

netloc

$url->netloc([netloc])

When invoked with no parameters, this method returns the network location for the URL defined in the object. The network location is a string composed of "user:password@host:port", where the user, password, and port may be

$\rightarrow$

Network Programming

omitted when not defined. When `netloc` is invoked with a parameter, the object's network location is defined to that value. Changes to the network location are reflected in the `user`, `password`, `host`, and `port` methods.

params

$url->params([param])

Same as `eparams`, except that the parameter that is set/returned is not escaped.

password

$url->password([passwd])

When invoked with no parameters, this method returns the password in the URL defined in the object. When invoked with a parameter, the object's password is assigned to that value.

path

$url->path([pathname])

Same as `epath`, except that the path that is set/returned is not escaped.

port

$url->port([port])

When invoked with no parameters, this method returns the port for the URL defined in the object. If a port wasn't explicitly defined in the URL, a default port is assumed. When invoked with a parameter, the object's port is assigned to that value.

query

$url->query([param])

Same as `equery`, except that the parameter that is set/returned is not escaped.

rel

$url->rel(base)

Given a base as a first parameter or a previous definition of the base, returns the current object's URL relative to the base URL.

scheme

*$url->***scheme***([scheme])*

When invoked with no parameters, this method returns the scheme in the URL defined in the object. When invoked with a parameter, the object's scheme is assigned to that value.

strict

URI::URL::strict*(bool)*

When set, the URI::URL module calls `croak` upon encountering an error. When disabled, the URI::URL module may behave more gracefully. The function returns the previous value of `strict`. This function is not exported explicitly by the module.

user

*$url->***user***([username])*

When invoked with no parameters, this method returns the user for the URL defined in the object. When invoked with a parameter, the object's user is assigned to that value.

PART VII

Perl/Tk

CHAPTER 18

Perl/Tk

Perl/Tk is an extension for writing Perl programs with a Graphical User Interface (GUI) on both Unix and Windows 95/NT. Tk was originally developed as an extension to the Tcl language, for use with the X Window System on Unix. With its port to Perl, Tk gives Perl programmers the same control over the graphical desktop that Tcl programmers have taken for granted.

The Tk extension makes it easy to draw a window, put widgets into it (such as buttons, checkboxes, entry fields, menus, etc.) and have them perform certain actions based on user input. A simple "Hello World" program would look like this:

```
#!/usr/bin/perl -w
use Tk;
my $mw = MainWindow->new;
$mw->Button(-text => "Hello World!", -command =>sub{exit})->pack;
MainLoop;
```

When you run it, it would look like Figure 18–1.

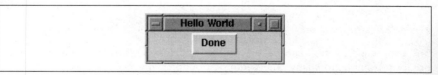

Figure 18–1: A simple Perl/Tk program

Pushing the "Hello World!" button exits the program, and your window disappears.

Let's walk through these few lines of code. After calling the Perl interpreter, the program calls the Tk module. Then it proceeds to build a generic, standard window (MainWindow) to act as a parent for any other widgets you create. Line 4 of the program creates a button and displays it using the pack geometry manager. It also gives the button something to do when pushed (in this case, exit the program).

The very last line tells the program to "go do it." MainLoop starts the event handler for the graphical interface, and the program draws any windows until it reaches the MainLoop statement. Everything up to that point is preparation; until you reach the MainLoop statement, the program simply prepares its windows and defines what to do when certain events happen (such as a mouse click on the "Hello World!" button). Nothing is drawn until the MainLoop statement is reached.

Widgets

Widgets in Perl/Tk are created with *widget creation commands*, which include Button, Canvas, CheckButton, Entry, Frame, Label, Listbox, Menu, Menubutton, Message, Radiobutton, Scale, Scrollbar, Text, and Toplevel.

Positioning widgets is done with *geometry managers*. In the "Hello World" example shown earlier, the pack command is the geometry manager. Geometry managers determine where in the window (or frame) the widget will sit. We'll talk more about the Perl/Tk geometry managers later in this chapter.

Widget Methods

Widgets can be configured, queried, or manipulated via various *widget methods*. For example, all widgets support the configure widget method for changing widget properties after the widget is created. In addition, most widgets have specialized methods associated with them for manipulating the widget as needed throughout the program. For example, widgets that scroll support the xview and yview methods for determining the viewable portion of the content when the scrollbar is moved. The Entry and Text widgets have methods for inserting and deleting values. The Canvas widget has a whole series of methods for drawing shapes and inserting text into the canvas. And so on.

Widget methods are listed in the discussion of each widget later in this chapter. However, since all widgets support the configure and cget methods, we're going to cover them now.

The configure method

The configure method can be used to set and retrieve widget configuration values. For example, to change the width of a button:

```
$button->configure(-width => 100);
```

To get the value for a current widget, just supply it without a value:

```
$button->configure(-width);
```

The result is an array of scalars; the values you care about are the last two, which represent the default value and its current value, respectively.

You can also call `configure` without any options at all, which will give you a listing of all options and their values.

The cget method

For simply retrieving the value of an option, `configure` returns more information than you generally want. The `cget` method returns just the current value.

Scrollbars

Many widgets have scrollbars associated with them. Scrollbars can be added to a widget in two ways: either using an independent Scrollbar widget or using the `Scrolled` method when creating a widget. For simple scrollbars, the `Scrolled` method is much easier and therefore preferable.

Using the Scrolled method

You use the `Scrolled` method to create both the widget and the scrollbar in a single command. For example:

```
$mainwindow->Scrolled('Entry', -scrollbars => 'os'
    -textvariable => \$address)->pack;
```

This creates an Entry widget with an "optional" scrollbar on the bottom. The first argument to `Scrolled` is the type of widget (in this case, an Entry widget). Then use the `-scrollbars` option to list the location of the scrollbar ("s" for the south, or bottom, edge of the widget). Here, we specify an "optional" scrollbar with "o", meaning that the scrollbar will only appear if needed.

Any additional options to the `Scrolled` method are taken as options to the widget itself. In this case, we're setting the `-textvariable` option to the Entry widget.

The Scrollbar widget

For more flexibility with a scrollbar, you can use the Scrollbar widget. To do so, you need to create the target widget to scroll, set the `-xscrollcommand` or `-yscrollcommand` option as appropriate, configure the scrollbar to talk to the widget, and position the scrollbar and target widget next to one another. For example:

```
$scrollbar = $mainwindow->Scrollbar(-orient => 'vertical');
$listbox = $mainwindow->Entry(-yscrollcommand => ['set' => $scrollbar]);
$scrollbar->configure(-command => ['yview' => $listbox]);
$scrollbar->pack(-side => 'right', -fill => 'y');
$listbox->pack(-side => 'left', -fill => 'both');
```

First, we create the scrollbar with vertical orientation (which is actually the default). Next, we create the Listbox widget with the `-yscrollcommand` option to define a callback when the widget is scrolled vertically. The scrollbar is then configured with a callback that says to inform the Listbox widget when it is clicked vertically. Finally, the Scrollbar and Listbox widgets are packed side-by-side. See further discussion of the Scrollbar widget later in this chapter for more information.

Perl/Tk

Callbacks

Many widgets allow you to define a *callback*, which is a command to execute when the widget is selected. For example, when you press an exit button, the callback might be to a routine that cleans up and quits the program. When you click on a radio button, you might want to change the window to reflect the new preferences.

Widgets that support callbacks have a -command option to provide the callback function. In the "Hello World!" example shown previously in this chapter, the callback is to sub {exit}. In that example, the callback is called as an anonymous subroutine. You could also use a reference to a subroutine (e.g., \&routine). If you want to provide arguments to a subroutine, you can call it as an anonymous list (e.g., [\&routine, $arg, $arg, ...]).

Colors and Fonts

Tk was originally created for the X Window System and is still primarily used in that environment. For that reason, it has inherited the font and color scheme used for the X Window System.

Colors that can be used with Tk widgets are identified either by an RGB value or by a name that has been associated with an RGB value. In general it is easiest to use a color name rather than an explicit RGB value; for a listing of the color names that are supported, see the *rgb.txt* file in your X distribution or use the *showrgb* command. (Most common color names are supported, so you can say things like "red," "pink," "green," and even "chartreuse" with confidence.)

Fonts are another matter. Under the X Window System, fonts are named things like *-adobe-helvetica-medium-o-normal--12-120-75-75-p-67-iso8859-1*. Wildcards can make the fonts easier to use, but they're still a mouthful. For a listing of fonts available for a particular X server, use the *xlsfonts* command. There are a few font "aliases" that have been defined for your convenience (such as fixed, 6x10, 9x15, etc.), and you might prefer to just stick to those.

Geometry Managers

Creating widgets and determining how to display them are done with separate commands. You can create a widget with one of the widget creation methods (such as Button, Canvas, etc.), but you display them using a geometry manager. The three geometry managers are pack, grid, and place. pack is by far the most commonly used.

You can either pack a widget as you create it, or you can create the widget object and pack it separately. For example, the previous "Hello World!" example might have read:

```
#!/usr/bin/perl -w
use Tk;
my $mw = MainWindow->new;
$button = $mw->Button(-text => "Hello World!", -command =>sub{exit});
```

```
$button->pack;
MainLoop;
```

The pack Geometry Manager

With the pack geometry manager, widgets cannot overlap or cover each other, either partially or completely. Once a widget is packed into a window, the next widget is packed in the remaining space around it. pack sets up an "allocation rectangle" for each widget, determined by the dimensions of the parent window and the positioning of the widgets already packed into it. This means that the order in which you pack your widgets is very important.

By default, pack places widgets at the top center of the allocation rectangle. However, you can use options to pack to control where a widget is placed and how much padding is placed around it. Options for pack are:

-side => *side*
> Puts the widget against the specified side of the window. Values for *side* are 'left', 'right', 'top', and 'bottom'. The default is 'top'.

-fill => *direction*
> Causes the widget to fill the allocation rectangle in the specified direction. Values for *direction* are 'none', 'x', 'y', and 'both'. The default is 'none'.

-expand => *boolean*
> Causes the allocation rectangle to fill the remaining space available in the window. Values are 'yes', 'no', 1, and 0. The default is 0 ('no').

-anchor => *position*
> Anchors the widget inside the allocation rectangle. Values for *position* are 'n', 'ne', 'e', 'se', 's', 'sw', 'w', 'nw', and 'center'. The default is 'center'.

-after => *$widget*
> Puts the widget after another widget in packing order.

-before => *$widget*
> Puts the widget before another widget in packing order.

-in => *$window*
> Packs the widget inside another window rather than inside its parent.

-ipadx => *amount*
> Increases the size of the widget horizontally by *amount* * 2. *amount* can be represented as a number followed by c (centimeters), i (inches), m (millimeters), and p (printer points). Pixels are the default units.

-ipady => *amount*
> Increases the size of the widget vertically by *amount* * 2. amount can be represented as a number followed by c (centimeters), i (inches), m (millimeters), and p (printer points). Pixels are the default units.

-padx => *amount*
> Places padding on the left and right of the widget. *amount* can be represented as a number followed by c (centimeters), i (inches), m (millimeters), and p (printer points). Pixels are the default units.

Perl/Tk

−pady => *amount*

Places padding on the top and bottom of the widget. *amount* can be represented as a number followed by c (centimeters), i (inches), m (millimeters),
and p (printer points). Pixels are the default units.

Pack methods

The following methods are associated with pack:

packForget

Causes a widget to be removed from view.

```
$widget->packForget;
```

The widget is not destroyed, but is no longer managed by pack. The widget is
removed from the packing order, so if it were repacked later, it would appear
at the end of the packing order.

packInfo

Returns a list containing all pack information about that widget.

```
$info = $widget->packInfo;
```

packPropagate

Suppresses automatic resizing of a Toplevel or Frame widget to accommodate
items packed inside of it. The following line turns off automatic resizing:

```
$widget->packPropagate(0);
```

packSlaves

Returns an ordered list of all the widgets packed into the parent widget.

```
$children = $widget->packSlaves;
```

The grid Geometry Manager

The grid geometry manager divides the window into a grid composed of columns
and rows starting at 0,0 in the upper left-hand corner. The resulting grid resembles
a spreadsheet, with each widget assigned a cell according to the options to grid.
To create a grid, create a frame that is packed inside the parent window and then
grid the widgets within the frame.

You can specify explicit rows and columns using options to grid. However, if several widgets are meant to appear in the same row, you can use a single grid command with a list of widgets rather than calling grid for each one. The first widget
invokes the grid command, and all other widgets for that column are specified as
options to grid. Any subsequent grid commands increment the row by one and
start again.

You can use special characters as placeholders:

− (minus sign)

The previous widget should span this column as well. May not follow ˆ or x.

x   Leave a blank space.

^   The widget above this one (same column, previous row) should span this row.

Options to grid are:

−column => *n*
: The column in which to place the widget. *n* is any integer >= 0.

−row => *m*
: The row in which to place the widget. *m* is any integer >= 0.

−columnspan => *n*
: The number of columns for the widget to span, beginning with the column specified with -column. *n* is any integer > 0.

−rowspan => *m*
: The number of rows for the widget to span, beginning with the column specified with -row. *m* is any integer > 0.

−sticky => *sides*
: Stick widget to specified side(s). *sides* contains characters n, s, e, or w.

−in => *$window*
: Grid widget inside another window instead of its parent.

−ipadx => *amount*
: Increases the size of the widget horizontally by *amount* * 2. *amount* can be represented as a number followed by c (centimeters), i (inches), m (millimeters), and p (printer points). Pixels are the default units.

−ipady => *amount*
: Increases the size of the widget vertically by *amount* * 2. *amount* can be represented as a number followed by c (centimeters), i (inches), m (millimeters), and p (printer points). Pixels are the default units.

−padx => *amount*
: Places padding on the left and right of the widget. *amount* can be represented as a number followed by c (centimeters), i (inches), m (millimeters), and p (printer points). Pixels are the default units.

−pady => *amount*
: Places padding on the top and bottom of the widget. *amount* can be represented as a number followed by c (centimeters), i (inches), m (millimeters), and p (printer points). Pixels are the default units.

Grid methods

The following methods are associated with grid:

gridColumnconfigure
: Configures the column specified by the first argument using -weight and -minsize arguments. The -weight argument determines the amount of space to allocate to that column, and the -minsize argument sets the minimum size in pixels. For example:

```
$widget->gridColumnconfigure(3, -weight => 1);
```

gridRowconfigure

Configures the row specified by the first argument using -weight and -min-size arguments. The -weight argument determines the amount of space to allocate to that row, and the -minsize argument sets the minimum size in pixels. For example:

```
$widget->gridRowconfigure(3, -weight => 1);
```

gridBbox

Returns the bounding box in pixels for the space occupied by the specified grid position (in the order of column, row). For example:

```
$widget->gridBbox(3,2);
```

gridForget

Causes the widget(s) to be removed from view. Additional widgets can be specified as arguments.

```
$widget1->gridForget($widget2, widget3, ...);
```

gridInfo

Returns information about the widget in list format.

```
$widget->gridInfo;
```

gridLocation

Returns the column and row of the widget nearest the specified x,y coordinates (in pixels).

```
$widget->gridLocation(120, 32);
```

gridPropagate

Turns off automatic resizing of the widget.

```
$widget->gridPropagate;
```

gridSize

Returns the size of the grid, i.e., the number of columns and rows.

```
$widget->gridSize;
```

gridSlaves

Returns a list of all widgets contained within a master widget. Optional -row and -column arguments restrict the response to the widget(s) within that row or column.

```
$children = $widget->gridSlaves(-row => 2);
```

The Place Geometry Manager

The place geometry manager lets you position a window at explicit x,y coordinates. With place, you can overlap widgets, which isn't allowed with grid or pack. For example, to position a button widget at the upper left corner of a window:

```
$button->place(-x => 0, -y => 0);
```

Options to place are:

−anchor => *position*
> The position in the widget that will be placed at the coordinates specified. Values for *position* are 'n', 'ne', 'e', 'se', 's', 'sw', 'w', 'nw', and 'center'. Default is 'nw'.

−bordermode => *location*
> Determines whether or not the border portion of the widget is included in the coordinate system. Values for *location* are 'inside', 'outside', and 'ignore'.

−height => *amount*
> Absolute height of the widget. *amount* can be represented as a number followed by c (centimeters), i (inches), m (millimeters), and p (printer points). Pixels are the default units.

−in => *$window*
> The child widget will be packed inside the specified window instead of the parent that created it. Any relative coordinates or sizes will still refer to the parent.

−relheight => *ratio*
> The height of the widget relates to the parent widget's height by the specified ratio.

−relwidth => *ratio*
> The width of the widget relates to the parent widget's width by the specified ratio.

−relx => *xratio*
> The widget will be placed relative to its parent by the specified ratio. *xratio* is a floating point number from 0.0 to 1.0, with 0.0 representing the left side of the parent widget and 1.0 representing the right side.

−rely => *yratio*
> The widget will be placed relative to its parent by the specified ratio. *yratio* is a floating point number from 0.0 to 1.0, with 0.0 representing the top of the parent widget and 1.0 representing the bottom.

−width => *amount*
> The width of the widget will be the specified amount. *amount* can be represented as a number followed by c (centimeters), i (inches), m (millimeters), and p (printer points). Pixels are the default units.

−x => *xcoord*
> The widget will be placed at the specified x coordinate.

−y => *ycoord*
> The widget will be placed at the specified y coordinate.

The following methods are associated with place:

placeForget
> Causes the widget to be removed from view.

Perl/Tk

placeInfo
> Returns information about the widget.

placeSlaves
> Returns a list of widgets managed by the specified parent widget.

Common Widget Configuration Options

In the remainder of this chapter, we'll be discussing each widget: the command used to create each widget, the options used to configure them, and the methods for manipulating them.

You'll find that there are many, many configuration options that are shared by multiple widgets. We could list them individually for each widget, but in the interest of saving a tree or two, we're instead going to list the shared options up front, rather than repeating them over and over. That way we can concentrate on the options that are crucial to the behavior of each particular widget, and save the reader from being lost in a sea of options.

The following options are supported by the widgets noted:

-activebackground => *color*
> Sets the background color when the mouse cursor is over the widget.
>
> Applicable widgets: Button, Checkbutton, Menu, Menubutton, Optionmenu, Radiobutton, Scale, Scrollbar

-activeforeground => *color*
> Sets the text color when the mouse cursor is over the widget.
>
> Applicable widgets: Button, Checkbutton, Menu, Menubutton, Optionmenu, Radiobutton

-anchor => *position*
> Causes the text to stick to that position in the widget. Values for *position* are 'n', 'ne', 'e', 'se', 's', 'sw', 'w', 'nw', and 'center'.
>
> Applicable widgets: Button, Checkbutton, Label, Menubutton, Optionmenu, Radiobutton

-background => *color*
-bg => *color*
> Sets the background of the widget to the specified color.
>
> Applicable widgets: Button, Canvas, Checkbutton, Entry, Frame, Label, Listbox, Menu, Menubutton, Optionmenu, Radiobutton, Scale, Scrollbar, Text, Toplevel

-bitmap => '*bitmapname*'
> Uses a bitmap instead of text in the widget. You can specify either a default bitmap or the location of a bitmap file (with @ in front of the path).
>
> Applicable widgets: Button, Checkbutton, Label, Menubutton, Optionmenu, Radiobutton

−borderwidth => *amount*
−bd => *amount*

> Changes the width of the edge drawn around the widget.

> Applicable widgets: Button, Canvas, Checkbutton, Entry, Frame, Label, List-box, Menu, Menubutton, Optionmenu, Radiobutton, Scale, Scrollbar, Text, Toplevel

−cursor => *'cursorname'*

> Mouse cursor will change to specified cursor when over the widget.

> Applicable widgets: Button, Canvas, Checkbutton, Entry, Frame, Label, List-box, Menu, Menubutton, Optionmenu, Radiobutton, Scale, Scrollbar, Text, Toplevel

−disabledforeground => *color*

> Sets the color of the text when the widget is disabled.

> Applicable widgets: Button, Checkbutton, Menu, Menubutton, Optionmenu, Radiobutton

−exportselection => *boolean*

> Determines whether selected text is exported to the window system's clip-board. (For a listbox, -exportselection => 1 means two listboxes cannot have selections at the same time.)

> Applicable widgets: Entry, Listbox, Text

−font => *'fontname'*

> Changes the font of all the text on the widget to *fontname*.

> Applicable widgets: Button, Checkbutton, Entry, Label, Listbox, Menu, Menubutton, Optionmenu, Radiobutton, Scale, Text

−foreground => *color*
−fg => *color*

> Changes the text color to *color*.

> Applicable widgets: Button, Checkbutton, Entry, Label, Listbox, Menu, Menubutton, Optionmenu, Radiobutton, Scale, Text

−height => *amount*

> Specifies the height of the widget. *amount* represents a number of characters if text is displayed, or a screen distance if an image or bitmap is displayed.

> Applicable widgets: Button, Canvas, Checkbutton, Frame, Label, Listbox, Menubutton, Optionmenu, Radiobutton, Text, Toplevel

−highlightbackground => *color*

> Sets the color of a non-focus rectangle.

> Applicable widgets: Button, Canvas, Checkbutton, Entry, Frame, Label, List-box, Menubutton, Optionmenu, Radiobutton, Scale, Scrollbar, Text, Toplevel

−highlightcolor => *color*

> Sets the color of the focus rectangle.

> Applicable widgets: Button, Canvas, Checkbutton, Entry, Frame, Label, List-box, Menubutton, Optionmenu, Radiobutton, Scale, Scrollbar, Text, Toplevel

Perl/Tk

-highlightthickness => *amount*

Sets the thickness of the black box around the widget that indicates focus.

Applicable widgets: Button, Canvas, Checkbutton, Entry, Frame, Label, Listbox, Menubutton, Optionmenu, Radiobutton, Scale, Scrollbar, Text, Toplevel

-image => *$imgptr*

Uses an image instead of text. *$imgptr* is a pointer to a Photo or Image object made using a GIF or PPM file. For example:

```
$image = $mainwindow->Photo(-file => "image.gif");
$mainwindow->Button(-image => $arrow,
                    -command => sub {exit})->pack;
```

Applicable widgets: Button, Checkbutton, Label, Menubutton, Optionmenu, Radiobutton

-insertbackground => *color*

Sets the color of the insert cursor.

Applicable widgets: Canvas, Entry, Text

-insertborderwidth => *amount*

Sets the width of the insert cursor's border.

Applicable widgets: Canvas, Entry, Text

-insertofftime => *milliseconds*

Defines the amount of time the insert cursor is "off."

Applicable widgets: Canvas, Entry, Text

-insertontime => *milliseconds*

Defines the amount of time the insert cursor is "on."

Applicable widgets: Canvas, Entry, Text

-insertwidth => *amount*

The width of the insert corner (default = 2 pixels).

Applicable widgets: Canvas, Entry, Text

-justify => *side*

Justifies text against the specified side. *side* can be 'left', 'right', or 'center'.

Applicable widgets: Button, Checkbutton, Entry, Label, Menubutton, Optionmenu, Radiobutton

-padx => *amount*

Adds extra space to left and right of the widget inside the widget edge.

Applicable widgets: Button, Checkbutton, Label, Menubutton, Optionmenu, Radiobutton, Text

-pady => *amount*

Adds extra space to top and bottom of the widget inside the widget edge.

Applicable widgets: Button, Checkbutton, Label, Menubutton, Optionmenu, Radiobutton, Text

`-relief => `*`type`*

> Changes the type of edges drawn around the widget. Values for *type* are `'flat'`, `'groove'`, `'raised'`, `'ridge'`, `'solid'`, and `'sunken'`.
>
> Applicable widgets: Button, Canvas, Checkbutton, Entry, Frame, Label, Listbox, Menu, Menubutton, Optionmenu, Radiobutton, Scale, Scrollbar, Text, Toplevel

`-selectbackground => `*`color`*

> Determines the background color of selected text in the entry widget.
>
> Applicable widgets: Canvas, Entry, Listbox, Text

`-selectborderwidth => `*`amount`*

> Determines the width of the selection highlight's border.
>
> Applicable widgets: Canvas, Entry, Listbox, Text

`-selectforeground => `*`color`*

> Determines the text color of selected text in the entry widget.
>
> Applicable widgets: Canvas, Entry, Listbox, Text

`-state => `*`state`*

> Sets the state of responsiveness of the widget. Values for *state* are `'normal'`, `'disabled'`, and `'active'`. (`disabled` makes it not respond.)
>
> Applicable widgets: Button, Checkbutton, Entry, Menubutton, Optionmenu, Scale, Text

`-takefocus => `*`focus`*

> Determines whether the widget gets focus. Values for *focus* are 0 (the widget will never get the focus), 1 (the widget always gets the focus), and the null string ("") (which lets the application decide).
>
> Applicable widgets: Button, Canvas, Checkbutton, Entry, Frame, Label, Listbox, Menu, Menubutton, Optionmenu, Scale, Scrollbar, Text, Toplevel

`-underline => `*`n`*

> Underlines the *n*th character in the text string. Allows keyboard input via that character when the widget has the focus.
>
> Applicable widgets: Button, Checkbutton, Label, Menubutton, Optionmenu, Radiobutton

`-width => `*`amount`*

> Width of the widget, represented in characters if text displayed, or as a screen distance if an image or bitmap is displayed.
>
> Applicable widgets: Button, Canvas, Checkbutton, Frame, Label, Listbox, Menubutton, Optionmenu, Radiobutton, Scale, Scrollbar, Text, Toplevel

`-wraplength => `*`amount`*

> Defines the maximum amount of text to be displayed on one line.
>
> Applicable widgets: Button, Checkbutton, Label, Menubutton, Optionmenu, Radiobutton

`-xscrollcommand => `*`callback`*

> Assigns a callback to use when scrolling back and forth.
>
> Applicable widgets: Canvas, Entry, Listbox, Text

`-yscrollcommand => callback`
    Determines a command to run when scrolled in the vertical direction.

    Applicable widgets: Canvas, Listbox, Text.

The Button Widget

Create a simple button with the `Button` method:

    `$parentwidget->Button (options)`

The standard configuration options that apply to `Button` are: `-activebackground`, `-activeforeground`, `-anchor`, `-background`, `-bg`, `-bitmap`, `-borderwidth`, `-bd`, `-cursor`, `-disabledforeground`, `-font`, `-foreground`, `-fg`, `-height`, `-highlight-background`, `-highlightcolor`, `-highlightthickness`, `-image`, `-justify`, `-padx`, `-pady`, `-relief`, `-state`, `-takefocus`, `-underline`, `-width`, and `-wraplength`.

Other options are:

`-command => callback`
    Pointer to a function that will be called when the button is pressed.

`-text => 'text'`
    Defines the text string displayed on the button. See also `-textvariable`.

`-textvariable => \$variable`
    Points to the variable containing text to be displayed in the button. Button text will change as `$variable` does.

Button Methods

In addition to `configure` and `cget`, the following methods can be used for `Button`:

`flash`
    Causes the button to flash from the normal to active state colors.

`invoke`
    Invokes the callback command as if the button were clicked.

The Checkbutton Widget

Creates a checkbutton with the `Checkbutton` command. A checkbutton has an indicator to the left of the label indicating whether the button is selected. The boolean status of the button ("0" or "1", or values as specified by the `-onvalue` and `-offvalue` options) is stored in the variable specified with the `-variable` option.

    `$parentwidget->Checkbutton (options)`

The standard configuration options that apply to `CheckButton` are: `-activeback-ground`, `-activeforeground`, `-anchor`, `-background`, `-bg`, `-bitmap`, `-borderwidth`, `-bd`, `-cursor`, `-disabledforeground`, `-font`, `-foreground`, `-fg`, `-height`, `-high-lightbackground`, `-highlightcolor`, `-highlightthickness`, `-image`, `-justify`, `-padx`, `-pady`, `-relief`, `-state`, `-takefocus`, `-underline`, `-width`, and `-wraplength`.

Other options are:

−command => *callback*

    Pointer to a function that will be called when the checkbutton is pressed.

−indicatoron => *boolean*

    Determines whether or not to display the indicator. Default is on (1).

−offvalue => *newvalue*

    Specifies the value used when the checkbutton is "off." Must be a scalar. Default is 0.

−onvalue => *newvalue*

    Specifies the value used when the checkbutton is "on." Must be a scalar. Default is 1.

−selectcolor => *color*

    Color of the indicator when the checkbutton is "on."

−selectimage => *imgptr*

    Defines the image to be displayed instead of text when the checkbutton is "on." Ignored if -image is not used.

−text => '*text*'

    Defines the text string displayed in the checkbutton. See also -textvariable.

−textvariable => *$variable*

    Points to the variable containing text to be displayed in the checkbutton. Button text will change as *$variable* does.

−variable => *$variable*

    Associates the on/off value of the indicator with the specified variable.

Checkbutton Methods

In addition to configure and cget, the following methods are supported by Checkbutton:

deselect

    Sets the indicator to the "off" state.

select

    Sets the indicator to the "on" state.

flash

    Causes the button to flash from the normal to active state colors.

invoke

    Invokes the callback command as if the checkbuttons were clicked.

toggle

    Toggles the indicator from "on" to "off," or from "off" to "on."

Perl/Tk

The Radiobutton Widget

Create a radiobutton with the Radiobutton method. A radiobutton has an indicator to the left of the label indicating whether the button is selected. It differs from a checkbutton in that only one button may be selected at the same time. Each button in a group of radiobuttons uses the same variable specified with the -variable option; when selected, the button assigns that variable the value specified by the -value option.

```
$parentwidget->Radiobutton (options)
```

The standard configuration options that apply to Radiobutton are: -activebackground, -activeforeground, -anchor, -background, -bg, -bitmap, -borderwidth, -bd, -cursor, -disabledforeground, -font, -foreground, -fg, -height, -highlightbackground, -highlightcolor, -highlightthickness, -image, -justify, -padx, -pady, -relief, -underline, -width, and -wraplength.

Other options are:

−command => callback
> Pointer to a function that will be called when the radiobutton is pressed.

−indicatoron => boolean
> Determines whether or not to display the indicator. Default is on (1).

−selectcolor => color
> Color of the indicator when the radiobutton is on.

−selectimage => imgptr
> Defines the image to be displayed instead of text when the radiobutton is on. Ignored if -image is not used.

−text => 'text'
> Defines the text string displayed in the radiobutton. See also -textvariable.

−textvariable => \$variable
> Points to the variable containing text to be displayed in the radiobutton. Button text will change as $variable does.

−value => value
> Sets $variable to the specified value when the radiobutton is selected (default is 1).

−variable => \$variable
> Associates the on/off value of the indicator with the specified variable.

Radiobutton Methods

In addition to configure and cget, the following methods are supported by Radiobutton:

deselect
> Deselects the button and sets the variable to the empty string.

select
> Sets the radio button.

`flash`
> Causes the button to flash from the normal to active state colors.

`invoke`
> Selects the button and invokes the callback command as if the radiobutton were clicked.

The Label Widget

Create a non-interactive label with the `Label` command.

> `$parentwidget->Label (options)`

The standard configuration options that apply to `Label` are: `-anchor`, `-background`, `-bg`, `-bitmap`, `-borderwidth`, `-bd`, `-cursor`, `-font`, `-foreground`, `-fg`, `-height`, `-highlightbackground`, `-highlightcolor`, `-highlightthickness`, `-image`, `-justify`, `-padx`, `-pady`, `-relief`, `-takefocus`, `-underline`, `-width`, and `-wraplength`.

Other options are:

`-text => 'text'`
> Defines the text string displayed in the label. See also `-textvariable`.

`-textvariable => \$variable`
> Points to the variable containing text to be displayed in the label. Label text will change as `$variable` does.

The Entry Widget

Create an entry widget with the `Entry` method. The value that the user has typed into the widget is stored in the variable pointed to by the `-textvariable` option.

> `$parent->Entry (options)`

The standard configuration options that apply to `Entry` are: `-background`, `-bg`, `-borderwidth`, `-bd`, `-cursor`, `-exportselection`, `-font`, `-foreground`, `-fg`, `-highlightbackground`, `-highlightcolor`, `-highlightthickness`, `-insertbackground`, `-insertborderwidth`, `-insertofftime`, `-insertontime`, `-insertwidth`, `-justify`, `-relief`, `-selectbackground`, `-selectborderwidth`, `-selectforeground`, `-state`, `-takefocus`, and `-xscrollcommand`.

Other options are:

`-show => x`
> Defines a character to be displayed in place of actual typed text (for use with passwords).

`-textvariable => \$variable`
> Points to the variable containing text to be displayed in the entry widget. Entry widget text will change as `$variable` does.

Perl/Tk

Text Indexes

In an Entry widget, several indexes are defined to identify positions in the entry text, for use by the methods used for retrieving or manipulating entry text. These indexes are:

n

> An integer representing a character position, with 0 as the first character in the string.

insert

> The character directly after the insert cursor.

sel.first

> The first character in the selection block.

sel.last

> The character after the last character in the selection block.

anchor

> The anchored position.

end

> The position just after the last character in the entry string.

@*x*

> The character containing the specified *x* coordinate.

Entry Methods

In addition to configure and cget, the following methods are supported for the Entry widget:

delete

> Deletes text from the widget. For example, to delete the selected text:
>
> ```
> $entry->delete('sel.first', 'sel.last');
> ```

get

> Gets the contents of the entry widget. For example:
>
> ```
> $input = $entry->get;
> ```

icursor

> Places the cursor at the specified index. For example, to move the cursor to the very end of the entry string:
>
> ```
> $entry->icursor('end');
> ```

index

> Converts a named index into a numeric one.
>
> ```
> $length = $entry->index('end');
> ```

insert
> Inserts text at the specified index. For example, to append the ".txt" string to the end of the entry string:
>
> ```
> $entry -> insert('end', '.txt');
> ```

selection
> Manipulates the selected block. The first argument can be any of:
>
> adjust
> > Extends selected text to the index specified in the second argument.
> >
> > ```
> > $entry->selection('adjust', 'end');
> > ```
>
> clear
> > Clears the selection block.
> >
> > ```
> > $entry->selection('clear');
> > ```
>
> from
> > Resets the "anchor" index to the index specified in the second argument.
> >
> > ```
> > $entry->selection('from',0);
> > ```
>
> present
> > Determines if any text is currently selected.
> >
> > ```
> > if ($entry->selection('present')) {
> >         $entry->delete('sel.first','sel.last');
> > }
> > ```
>
> range
> > Changes the selection range to the indexes specified in the second and third arguments. For example, to change the selection to include the entire entry string:
> >
> > ```
> > $entry->selection('range',0,'end');
> > ```
>
> to Extends the selection from the current anchor position to the specified index.
> >
> > ```
> > $entry->selection('to','insert');
> > ```

xview
> Manipulates the text in view. With no arguments, returns a list of two numbers between 0 and 1, defining what portion of the entry text is currently hidden on the left and right sides, respectively. With arguments, the function of xview changes:
>
> *index*
> > If the first argument is an index, that position becomes the leftmost position in view. For example, to reset the visible portion to the beginning of the string:
> >
> > ```
> > $entry->xview(0);
> > ```

moveto

> Moves the specified fraction of the entry text to the left of the visible portion. For example, to hide the first 10% of the entry text:

```
$entry->xview('moveto',0.1);
```

scroll

> Scrolls the text left or right by the specified number of units (characters, in this context) or pages. Used mainly as a callback to a scrollbar; pressing on an arrow moves by units (characters), and pressing on the trough moves by pages. The number is either 1 or −1, to move forwards or backwards, respectively. For example:

```
$entry->xview('scroll',1,'units');
```

The Scrollbar Widget

Create a scrollbar with the Scrollbar method.

```
$parentwidget->Scrollbar (options)
```

The standard configuration options that apply to Scrollbar are: -activebackground, -background, -bg, -borderwidth, -bd, -cursor, -highlightbackground, -highlightcolor, -highlightthickness, -relief, -takefocus, and -width.

Other options are:

−activerelief => type

> Changes how active elements (arrow1, arrow2, and the slider) in the scrollbar are drawn. Values for type are 'flat', 'groove', 'raised', 'ridge', and 'sunken'. The default is 'raised'.

−command => callback

> Pointer to a function that will be called when the scrollbar is clicked on.

−elementborderwidth => amount

> The width of the borders of the arrow1, arrow2, and slider elements.

−jump => boolean

> Determines whether the scrollbar will jump scroll. Default is 0 (jump scroll disabled).

−orient => orientation

> Determines the orientation of the scrollbar. Possible orientations are 'horizontal' and 'vertical' (default).

−repeatdelay => milliseconds

> Determines the number of milliseconds to hold down an arrow before it will auto-repeat. Default is 300.

−repeatinterval => milliseconds

> Determines the number of milliseconds between auto-repeats once it is started. Default is 100.

−troughcolor => color

> Changes the color of the trough.

Scrollbar Methods

In addition to `configure` and `cget`, the following methods are supported by the Scrollbar widget:

set
> Changes the viewable portion of the data, with the two arguments being numbers between 0 and 1 representing the portions of the data to be visible.
>
> ```
> $scrollbar->set(0.2,0.6);
> ```

get
> Returns the latest arguments to `set`.

activate
> With no arguments, returns the name of the current active element. With an argument of `arrow1`, `arrow2`, or `slider`, changes the color of the specified element to the active foreground color and relief type.

delta
> Given a number of pixels in the first argument, returns the fractional change needed to move the slider that amount.

fraction
> Given an x,y coordinate as the first and second arguments, returns a number between 0 and 1 representing what fraction of the scrollbar that coordinate would fall under.

identify
> Given an x,y coordinate as the first and second arguments, returns the name of the element at those coordinates.

The Listbox Widget

Create a listbox with the `Listbox` method. You can then insert items into the listbox using the `insert` method.

```
$parentwidget->Listbox (options)
```

The standard configuration options that apply to `Listbox` are: `-background`, `-bg`, `-borderwidth`, `-bd`, `-cursor`, `-exportselection`, `-font`, `-foreground`, `-fg`, `-height`, `-highlightbackground`, `-highlightcolor`, `-highlightthickness`, `-relief`, `-selectbackground`, `-selectborderwidth`, `-selectforeground`, `-takefocus`, `-width`, `-xscrollcommand`, and `-yscrollcommand`.

Other options are:

−selectmode => mode
> Determines how many items can be selected at once, as well as key/mouse bindings. mode can be any of:
>
> 'single'
> > Only one item can be selected at a time.
>
> 'browse'
> > Only one item can be selected at a time. (Default).

Perl/Tk

'multiple'

>Multiple items can be selected at a time.

'extended'

>Multiple items can be selected at a time.

-setgrid => *boolean*

>Turns on gridding for the listbox. If the widget is resized, only complete lines and characters are displayed. Default is 0 (off).

Listbox Indexes

In a Listbox widget, several indexes are defined to identify positions in the listbox, for use by the methods used for retrieving or manipulating listbox entries. These indexes are:

n

>An integer representing a position in the list, with 0 as the first item.

active

>The item with the keyboard focus.

anchor

>The anchored position.

end

>The last element in the listbox.

@*x*,*y*

>The listbox item containing the specified x,y coordinate.

Listbox Methods

In addition to configure and cget, the following methods are supported by List-box:

insert

>Adds items to a listbox at the specified index. For example, to insert items at the end of a list:

>```
>$listbox->insert('end', "Puerto Rico", "Virgin Islands", "Guam");
>```

delete

>Deletes items from a listbox. To delete all items:

>```
>$listbox->delete(0,'end');
>```

get

>Returns a list of elements within the specified range of indexes. For a list of all elements:

>```
>@items = $listbox->get(0,'end');
>```

curselection

>Returns a list of all currently selected elements in the listbox.

activate

Sets the specified item to be the active element.

bbox

Returns the location and dimensions of the bounding box surrounding the specified listbox element. The returned list contains four numbers representing (respectively) the x coordinate of the upper-left corner, the y coordinate of the upper-left corner, the width of the text in pixels, and the height of the text in pixels.

index

Converts a named index into a numeric one.

nearest

Gets the index of the listbox item nearest to a given y coordinate.

see

Pages the listbox up or down to display the specified item.

selection

Manipulates the selected block of list items. The first argument can be any of:

> **anchor**
>
> > Sets the anchor index to the specified index.
>
> **clear**
>
> > Clears any selected list items in the specified range. For example, to clear all selections:
> >
> > ```
> > $listbox->selection('clear', 0, 'end');
> > ```
>
> **includes**
>
> > Returns 0 or 1 depending on whether the specified item is already selected.
> >
> > ```
> > $listbox->selection('includes', 'end');
> > ```
>
> **set** Selects a range of items in the listbox.
>
> > ```
> > $listbox->selection('set', 0, 'end');
> > ```

size

Returns the total number of items in the listbox.

xview

Manipulates the text in view. With no arguments, returns a list of two numbers between 0 and 1, defining what portion of the list text is currently hidden on the left and right sides, respectively. With arguments, the function of xview changes:

> *index*
>
> > If the first argument is an index, that position becomes the leftmost position in view.
>
> **moveto**
>
> > Moves the specified fraction of the listbox to the left of the visible portion.

scroll

> Scrolls the text left or right by the specified number of units (characters, in this context) or pages. Used primarily as a callback to a scrollbar; pressing on an arrow would move by units (characters), and pressing on the trough would move by pages. The number is either 1 or −1, to move forwards or backwards, respectively.

yview

Manipulates the text in view. With no arguments, returns a list of two numbers between 0 and 1, defining what portion of the list text is currently hidden on the top and bottom, respectively. With arguments, the function of yview changes:

> index
>
>> If the first argument is an index, that position becomes the topmost position in view.
>
> moveto
>
>> Moves the specified fraction of the listbox to the top of the visible portion.
>
> scroll
>
>> Scrolls the text up or down by the specified number of units (lines, in this context) or pages. Used primarily as a callback to a scrollbar; pressing on an arrow would move by units (lines), and pressing on the trough would move by pages. The number is either 1 or −1, to move forwards or backwards, respectively.

The Text Widget

Create a text widget with the Text method:

```
$parentwidget->Text ( options )
```

The standard configuration options that apply to Text are: -background, -bg, -borderwidth, -bd, -cursor, -exportselection, -font, -foreground, -fg, -height, -highlightbackground, -highlightcolor, -highlightthickness, -insertbackground, -insertborderwidth, -insertofftime, -insertontime, -insertwidth, -padx, -pady, -relief, -selectbackground, -selectborderwidth, -selectforeground, -state, -takefocus, -width, -xscrollcommand, and -yscrollcommand.

Other options are:

−setgrid => *boolean*

Turns on gridding for the text widget. Default is 0 (off).

−spacing1 => *amount*

Defines the amount of space left on the top of a line of text that starts on its own line. Default is 0.

−spacing2 => *amount*

Defines the amount of space left on the top of a line of text after it has been automatically wrapped by the text widget. Default is 0.

−spacing3 => *amount*
>   Defines the amount of space left after a line of text that has been ended by
>   "\n". Default is 0.

−tabs => *list*
>   Specifies a list of tab stops to use in the text widget. Default is undefined (no
>   tab stops).

−wrap => *mode*
>   Sets the mode for determining automatic line wrapping. Values are "none" (no
>   wrapping), "char" (wrap at any character), or "word" (wrap at a word bound-
>   ary). Default is "char".

Text Indexes and Modifiers

In a Text widget, several indexes are defined to identify positions in the text widget, for use by the methods used for retrieving or manipulating text. These indexes
are:

n.m
>   Numbers representing character *m* on line *n*.

@*x,y*
>   The character closest to the *x,y* coordinate.

end
>   The end of the text.

insert
>   The character after the insert cursor.

current
>   The position closest to the mouse cursor.

mark
>   Other marks defined for the widget (see discussion of text marks later in this
>   section).

sel.first
>   The first selected character.

sel.last
>   The character just after the last selected character.

tag.first
>   The first character in the widget of the specified tag type.

tag.last
>   The character just after the last character of the specified tag type.

widget
>   The location of an embedded widget.

There are also several modifiers to use with text indexes. They are:

+ *n* lines
− *n* lines
>   *n* lines before or after the index.

+ *n* chars
− *n* chars
> *n* characters before or after the index.

linestart
> The first character on the line.

lineend
> The last character on the line (often a newline).

wordstart
> The first character in the word.

wordend
> The character after the last character in the word.

Text Methods

In addition to configure and cget, the following methods are defined for the Text widget.

bbox
> Returns the location and dimensions of the bounding box surrounding the character at the specified index. The returned list contains four numbers representing (respectively) the x coordinate of the upper-left corner, the y coordinate of the upper-left corner, the width of the text in pixels, and the height of the text in pixels.

compare
> Performs a comparison on two indexes. For example:
>
> ```
> if ($text->compare('insert', '==', 'end') {
>         # we're at the end of the text
> }
> ```
>
> The valid operators are <, <=, ==, >=, and !=.

debug
> Given a boolean, turns debugging on or off.

delete
> Deletes text from the text widget. To delete everything:
>
> ```
> $text->delete(0, 'end');
> ```

dlineinfo
> Returns the location and dimensions of the bounding box surrounding the line at the specified index. The returned list contains five numbers representing (respectively) the x coordinate of the upper-left corner, the y coordinate of the upper-left corner, the width of the text in pixels, the height of the text in pixels, and the baseline position of the line.

get
> Returns the text located in the given index range.

`index`

Given a named index, returns its numeric equivalent in the format *line.char*.

`insert`

Inserts text into the widget at the specified location. The second argument is the text to insert and the third argument is either a single tag or a list reference containing the names of multiple tags to apply to the text. Subsequent arguments alternate between text and tags. For example:

```
$text->insert('end', 'You want to do ', 'normal',
              'what?!', ['bold','red']);
```

`search`

Returns the index containing a particular string in the text widget. For example, to search backwards for a case-insensitive hostname starting from the end of the text:

```
$hostindex = $text->search(-nocase, -backwards, $hostname, 'end');
```

The `search` method takes several switches to modify the search, each starting with "–". The first argument that does not start with "–" is taken to be the search string. The switches are:

-forwards

Search forwards starting at the specified index.

-backwards

Search backwards starting at the specified index.

-exact

Match the string exactly (default).

-regexp

Treat the pattern as a regular expression.

-nocase

Ignore case.

-count => \$variable

Store the number of matches into the specified variable.

–

Interpret the next argument as the pattern. (Useful when the pattern starts with a "-".)

`see`

Scrolls the text so that the portion of the text containing the specified index is visible.

`window`

Embeds widgets within the Text widget. The first argument can be any of: 'create', 'names', 'cget', and 'configure'.

create

Inserts an embedded widget at a specified index. Each widget occupies one character in the text widget. The widget must have already been created as a child of the text widget. For example:

```
$button = $text->Label(-text => "How ya doing?");
$text->window('create','end', -window => $button);
```

Here, the -window option is used to identify the widget to embed. The list of options to window ('create') is:

-align

Determines the positioning within the line of text. Values are 'baseline', 'bottom', 'top', or 'center' (default).

-padx

Adds padding in the x direction.

-pady

Adds padding in the y direction.

-window

Identifies the widget to embed.

names

Returns a list of widget types embedded into the text widget.

cget

Returns information on the widget at the specified index.

```
$text->window('cget',0);
```

configure

Configures widget at the specified index.

```
$text->window('configure',0,-background => "green");
```

xview

Manipulates the text in view. With no arguments, returns a list of two numbers between 0 and 1, defining what portion of the text is currently hidden on the left and right sides, respectively. With arguments, the function of xview changes:

index

If the first argument is an index, that position becomes the leftmost position in view.

moveto

Moves the specified fraction of the text to the left of the visible portion.

scroll

Scrolls the text left or right by the specified number of units (characters, in this context) or pages. Used primarily as a callback to a scrollbar; pressing on an arrow would move by units (characters), and pressing on the trough would move by pages. The number is either 1 or -1, to move forwards or backwards, respectively.

yview

Manipulates the text in view. With no arguments, returns a list of two numbers between 0 and 1, defining what portion of the text is currently hidden on the top and bottom, respectively. With arguments, the function of yview changes:

index

If the first argument is an index, that position becomes the topmost position in view.

moveto

> Moves the specified fraction of the text to the top of the visible portion.

scroll

> Scrolls the text up or down by the specified number of units (lines, in this context) or pages. Used primarily as a callback to a scrollbar; pressing on an arrow would move by units (lines), and pressing on the trough would move by pages. The number is either 1 or -1, to move forwards or backwards, respectively.

Tags

You can associate a distinct set of format properties to a portion of the text using *tags*. A tag is defined with the tagConfigure method, and text is associated with a tag via an option to the insert or tagAdd method. For example:

```
$text->Text->pack;
$text->tagConfigure('bold', -font =>
'-*-Courier-Medium-B-Normal--*-120-*-*-*-*-*-*");
$text->insert('end', "Normal text0);
$text->insert('end', "Bold text0, 'bold');
```

There are several methods defined for manipulating text tags. They are:

tagAdd

> Adds a tag to the text within the specified index range. For example, to assign the "bold" tag defined above to the current selection:
>
> ```
> $text->tagAdd('bold','sel.first','sel.last');
> ```
>
> You can supply multiple ranges as arguments to tagAdd.

tagBind

> Executes a callback when a specified event happens on the tagged text. For example:
>
> ```
> $text->tagBind('goto_end', "<Button-1>", sub {shift->see('end');} );
> ```

tagConfigure

> Creates or changes settings for a text tag, for example:
>
> ```
> $text->tagConfigure('link', -foreground => 'red');
> ```
>
> Options for configuring text tags are:
>
> −background => *color*
> > The color to use behind the text.
>
> −bgstipple => *bitmap*
> > A pattern to draw behind the text.
>
> −borderwidth => *amount*
> > The width of the edge drawn around the text.
>
> −fgstipple => *bitmap*
> > A pattern used to draw the text.

−font => *fontname*

The font used for the text.

−foreground => *color*

The color of the text.

−justify => *position*

The justification of the text (any of `'left'`, `'right'`, and `'center'`). The default is `'left'`.

−lmargin1 => *amount*

The indentation for the first line of a paragraph.

−lmargin2 => *amount*

The indentation for subsequent lines of a paragraph (for hanging indents).

−offset => *amount*

The amount the text is raised or lowered from the baseline (for subscripts and superscripts).

−overstrike => *boolean*

Draws the text with a line through it.

−relief => *type*

The type of edges drawn around the text. Values for *type* can be `'flat'`, `'groove'`, `'raised'`, `'ridge'`, and `'sunken'`. Default is `'flat'`.

−rmargin => *amount*

The right margin.

−spacing1 => *amount*

The amount of space left on the top of a line of text that starts on its own line.

−spacing2 => *amount*

The amount of space left on the top of a line of text after it has been automatically wrapped by the text widget.

−spacing3 => *amount*

The amount of space left after a line of text that has been ended by "\n".

−tabs => *list*

A list of tab stops to use in the text widget.

−underline => *boolean*

Whether to underline the text.

−wrap => *mode*

Sets the mode for determining automatic line wrapping. Values are `"none"` (no wrapping), `"char"` (wrap at any character), or `"word"` (wrap at a word boundary).

tagCget

Returns configuration settings for a tag.

tagDelete

Deletes the specified tag(s).

tagRemove

Removes the tags from the text in the specified index range. (The tag itself remains defined, but is no longer applied to that text.)

tagRaise

Increases priority for a specified tag. With only one argument, the tag takes highest priority over all others; with a second argument of another tag, the tag's priority is just higher than the second tag. For example:

```
$text->tagRaise('bold','italic');
```

tagLower

Decreases priority for a specified tag. With only one argument, the tag takes lowest priority to all others; with a second argument of another tag, the tag's priority is just lower than the second tag. For example:

```
$text->tagLower('italic','bold');
```

(The outcome of this code is effectively identical to that of the previous example.)

tagNames

Returns the names of all tags applying to the specified index. With no index specified, returns all tags defined for the text widget, regardless of whether they have been applied.

```
@defined_tags = $text->tagNames;
```

tagRanges

Returns a list of index ranges to which the specified tag is defined. The returned list contains pairs of starting and ending indexes for the ranges.

```
@bold_indexes = $text->tagRanges('bold');
```

tagNextrange

Given a tag name and an index, returns the next index range to which the specified tag is defined.

```
@next_bold = $text->tagRanges('bold', 'insert');
```

Marks

A *mark* refers to a particular position in between characters in a text widget. Once you create a mark, you can use it as an index. The gravity of the mark affects which side the text is inserted. "Right" gravity is the default, in which case the text is inserted to the right of the mark.

The two marks that are automatically set are "insert" and "current". The "insert" mark refers to the position of the insert cursor. The "current" mark is the position closest to the mouse cursor.

Perl/Tk

The following methods are defined for marking:

markGravity

Sets the gravity of a mark. For example:

```
$text->markGravity('insert', 'left');
```

markNames

Returns a list of all marks defined for the text widget.

markSet

Creates a mark at a specified index.

```
$text->markSet('saved', 'insert');
```

markUnset

Deletes mark(s) from the text widget.

```
$text->markUnset('saved');
```

Note that you cannot delete the "insert" or "current" marks.

The Canvas Widget

Create a canvas for drawing with the Canvas method. The Canvas widget uses a coordinate system with the x coordinate increasing as you move right, and the y coordinate increasing as you move *down* (i.e., the y coordinate is mathematically upside-down). The x and y coordinates are specified in pixels by default.

```
$parentwidget->Canvas ( options)
```

The standard configuration options that apply to Canvas are: -background, -borderwidth, -cursor, -height, -highlightbackground, -highlightcolor, -highlightthickness, -insertbackground, -insertborderwidth, -insertofftime, -insertontime, -insertwidth, -relief, -selectbackground, -selectborderwidth, -selectforeground, -takefocus, -width, -xscrollcommand, and -yscrollcommand.

Other options are:

−closeenough => *amount*

The distance considered "close enough" to an item to be judged to be within it. Default is 1 pixel.

−confine => *boolean*

Whether to limit the canvas to the scroll region. Default is 1.

−scrollregion => [*x, y, w, h*]

Sets the region that the user is allowed to scroll. The option is a list reference that conveniently corresponds to the return value of the bbox method.

−xscrollincrement => *amount*

The distance to use for scrolling in the x direction.

−yscrollincrement => *amount*

The distance to use for scrolling in the y direction.

Canvas Creation Methods

To place graphic elements in a canvas, there are several item creation commands:

createArc

> Creates an arc contained within the given bounding box. For example, to create an oval bounded by the box from (0,0) to (40,100):
>
> ```
> $canvas->createArc(0,0,40,100, -extent => 360);
> ```
>
> The -extent option gives a number between 0 and 360 defining the length of the arc. The default -extent is 90, or 1/4 of an oval; an extent of 360 gives you a full oval. The complete list of options to createArc is:
>
> -extent => degrees
> > Creates an arc of the specified extent. *degrees* can be any number between 0 and 360, as described above.
>
> -fill => color
> > Fills the arc with the specified color.
>
> -outline => color
> > Draws the arc with the specified color (default = black).
>
> -outlinestipple => bitmap
> > Draws the outline with the specified bitmap pattern.
>
> -start => degrees
> > Starts drawing the arc from the specified position, where the position is represented by a number from 0 to 360. The default is 0, which means to start drawing at the 3 o'clock position.
>
> -stipple => bitmap
> > Uses the specified bitmap to fill the arc (if -fill is also specified).
>
> -style => type
> > Draws the arc as specified. Values are:
> >
> > 'pieslice'
> > > Draws lines from the center to the ends of the arc (the default).
> >
> > 'chord'
> > > Draws a line connecting the two ends of the arc.
> >
> > 'arc'
> > > Draws the arc with no other lines.
>
> -tags => tagnames
> > Associates the arc with the specified tag(s). Multiple tag names can be supplied as an anonymous list.
>
> -width => amount
> > The width of the outline. Default is 1.

createBitmap

> Inserts a bitmap. For example, to place the "calculator" bitmap at the (0,0) coordinates:
>
> ```
> $canvas -> createBitmap(0, 0, -bitmap => 'calculator');
> ```

Perl/Tk

Options are:

  −anchor => *position*
  > Anchors the bitmap at the specified position. Values are "center"
  > (default), "n", "e", "s", "w", "ne", "nw", "se", and "sw".

  −background => *color*
  > Specifies the color to use for the "0" pixels in the bitmap (default is
  > to be transparent).

  −bitmap => *bitmap*
  > Specifies the bitmap name. For a built-in bitmap, just specify the
  > name; for a local bitmap file, specify the name with an "@" symbol
  > preceding it.

  −foreground => *color*
  > Specifies the color to use for the "1" pixels in the bitmap (default is
  > black).

  −tags => *tagnames*
  > Associates the bitmap with the specified tag(s). Multiple tag names
  > can be supplied as an anonymous list.

createImage
  > Creates an image. For example, to place an image at (0,0):

```
$canvas->createImage(0,0, -image => $imgptr);
```

  Options are:

  −anchor => *position*
  > Anchors the image at the specified position. Values are "center"
  > (default), "n", "e", "s", "w", "ne", "nw", "se", and "sw".

  −image => *$imgptr*
  > *$imgptr* is a pointer to a Photo or Image object made using a GIF or
  > PPM file. For example:

```
$imgptr = $mainwindow->Photo(-file => "doggie.gif");
```

  −tags => *tagnames*
  > Associate the image with the specified tag(s). Multiple tag names can
  > be supplied as an anonymous list.

createLine
  > Creates a line or several adjoining lines. For example, to create a line from
  > (0,0) to (100, 100) and then back to (100, 0):

```
$canvas->createLine (0,0,100,100,100,0);
```

The first four coordinates are required. Any additional coordinates are taken
to represent a continuation of that line. Options are:

  −arrow => *position*
  > Specifies where to place arrowheads. Values are 'none' (default),
  > 'first', 'last', and 'both'.

-arrowshape => [*head, length, flare*]
Specifies the dimensions of the arrow as a three-element anonymous list, describing (in order) the distance from the base to the "head" of the arrow, the distance from the rear point(s) to the head of the arrow, and the distance from the rear point(s) to the line.

-capstyle => *type*
Defines the type of arrowhead. Values are "butt" (the default), "projecting", and "round".

-fill => *color*
The color to use to draw the line.

-joinstyle => *type*
Defines how multiple lines are joined. Values are "miter" (default), "bevel", and "round".

-smooth => *boolean*
Determines whether the lines are drawn with a Bezier spine. Default is 0.

-splinesteps => *n*
Determines how smooth the Bezier curve is.

-stipple => *bitmap*
Draws the line with the specified bitmap pattern.

-tags => *tagnames*
Associates the line with the specified tag(s). Multiple tag names can be supplied as an anonymous list.

-width => *amount*
The width of the line (default = 1 pixel).

createOval
Creates an oval. For example, to create a circle bounded by the box from (50,50) to (150,150):

```
$canvas->createOval(50,50,150,150);
```

Options are:

-fill => *color*
Fills the arc with the specified color.

-outline => *color*
Specifies the color for the outline (default = black).

-stipple => *bitmap*
Specifies a bitmap to fill the oval with.

-tags => *tagnames*
Associates the oval with the specified tag(s). Multiple tag names can be supplied as an anonymous list.

-width => *amount*
The width of the outline (default = 1 pixel).

Perl/Tk

createPolygon

Creates a polygon. At least three sets of coordinates are required; the first point is automatically connected to the last point to complete the polygon.

```
$canvas -> createPolygon(0,0,130, 20, 90, -35);
```

-fill => *color*
The color to use to fill the polygon.

-outline => *color*
Specifies the color for the outline (default = black).

-smooth => *boolean*
Determines whether the outline is drawn with a Bezier spine. Default is 0.

-splinesteps => *n*
Determines how smooth the Bezier curve is.

-stipple => *bitmap*
Fills the polygon with the specified bitmap pattern.

-tags => *tagnames*
Associates the polygon with the specified tag(s). Multiple tag names can be supplied as an anonymous list.

-width => *amount*
The width of the outline (default = 1 pixel).

createRectangle

Creates a rectangle. For example, to create a square with one corner at (0,0) and another at (100,100):

```
$canvas->createRectangle(0,0,100,100);
```

Options are:

-fill => *color*
The color to use to fill the rectangle.

-outline => *color*
Specifies the color for the outline (default = black).

-stipple => *bitmap*
Fills the rectangle with the specified bitmap pattern.

-tags => *tagnames*
Associates the rectangle with the specified tag(s). Multiple tag names can be supplied as an anonymous list.

-width => *amount*
The width of the outline (default = 1 pixel).

createText

Places text in a canvas widget. For example, to write "Broadway" centered at the position (130,-40):

```
$canvas->createText(130,-40, -text => "Broadway");
```

Options are:

−anchor => *position*

Anchors the text at the specified position. Values are "center" (default), "n", "e", "s", "w", "ne", "nw", "se", and "sw".

−fill => *color*

The color to use for the text.

−font => *fontname*

The font for the text.

−justify => *position*

The justification of the text (any of 'left', 'right', and 'center'). The default is 'left'.

−stipple => *bitmap*

Fills the text with the specified bitmap pattern.

−tags => *tagnames*

Associates the text with the specified tag(s). Multiple tag names can be supplied as an anonymous list.

−text => *string*

Specifies the text to display.

−width => *amount*

The maximum length of each line of text. Default is 0, which means that lines are only broken at explicit newline characters.

There is a set of methods for manipulating text items within a Canvas widget. For each of these methods, the first argument is the tag name or tag ID, and subsequent arguments use text indexes as described for the Text widget.

dchars

Deletes characters from a text item, given the tag name or ID, and indexes of the first and last characters to delete.

icursor

Places the insert cursor at the specified index.

index

Gets a numerical index from a named one.

insert

Adds a string to the text item.

createWindow

Embeds another widget inside of a canvas. The widget must have been already created as a child of the canvas or of the canvas's parent. Options are:

−anchor => *position*

Anchors the widget at the specified position. Values are "center" (default), "n", "e", "s", "w", "ne", "nw", "se", and "sw".

−height => *amount*

Specifies the height of the widget.

```
-tags => tagnames
```
Associates the widget with the specified tag(s). Multiple tag names can be supplied as an anonymous list.

```
-width => amount
```
The width of the widget.

```
-window => $widget
```
Specifies the widget to embed.

Item Tags and IDs

Each item in a Canvas Widget is given a unique ID when it is created. This ID is returned from the canvas creation command. In addition, each item can have a tag associated with it, either when created or with the `addtag` method. You can use either the ID or the tag to refer to an item in the canvas. Unlike IDs, tags do not have to be unique, which makes it possible to configure several items as a group.

Two special tags are created automatically. The "all" tag refers to all items in the canvas. The "current" tag refers to the item that the cursor is currently over, if any.

Canvas Methods

In addition to `configure` and `cget`, the following methods are supported by the Canvas widget.

`addtag`

Defines a tag for an already-created canvas item. For example, to assign a tag called "everything" to all items in a canvas:

```
$canvas->addtag("everything", "all");
```

To change the tag for an item from "tmp" to "circle":

```
$canvas->addtag("circle", "withtag", "tmp");
```

To assign the tag "origin" to the item closest to the coordinates (0,0):

```
$canvas->addtag("origin", "closest", 0, 0);
```

The full list of identifiers is:

`above`

Assigns the tag to the item above the specified item in the display list.

`all` Assigns the tag to all items in the canvas.

`below`

Assigns the tag to the item below the specified item in the display list.

`closest`

Assigns the tag to the item closest to the specified x,y coordinate.

enclosed

    Assigns the tag to all items that are completely enclosed within the specified bounding box.

overlapping

    Assigns the tag to all items that are even partially inside the specified bounding box.

withtag

    Assigns the tag to all items with the specified tag.

bind

Binds a callback to an item. (To bind a callback to the canvas widget itself, you must specify Tk::bind.)

bbox

Returns the bounding box of an item. For example, to get the bounding box for all items in the canvas:

```
$canvas->bbox("all");
```

itemconfigure

Configures one of the items within the canvas. Works just like the configure method for widgets, but the first argument is the tag name or ID for the canvas item.

itemcget

Gets configuration information for one of the items within the canvas. Works just like the cget method for widgets, but the first argument is the tag name or ID for the canvas item.

move

Moves an item on the canvas by adding the specified x and y distances to it.

```
$canvas->move("circle1", 100, 100);
```

coords

Gets the current x,y coordinates for an item, or moves an item to an explicit x,y coordinate.

lower

Sets the priority for the item in the display list to be lower than the item identified by the specified tag or ID.

raise

Sets the priority for the item in the display list to be higher than the item identified by the specified tag or ID.

delete

Removes an item from the canvas. You can specify as many tags or IDs in the argument list as you want.

find

Finds the specified items. The first argument can be any of:

above

    Finds the item above the specified item in the display list.

Perl/Tk

all Finds all items in the canvas.

below
> Finds the item below the specified item in the display list.

closest
> Finds the item closest to the specified x,y coordinate.

enclosed
> Finds all items that are completely enclosed within the specified bounding box.

overlapping
> Finds all items that are even partially inside the specified bounding box.

withtag
> Finds all items with the specified tag.

gettags
> Retrieves a list of all tags associated with an item.

type
> Determines the type of the specified item.

focus
> Assigns the keyboard focus to the specified item.

postscript
> Renders the canvas as PostScript. Options are:

> -colormap => \@colorcommand
>> Specifies a PostScript command for setting color values.

> -colormode => mode
>> Sets the mode to "color" (full color), "gray" (grayscale), or "mono" (black and white).

> -file => filename
>> The name of the file to store the PostScript output.

> -fontmap => \@fontspec
>> Specifies a font name and point size.

> -height => size
>> The height of the area to print.

> -pageanchor => position
>> The anchor position of the page. Values are "center" (default), "n", "e", "s", and "w".

> -pageheight => height
>> The height of the printed page.

> -pagewidth => width
>> The width of the printed page.

> -pagex => x
>> The x positioning point.

-pagey => *y*
> The y positioning point.

-rotate => *boolean*
> Whether to rotate to landscape orientation. Default is 0.

-width => *size*
> The width of the area to print.

-x => *x*
> The left edge of the canvas.

-y => *y*
> The top edge of the canvas.

scale
> Changes the scaling of the canvas or any individual items. For example, to scale the entire canvas to half its dimensions:
>
> ```
> $canvas->scale("all", 0, 0, .5, .5);
> ```

xview
> Manipulates the canvas area in view. With no arguments, returns a list of two numbers between 0 and 1, defining what portion of the canvas is currently hidden on the left and right sides, respectively. With arguments, the function of xview changes:
>
> moveto
> > Moves the specified fraction of the text to the left of the visible portion.
>
> scroll
> > Scrolls the canvas left or right by the specified number of units or pages. Used primarily as a callback to a scrollbar; pressing on an arrow would move by units (characters), and pressing on the trough would move by pages. The number is either 1 or −1, to move forwards or backwards, respectively.

yview
> Manipulates the canvas in view. With no arguments, returns a list of two numbers between 0 and 1, defining what portion of the canvas is currently hidden on the top and bottom, respectively. With arguments, its function changes:
>
> moveto
> > Moves the specified fraction of the canvas area to the top of the visible portion.
>
> scroll
> > Scrolls the canvas up or down by the specified number of units or pages. Used primarily as a callback to a scrollbar; pressing on an arrow would move by units (lines), and pressing on the trough would move by pages. The number is either 1 or −1, to move forwards or backwards, respectively.

Perl/Tk

The Scale Widget

Create a "slider" widget representing a numeric value with the Scale method.

```
$parent->Scale(options);
```

The standard configuration options that apply to Scale are: -activebackground, -background, -bg, -borderwidth, -bw, -cursor, -font, -foreground, -fg, -high-lightbackground, -highlightcolor, -highlightthickness, -relief, -state, -takefocus, and -width.

Other options are:

−bigincrement => *amount*
> The amount to change the slider when using large increments. Default is 0, which means 1/10 of the scale.

−command => *callback*
> Pointer to a function that will be called for every incremental change in the slider.

−digits => *amount*
> The number of digits to keep when converting from a number to a string.

−from => *n*
> Low end of the scale (default = 0).

−label => *string*
> The string to use as a label for the slider.

−length => *amount*
> The length of the slider.

−orient => *direction*
> The orientation of the slider. Values can be either 'vertical' (default) or 'horizontal'.

−repeatdelay => *milliseconds*
> Determines the number of milliseconds to hold down an arrow before it will auto-repeat. Default is 300.

−repeatinterval => *milliseconds*
> Determines the number of milliseconds between auto-repeats once it is started. Default is 100.

−resolution => *value*
> The increments that the scale will change by (default = 1).

−showvalue => *boolean*
> Whether to show the current value of the slider (default = 1).

−sliderlength => *amount*
> The size of the slider. Default is 25 pixels.

−tickinterval => *n*
> The number of "ticks" to display for the slider. Default is 0 (no ticks).

−to => *n*
> The top value of the scale (default is 100).

`-troughcolor => color`
Changes the color of the trough.

`-variable => \$variable`
Assigns the value of the slider to the specified variable.

Scale Methods

In addition to `configure` and `cget`, the following methods are defined for the Scale widget:

`get`
Returns the current value if given no arguments. If given x and y coordinates as the first and second arguments, returns the value of the scale at that position.

`set`
Assigns the value associated with the scale.

`coords`
Returns the x and y coordinates associated with the value given in the first argument.

`identify`
Returns `"slider"`, `"trough1"`, `"trough2"`, or `""`, depending on which part of the scale corresponds to the given x, y coordinates.

The Menubutton Widget

Create a menubutton with the `Menubutton` method. For example:

```
$mainwindow->Menubutton(-text => "File",
        -menuitems => [ [ 'command' => "New",
                          "-command" => \&newfile,
                          "-underline" => 0 ],
                        [ 'command' => "Open",
                          "-command" => \&openfile,
                          "-underline" => 0 ],
                        "-",
                        [ 'command' => "Save",
                          "-command" => \&savefile,
                          "-underline" => 0 ],
                        [ 'command' => "SaveAs",
                          "-command" => \&saveasfile,
                          "-underline" => 4 ] ] );
```

The `-menuitems` option takes a list of lists describing the menu items. For each menu item, an embedded anonymous list describes the type of menu item, the label to use, and the action to take when it is selected along with any other options desired to configure the menu item. In this example, each of the menu items is the `'command'` type, and we use the `-command` option for each item to point to the callback to execute when the menu item is selected. We also use the `-underline` option to enable the user to select a menu item using keystrokes. (The `"-"` represents a separator between menu items.)

In addition to `'command'`, other types of menus are:

`'cascade'`
> Embeds a cascade menu.

`'checkbutton'`
> Treats the menu item as a checkbutton.

`'command'`
> Executes a callback.

`'radiobutton'`
> Treats the menu item as a radiobutton.

You can configure both the menu itself and the individual menu items. The configuration options that apply to Menubutton are: `-activebackground`, `-activeforeground`, `-anchor`, `-background`, `-bg`, `-bitmap`, `-borderwidth`, `-bw`, `-cursor`, `-disabledforeground`, `-font`, `-foreground`, `-fg`, `-height`, `-highlightbackground`, `-highlightcolor`, `-highlightthickness`, `-image`, `-justify`, `-padx`, `-pady`, `-relief`, `-state`, `-takefocus`, `-underline`, `-width`, and `-wraplength`.

Other Menubutton options are:

`-indicatoron => boolean`
> Determines whether or not to display an indicator.

`-menu => $menu`
> Display the menu associated with `$menu`.

`-menuitems => list`
> Specifies items to create in the menu as a list of lists. See the description at the beginning of this section.

`-tearoff => boolean`
> Whether or not to allow the menu to be "torn off." Default is 1.

`-text => string`
> Specifies the text to display as a label for the button.

`-textvariable => \$variable`
> Points to the variable containing text to be displayed in the menubutton. Button text will change as `$variable` does.

Menu Item Options

In addition to the menu itself, each individual menu item can be configured. The widget configuration options that apply to menu items are: `-activebackground`, `-background`, `-bg`, `-bitmap`, `-font`, `-foreground`, `-fg`, `-image`, `-state`, and `-underline`. Other options are:

`-accelerator`
> Displays an accelerator key sequence for the menu item. The key sequence must be independently defined with a `bind`.

`-command => callback`
> Pointer to a function that will be called when the menu item is selected.

`-indicatoron => boolean`

Determines whether or not to display an indicator.

`-label => string`

The string to use as a label for the menu item.

`-menu => $submenu`

For a cascade menu, points to the menu to embed.

`-offvalue => newvalue`

For a checkbutton, specifies the value used when the checkbutton is "off."

`-onvalue => newvalue`

For a checkbutton, specifies the value used when the checkbutton is "on."

`-selectcolor => color`

For a checkbutton or radiobutton, color of the indicator when "on."

`-selectimage => imgptr`

For a checkbutton or radiobutton, defines the image to be displayed instead of text when the radiobutton is "on". Ignored if `-image` is not used.

`-value => value`

For a radiobutton, sets `$variable` to the specified value when the radiobutton is selected (default is 1).

`-variable => \$variable`

Associates the value of the menu item to the specified variable.

Menubutton Methods

In addition to `configure` and `cget`, the following methods are defined for Menubutton widgets:

`AddItems`

Adds menu items to the end of the menu. The arguments to `AddItems` are lists configuring each menu item, similar to the lists defined with the `-menuitem` option.

```
$menubutton->AddItems(["command" => "Print",
                       "-command" => \&printscreen ],
                      ["command" => "Exit",
                       "-command" => \&exitclean ]);
```

`command`

Adds a command item to the end of the menu. The above example could have read:

```
$menubutton->command(-label => "Print", -command => \&printscreen);
$menubutton->command(-label => "Exit", -command => \&exitclean);
```

`checkbutton`

Adds a checkbutton item to the end of the menu.

```
$menubutton->checkbutton(-label => "Show Toolbar",
            [-variable => \$toolbar");
```

Perl/Tk

```
radiobutton
```
Adds a radiobutton item to the end of the menu.

```
    $menubutton->radiobutton(-label => "Red", -variable => \$color");
    $menubutton->radiobutton(-label => "Blue", -variable => \$color");
```

```
separator
```
Adds a separator line to the end of a menu.

```
cascade
```
Adds a cascade item to the end of the menu.

```
menu
```
Returns a reference to the menu.

```
entrycget
```
Gets information on a menu entry given an index and option to query.

```
entryconfigure
```
Changes information on a specific menu item given an index.

The Menu Widget

Create a menu with the Menu method, to be displayed later with the post method.

```
    $menu = $parent->Menu(options)
```

The standard configuration options that apply to Menu are: -activebackground, -activeforeground, -background, -bg, -borderwidth, -bw, -cursor, -disabled-foreground, -font, -foreground, -fg, -relief, and -takefocus.

Other options are:

```
-activeborderwidth => amount
```
Sets the width of the edges for the active menu item.

```
-menuitems => list
```
Specifies items to create in the menu as a list of lists.

```
-postcommand => callback
```
The command to invoke before the menu is posted, for example, to update the state of the menu items.

```
-tearoff => boolean
```
Whether or not to allow the menu to be "torn off." Default is 1.

```
-selectcolor => color
```
Color of the selection box for checkbuttons or radiobuttons.

Menu Indexes

Menus have indexes for manipulating individual menu items. They are:

n   Menu item *n*, with 0 representing the first item.

```
'active'
```
The current menu item.

'end' or 'last'
> The last menu item.

'none'
> No menu item.

@n The menu item closest to the y coordinate specified by *n*.

'pattern'
> The first menu item whose text matches the pattern.

Menu Methods

In addition to `configure` and `cget`, the following methods are defined for the Menu widget:

add
> Adds items to the end of a menu. The first argument is the type of menu item to add, and additional arguments are options to the menu item. For example:
>
> ```
> $menu = $mainwindow->Menu;
> $menu->add( 'commnd', -label => "New", "-command" => \&newfile );
> ```

entrycget
> Gets information on a specific menu item given an index.

entryconfigure
> Changes information on a specific menu item given an index.

post
> Displays the menu widget.

unpost
> Removes the menu widget from display.

postcascade
> Unposts a submenu and then posts the cascade menu associated with the menu item at the specified index.

delete
> Removes menu items from the menu.

index
> Given a named index, returns the numerical index for that menu item.

insert
> Inserts a menu item at the specified index. Same as `add`, except that it takes an index as the first argument.

invoke
> Invokes the menu item at the specified index as if it were selected.

type
> Returns the type of menu item at the specified index.

yposition
> Returns the y coordinate of the top-most pixel of the menu item.

Perl/Tk

The Optionmenu Widget

Use the `Optionmenu` method to create an option menu, in which the selected item is the value displayed. For example:

```
$mainwindow->OptionMenu(-textvariable => \$platform,
        -options => [ [ "UNIX", "unix" ],
                      [ "Windows NT", "winnt" ],
                      [ "Macintosh", "mac" ] ]) -> pack;
```

The `-options` argument takes a list of menu items. If the description of the menu items that are displayed are different from the values stored, the menu items are themselves written as two-item lists.

The standard configuration options that apply to `Optionmenu` are: `-activebackground`, `-activeforeground`, `-background`, `-bg`, `-bitmap`, `-borderwidth`, `-bw`, `-cursor`, `-disabledforeground`, `-font`, `-foreground`, `-fg`, `-highlightbackground`, `-highlightcolor`, `-highlightthickness`, `-image`, `-justify`, `-relief`, `-state`, `-takefocus`, `-underline`, `-width`, and `-wraplength`.

Other options are:

`−command => callback`
> The command to execute when a selection is made, with its arguments being the values of the `-textvariable` and `-variable` options.

`−indicatoron => boolean`
> Determines whether or not to display an indicator.

`−menu => $menu`
> Displays the menu associated with `$menu`.

`−options => list`
> Lists the menu options, as described above.

`−tearoff => boolean`
> Whether or not to allow the menu to be "torn off." Default is 1.

`−text => string`
> Specifies the text to display as a label for the option menu.

`−textvariable => \$variable`
> Points to the variable containing text to be displayed in the option menu.

`−variable => \$variable`
> Points to a variable containing a stored value, distinct from the value shown in the option menu.

The Frame Widget

Create a frame for enclosing other widgets using the `Frame` method. For example:

```
$parent->Frame( options )
```

The standard configuration options that apply to `Frame` are: `-background`, `-bg`, `-borderwidth`, `-bw`, `-cursor`, `-height`, `-highlightbackground`, `-highlightcolor`, `-highlightthickness`, `-relief`, `-takefocus`, and `-width`.

Other options are:

−class => *name*
>   The class associated with the frame.

−colormap => *\$window*
>   Specifies another window to share the colormap with. You can point to another window or use the value "new" to specify a new colormap. Default is undef.

−label => *string*
>   The string to use as a label for the frame.

−labelPack => *options*
>   Specifies options for the pack command.

−labelVariable => *\$variable*
>   Specifies a variable containing the text for the label.

−visual => *type n*
>   For the X Window System, changes the depth of colors.

The Toplevel Widget

Create a toplevel widget, displayed independently from the main window with the same decoration as the window system, using the Toplevel method.

The standard configuration options that apply to Toplevel are: -background, -bg, -borderwidth, -bw, -cursor, -height, -highlightbackground, -highlightcolor, -highlightthickness, -relief, -takefocus, and -width.

Other options are:

−class => *name*
>   The class associated with the toplevel widget.

−colormap => *\$window*
>   Specifies another window to share the colormap with. You can point to another window or use the value "new" to specify a new colormap. Default is undef.

−screen => *screen*
>   The screen to place the toplevel widget on.

−visual => *type n*
>   For the X Window System, changes the depth of colors.

Toplevel Methods

In addition to cget and configure, the following methods are supported by the Toplevel widget. Note that since the MainWindow is a Toplevel widget, each of these methods applies to the MainWindow as well.

aspect
>   Returns the constraints to the aspect of the window. The four-item list returned corresponds to the minimum width, the minimum height, the maximum width, and the maximum height.

Perl/Tk

`client`
> Assigns a name to the toplevel window.

`colormapwindows`
> For the X Window System, passes a list of windows to the window manager that have private colormaps. Controls the WM_COLORMAP_WINDOWS property.

`command`
> For the X Window System, returns the command used to start the application.

`deiconify`
> Displays an iconified window.

`focusmodel`
> Gives up the keyboard focus to another window.

`frame`
> Returns the ID of the parent widget as a hexadecimal string.

`geometry`
> For the X Window System, gets the geometry of the toplevel widget.

`grid`
> Changes the size of the toplevel's grid.

`group`
> Makes the widget the group leader of a set of related windows.

`iconbitmap`
> Identifies a bitmap to use as an icon when the window is iconified.

`iconify`
> Iconifies the window.

`iconmask`
> Specifies a mask for the icon bitmap.

`iconname`
> Assigns text to be associated with the icon.

`iconposition`
> Specifies a position for the icon on the desktop.

`iconwindow`
> Specifies a widget to use in place of an icon when iconified.

`maxsize`
> Specifies the largest size for the window.

`minsize`
> Specifies the smallest size for the window.

`overrideredirect`
> Removes window decorations from the window.

`positionfrom`
> Returns either "program" or "user", to tell you whether the user or window manager requested its current position.

`protocol`
> Given one of the window managers WM_DELETE_WINDOW, WM_SAVE_YOURSELF, or WM_TAKE_FOCUS, allows you to define a callback to execute when an associated event is detected.

`resizable`
> Takes boolean values representing whether the window can be resized in width and height, respectively.

`sizefrom`
> Returns either "program" or "user", to tell you whether the user or window manager requested its current size.

`state`
> Returns `"normal"`, `"iconic"`, or `"withdrawn"`, indicating the current state of the window.

`title`
> Changes the title at the top of the window.

`transient`
> Indicates to the window manager that the window is transient.

`withdraw`
> Makes the window non-visible.

Perl/Tk

PART VIII

Win32

CHAPTER 19

Win32 Modules and Extensions

If you use Perl on a Win32 system, a number of extension modules are available to provide Windows-specific functionality. Extension modules consist of a regular module written in Perl and a library written in C or C++ that can implement native Windows calls. The core of available modules is bundled together as *lib-win32* on CPAN, and with ActivePerl, Activestate's version of Perl for Win32. They provide such functionality as managing Windows processes, NT user administration, registry modification, and OLE automation.

The Win32 modules were originally written for Windows NT systems, so much of the functionality of the Win32 library is only applicable to Perl running on Windows NT. Many modules check to see which system they are on before installing. Many of the NT-specific modules such as NetAdmin and EventLog do not install at all on Windows 95. Modules like Registry do their best to work on both systems, despite the differences in their registries.

This chapter covers most of the modules and extensions included in *lib-win32* and distributed with ActivePerl. Additional Windows modules are available at CPAN.

The following modules are described in this chapter:

Win32::Clipboard
    Provide Windows clipboard interaction

Win32::Console
    Provide Windows console interaction

Win32::ChangeNotification
    Create and use ChangeNotification objects

Win32::EventLog
    Read from and write to the Windows NT event log

Win32::File
    Manage file attributes (read-only, system, hidden . . .)

Win32

Win32::FileSecurity
Manage ACLs in Perl

Win32::Internet
Provide extensions for Internet services

Win32::IPC
Wait for objects (processes, mutexes, semaphores)

Win32::Mutex
Create and use mutexes

Win32::NetAdmin
Administer users and groups

Win32::NetResource
Manage resources (servers, file shares, printers)

Win32::Process
Start and stop Win32 processes

Win32::Registry
Read and manage the Win32 Registry

Win32::Semaphore
Create and use semaphores

Win32::Service
Manage Windows NT services

Win32::Shortcut
Provide shell link interface

The reference material for the Clipboard, Console, Internet, and Shortcut modules was graciously provided by Aldo Capini, author and maintainer of many Win32 modules (*http://www.divinf.it/dada/perl/*).

The final section of this chapter describes OLE automation in Perl programs and details the Win32::OLE modules.

Win32::Clipboard

The Win32::Clipboard module allows you to manipulate the Windows clipboard. You can use the clipboard as an object with the following syntax:

```
$clip = Win32::Clipboard();
```

This functions as an implicit constructor. If you include a text string as an argument, that text will be placed on the clipboard. You can just use the package-qualified method names instead of the object syntax, since the clipboard is a single entity.

```
$text = Win32::Clipboard::Get();
Win32::Clipboard::Set("blah blah blah");
Win32::Clipboard::Empty();
```

Alternatively, you can use the clipboard as an object with this syntax:

```
$Clip = Win32::Clipboard();
$text = $Clip->Get();
$Clip->Set("blah blah blah");
$Clip->Empty();
```

Win32::Console

Win32::Console implements the Win32 console and character mode functions. They give you full control on the console input and output, including: support of off-screen console buffers (e.g., multiple screen pages); reading and writing of characters, attributes, and whole portions of the screen; and complete processing of keyboard and mouse events.

The new constructor is used to create a console object. It can take two forms:

```
$con = Win32::Console->new(standard_handle);
$con = Win32::Console->new(accessmode, sharemode);
```

The first form creates a handle to a standard channel. *standard_handle* can be one of STD_OUTPUT_HANDLE, STD_ERROR_HANDLE, or STD_INPUT_HANDLE.

The second form creates a console screen buffer in memory, which you can access for reading and writing as a normal console, and then redirect on the standard output (the screen) with Display. In this case, you can specify *accessmode* to be GENERIC_READ, GENERIC_WRITE, or both, determining the permissions you will have on the created buffer.

sharemode affects the way the console can be shared. It can be specified either as FILE_SHARE_READ, FILE_SHARE_WRITE, or both. If you don't specify any of those parameters, all four flags will be used.

Methods supported by the Win32::Console module are:

Alloc

$cons->Alloc

Allocates a new console for the process. Returns undef on error or a nonzero value on success. A process cannot be associated with more than one console, so this method will fail if there is already an allocated console. Use Free to detach the process from the console, and then call Alloc to create a new console.

Attr

$cons->Attr(*[attr]*)

Gets or sets the current console attribute. This attribute is used by the Write method.

Win32

Cls

$cons->Cls([attr])

Clear the console, with the specified *attr* if given, or using ATTR_NORMAL otherwise.

Cursor

$cons->Cursor([x, y, size, visible])

Gets or sets cursor position and appearance. Returns undef on error, or a four-element list containing: *x, y, size, visible. x* and *y* give the current cursor position.

Display

$cons->Display

Displays the specified console on the screen. Returns undef on error or a nonzero value on success.

FillAttr

$cons->FillAttr([value, number, col, row])

Fills the specified *number* of consecutive attributes, beginning at *col, row*, with the *value* specified. Returns the number of attributes filled, or undef on error.

FillChar

$cons->FillChar(*char, number, col, row*)

Fills the specified *number* of consecutive characters, beginning at *col, row*, with the character specified in *char*. Returns the number of characters filled, or undef on error.

Flush

$cons->Flush

Flushes the console input buffer. All the events in the buffer are discarded. Returns undef on error, a nonzero value on success.

Free

$cons->Free

Detaches the process from the console. Returns undef on error, a nonzero value on success.

GenerateCtrlEvent

$cons->**GenerateCtrlEvent(***[type, processgroup]***)**

Sends a break signal of the specified type to the specified process group. *type* can be one of CTRL_BREAK_EVENT or CTRL_C_EVENT, signaling, respectively, the pressing of CTRL + Break and of·CTRL + C. If not specified, *type* defaults to CTRL_C_EVENT. *processgroup* is the PID of a process sharing the same console. If omitted, it defaults to 0 (the current process), which is also the only meaningful value that you can pass to this function. Returns undef on error, a nonzero value on success.

GetEvents

$cons->**GetEvents**

Returns the number of unread input events in the console's input buffer, or undef on error.

Info

$cons->**Info**

Returns an array of information about the console, which contains:

- Number of columns (X size) of the console buffer

- Number of rows (Y size) of the console buffer

- Current column (X position) of the cursor

- Current row (Y position) of the cursor

- Current attribute used for Write

- Left column (X of the starting point) of the current console window

- Top row (Y of the starting point) of the current console window

- Right column (X of the final point) of the current console window

- Bottom row (Y of the final point) of the current console window

- Maximum number of columns for the console window, given the current buffer size, font, and screen size

- Maximum number of rows for the console window, given the current buffer size, font, and screen size

This example prints the cursor's current position:

```
@info = $CONSOLE->Info();
print "Cursor at $info[3], $info[4].0";
```

Input

$cons->Input

Reads an event from the input buffer. Returns a list of values, determined by the type of event. A keyboard event will contain the following values, in order:

- Event type (1 for keyboard)
- Key state—true if the key is being pressed, false if the key is being released
- Repeat count—the number of times the key is being held down
- Virtual keycode of the key
- Virtual scancode of the key
- ASCII code of the character (if the key is a character key, 0 otherwise)
- State of the control keys (SHIFTs, CTRLs, ALTs, etc.)

A mouse event will return the following values, in order:

- Event type (2 for mouse)
- X coordinate (column) of the mouse location
- Y coordinate (row) of the mouse location
- Button state—the mouse button(s) which are pressed
- State of the control keys (SHIFTs, CTRLs, ALTs, etc.)
- Event flags for the type of the mouse event

This method will return undef on error.

Note that the events returned depend on the input mode of the console; for example, mouse events are not intercepted unless ENABLE_MOUSE_INPUT is specified.

InputChar

$cons->InputChar(*number*)

Reads and returns number characters from the console input buffer, or returns undef on error.

InputCP

$cons->InputCP(*[codepage]*)

Gets or sets the input code page used by the console. Note that this doesn't apply to a console object, but to the standard input console. This attribute is used by the Write method.

MaxWindow

$cons->MaxWindow

Returns the size of the largest possible console window, based on the current font and the size of the display. The result is undef on error; otherwise, a two-element list containing the number of columns and rows is returned.

Mode

$cons->Mode(*[flags]*)

Gets or sets the input or output mode of a console. *flags* can be a combination of the following constants:

```
ENABLE_LINE_INPUT
ENABLE_ECHO_INPUT
ENABLE_PROCESSED_INPUT
ENABLE_WINDOW_INPUT
ENABLE_MOUSE_INPUT
ENABLE_PROCESSED_OUTPUT
ENABLE_WRAP_AT_EOL_OUTPUT
```

MouseButtons

$cons->MouseButtons

Returns the number of the buttons on your mouse, or undef on error.

OutputCP

$cons->OutputCP(*[codepage]*)

Gets or sets the output code page used by the console. Note that this doesn't apply to a console object, but to the standard output console. You may want to use the non-instantiated form to avoid confusion:

```
$codepage = Win32::Console::OutputCP();
Win32::Console::OutputCP(437);
```

PeekInput

$cons->PeekInput

Does exactly the same as Input, except that the event read is not removed from the input buffer.

ReadAttr

$cons->ReadAttr(*[number, col, row]*)

Reads the specified *number* of consecutive attributes from the console, beginning at *col, row*. Returns the attributes read (a variable containing one charac-

$\rightarrow$

Win32

ter for each attribute), or undef on error. You can then pass the returned variable to WriteAttr to restore the saved attributes on screen.

ReadChar

$cons->ReadChar([number, col, row])

Reads the specified *number* of consecutive characters from the console, beginning at *col* and *row*. Returns a string containing the characters read, or undef on error. You can then pass the returned variable to WriteChar to restore the saved characters on screen.

ReadRect

$cons->ReadRect(left, top, right, bottom)

Reads the content (characters and attributes) of the rectangle specified by *left, top, right, bottom* from the console. Returns a string containing the rectangle read, or undef on error. You can then pass the returned variable to WriteRect to restore the saved rectangle on screen (or on another console).

Scroll

$cons->Scroll(left, top, right, bottom, col, row, char, attr, [cleft, ctop, cright, cbottom])

Moves a block of data in a console buffer; the block is identified by the *left, top, right,* and *bottom* positions.

row and *col* identify the new location of the block. The cells left empty as a result of the move are filled with the character *char* and attribute *attr.*

Optionally, you can specify a clipping region with *cleft, ctop, cright, cbottom,* so that the contents of the console outside this rectangle are unchanged. Returns undef on error or a nonzero value on success.

```
# scrolls the screen 10 lines down, filling with black spaces
$CONSOLE->Scroll(0, 0, 80, 25, 0, 10, " ", $FG_BLACK | $BG_BLACK);
```

Select

$cons->Select(standard_handle)

Redirects a standard handle to the specified console. *standard_handle* can have one of the following values:

```
STD_INPUT_HANDLE
STD_OUTPUT_HANDLE
STD_ERROR_HANDLE
```

Returns undef on error or a nonzero value on success.

Size

$cons->Size([col, row])

Gets or sets the console buffer size.

Title

$cons->Title([title])

Gets or sets the title bar string of the current console window.

Window

$cons->Window([flag, left, top, right, bottom])

Gets or sets the current console window size. If called without arguments, returns a four-element list containing the current window coordinates in the form of *(left, top, right, bottom)*. To set the window size, you have to specify an additional flag parameter. If it is 0 (zero), coordinates are considered relative to the current coordinates; if it is non-zero, coordinates are absolute.

Write

$cons->Write(string)

Writes *string* on the console, using the current attribute, which you can set with Attr, and advancing the cursor as needed. This isn't so different from Perl's print statement. Returns the number of characters written, or undef on error.

WriteAttr

$cons->WriteAttr(attrs, col, row)

Writes the attributes contained in the string *attrs*, beginning at *col, row*, without affecting the characters that are on screen. The string *attrs* can be the result of a ReadAttr function, or you can build your own attribute string; in this case, keep in mind that every attribute is treated as a character, not a number (see example). Returns the number of attributes written, or undef on error.

```
$CONSOLE->WriteAttr($attrs, 0, 0);

# note the use of chr()...
$attrs = chr($FG_BLACK | $BG_WHITE) x 80;
$CONSOLE->WriteAttr($attrs, 0, 0);
```

WriteChar

*$cons->*WriteChar(*chars, col, row*)

Writes the characters in the string *attr*, beginning at *col, row*, without affecting the attributes that are onscreen. The string chars can be the result of a Read-Char function or a normal string. Returns the number of characters written, or undef on error.

WriteInput

*$cons->*WriteInput(*event*)

Pushes data in the console input buffer. *event* is a list of values; for more information, see Input. The string chars can be the result of a ReadChar function or a normal string. Returns the number of characters written, or undef on error.

WriteRect

*$cons->*WriteRect(*rect, left, top, right, bottom*)

Writes a rectangle of characters and attributes (contained in *rect*) on the console at the coordinates specified by *left, top, right, bottom. rect* can be the result of a ReadRect function. Returns undef on error; otherwise, a four-element list containing the coordinates of the affected rectangle, in the format *(left, top, right, bottom)*.

Constants

The following constants are exported in the main namespace of your script using Win32::Console:

BACKGROUND_BLUE	BACKGROUND_GREEN
BACKGROUND_INTENSITY	BACKGROUND_RED
CAPSLOCK_ON	CONSOLE_TEXTMODE_BUFFER
ENABLE_ECHO_INPUT	ENABLE_LINE_INPUT
ENABLE_MOUSE_INPUT	ENABLE_PROCESSED_INPUT
ENABLE_PROCESSED_OUTPUT	ENABLE_WINDOW_INPUT
ENABLE_WRAP_AT_EOL_OUTPUT	ENHANCED_KEY
FILE_SHARE_READ	FILE_SHARE_WRITE
FOREGROUND_BLUE	FOREGROUND_GREEN
FOREGROUND_INTENSITY	FOREGROUND_RED
LEFT_ALT_PRESSED	LEFT_CTRL_PRESSED
NUMLOCK_ON	GENERIC_READ
GENERIC_WRITE	RIGHT_ALT_PRESSED
RIGHT_CTRL_PRESSED	SCROLLLOCK_ON
SHIFT_PRESSED	STD_INPUT_HANDLE
STD_OUTPUT_HANDLE	STD_ERROR_HANDLE

Additionally, the following variables can be used:

```
$FG_BLACK              $FG_BLUE
$FG_LIGHTBLUE          $FG_RED
$FG_LIGHTRED           $FG_GREEN
$FG_LIGHTGREEN         $FG_MAGENTA
$FG_LIGHTMAGENTA       $FG_CYAN
$FG_LIGHTCYAN          $FG_BROWN
$FG_YELLOW             $FG_GRAY
$FG_WHITE

$BG_BLACK              $BG_BLUE
$BG_LIGHTBLUE          $BG_RED
$BG_LIGHTRED           $BG_GREEN
$BG_LIGHTGREEN         $BG_MAGENTA
$BG_LIGHTMAGENTA       $BG_CYAN
$BG_LIGHTCYAN          $BG_BROWN
$BG_YELLOW             $BG_GRAY
$BG_WHITE

$ATTR_NORMAL           $ATTR_INVERSE
```

ATTR_NORMAL is set to gray foreground on black background (DOS's standard colors).

Win32::ChangeNotification

This module provides access to Win32 change-notification objects, letting you monitor events relating to files and directory trees. The constructor for this class is new, which creates a ChangeNotification object for a specified directory and indicates how it should be monitored:

```
$ntfy = Win32::ChangeNotification->new(directory, subtree, filter);
```

The function returns a reference to the object as $ntfy. *directory* is the pathname of the directory to monitor. *subtree* is a Boolean value that, if true, forces the object to monitor all subdirectories of the object's path. The *filter* parameter indicates what type of events will trigger a notification. It can be one of the following string values:

Value	Description
ATTRIBUTES	Any attribute change
DIR_NAME	Any directory name change
FILE_NAME	Any filename change (creating/deleting/renaming)
LAST_WRITE	Any change to a file's last write time
SECURITY	Any security descriptor change
SIZE	Any change in a file's size

The following methods are used on notification objects created by new:

close

$ntfy->close()

Stops the monitoring done by the notification object and destroys the object. This happens automatically when the program exits.

reset

$ntfy->reset()

Resets the object to begin monitoring again after a change has occurred.

wait

$ntfy->wait([timeout])

The wait method is inherited from the Win32::IPC package. It waits for the notification object to become signaled when it detects a change. *timeout* is the maximum time to wait (in milliseconds). If *timeout* is omitted, the method waits forever. If *timeout* is 0, the function returns immediately. The function returns the following values:

+1   The object is signaled

0   Timed out

undef
    An error occurred

Use reset on the object after wait if you wish to continue monitoring.

Win32::Eventlog

This module makes the Windows NT event log accessible to your Perl programs. It allows you to create new records, read records, and create backup logfiles. The new constructor opens a server's event log as an object.

```
$log = Win32::EventLog->new(source, [server]);
```

This function opens an event log and returns an object reference. *source* specifies the name of the source event, and *server* specifies the name of the server (local is assumed if no server name is given).

Many of the methods for this module require a reference to an empty variable as an argument. This is where the return value of the method will be placed, whether it is a hash or a scalar. The following methods can be used on event log objects:

Backup

$log->Backup(*filename*)

Saves the current open event log to a file named by *filename*.

Read

$log->Read(*flags, offset,* \%*eventinfo*)

Reads an entry from the event log and returns the information in the *eventinfo* hash. *offset* specifies the record number you want to start at in the log.

$\rightarrow$

flags sets options for how you want to read the log, which can be any combination of the following:

EVENTLOG_FORWARDS_READ

> Eventlog is read in forward chronological order.

EVENTLOG_BACKWARDS_READ

> Eventlog is read in reverse chronological order.

EVENTLOG_SEEK_READ

> The read begins at the record specified by the $RecordOffset parameter. Must also specify EVENT_LOG_FORWARDS_READ or EVENTLOG_BACK-WARDS_READ.

EVENTLOG_SEQUENTIAL_READ

> The read continues sequentially from the last read call.

The final argument is the output object for the event read. \%*eventinfo* is a reference to a hash that contains keys for each part of the event description. This same structure is used when you report new events to the event log using the Report method. The *eventinfo* hash looks like this:

```
%event = (
        EventID             => val,
        EventType           => val,
        Category            => val,
        ClosingRecordNumber => val,
        Source              => val,
        Computer            => val,
        Strings             => val,
        Data                => val,
);
```

Report

$log->Report(\%eventinfo)

Reports an event to the event log. The information for the event to be recorded is given in a hash, %eventinfo, which should contain values for at least the following keys:

EventType

> A string describing the type of event to be reported. The options for EventType are:
>
> | | |
> |---|---|
> | EVENTLOG_ERROR_TYPE | Error event |
> | EVENTLOG_WARNING_TYPE | Warning event |
> | EVENTLOG_INFORMATION_TYPE | Information event |
> | EVENTLOG_AUDIT_SUCCESS_TYPE | Success Audit event |
> | EVENTLOG_AUDIT_FAILURE_TYPE | Failure Audit event. |

Category

> An integer value for the category of the event, defined by the application.

EventID

> Source-specific ID for the event.

→

Win32

Data
> Raw binary data for the event.

Strings
> Any text strings to merge that provide a description of the event.

GetOldest

$log->**GetOldest***(\ $record)*

Returns the record number of the oldest record in the event log to the scalar *$record*.

GetNumber

$log->**GetNumber***(\ $number)*

Returns the number of events as the value of the scalar variable *number*.

Clear

$log->**Clear***([filename])*

Writes the current event log to the file *filename* (if supplied), and clears the event log.

Win32::File

The Win32::File module allows you to view or set the attributes for files. There are two functions that allow you to do this, which must be explicitly imported to your namespace:

```
use Win32::File qw/GetAttributes SetAttributes/;
```

The constant values for the attributes are exported by default.

GetAttributes (*filename*, \ *$atts*)
> Returns the attribute settings for file *filename* and saves them as the variable referenced by *$atts*, which will contain an ORed combination of one or more of the following values:
>
> ```
> ARCHIVE
> DIRECTORY
> HIDDEN
> NORMAL
> READONLY
> SYSTEM
> ```

SetAttributes (*filename*, *atts*)
> Set the attributes for the file *filename* to the values contained in *atts*. The attributes are given as an ORed combination of one or more of the attribute values shown above.

Win32::FileSecurity

The Win32::FileSecurity module allows you to work with NT File System (NTFS) file permissions. File permissions are stored as Discretionary Access Control Lists (DACLs) for each file or directory. These lists contain a bitmask specifying the permission rights for users on the file or directory. This module implements a DACL as a *permissions* hash in which each key is a username and the value is the bitmask for the permissions.

The FileSecurity module exports the following constants to describe user permissions:

```
ACCESS_SYSTEM_SECURITY      READ or R
CHANGE or C                 SPECIFIC_RIGHTS_ALL
DELETE                      STANDARD_RIGHTS_ALL
FULL or F                   STANDARD_RIGHTS_EXECUTE
GENERIC_ALL                 STANDARD_RIGHTS_READ
GENERIC_EXECUTE             STANDARD_RIGHTS_REQUIRED
GENERIC_READ                STANDARD_RIGHTS_WRITE
GENERIC_WRITE               SYNCHRONIZE
MAXIMUM_ALLOWED             WRITE_DAC
READ_CONTROL                WRITE_OWNER
```

Using the constant function on one of these constants gives its value, and bitmasks or multiple permissions settings can be made by supplying a list of these constants to the MakeMask function.

The functions exported by the Win32::FileSecurity module are:

---

constant

constant *(name $val)*

Takes the *name* of a permission constant and saves its value in the variable *val*.

EnumerateRights

EnumerateRights *(mask, \@rights)*

Takes a permissions bitmask (as returned by MakeMask or constant) and saves the corresponding list of string constants in *rights*.

Get

Get *(filename, \%permissions)*

Gets the access control list for *filename* (or directory) and saves in the specified *permissions* hash.

MakeMask

> **MakeMask** *(stringlist)*
>
> Takes a list of permission string constants and returns the bitmask.

Set

> **Set** *(filename, \%permissions)*
>
> Sets the access control list for the given *filename* (or directory) to the settings in the specified *permissions* hash.

===

Win32::Internet

The Win32::Internet extension implements the Win32 Internet APIs (found in *WININET.DLL*), providing support for HTTP, FTP, and Gopher connections.

All types of connections start as a basic Internet connection that must be opened with the following command:

```
use Win32::Internet;
$Connection = Win32::Internet->new();
```

This creates an Internet object in Perl on which you use the functions provided in this module to create more specific connection objects. The objects and functions that create them are:

- Internet connections (the main object, with new)

- URLs (with OpenURL)

- FTP sessions (with FTP)

- HTTP sessions (with HTTP)

- HTTP requests (with OpenRequest)

This module provides different levels of implementation of the Win32 Internet functions. Some routines use several Win32 API functions to perform a complex task in a single call; they are simpler to use, but less powerful. Other functions implement nothing more and nothing less than the corresponding API function, so you can use all of their power, but with some additional programming steps.

For example, the function FetchURL fetches the contents of any HTTP, FTP, or Gopher URL with a simple command:

```
$inet = new Win32::Internet();
$file = $inet->FetchURL("http://www.yahoo.com");
```

You can achieve the same result with this series of commands, which is what FetchURL actually does:

```
$inet = new Win32::Internet();
$url = $inet->OpenURL("http://www.yahoo.com");
$file = $url->ReadFile();
$url->Close();
```

General Internet Methods

The methods described in this section are used on Internet connection objects created with new:

```
$inet = Win32::Internet->new();
```

You can supply new with an optional list of arguments (or a reference to a hash containing them) that looks like this:

```
Win32::Internet->new [useragent, opentype, proxy, proxybypass, flags]
Win32::Internet->new [$hashref]
```

The parameters and their values are:

useragent
> The user-agent string passed to HTTP requests. Default is Perl-Win32::Internet/version.

opentype
> How to access the Internet (e.g., directly or using a proxy). Default is INTERNET_OPEN_TYPE_DIRECT.

proxy
> Name of the proxy server (or servers) to use. Default is none.

proxybypass
> Optional list of host names or IP addresses that are known locally. Default is none.

flags
> Additional flags affecting the behavior of the function. Default is none.

If you pass a hash reference to the function, the following values are taken from the hash:

```
%hash=(
    "useragent"    => "useragent",
    "opentype"     => "opentype",
    "proxy"        => "proxy",
    "proxybypass"  => "proxybypass",
    "flags"        => flags,
);
```

The following methods can be used on Internet connection objects:

CanonicalizeURL

*$inet->*CanonicalizeURL(*URL, [flags]*)

Converts a URL to a canonical format, which includes converting unsafe characters to escape sequences. Returns the canonicalized URL, or undef on error.

→

For the possible values of flags, refer to the Microsoft Win32 Internet Functions documentation.

Close

$inet->**Close**(*[$obj]*)

Closes an Internet connection. This can be applied to any Win32::Internet object. Note that it is not strictly required to close the connections you create, since the Win32::Internet objects are automatically closed when the program ends (or when such an object is destroyed by other means).

CombineURL

$inet->**CombineURL**(*baseURL, relativeURL, [flags]*)

Combines a base and relative URL into a single URL. Returns the (canonicalized) combined URL, or undef on error. For the possible values of flags, refer to the Microsoft Win32 Internet Functions documentation.

ConnectBackoff

$inet->**ConnectBackoff**(*[value]*)

Reads or sets the delay value, in milliseconds, to wait between connection retries. If no value parameter is specified, the current value is returned; otherwise, the delay between retries is set.

ConnectionRetries

$inet->**ConnectRetries**(*[value]*)

Reads or sets the number of times a connection is retried before considering it failed. If no value parameter is specified, the current value is returned; otherwise, the number of retries is set. The default value is 5.

ConnectTimeout

$inet->**ConnectTimeout**(*[value]*)

Reads or sets the timeout value (in milliseconds) before a connection is considered failed. If no value parameter is specified, the current value is returned; otherwise, the timeout is set to *value*. The default value is infinity.

ControlReceiveTimeout

$inet->**ControlReceiveTimeout**(*[value]*)

Reads or sets the timeout value (in milliseconds) to use for non-data (control) receive requests before they are cancelled. Currently, this value has meaning only for FTP sessions. If no value parameter is specified, the current value is returned; otherwise, the timeout is set. The default value is infinity.

ControlSendTimeout

*$inet->*ControlSendTimeout*([value])*

Reads or sets the timeout value (in milliseconds) to use for non-data (control) send requests before they are cancelled. Currently, this value has meaning only for FTP sessions. If no value parameter is specified, the current value is returned; otherwise, the timeout is set. The default value is infinity.

CrackURL

*$inet->*CrackURL*(URL, [flags])*

Splits a URL into its component parts and returns them in an array. Returns undef on error. The array will contain the following values: *(scheme, host, port, username, password, path, extrainfo)*.

For example, the URL *http://www.divinf.it/index.html#top* can be split into:

```
http, www.divinf.it, 80, anonymous, dada@divinf.it, /index.html, #top
```

If you don't specify a flags parameter, ICU_ESCAPE will be used by default; for the possible values of flags refer to the Microsoft Win32 Internet Functions documentation.

CreateURL

*$inet->*CreateURL*(scheme, hostname, port, username, password, path, extrainfo, [flags])*

$inet->*CreateURL*($hashref, [flags])

Creates a URL from its component parts. Returns undef on error and the created URL if successful. If you pass a hash reference, the following values are taken from the array:

```
%hash=(
    "scheme"    => "scheme",
    "hostname"  => "hostname",
    "port"      => port,
    "username"  => "username",
    "password"  => "password",
    "path"      => "path",
    "extrainfo" => "extrainfo",
);
```

If you don't specify a flags parameter, ICU_ESCAPE will be used by default; for the other possible values of flags, refer to the Microsoft Win32 Internet Functions documentation.

DataReceiveTimeout

*$inet->*DataReceiveTimeout(*[value]*)

Reads or sets the timeout value (in milliseconds) to use for data receive requests before they are cancelled. If no value parameter is specified, the current value is returned; otherwise, the timeout is set. The default value is infinity.

DataSendTimeout

*$inet->*DataSendTimeout(*[value]*)

Reads or sets the timeout value (in milliseconds) to use for data send requests before they are cancelled. If no value parameter is specified, the current value is returned; otherwise, the timeout is set. The default value is infinity.

Error

*$inet->*Error()

Returns the last recorded error in the form of an array or string (depending upon the context) containing the error number and an error description. Can be applied on any Win32::Internet object (FTP sessions, etc.). There are three types of errors you can encounter, recognizable by the error number returned:

−1 A "trivial" error has occurred in the package. For example, you tried to use a method on the wrong type of object.

1 through 11999
   A generic error has occurred and the Win32::GetLastError error message is returned.

12000 and higher
   An Internet error has occurred; the extended Win32 Internet API error message is returned.

FetchURL

*$inet->*FetchURL(*URL*)

Fetch the content of an HTTP, FTP, or Gopher URL. Returns the contents of the file read (or undef if there was an error and nothing was read).

FTP

$inet->FTP($ftpobject, server, username, pwd, [port, pasv, context])

$inet->FTP($ftpobject, $hashref)

Opens an FTP connection to *server*, logging in with the given username and password. The new connection object is saved to *ftpobject*. The parameters and their values are:

server
> The server to connect to.

username
> The username used to log in to the server. Default is anonymous.

pwd
> The password used to log in to the server. Default is none.

port
> The port of the FTP service on the server. Default is 21.

pasv
> If it is a value other than 0, use passive transfer mode. Otherwise, it is taken from the parent Internet connection object; you can set this value with the Pasv method.

context
> A number to identify this operation if it is asynchronous. See SetStatus-Callback and GetStatusCallback for more info on asynchronous operations.

> If you pass a hash reference, the following values are taken from the hash:

```
%hash=(
  "server"   => "server",
  "username" => "username",
  "password" => "password",
  "port"     => port,
  "pasv"     => pasv,
  "context"  => context,
);
```

> The FTP method returns undef if the connection failed, a number otherwise. You can then call any of the FTP functions as methods of the newly-created FTP object.

GetResponse

$inet->GetResponse()

Returns the text sent by a remote server in response to the last function executed. It applies to any Win32::Internet object, particularly FTP sessions.

Win32

GetStatusCallback

*$inet->*GetStatusCallback(*context*)

Returns information about the progress of the asynchronous operation identified by context; this information consists of two values: a status code (one of the INTERNET_STATUS_* constants) and an additional value depending on the status code. For example, if the status code returned is INTERNET_STATUS_HAN-DLE_CREATED, the second value will hold the handle just created. For more information on these values, please refer to the Microsoft Win32 Internet Functions documentation.

HTTP

*$inet->*HTTP(*httpobject, server, username, password, [port, flags, context]*)

$inet->*HTTP(*$httpobject, $hashref)

Opens an HTTP connection to *server*, logging in with the given username and password. The new connection object is saved as *httpobject*. The parameters and their values are:

server
  The server to connect to.

username
  The username used to log in to the server. Default is anonymous.

password
  The password used to log in to the server. Default is none.

port
  The port of the HTTP service on the server. Default is 80.

flags
  Additional flags affecting the behavior of the function.

context
  A number to identify this operation if it is asynchronous.

If you pass a hash reference, the following values are taken from the hash:

```
%hash=(
  "server"   => "server",
  "username" => "username",
  "password" => "password",
  "port"     => port,
  "flags"    => flags,
  "context"  => context,
);
```

The HTTP method returns undef if the connection failed, a number otherwise. You can then call any of the HTTP functions as methods of the newly-created *httpobject*.

OpenURL

$inet->**OpenURL**(*urlobject, URL*)

Opens a connection to an HTTP, FTP, or Gopher URL. Returns undef on error, or a number if the connection was successful. You can then retrieve the URL content by applying the methods QueryDataAvailable and ReadFile on the newly-created *urlobject*. See also FetchURL.

Password

$inet->**Password**(*[password]*)

Reads or sets the password used for an FTP or HTTP connection. If no password parameter is specified, the current value is returned.

QueryDataAvailable

$inet->**QueryDataAvailable**()

Returns the number of bytes of data that are available to be read immediately by a subsequent call to ReadFile (or undef on error). Can be applied to URL or HTTP request objects.

QueryOption

$inet->**QueryOption**(*option*)

Queries an Internet option. For the possible values of *option*, refer to the Microsoft Win32 Internet Functions documentation.

ReadEntireFile

$inet->**ReadEntireFile**()

Reads all the data available from an opened URL or HTTP request object. Returns what has been read, or undef on error.

ReadFile

$inet->**ReadFile**(*bytes*)

Reads and returns the specified number of bytes of data from an opened URL or HTTP request object. Returns undef on error. Be careful to keep *bytes* to an acceptable value.

SetOption

$inet->**SetOption**(*option, value*)

Sets an Internet option. For the possible values of *option*, refer to the Microsoft Win32 Internet Functions documentation.

Win32

SetStatusCallback

$inet->SetStatusCallback()

Initializes the callback routine that is used to return data about the progress of an asynchronous operation. This is one of the steps required to perform asynchronous operations; the complete procedure is:

```
# use the INTERNET_FLAG_ASYNC when initializing
$params{'flags'}=INTERNET_FLAG_ASYNC;
$inet = new Win32::Internet(params);

# initialize the callback routine
$inet->SetStatusCallback();

# specify the context parameter (the last 1 in this case)
$inet->HTTP($http, "www.yahoo.com", "anonymous", "dada\@divinf.it",
            80, 0, 1);
```

At this point, control returns immediately to Perl and $inet->Error() will return 997, which means an asynchronous I/O operation is pending. Now, you can call:

```
$http->GetStatusCallback(1);
```

in a loop to verify what's happening; see also GetStatusCallback.

TimeConvert

$inet->TimeConvert(*time*)

Takes an HTTP date/time string and returns the date/time converted in the following array: *(seconds, minute, hours, day, month, year, day_of_week)*.

UserAgent

$inet->UserAgent(*[name]*)

Reads or sets the user agent name used for HTTP requests. If no name is specified, the current value is returned.

Username

$inet->Username(*[name]*)

Reads or sets the username used for an FTP or HTTP connection. If no name parameter is specified, the current value is returned.

Version

$inet->Version()

Returns the version numbers for the Win32::Internet package and the *WININET.DLL* version, as an array or string, depending on the context. The

→

string returned will contain "package_version/DLL_version", while the array will contain: "package_version", "DLL_version". For example:

```
$version = $inet->Version(); # should return "0.06/4.70.1215"
@version = $inet->Version(); # should return ("0.06", "4.70.1215")
```

FTP Functions

The methods described in this section are used to control FTP sessions. They apply to FTP session objects created by the FTP method on an Internet connection object. FTP creates an open FTP session and assigns it to an object ($FTP):

```
use Win32::Internet;
$inet = new Win32::Internet();
$inet->FTP($FTP, "hostname", "username", "password");
```

The following methods are used on FTP session objects:

Ascii

$FTP->**Ascii**()

$FTP->**Asc**()

Sets the ASCII transfer mode for this FTP session. It will be applied to subsequent Get functions.

Binary

$FTP->**Binary**()

$FTP->**Bin**()

Sets the binary transfer mode for this FTP session. It will be applied to subsequent Get functions.

Cd

$FTP->**Cd**(*path*)

$FTP->**Cwd**(*path*)

$FTP->**Chdir**(*path*)

Changes the current directory on the FTP remote host. Returns *path*, or undef on error.

Delete

$FTP->**Delete**(*file*)

$FTP->**Del**(*file*)

Deletes *file* on the FTP remote host. Returns undef on error.

Win32

Get

$FTP->Get(file, [local, overwrite, flags, context])

Gets the remote FTP *file* and saves it locally in *local*. If *local* is not specified, it will be the same name as *file*. Returns undef on error. The parameters and their values are:

file The name of the remote file on the FTP server.

local
  The name of the local file to create.

overwrite
  If 0, overwrites *local* if it exists. With any other value, the function fails if the local file already exists. Default is 0.

flags
  Additional flags affecting the behavior of the function. None by default.

context
  A number to identify this operation if it is asynchronous. See SetStatus-Callback and GetStatusCallback for more information on asynchronous operations. None by default.

List

$FTP->List([pattern, listmode])

$FTP->Ls([pattern, listmode])

$FTP->Dir([pattern, listmode])

Returns a list containing the files found in the current directory, matching the given *pattern*, if specified. The content of the returned list depends on the *listmode* parameter, which can have the following values:

1 *(default)*
  The list contains the names of the files found.

2   The list contains seven values for each file:

  - The file name

  - The DOS short file name, a.k.a. 8.3

  - The size

  - The attributes

  - The creation time

  - The last access time

  - The last modified time

$\rightarrow$

3   The list contains a reference to a hash for each found file. Each hash contains the following key/value pairs:

```
name => file name
altname => DOS short file name, a.k.a. 8.3
size => size
attr => attributes
ctime => creation time
atime => last access time
mtime => last modified time
```

All times are reported as strings of the following format: second, hour, minute,
day, month, year. For example:

```
$file->{'mtime'} == "0,10,58,9,12,1996"
# stands for 09 Dec 1996 at 10:58:00
```

Mkdir

$FTP->Mkdir(name)

$FTP->Md(name)

Creates the directory *name* on the FTP remote host. Returns undef on error.

Mode

$FTP->Mode([mode])

If called with no arguments, returns the current transfer mode for this FTP
session ("asc" for ASCII or "bin" for binary). The *mode* argument can be asc
or bin, in which case the appropriate transfer mode is selected. Returns undef
on error.

Pasv

$FTP->Pasv([mode])

If called with no arguments, returns 1 if the current FTP session has passive
transfer mode enabled; 0 if not. You can call it with a *mode* parameter (0/1)
only as a method of a Internet object, in which case it will set the default
value for the next FTP object you create (i.e., set it before, because you can't
change this value once you open the FTP session).

Put

$FTP->Put(file, [remote, context])

Upload the local *file* to the FTP server, saving it under the name *remote*,
which if omitted is the same name as *file*. Returns undef on error. *context* is a
number to identify this operation if it is asynchronous. See SetStatusCall-
back and GetStatusCallback for more information on asynchronous operations.

Pwd

*$FTP->*Pwd()

Returns the current directory on the FTP server, or undef on error.

Rename

*$FTP->*Rename(*oldfile, newfile*)

*$FTP->*Ren*(oldfile, newfile)*

Renames a file on the FTP remote host. Returns undef on error.

Rmdir

*$FTP->*Rmdir(*name*)

*$FTP->*Rd*(name)*

Removes the directory *name* on the FTP remote host. Returns undef on error.

HTTP Functions

The methods described in this section are used to create and control an HTTP session. You open an HTTP session using the HTTP method on an Internet connection object:

```
use Win32::Internet;
$inet = new Win32::Internet();
$inet->HTTP($http, "hostname", "username", "password");
```

This opens the session and creates the HTTP session object $http. The following methods can be used on HTTP session objects:

AddHeader

*$request->*AddHeader(*header, [flags]*)

Adds HTTP request headers to an HTTP request object created with OpenRequest. For the possible values of flags, refer to the Microsoft Win32 Internet Functions documentation.

OpenRequest

*$http->*OpenRequest*(requestobject, [path, method, version, referer, accept, flags, context])*

$http->*OpenRequest*($requestobject, hashref)

Opens an HTTP request and saves it as *$requestobject*. Returns undef on error, or a number if the connection was successful. You can then use one of the AddHeader, SendRequest, QueryInfo, QueryDataAvailable, and ReadFile

→

methods on the newly-created *requestobject.* The optional parameters and their values are:

path

The object to request. This is generally a filename, an executable module, etc. The default is "/".

method

The method to use, which can be GET, POST, HEAD, or PUT. Default is ˙GET.

version

The HTTP version. Default is HTTP/1.0.

referer

The URL of the document from which the URL in the request was obtained.

accept

The content types accepted. They must be separated by a "\0" (ASCII zero). Default types are "text/* image/gif image/jpeg."

flags

Additional flags affecting the behavior of the function.

context

A number to identify this operation if it is asynchronous. See `SetStatus-Callback` and `GetStatusCallback` for more information on asynchronous operations.

A reference to a hash containing the previous list of parameters can also be supplied to this method.

```
%hash=(
   "path"       => "path",
   "method"     => "method",
   "version"    => "version",
   "referer"    => "referer",
   "accept"     => "accept",
   "flags"      => flags,
   "context"    => context,
);
```

QueryInfo

*$request->*__QueryInfo__*(header, [flags])*

Queries information about an HTTP request object (`$request`) created with `OpenRequest`. You can specify a header (for example, "Content-type") and/or one or more flags. If you don't specify flags, `HTTP_QUERY_CUSTOM` will be used by default; this means that the header should contain a valid HTTP header name. For the possible values of flags, refer to the Microsoft Win32 Internet Functions documentation.

Win32

Request

*$http->***Request** *([path, method, version, referer, accept, flags])*

*$http->***Request** *(hashref)*

Performs an HTTP request and returns an array containing the status code, the headers, and the content of the file. It is a one-step procedure that executes `OpenRequest`, `SendRequest`, `QueryInfo`, `ReadFile`, and finally `Close`. For a description of the parameters, see `OpenRequest`.

SendRequest

*$request->***SendRequest** *([postdata])*

Sends an HTTP request to the destination server. *postdata* contains any optional data to send immediately after the request header; this is generally used for POST or PUT requests. Your request object must contain the following content header for post data to be processed. You can add the header with `AddHeader`:

```
$request->AddHeader("Content-Type: application/x-www-form-urlencoded");
$request->SendRequest("key1=value1&key2=value2&key3=value3");
```

Win32::IPC

The Win32::IPC module provides synchronization for multiple objects created from the Semaphore, Mutex, Process, and ChangeNotify classes. This `wait` method of this class is inherited by objects of the preceding modules, as well as the functions `wait_all` and `wait_any`. You should not need to call Win32::IPC directly.

`$obj->wait([timeout])`

This method is used on any synchronization object. It waits for the object to become signaled. It returns 1 if the object is signaled, −1 if the object is an abandoned mutex, 0 if the call times out, and `undef` on error. `timeout` is the time to wait (in milliseconds). If no `timeout` is specified, the method waits indefinitely.

Win32::IPC also defines the two functions `wait_all` and `wait_any`:

`wait_all(@objects, [timeout])`

Waits for all the synchronization objects contained in `@objects` to be signaled. The optional `timeout` parameter is the same as described for `wait`. The return value will be an integer that identifies the last object to be signaled (the *n*th object in the list, starting from 1). A negative integer (−*n*) indicates that the *n*th object was an abandoned mutex. A return of 0 means that the function timed out; and `undef` is returned on error.

```
wait_any(@objects, [timeout])
```
    Waits for at least one of the objects contained in *@objects* to be signaled.
Return values are the same as for wait_all, above, indicating which object
signaled.

Win32::Mutex

This module provides access to Win32 mutex objects, which control access to
common resources. The new constructor creates the mutex and determines its initial availability. It has the following syntax:

```
$mut = Win32::Mutex->new(init, [name]);
```

The first argument determines the initial status of the mutex. If *init* is non-zero,
the calling process has immediate ownership of the mutex object. A zero value
means that the mutex is available. The second argument assigns a name to the
mutex that allows this object to be referenced by others via the open function.

Another object constructor for Win32::Mutex is open:

```
$mut = Win32::Mutex->open(name);
```

This call creates a new mutex object to access an existing mutex identified by
name.

The following methods can be used on Win32::Mutex objects:

release

$mut->Release()

Releases ownership of the mutex from the calling process, allowing anyone
waiting on the mutex to take ownership.

wait

$mut->wait([timeout])

The Win32::IPC method inherited by this module. Makes the calling process
wait for ownership of the mutex object for the number of milliseconds specified by *timeout*. If the mutex doesn't become available before the timeout, the
call returns 0.

Win32::NetAdmin

The Win32::NetAdmin module provides extensive functionality for administering
users and groups on Windows NT servers. This module does not implement an
object interface for administration; it exports several functions that execute admin-
istrative commands. (This module does not load on Windows 95 systems.)

Win32

The following functions are provided by the Win32::NetAdmin module. The *server* argument of each function is optional; however, a placeholder for the argument must be used if you don't supply a name. An empty string ("") will work, indicating that the local machine is to be used.

GetDomainController

GetDomainController *(server, domain, $name)*

Returns the name of the domain controller for the specified *server* and *domain* to the variable *$name*.

UserCreate

UserCreate *(server, username, password, passwordage, privilege, homedir, comment, flags, scriptpath)*

Creates a new user with the specified settings:

server
> Name of the server

username
> Name of new user

password
> The user's password

passwordage
> Amount of time before password expires

privilege
> Privilege settings of the new user, which can be one of the following:
>
> ```
> USER_PRIV_MASK
> USER_PRIV_GUEST
> USER_PRIV_USER
> USER_PRIV_ADMIN
> ```

homedir
> Pathname of the user's home directory

comment
> A string containing a comment about the user

flag
> A flag containing user creation settings, which can be one of the following:
>
> ```
> UF_TEMP_DUPLICATE_ACCOUNT
> UF_NORMAL_ACCOUNT
> UF_INTERDOMAIN_TRUST_ACCOUNT
> UF_WORKSTATION_TRUST_ACCOUNT
> UF_SERVER_TRUST_ACCOUNT
> UF_MACHINE_ACCOUNT_MASK
> UF_ACCOUNT_TYPE_MASK
> UF_DONT_EXPIRE_PASSWD
> UF_SETTABLE_BITS
> ```

$\rightarrow$

```
UF_SCRIPT
UF_ACCOUNTDISABLE
UF_HOMEDIR_REQUIRED
UF_LOCKOUT
UF_PASSWD_NOTREQD
UF_PASSWD_CANT_CHANGE
```

scriptpath
> Pathname for the user's login script

UserDelete

UserDelete *(server, username)*

Deletes a user with *username* from *server*.

UserGetAttributes

UserGetAttributes *(server, username, $password, $passwordage, $privilege, $homedir, $comment, $flags, $scriptpath)*

Retrieves information from a user profile for the user identified by *username* on *server*, and stores each piece in the corresponding variables you provide as arguments. The elements and order of user information are the same as described in the `UserCreate` function.

UserSetAttributes

UserSetAttributes *(server, username, password, passwordage, privilege, homedir, comment, flags, scriptpath)*

Sets attributes for user *username* on *server*. The attributes are those described for the `UserCreate` function.

GroupCreate

GroupCreate *(server, name, comment)*

Creates a group with the specified *name* on *server*. *comment* is a string used to provide a description about the group.

GroupDelete

GroupDelete *(server, name)*

Deletes a group named *name* from *server*.

GroupGetAttributes

GroupGetAttributes *(server, name, comment)*

Returns the comment for group *name* on *server* to the variable *comment*.

Win32

GroupSetAttributes

GroupSetAttributes *(server, name, comment)*

Sets the comment for group *name* on *server* to the string provided in *comment*.

GroupAddUsers

GroupAddUsers *(server, name, users)*

Adds users to group *name* on *server*. *users* can be a list of usernames or a list variable containing multiple usernames.

GroupDeleteUsers

GroupDeleteUsers *(server, name, users)*

Deletes a list of *users* from the group *name* on *server*.

GroupIsMember

GroupIsMember *(server, name, user)*

Queries group *name* on *server* to see if *user* is a member. Returns true if *user* is a member, false if not.

GroupGetMembers

GroupGetMembers *(server, name, $users)*

Returns the usernames that are members of group *name* on *server* to the array referenced by *users*.

LocalGroupCreate

LocalGroupCreate *(server, name, comment)*

Creates a local group with the specified *name* on *server*. *comment* is a string used to provide a description about the group.

LocalGroupDelete

LocalGroupDelete *(server, name)*

Deletes a local group named *name* from *server*.

LocalGroupGetAttributes

LocalGroupGetAttributes *(server, name, $comment)*

Returns the comment for local group *name* on *server* to the variable *$comment*.

LocalGroupSetAttributes

LocalGroupSetAttributes *(server, name, comment)*

Sets the comment for local group *name* on *server* to the string provided in *comment*.

LocalGroupAddUsers

LocalGroupAddUsers *(server, name, users)*

Adds users to local group *name* on *server*. *users* can be a list of usernames or a list variable containing multiple usernames.

LocalGroupDeleteUsers

LocalGroupDeleteUsers *(server, name, users)*

Deletes a list of *users* from the local group *name* on *server*.

LocalGroupIsMember

LocalGroupIsMember *(server, name, user)*

Queries local group *name* on *server* to see if *user* is a member. Returns TRUE if *user* is a member, FALSE if not.

LocalGroupGetMembers

LocalGroupGetMembers *(server, name, \@users)*

Returns the usernames that are members of local group *name* on *server* to the array referenced by *users*.

Win32::NetResource

The Win32::NetResource module allows you to manage shared resources on a network, such as printers, disks, etc. Two data structures are used to provide or store information for many of the NetResource functions. The first is the share_info hash. This hash contains parameters for setting up a share, using the following structure:

Win32

```
%share_info = (
        netname         => "name of share",
        type            => "type of share",
        remark          => "a string comment",
        permissions     => "permissions value",
        maxusers        => "the max number of users",
        current-users   => "the current number of users",
        path            => "the path of the share",
        passwd          => "password, if required"
);
```

A netresource data structure contains information about the shared resource or device. It has the following structure:

```
%netresource = (
        'Scope'        => "Scope of a resource connection (see table below for
                          values)",
        'Type'         => "The type of resource (see table below)",
        'DisplayType'  => "How the resource should be displayed (see table
                          below)",
        'Usage'        => "How the resource should be used",
        'LocalName'    => "Name of the local device the resource is connected
                          to",
        'RemoteName'   => "Network name of the resource",
        'Comment'      => "Comment string",
        'Provider'     => "Provider of the resource"
);
```

The first three elements of the netresource hash contain values described in the following tables. The Scope value can be one of the following:

RESOURCE_CONNECTED	*Resource is already connected.*
RESOURCE_REMEMBERED	*Resource is reconnected each time the user logs on.*
RESOURCE_GLOBALNET	*Resource is available to the entire network.*

The Type element takes one of the following values:

RESOURCETYPE_ANY	*All resources*
RESOURCETYPE_DISK	*Disk resources*
RESOURCETYPE_PRINT	*Print resources*

The Display element can be one of these values:

RESOURCEDISPLAYTYPE_DOMAIN	*The object is displayed as a domain.*
RESOURCEDISPLAYTYPE_SERVER	*The object is displayed as a server.*
RESOURCEDISPLAYTYPE_SHARE	*The object is displayed as a sharepoint.*
RESOURCEUSAGE_CONNECTABLE	*The resource can be connected to a local device.*
RESOURCEUSAGE_CONTAINER	*The resource contains more resources.*

The functions in Win32::NetResource use the share_info and netresource structures as input and output arguments. These arguments are used in the description of the functions below; you should name them whatever you want.

GetSharedResources

GetSharedResources *(\@resources, type)*

Gets a list of all network resources and saves the list as references to *%netresource* hashes in *@resources*. *type* is the type of enumeration.

AddConnection

AddConnection (\%netresource, password, username, connection)

Connects to the resource described in *%netresource*, with the *password* and *username* of the user. The *connection* flag indicates whether the connection should be remembered for the user for all logins.

CancelConnection

CancelConnection (name, connection, force)

Cancels a connection to a resource connected to the local device specified by *name*. *connection* indicates the type of connection, with 1 being a persistent connection and 0 being non-persistent. The *force* value is a Boolean indicating whether or not to force the connection.

WNetGetLastError

WNetGetLastError ($code, $description, $name)

Gets the extended network error and saves its information to the variables named by *code*, *description*, and *name*. An extended network error is given only when Win32::GetLastError returns ERROR_EXTENDED_ERROR.

GetError

GetError ($code)

Gets the last error caused by a Win32 network call and saves it in the variable named by *code*.

GetUNCName

GetUNCName ($uncname, path)

Gets the UNC name of the share connected to the local *path* and saves it to the variable specified by *uncname*.

NetShareAdd

NetShareAdd (\%shareinfo, $error, [server])

Makes a disk resource described by *shareinfo* available for sharing on the network. *server* is the name of the server for the shared resource (local is assumed if not specified). Any error that occurs is saved in the variable named by *error*.

NetShareCheck

NetShareCheck *(device, $type, [server])*

Returns true if a share on *device* is available for connection. The type of share is saved in the variable named by *type* (if the function returns true).

NetShareDel

NetShareDel *(name, [server])*

Removes the share named *name* on optional *server* from a machine's list of shares.

NetShareGetInfo

NetShareGetInfo *(name, \%shareinfo, [server])*

Gets the share information for the share *name* on optional *server* and saves it in the specified *shareinfo* variable.

NetShareSetInfo

NetShareSetInfo *(name, \%shareinfo, $error, [server])*

Sets the information for the share *name* on *server* to the parameters given by *shareinfo*. The error status is saved to the variable named by *error*.

Win32::Process

This module provides access to extended Win32 process creation and management abilities. Process objects are created with the `Create` method (the constructor). Additional methods can be used on objects to kill, suspend, resume, and set the priorities of processes.

The `Create` constructor has the following syntax:

```
Win32::Process->Create($Proc, app, cmnd, hndls, opts, dir)
```

The arguments to `Create` are as follows:

$Proc
    Name of the reference for the created process object.

app Full pathname of the executable.

cmnd
    Command line for executable.

hndls

>Determines handle inheritance. A value of 1 turns on inheritance; a 0 value turns it off.

opts

>Sets options to implement when the process is created. The available options for this argument are listed below.

dir The working directory for the executable.

The process is created by passing the command line in *cmnd* to the executable named in *app*. For example, a process object for a text file running in Notepad is created like this:

```
use Win32::Process;
Win32::Process->Create($proc, 'C:\\windows\\Notepad.exe',
                "Notepad perlnut.txt", 1,
                DETACHED_PROCESS, ".");
```

The process creation options given by the *opts* argument to Create are:

CREATE_DEFAULT_ERROR_MODE	*Give the process the default error mode.*
CREATE_NEW_CONSOLE	*Create a new console for the process.*
	Can't be used with DETACHED_PROCESS.
CREATE_NEW_PROCESS_GROUP	*Create process as root of a new process group.*
CREATE_SEPARATE_WOW_VDM	*Run process in its own Virtual DOS Machine (VDM).*
	Only applicable to 16-bit apps.
CREATE_SUSPENDED	*Start process in a suspended state. The process*
	can be started with the Resume method.
CREATE_UNICODE_ENVIRONMENT	*Use UNICODE characters in the environment block of*
	the new process.
DEBUG_PROCESS	*Debug the new process with the calling process.*
DEBUG_ONLY_THIS_PROCESS	*Don't debug the new process if calling process*
	is being debugged.
DETACHED_PROCESS	*Create a process with no access to the console*
	of the calling process.

Methods

The following methods are provided for objects of created by Win32::Process:

Kill

>*$proc->**Kill**(exitcode)*

>Kills the process with the given *exitcode*, which is returned by the process.

Suspend

>*$proc->**Suspend***

>Suspends the process.

Resume

$proc->**Resume**

Resumes a suspended process. This method can also be used on processes created with the CREATE_SUSPENDED flag.

GetPriorityClass

$proc->**GetPriorityClass**(*$ref*)

Gets the priority class of the process and stores it in *$ref.*

SetPriorityClass

$proc->**SetPriorityClass**(*$priority*)

Sets the priority class of the object to *$priority.* The priority can be one of the following:

IDLE_PRIORITY_CLASS
:   A process whose threads run only when the system is idle.

NORMAL_PRIORITY_CLASS
:   A process with normal scheduling.

HIGH_PRIORITY_CLASS
:   A process that performs time-critical tasks that must be executed immediately.

REALTIME_PRIORITY_CLASS
:   The highest priority process, even preempts OS threads.

GetExitCode

$proc->**GetExitCode**(*$ref*)

Gets the exit code of a process and saves it to *$ref.*

Wait

$proc->**Wait**(*n*)

Waits *n* milliseconds for the process to exit. If the process times out, the method returns false and sets $! to WAIT_FAILED. For no timeout, set *n* to INFINITE.

Win32::Registry

This module provides access to the Windows Registry, the database that stores information about all parts of your system and software. Many operating system and application behaviors are controlled by Registry data. The Win32::Registry module gives you a way to access and update registry information with Perl. (Warning: Always be careful when making changes to the registry. If vital system information gets changed by mistake, your system could become inoperable. Always make certain you have a backup of your registry before you start to make modifications.)

The Registry module automatically creates objects for the top-level registry trees. These objects are created in the `main::` namespace, and each key that you open or create is accessed via one of these root objects. The four top-level objects are:

```
$HKEY_CLASSES_ROOT
$HKEY_CURRENT_USER
$HKEY_LOCAL_MACHINE
$HKEY_USERS
```

If you are outside of the main (default) namespace, you should package declare the keys, i.e., `$main::HKEY_USERS`.

The `Open` method creates new key objects for subtrees or subkeys under another open key object. Initially, a new key is opened from one of the main key objects, for example:

```
use Win32::Registry;
$p = "SOFTWARE\Microsoft\Windows NT\CurrentVersion";
$HKEY_LOCAL_MACHINE->Open($p, $CurrVer) || die "Open $!";
```

This example creates a key object $CurrVer for the CurrentVersion key for Windows NT. This key contains several values for the version of the operating system. With the new key open, you can read or change the values it contains (every key has at least one unnamed, default value), or open and create subkeys. The `Open` method can only create key objects for existing keys.

Registry values are represented in Win32::Registry functions by three elements: the name of the value, the data type of the value, and the value itself. There are several different data types for the values. Win32::Registry defines the following constants for these types:

```
REG_SZ           String data
REG_DWORD        Unsigned four-byte integer
REG_MULTI_SZ     Multiple strings delimited with NULL
REG_EXPAND_SZ    Strings that expand (e.g., based on environment variables)
REG_BINARY       Binary data (no particular format is assumed)
```

Methods

The following methods can be used on key objects, either the preopened main keys or subkeys that you have already opened.

Win32

Open

$parent->Open(*keyname, $key*)

Opens a registry key named in *keyname* and saves it as the object reference named by *$key*. *keyname* is the name of a key relative to the object on which Open is used ($parent).

Create

$key->Create(*$newkey, name*)

Creates a new key identified by *name* and saves it as the object reference named by *$newkey*. If the key already exists, this function simply opens the key. New keys can only be created one level below the key on which Create is used.

SetValue

$key->SetValue(*subkey, type, value*)

Sets the default (unnamed) value for the specified subkey of the key object on which SetValue is used.

subkey
Name of the subkey

type
One of the type constants (listed above) describing the value

value
The value of the key

SetValueEx

$key->SetValueEx(*name, res, type, value*)

Sets a value specified by *name* in the current key (or creates the value if it doesn't already exist).

res A reserved argument for future use (use a 0 as a placeholder).

type
The data type constant (listed above) describing the value.

value
The value of the key.

QueryValue

$key->QueryValue(*name, $var*)

Returns the value of the registry value specified by *name* and saves it in the scalar variable *$var*.

QueryKey

$key*->**QueryKey(** *$class, $subs, $vals **)**

Retrieves information about the current key and returns it to the named scalar variables. The key class is saved in the *class* variable (it will be the null string " " on Win95 since it doesn't use key classes). The number of subkeys is saved in the *$sub* variable, and the number of values in the current key is saved in *$vals*.

GetKeys

$key*->**GetKeys(** *$listref **)**

Returns the names of the subkeys of the current key to the list referenced by *listref*.

GetValues

$key*->**GetValues(** *$hashref **)**

Returns the values contained in the current key to the hash referenced by *hashref*. Each registry value name is a hash key, while the hash value is a reference to a three-element list containing the name of the value, the data type, and the value.

Save

$key->**Save(** *filename* **)**

Saves the registry tree root and the current key to a file, *filename*.

Load

$key->**Load(** *subkey, filename* **)**

Loads a registry file to the named *subkey* from file *filename*.

DeleteKey

$key->**DeleteKey(** *subkey* **)**

Deletes a subkey of the current key. This function will delete all values in the subkey and the subkey itself. A key cannot be deleted if it contains any subkeys.

DeleteValue

$key->**DeleteValue(** *name* **)**

Deletes a value identified by *name* from the current key.

Win32::Semaphore

The Win32::Semaphore module implements semaphores, synchronizing access to shared resources. The constructor new creates a new semaphore object and sets the initial count and the maximum count of the semaphore. The constructor has the following syntax:

```
$sem = Win32::Semaphore->new(init, max, [name]);
```

The arguments are defined as follows:

init
> The initial count of the semaphore.

max The maximum count of the semaphore.

name
> A string containing a name of the semaphore.

The open constructor opens an existing semaphore object specified by *name*:

```
$sem = Win32::Semaphore->open(name);
```

The following methods can be used on Win32::Semaphore objects:

---

wait

*$sem->***wait***([timeout])*

The inherited Win32::IPC call. Waits for the semaphore's count to be nonzero, then decrements it. Optional *timeout* is given in milliseconds.

---

release

$sem->***release***(inc, [$var])

Releases a semaphore and increments the count by the amount specified in *inc*. The last count (before the increment) is returned in the *$var* variable, if provided.

Win32::Service

The Win32::Service module provides a service control interface. It allows you to start, pause, resume, and stop Windows NT system services from Perl scripts.

The following functions are exported by this module. The *host* argument in each function gives the hostname of the machine a service is running (or will run) on. If you supply a null string (""), the local machine will be assumed.

StartService

StartService *(host, service)*

Starts the named *service* on the machine *host*. The specified service must be registered with the Service Control Manager.

StopService

StopService *(host, service)*

Stops the named *service* on machine *host*.

GetStatus

GetStatus *(host, service, \%status)*

Returns the status of *service* as a hash referenced by *status*. The keys for this hash are:

```
ServiceType
CurrentState
ControlsAccepted
Win32ExitCode
ServiceSpecificExitCode
CheckPoint
WaitHint
```

PauseService

PauseService *(host, service)*

Pauses the named *service* on machine *host* (only if the service is able to pause).

ResumeService

ResumeService *(host, service)*

Resumes a paused *service* on *host*.

GetServices

GetServices *(host, \%hash)*

Returns a list of services on *host* to the hash referenced by *hash*.

Win32

Win32::Shortcut

This module allows you to create and manipulate Windows shortcut files (*.lnk* files) through Perl. The methods and properties of this module apply to shortcut objects created by new:

```
use Win32::Shortcut;
$link = Win32::Shortcut->new();
```

This creates the shortcut object $link, on which you can set properties and save into a file. If you supply a filename as an argument to new, the file will be loaded into the shortcut object.

The object can also be accessed as if it were a normal hash reference. The following properties (hash keys) are available:

```
$link->{'File'}
$link->{'Path'}
$link->{'ShortPath'}
$link->{'WorkingDirectory'}
$link->{'Arguments'}
$link->{'Description'}
$link->{'ShowCmd'}
$link->{'Hotkey'}
$link->{'IconLocation'}
$link->{'IconNumber'}
```

See the section on shortcut properties, below, for a description of each property.

The following example assumes you have a shortcut file named *test.lnk* in your current directory. This simple script will tell you where this shortcut points to:

```
use Win32::Shortcut;
$link=new Win32::Shortcut();
$link->Load("test.lnk");
print "Shortcut to: $link->{'Path'} $link->{'Arguments'} 0;
$link->Close();
```

But you can also modify its values:

```
use Win32::Shortcut;
$link=new Win32::Shortcut();
$link->Load("test.lnk");
$link->{'Path'}=~s/C:/D:/i; # move the target from C: to D:
$link->{'ShowCmd'}=SW_NORMAL; # runs in a normal window
```

The methods provided by Win32::Shortcut are as follows:

Close

$link>Close()

Closes a shortcut object. It is not strictly required to close the objects you created, since the Win32::Shortcut objects are automatically closed when the program ends (or when you otherwise destroy such an object).

$\rightarrow$

Also note that a shortcut is not automatically saved when it is closed, even if you modified it. You have to call Save in order to apply modifications to a shortcut file.

Load

$link->Load(file)

Loads the content of the shortcut file named *file* in a shortcut object and fills the properties of the object with its values. Returns undef on error, or a true value if everything was successful.

new

new Win32::Shortcut [file]

Creates a new shortcut object. If a filename is passed in *file*, automatically Loads this file also. Returns the object created, or undef on error.

Resolve

$link->Resolve([flag])

Attempts to automatically resolve a shortcut and returns the resolved path, or undef on error; if there is no resolution, the path is returned unchanged. Note that the path is automatically updated in the Path property of the shortcut.

By default, this method acts quietly, but if you pass a value of 0 (zero) in the *flag* parameter, it will eventually post a dialog box prompting the user for more information. For example:

```
# if the target doesn't exist...
if(! -f $link->Path) {

# save the actual target for comparison
$oldpath = $link->Path;

# try to resolve it (with dialog box)
$newpath = $link->Resolve(0);

die "Not resolved..." if $newpath == $oldpath;

}
```

Save

$link->Save([file])

Saves the content of the shortcut object into the file named *file*. If *file* is omitted, the filename is taken from the File property of the object (which, if not changed, is the name of the last Loaded file).

If no file was loaded and the File property doesn't contain a valid filename, the method returns undef, which is also returned on error. A true value is returned if everything was successful.

Set

$link->Set(path, arguments, workingdirectory, description, showcmd, hotkey, iconlocation, iconnumber)

Sets all the properties of the shortcut object with a single command. This method is supplied for convenience only; you can also set these values by changing the values of the properties. For example:

```
$link->Set("C:\PERL5\BIN\PERL.EXE",
           "-v",
           "C:\PERL5\BIN",
           "Prints out the version of Perl",
           SW_SHOWMAXIMIZED,
           hex('0x0337'),
           "C:\WINDOWS\SYSTEM\COOL.DLL",
           1);
```

This is the same as:

```
$link->Path("C:\PERL5\BIN\PERL.EXE");
$link->Arguments("-v");
$link->WorkingDirectory("C:\PERL5\BIN");
$link->Description("Prints out the version of Perl");
$link->ShowCmd(SW_SHOWMAXIMIZED);
$link->Hotkey(hex('0x0337'));
$link->IconLocation("C:\WINDOWS\SYSTEM\COOL.DLL");
$link->IconNumber(1);</PRE>
```

Shortcut properties

The properties of a shortcut object can be accessed as:

```
$link->{'property'}
```

For example, assuming that you have created a shortcut object with:

```
$link=new Win32::Shortcut();
```

you can see its description with:

```
print $link->{'Description'};
```

You can of course also set it like this:

```
$link->{'Description'}="This is a description";
```

The shortcut properties also have corresponding methods which can also set or read their values.

The properties of a shortcut reflect the content of the Shortcut Properties dialog box, which can be obtained by clicking the right mouse button on a shortcut file in the Windows 95 (or NT 4.0) Explorer and choosing "Properties." Shortcut properties are:

Arguments

The arguments associated with the shell link object. They are passed to the targeted program (see *Path*) when it gets executed. In fact, joined with *Path*, this parameter forms the "Target" field of a Shortcut Properties dialog box.

Description

An optional description given to the shortcut. Not implemented in Shortcut Properties dialog box.

File

The filename of the shortcut file opened with Load, and/or the filename under which the shortcut will be saved with Save (if the *file* argument is not specified).

Hotkey

The hotkey associated with the shortcut, in the form of a 2-byte number, of which the first byte identifies the modifiers (Ctrl, Alt, Shift, etc.), and the second is the ASCII code of the character key. Corresponds to the "Shortcut key" field of a Shortcut Properties dialog box.

IconLocation

The file that contains the icon for the shortcut.

IconNumber

The number of the icon for the shortcut in the file pointed by *IconLocation*, in case more that one icon is contained in that file.

Path

The target of the shortcut. This (joined with *Arguments*) is the content of the "Target" field in a Shortcut Properties dialog box.

ShortPath

Same as *Path*, but expressed in a DOS-readable format (8.3-character filenames). It is available as read-only (well, you can change it, but it has no effect on the shortcut; change *Path* instead) once you Load a shortcut file.

ShowCmd

The condition of the window in which the program will be executed (can be Normal, Minimized or Maximized). Corresponds to the "Run" field of a Shortcut Properties dialog box. Allowed values are:

Value	Meaning	Constant
1	Normal window	SW_SHOWNORMAL
3	Maximized	SW_SHOWMAXIMIZED
7	Minimized	SW_SHOWMINNOACTIVE

WorkingDirectory

The directory in which the targeted program will be executed. Corresponds to the "Start in" field of a Shortcut Properties dialog box.

Win32 Extensions

In addition to the modules listed above, Perl for Win32 can use an additional set of functions from the Win32 extension. These functions provide useful tools for some Windows-specific tasks that don't require their own modules. They are exported from the Win32 package with:

```
use Win32;
```

Many of these functions do not take arguments, and they return the value (or values) of the requested information, unless otherwise noted.

Win32::GetLastError()
> Returns the last error value generated by a call to a Win32 API function.

Win32::OLELastError()
> Returns the last error value generated by a call to a Win32 OLE API function.

Win32::BuildNumber()
> Returns the build number of Perl for Win32.

Win32::LoginName()
> Returns the username of the owner of the current Perl process.

Win32::NodeName()
> Returns the Microsoft network node-name of the current machine.

Win32::DomainName()
> Returns the name of the Microsoft network domain that the owner of the current Perl process is logged into.

Win32::FsType()
> Returns a string naming the filesystem type of the currently active drive.

Win32::GetCwd()
> Returns the current active drive and directory. This function does not return a UNC path, since the functionality required for such a feature is not available under Windows 95.

Win32::SetCwd(*newdir*)
> Sets the current active drive and directory to *newdir*. This function does not work with UNC paths, since the functionality required for such a feature is not available under Windows 95.

Win32::GetOSVersion()
> Returns a list of elements describing the version of the operating system. The elements of the list are: an arbitrary descriptive string, the major version number of the operating system, the minor version number, the build number, and a digit indicating the actual operating system, which will be 0 for Win32s, 1 for Windows 95, and 2 for Windows NT. For example:
>
> ```
> use Win32;
> ($string, $major, $minor, $build, $id) = Win32::GetOSVersion();
> ```

`Win32::FormatMessage(error)`
Converts the Win32 error number supplied by *error* into a descriptive string. The error number can be retrieved using `Win32::GetLastError` or `Win32::OLELastError`.

`Win32::Spawn(command, args, $pid)`
Spawns a new process for the given *command*, passing the arguments in *args*. The ID of the new process in saved in the variable named by *pid*.

`Win32::LookupAccountName(sys, acct, $domain, $sid, $type)`
Returns the domain name, SID, and SID type to the specified variables for the account *acct* on system *sys*.

`Win32::LookupAccountSID(sys, sid, $acct, $domain, $type)`
Returns the account name, domain name, and SID type to the specified variables for the SID *sid* on system *sys*.

`Win32::InitiateSystemShutdown(machine, message, timeout, forceclose, reboot)`
Shuts down the specified *machine* in the specified *timeout* interval. *message* is broadcast to all users. If *forceclose* is true, all documents are closed (forcefully) without prompting the user. If *reboot* is true, the machine is rebooted.

`Win32::AbortSystemShutdown(machine)`
Aborts a shutdown on the specified *machine*.

`Win32::GetTickCount()`
Returns the Win32 tick count.

`Win32::IsWinNT()`
Returns true (non-zero) if the Win32 subsystem is Windows NT.

`Win32::IsWin95()`
Returns true (non-zero) if the Win32 subsystem is Windows 95.

`Win32::ExpandEnvironmentStrings(envstring)`
Returns a string in which any environment variables in the given *envstring* are replaced with their values.

`Win32::GetShortPathName(longpathname)`
Returns the short (8.3) path name of *longpathname*.

`Win32::GetNextAvailDrive()`
Returns a string in the form of `"d:\"`, where *d* is the first available drive letter.

`Win32::RegisterServer(libraryname)`
Loads the DLL *libraryname* and calls the function `DllRegisterServer`.

`Win32::UnregisterServer(libraryname)`
Loads the DLL *libraryname* and calls the function `DllUnregisterServer`.

`Win32::Sleep(time)`
Pauses for the number of milliseconds specified by *time*.

Win32

OLE Automation

The Win32::OLE modules give Perl support for OLE automation. OLE automation is a Microsoft technology based on COM that allows objects created by another application to be used and manipulated by a program through a common interface.

The application (or DLL) that implements the automation interface is called the *automation server*. The application that creates and uses the interface is called the *automation controller* or *automation client*. Many popular applications expose their objects through automation. Microsoft Word, Excel, and other Office applications can be used as automation servers. Automation is widely used by Active Server Pages (ASP) and CGI scripts to access data repositories, perhaps via ActiveX Data Objects (ADO). You can even use automation to control many development environments and editors.

In order to create an automation object, the server needs to be *registered* on the system. This is typically done by the server's installation program, but can be done manually using a utility like *regsvr32.exe*. This involves adding entries to the system registry to tell COM how to find the component, what types of interfaces it provides, what type of server it is, etc. You should be able to find the object model, available methods and properties of the interface in the documentation provided by the application. This object model can be used via Perl's object syntax to create and control objects in your programs.

Four modules provide automation functionality to Perl:

Win32::OLE
> Provides the main interface for OLE automation. You can create or open automation objects, use their methods, and set their properties.

Win32::OLE::Enum
> Creates objects for collections and defines an interface for enumerating them.

Win32::OLE::Variant
> Allows you to convert the Variant data type used in OLE.

Win32::OLE::Const
> Imports constants from an automation object into your script.

There are a few limitations to Win32::OLE to note. There is currently no support for OCXs or OLE events (notifications generated by the automation server). Win32::OLE implements the IDispatch interface only, and therefore cannot access a custom OLE interface.

Creating Objects

Automation objects are represented in Perl as instances of Win32::OLE objects. The module provides three constructors for creating objects from a registered automation server.

new

Win32::OLE->new(*progid*, [*destructor*])

Creates a new automation object. This method always creates a new instance of the server, even if a previous instance of the server is running. If the object cannot be created, new returns undef.

progid, the program identifier (ProgID), is a string that uniquely identifies an automation object. *progid* is used to look up the object's class ID (CLSID), which is stored in the registry.

The second, optional argument to the new method describes a way to destroy the object in case the Perl program dies unexpectedly. *destructor* can be either a string with the name of the defined OLE destructor method, or a code reference that will destroy the object. You should use some form of destructor to close out all your objects, for they can be extremely expensive in terms of system resources. You can explicitly destroy an object using the undef function. If you don't explicitly destroy the object, Perl takes care of it for you when the last reference to the object goes away.

Here is what new would look like with the destructor arguments:

```
# Quit is the OLE-defined destructor method
$x1 = Win32::OLE->new("Excel.Application", 'Quit');

# The object reference is the first argument ($_[0]) passed to new.
# The code reference will undef it to destroy the object.
$x2 = Win32::OLE->new("Excel.Application", sub{undef $_[0];})
```

Notice that we're supplying Excel.Application as the ProgID. Excel supports several different automation objects, including an Application object, Work-Book objects, and several more. You don't necessarily have to create the top-level object (Application, in this case) when dealing with automation objects (this is determined by the automation server). In Excel's case, we could have directly created a WorkSheet object (e.g., Excel.Sheet) or a Chart object, for example.

GetActiveObject

Win32::OLE->GetActiveObject(*progid*)

Creates an object for a currently active instance of a server, if one exists. If the server is registered, but no instance of it is running, the method returns undef. If the server is not registered, the method will croak.

You should probably call GetActiveObject inside an eval so that you can do exception handling in the event that the server is unregistered or is not currently running. If the method returns undef, you can just create a new instance of the server and the object with new.

Win32

GetObject

Win32::OLE->GetObject *(filename)*

Creates an automation object based on a document. *filename* is the full pathname of the document, which can be optionally followed by additional item subcomponents separated by exclamation marks (!). For example:

```
$doc = 'c:estest.xls';
$xl = Win32::OLE->GetObject($doc);
```

This code creates an Excel instance based on an Excel file. It is not always clear what type of object GetObject will return from a document since applications may register for than one document type (e.g., worksheets, charts, macro files, etc. for Excel). You can use QueryObjectType on an object to get the class name of the object.

Automation Methods and Properties

Once you have created an automation object, you can use its methods or adjust its properties as you require. Automation methods are implemented as you'd expect with the Perl object syntax:

```
$obj->some_method(args);
```

Automation methods can often take a number of optional parameters. You can pass undef for any unwanted parameters in the arguments list. For example, you can save a WorkBook in Excel with SaveAs. Additional settings allow you to add the WorkBook to the MRU list and create a backup copy:

```
$xl->WorkBooks(1)->SaveAs($f, undef, undef, undef, undef, 1, undef, undef, 1);
```

For simplification, you can also use just the named parameters you want to set by passing a reference to a hash containing them. You can do this right in the argument list by creating an anonymous hash reference with {}. The previous example can therefore be written like this:

```
$xl->WorkBooks(1)->SaveAs($f, {AddtoMru => 1, CreateBackup => 1});
```

Properties of automation objects are accessed via hash reference notation on the object. For example:

```
$val = $obj->{"property"};      # get a property value
$obj->{"property"} = $val;      # set a property value
```

Be aware that properties may not be writable (or even readable). Many automation objects have read-only properties and will generate an exception if you try to write to them. You'll need to consult the documentation for the object to find out which properties you can safely set.

You can enumerate the properties of an automation object using the normal methods for enumerating hashes, which are keys and each. Here's how you can print the properties and values contained within an object:

```
$xl = Win32::OLE->new('Excel.Application', 'Quit');
while( ($key,$value) = each %$xl ) {
    print "$key=$value\n";
}
```

Win32::OLE methods

Win32::OLE defines a couple of its own methods for dealing with the automation
interface. These are not automation-defined methods, although they look the
same. If a given method is not defined in Win32::OLE, the method call is dis-
patched to the automation object. If the method doesn't exist there, you will get
an OLE error.

The following methods are defined by Win32::OLE:

Invoke

$obj->Invoke(method, args)

This object method calls the given *method* for *$obj* with *args* as arguments. It
is useful for invoking methods that would interfere with predefined names in
Perl, or methods that contain characters that Perl can't recognize. You can also
use Invoke to call an object's default method by using either undef or an
empty string (' ') as the first argument.

LastError

Win32::OLE->LastError()

This class method returns the last OLE error. In a numeric context, the error
number is returned, while in a string context, the error message is returned.

QueryObjectType

Win32::OLE->QueryObjectType($obj)

This class method returns the type of object queried (*$obj*). In list context, a
two-element list of the type library name and the class name of the object is
returned. In scalar context, just the class name is returned.

Win32::OLE functions

The following functions are defined by Win32::OLE. They are not exported by
default.

in

in($coll)

Returns a list of all the members of a collection referenced by the collection
object *$coll*. Same as Win32::OLE::Enum->All().

valof

valof(obj)

Dereferences an automation object (*$obj*), calls the default method of the object, and returns the value.

with

with($obj, property1* => *value1*, . . .)

Sets the values of multiple properties on an object (*$obj*). The function calls `$obj->{`*property*`}=`*value* for each property/value pair.

Win32::OLE class variables

The Win32::OLE module defines certain class variables that set default behavior for automation usage.

`$Win32::OLE::CP`

Determines the codepage used by all translations between Perl strings and Unicode strings used by the OLE interface. The default value is CP_ACP, which is the default ANSI codepage. It can also be set to CP_OEMCP, which is the default OEM codepage. Both constants are not exported by default.

`$Win32::OLE::LCID`

Controls the locale identifier used for all OLE calls. It is set to LOCALE_NEUTRAL by default. Check the Win32 module for other locale-related information.

`$Win32::OLE::Warn`

Determines the behavior of the Win32::OLE module when an error happens. Valid values are:

0   Ignore error, return `undef`.

1   Use `Carp::carp` if `$^W` is set (*–w* option).

2   Always use `Carp::carp`.

3   Use `Carp::croak`.

The error number and message (without `Carp` line/module info) are also available through the `Win32::OLE->LastError` method.

Win32::OLE::Enum

The Win32::OLE::Enum module provides special support for collections. Collections are special automation data types that contain an array of objects or data. A collection supports enumeration—you can iterate through each item through a standard interface.

Collection objects should always provide a Count property (the number of items in the collection) and an Item method. The Item method is used to access a particular collection item using a subscript, which may be an integer or a string, depending on the server. Collection objects may also optionally contain an Add and a Remove method.

Collection objects also support a standard COM interface (IEnumVARIANT) that allows you to enumerate each item in a collection. It defines methods that let you advance the iteration to the next item, skip a given item, restart the enumeration, and create a new copy of the iterator. While all servers are supposed to provide this interface, some servers don't implement all of the methods (often Reset and Clone).

Win32::OLE::Enum defines these methods for enumerating collections. The collection object should provide the Count and Item methods, which are often all you need to use on collections. For example:

```
$cnt = $coll->Count();
if( $cnt) {
    $obj = $coll->Item(0);
    $obj->do_something();
}
```

Count will tell you how many items are in the collection, and Item will return the desired item as a Win32::OLE object.

For the enumeration methods, you need to create an enumeration object for the collection object:

```
$coll = $obj->some_coll();
$enum = Win32::OLE::Enum->new($coll);
```

Now you can use the enumeration methods on the object.

Win32::OLE::Enum methods

The following methods are defined in Win32::OLE::Enum:

---

new

Win32::OLE::Enum->new(*$obj*)

Creates a new Win32::OLE::Enum object. Provides it with either a collection object or and existing Enum object, in which case it calls Clone.

All

*$Enum->*All()

Returns a list of all objects in the collection. Note that in order to use All again, you need to first call Reset.

Clone

*$Enum->*Clone()

Returns a copy of the current iterator. This method is supposed to maintain the same iteration position, if possible, but may be unimplemented.

Next

*$Enum->*Next(*[count]*)

Returns the next item in the collection. You can optionally provide Next with a count (which must be greater than zero), in which case it returns a list of the next count items. Note that if you provide a scalar context in conjunction with a count, you'll only get the last item in the list of returned items. Next returns undef if it is currently on the last item in the collection.

Reset

*$Enum->*Reset()

Restarts the enumeration with the first item in the collection. Reset returns true if it succeeds, false if it fails. Note that this method may be unimplemented.

Skip

*$Enum->*Skip(*[count]*)

Skips the next *count* number of items of the enumeration (again, *count* must be positive and defaults to 1). Skip returns false if there are not at least *count* number of items left.

Win32::OLE::Variant

All automation data has to be coerced into a special type called a Variant. Most of the time, you don't need to worry about explicit type coercion. You just provide your scalar data and the magic of automation takes care of the rest of it. However, there are cases when you want to control the exact type of data you're sending to the automation server. The Win32::OLE::Variant module provides access to the Variant data type and lets you control exactly how the data is represented.

A Variant is an OLE data structure that contains a type field and a data field. The flags are implemented in Perl (as are many constants) as subroutines that return an integer value. The table below lists the Variant type flags, along with a brief description of each.

Type	Description
VT_EMPTY	No value specified. Incidentally, automation does not use VT_EMPTY for empty optional parameters. Rather, it uses VT_ERROR with a value of DISP_E_PARAM- NOTFOUND (which isn't exported by Perl: the value in current Win32 SDK headers is 0x80020004).
VT_NULL	A propagating NULL value was specified (not to be confused with a null pointer). This is used for things like the NULL in SQL.
VT_I2	A 2-byte integer value.
VT_I4	A 4-byte integer value.
VT_R4	An IEEE 4-byte real value.
VT_R8	An IEEE 8-byte real value.
VT_CY	An automation currency value.
VT_DATE	An automation date value.
VT_BSTR	A string value.
VT_DISPATCH	The value contains another automation object.
VT_ERROR	An error code was specified. The type of the error is determined by the actual value. As mentioned earlier, this is used to implement empty optional parameters.
VT_BOOL	A Boolean (true/false) value. If all bits are 1, it's true, if all bits are 0, it's false. Any other value is invalid.
VT_VARIANT	The value contains another Variant.
VT_UNKNOWN	The value contains an IUnknown pointer (the base class of COM objects).
VT_UI1	An unsigned 1-byte character.
VT_BYREF	Can be combined with some fields to indicate that the data is being passed by reference, rather than by value.
VT_ARRAY	The value contains an OLE SAFEARRAY (this flag is not currently exported by Perl).

To convert data to a specific variant type, you create a variant object with either the new constructor method or the convenience function Variant:

```
$vnt = Win32::OLE::Variant->new(type, data);
$vnt = Variant(type, data);
```

For example, to force a string to be interpreted as a date, create a variant object and set it to the VT_DATE type:

```
$dt = Variant(VT_DATE, "August 24, 1970");   # create an explicit data type
$sheet->Cells(1,1)->{Value} = $dt;           # set it to a spreadsheet cell
```

Win32::OLE::Variant methods

The following methods are defined by Win32::OLE:Variant for working with Variant data types:

As

$vnt->As(type)

Takes a *type* flag argument and converts the Variant object to the supplied type before converting it to a Perl value.

ChangeType

$vnt->ChangeType(type)

Takes a type flag argument and converts the Variant object (in place) to the supplied type.

Type

$vnt->Type()

Returns the type of the variant *$vnt*.

Value

$vnt->Value()

Returns the value of the variant *$vnt* as a Perl value. The conversion is performed in the same manner as all return values of Win32::OLE method calls are converted.

Win32::OLE::Const

While browsing through the documentation for an automation object, you may have come across references to constant values. For example, if you're trying to save an Excel workbook to a different file format, you need to provide a file format constant. Since the server documentation typically provides symbolic constants (e.g., xlExcel5 or xlTemplate), we need a way to access those from Perl. This is the purpose of Win32::OLE::Const, which imports the constants from an automation object into your script.

You can either import the constants directly into your namespace as subs that return the constant value, or you can have them returned as a hash reference with the constant name as the key and its value as the value. Here's an example of the former:

```
use Win32::OLE::Const ("Microsoft Excel");
print "xlExcel5 = ", xlExcel5, "0;
```

which produces something like:

```
xlExcel5 = 39
```

Here's an example using the Load method to return a hash reference populated with the constants and their values (this produces the same output as the previous example, of course):

```
use Win32::OLE::Const;

my $constants = Win32::OLE::Const->Load("Microsoft Excel");
print "xlExcel5 = $constants->{xlExcel5}0;
```

Notice that, in both cases, we're supplying a regular expression for the name of the type library from which we want to import. Win32::OLE::Const searches the registry for matching type libraries and loads the one with the highest version number (you can override this by supplying the version you want). You can also specify the language you'd like. The parameters (for either Load or Win32::OLE::Const) are the typelib regular expression, the major version number, the minor version number, and the locale (LCID).

You can also provide the Load method with an automation object, which is then queried for its type library. Interestingly, the documentation notes that this seems to be slower than searching the Registry (though neither is really speedy with a large automation server like Excel). Here's an example of that:

```
use Win32::OLE;
use Win32::OLE::Const;

# create an Excel application object
my $xl = Win32::OLE->new('Excel.Application', 'Quit') ||
    die "Can't create Excel: ", Win32::OLE->LastError;

# import the constants from it
my $constants = Win32::OLE::Const->Load($xl);
```

Using Load (to get a hash reference for the constants) may be preferable to importing all of the constants into your namespace. Some automation servers pro- vide a large number of constants (the current version of Excel has some 900+), so importing them into your namespace can clutter things considerably.

CHAPTER 20

PerlScript

PerlScript is an ActiveX scripting engine that allows you to incorporate Perl within any ActiveX scripting host. PerlScript can be used on the client side (Internet Explorer 4.0) or in Active Server Pages (ASP) generated by web servers like IIS or WebSite Pro. To use PerlScript with these applications, you must have Active State's ActivePerl with PerlScript installed on the local machine (or you can use a network-based installation of each).

Since a local Perl and PerlScript installation is required, it is not practical to deploy applications that use client-side PerlScript across the Internet. Nevertheless, in situations where you have control over the desktop configurations, as in an Intranet environment, client-side PerlScript offers tremendous opportunities for browser-based application development.

Server-side PerlScript does not have this limitation. To use PerlScript on your web server, you don't need to worry about how the end user's desktop is configured. As long as you are running a web server that can use ASP, you can use PerlScript on your web server.

With the free distribution of Netscape Navigator source code, the availability of PerlScript is likely to broaden significantly. This is an area of development that you should keep an eye on if you like the idea of extending Perl's power to web authoring.

PerlScript is implemented into HTML pages or ASP pages via the Document Object Model used by the ActiveX scripting engine. Scripts are virtually the same as any other Perl script. They use Perl's object-oriented features on an object hierarchy defined by the script engine. The object model is different for clients and servers, but the same scheme is used throughout: top-level objects with sub-objects, each containing their own properties and methods.

Properties of objects, like the name of a frame or the background color of a window, are available as hash elements from a referenced object. For example:

```
$object->subobject{'property'} = "value";
$val = $object->subobject->{'property'};
```

Thus, properties can be set or retrieved.

Objects have a predefined set of methods available to them as well. Methods define actions such as writing to a document or performing actions on a mouse click. Methods are accessible in the usual way:

```
$object->method(args);
```

This chapter provides information on the parts of the object model that you will use most often. A complete reference for the object models for both ASP and ActiveX scripting clients is beyond the scope of this book. For more detailed information, consult the documentation for your server, or the Microsoft web site, which has complete client and server information.

Client-Side PerlScript

All PerlScript code must be contained within a <SCRIPT LAN-GUAGE="PerlScript"></SCRIPT> element. You may include any number of these elements in your program, so it is possible to intersperse Perl and HTML freely. For example:

```
<HTML>
<HEAD>
<TITLE>Hello, World</TITLE>
</HEAD>
<BODY>

<H1>Hello, from the Old Edition!</H1>

<SCRIPT LANGUAGE="PerlScript">

    my @one_hit = ('Bel', 'Biv', 'DeVoe');

    foreach (@one_hit) {
        $window->document->write(qq[$_ says "Hello"!<BR>]);
        }

    $window->document->write(qq[<P><I>"That girl is Poison!"</I></P>]);

</SCRIPT>

</BODY>
</HTML>
```

The write method is used on the document object to "write" HTML and text to the document displayed in the window.

The top-level object is the window. This is the default object that contains the script. (Even though the script is contained in the HTML file, the script object is a level below the window, just like the document object.)

Win32

Every window contains the following objects:

Frame
> This object contains an array of frames in the window. Each frame object is accessible via the index, i.e., `$window->frame[2]` is the third frame object. Each frame object is a container that acts like its own window object.

History
> This object stores the browser history—all the sites a client has been to in its current session.

Navigator
> This object contains information about the client application, like the User-Agent header it provides.

Location
> This object contains information about the current URL for the window.

Script
> This object contains any script elements in the current window scope.

Document
> This object contains all of the displayed content in a window: the HTML, text, forms, objects, etc.

The most important object in this hierarchy is the document object. The following section explains the objects it contains, their properties, and their methods.

The Document Object

The document object represents what is displayed within the client window. In the example above, we showed that the `write` method tells the client to show the given HTML and text. The document object contains a number of methods and properties that can be manipulated within a script. It also is a container for other objects that hold information about the document:

Anchor
> An array of anchors (`<a name="string"> </a>` tags) in the document.

Form
> An array of forms contained in the document.

Link
> An array of hyperlinks (`<a href="url"> </a>` in the document.

The anchor and link objects both provide arrays. Each element in the array is a string with the name of the anchor or location of the hyperlink. The elements in the link array are read-only. Anchor names can be manipulated by the script.

The form object provides access to the elements of the forms within your document. Each form is an indexed element of the form object array and can be accessed like this:

```
$obj = $window->document->form[1];
```

This would be the second form in the document. Under this form object are objects representing the various parameters of the form and input tags. They are accessible by the names of the attributes used in the HTML tags.

Document methods

The following methods can be used on the document object. They are accessed using the usual object-method syntax: $obj->method(args).

write *(string)*

Places the given *string* into the document at the current position. The string can contain HTML tags and text that will be interpreted by the browser or other HTML-capable client.

writeLn *(string)*

Same as the write method, except that it places a new line after the given *string*.

open

Opens a document object for writing. The current document is already open for writing. This method may be used on another document object from another frame or window to send output to. After open is called, output to a document is not displayed immediately; it displays only after a close call is used on the document.

close

Closes a document and writes all output to it.

clear

Clears an output stream on a document.

Document properties

The document object contains a set of properties described below. Properties can be set or retrieved, and are accessed as hash variables under the document object. They are accessible via the following syntax:

```
$val = $window->document->{property};
```

linkColor

The color of hyperlinks in the document, given by an RGB-color value.

vLinkColor

The color of visited hyperlinks in the document, given by an RGB-color value.

bgColor

The background color of a document, given by an RGB-color value.

fgColor

The foreground color of a document, given by an RGB-color value.

location

The URL of the current document.

Win32

`lastModified`
> The timestamp for the last modification of the document.

`title`
> The title of the document as given by the <TITLE> tag.

`cookie`
> The string value of the cookie for the document, if there is one.

Server-Side PerlScript

PerlScript on the server-side of business is a much more viable method of incorporating Perl into your web applications. You can use PerlScript as the scripting language for Active Server Pages (ASP), which are used by such applications as Microsoft's IIS and O'Reilly's WebSite Pro. See the documentation for these products to properly set up ASP on your server. ActivePerl with PerlScript must be installed on the server machine to be used with ASP.

Active Server Pages use PerlScript in pages much like client-side scripting except that the object model is different, and most importantly, the script is executed on the server. When an Active Server Page is requested, the *.asp* file is processed, scripts are executed, and an HTML page is produced and delivered to the client.

Each script is contained within <SCRIPT> tags. PerlScript must be declared as the default scripting language for each file with:

```
<SCRIPT LANGUAGE="PerlScript" RUNAT=Server>
```

The RUNAT attribute signals that the script is to be executed on the server and not the client. The lines of the script follow, and the script is closed with an ending </SCRIPT> tag.

An alternative syntax to the <SCRIPT> tags are the <% %> delimiters. These are not HTML tags, but indicate that whatever happens between them is to be executed. There are also special constructs used with these delimiters. Since they can be interspersed with HTML throughout a file, the default language must be declared at the top of the file with the <%@ %> tag:

```
<%@ PerlScript%>
```

This delimiter syntax completely replaces the declarative <SCRIPT> tag shown above, but it must be placed at the top of any file using the <% %> syntax for scripting. In addition to this tag, you can use the <%= %> tag throughout your file to automatically assign a value to the output of your file (i.e., a $Response->write function). Here is an example:

```
<%@ PerlScript>
<HTML>
<HEAD></HEAD>
<BODY>
<H1>Say Hello, Boys!</H1>

<% my @onehit = ("Bel", "Biv", "DeVoe"); %>

<P>
```

```
<%= $onehit[0] %> says "Hello."
<BR>
<%= $onehit[1] %> says "Hello."
<BR>
<%= $onehit[2] %> says "Hello."

</P>
</BODY>
</HTML>
```

The return value of any code within <%= %> is placed into the output HTML returned to the client. This syntax makes it very easy to intersperse the output of commands with HTML throughout the ASP file.

The scripting object model for ASP contains the following top-level objects:

Application
>Application objects can be created to share data among multiple users of defined groups of *.asp* files under a virtual directory on the server.

Request
>The Request object encapsulates all of the information about the browser and any data it supplies in its request, such as POST data from a form. It is equivalent to the information contained in an HTTP request.

Response
>The Response object represents information and data sent to a client after a request. It is equivalent to an HTTP server response.

Server
>The Server object contains certain control parameters for the server and provides methods for creating connections to other applications.

Session
>The Session object uses cookies to store state information for a user across multiple pages accessed during a session.

The Request and Response objects provide an ASP interface to the HTTP protocol used in web transactions. The other objects encapsulate special server features and connections to outside applications.

The Request Object

The Request object contains all the information sent to the server in the client's request. This object has only one property, TotalBytes, which is read-only and gives the number of bytes sent in the body of a client request. The BinaryRead method of the Request object retrieves the client request as raw binary data.

The information contained in a request is stored in various collection objects. Collections contain objects that represent the important pieces of a request, for example, form or cookie data. There are five collections under the Request object:

ClientCertificate
>Contains information from a client certificate sent in the request.

Win32

Cookies

Contains the data from any cookies sent in the request.

Form

Contains POST data from forms.

QueryString

Contains form data passed in the query string of the URL.

ServerVariables

Contains the values of environment variables and header values in the request.

To access the objects in the collection, the name of an object is given as the argument to the Collection object. For example, to access a form variable named "birthday" from the Form collection, you would use:

```
$object = $Request->Form("birthday");
```

This returns an object for the "birthday" form variable. To get the value, you use the Item method on the object:

```
$data = $Request->Form("birthday")->Item;
```

This returns the value assigned to "birthday" in the request. Since ASP collection objects are OLE collections, the functionality of the Win32::OLE modules can be employed. See Chapter 19, *Win32 Modules and Extensions*, for more information on OLE collections.

The QueryString collection contains form data input by the GET method and transmitted at the end of the requested URL. Values are retrieved from the QueryString object the same way they are retrieved from the form object, for example:

```
$data = $Request->QueryString("birthday")->Item;
```

Cookies sent within a client request are stored the same way. The name of the cookie variable retrieves the cookie object from the collection, and **Item** retrieves the value:

```
$data = $Request->Cookie("birthday")->Item;
```

The ServerVariables collection stores both environment variables relevant to the transaction and HTTP headers sent in the request. The header objects are accessible by using the syntax: HTTP_*HeaderName*. Underscores contained within *HeaderName* are interpreted as dashes.

The Response Object

The Response object contains the information output to the client. The Write method is primarily used to write the output of code to the client, but the Response object is also used to create and send cookies to the client, as well as manipulate headers, update server logs, and set control parameters for the document.

Setting cookies

The Response object contains one collection for setting cookies with the client. The Cookies collection allows you to create cookies and sets the information that is delivered to the client in the Set-Cookie header of the HTTP response.

In the ASP file, you can check for a returned cookie in the request, and if there is none, you can set a new cookie:

```
<%
if ( defined($Request->Cookie("user") )
  { $userid = $Request->Cookie("user")->Item; }
else
  { $Response->Cookie("user") = 123; };
%>
```

This will check to see if a cookie named user was sent in the request. If it was not, a new cookie is sent in the response and set on the client machine.

The Response cookie collection uses a number of properties to set the standard attributes used with cookies. For example, to set the expiration of a cookie, you would use the Expires attribute:

```
$Response->Cookie("user")->{Expires} = "Tuesday, 31-Dec-99 00:00:00 GMT";
```

The client will no longer return a cookie after its expiration date.

The following properties are used to set attributes on a response cookie:

Domain
> If specified, the cookie will be sent in any request to this domain. The value must contain at least two dots, e.g., .oreilly.com. This value would cover both www.oreilly.com and software.oreilly.com.

Expires
> Sets the expiration date for the cookie.

Path
> Sets the URL range for which the cookie is valid. If the value is set to /pub, for example, the cookie will be returned for URLs in /pub as well as subpaths such as /pub/docs and /pub/images. A path value of "/" indicates that the cookie will be used for all URLs at the originating site. If no path value is set, the cookie will be returned only for the originating URL.

Secure
> If set to true, this attribute instructs the client to return the cookie over only a secure connection (via SHTTP or SSL).

Response properties

The following properties can be set on the Response object. The property syntax is as follows:

```
$Response->{property} = value;
```

Win32

Buffer

If set to false, output is sent the client immediately as it is processed by the script. If set to true, output is buffered and sent only when the entire page has been processed, or upon calls to the Flush or End methods.

CacheControl

If set to Private, output from this ASP page will not be cached by a proxy server. If set to Public, the output can be cached by a proxy server.

Charset

Appends the given character set name to the Content-Type header.

ContentType

Specifies the HTTP content type of the response; for example, text/html.

Expires

Specifies the length of time in minutes before a client-cached page expires. After this time, the page will be requested again. A setting of 0 forces the page to expire immediately.

ExpiresAbsolute

Specifies the date and time on which a client-cached page expires. The date and time are given in a format such as "June 18,1999 00:00:00", where the time is GMT.

IsClientConnected

Returns true if the client is still connected to the server (possibly waiting on a request); false, otherwise.

Pics

Adds a PICS-label header to the response with the given PICS formatted string.

Status

Sets the status code and explanation string in a server response, for example "403 Forbidden".

Response methods

The following methods can be used on the Response object.

AddHeader (*header, value*)

Adds an HTTP *header* with assigned *value* to the header of the HTTP response. The specified header will simply be added to the response; it will not replace an existing header. This method must be used in the ASP file before any page content is output. For buffered pages, it can be used anywhere before the first Flush call.

AppendToLog (*string*)

Appends *string* to the server log (if extended logging is properly configured). *string* can be a maximum of 80 characters and should not contain commas.

BinaryWrite (*data*)

Writes the given binary *data* to the HTTP output without any conversion.

`Clear ()`

Clears any response content from the output buffer. This method will not clear header information, and will cause a runtime error if `$Response->Buffer` has not been set to true.

`End ()`

Stops all processing of the ASP file and outputs any buffered content.

`Flush ()`

If buffering has been enabled with `$Response->Buffer`, this call clears the buffer and outputs its contents.

`Redirect (url)`

Instructs the client to connect to the specified *url*.

`Write (data)`

Writes the *data* to the HTML output stream.

Index

Numbers

-0 option (perl), 33
\007 (octal value) sequence, 66

Symbols

@_ array, 70
& (ampersand)
  AND bitwise operator, 62
  calling subroutines, 70
  in encoded URLs, 325
  prototype symbol, 71
  && (logical AND) operator, 61
  &&= (assignment) operator, 60
  &= (assignment) operator, 60
<> (angle brackets), 76
  greater-than operator, 59
  < Perl debugger command, 150
  << Perl debugger command, 150
  <<= (assignment) operator, 60
  <= (less-than-or-equal) operator, 59
  <=> (comparison) operator, 59
  > Perl debugger command, 150
  < . . . > line-input operator, 75
  >> to open file for appending, 74
  >> Perl debugger command, 150
  >>= (assignment) operator, 60
  >= (greater-than-or-equal) operator,
    59

* (asterisk)
  metacharacter, 65
  multiplication operator, 59
  prototype symbol (typeglob), 71
  ** (exponentiation) operator, 59
  **= (assignment) operator, 60
  *= (assignment) operator, 60
  *? regular expression quantifier, 68
@ (at sign)
  dereferencing with, 73
  format fieldholders, 76
  prototype symbol (list), 71
  signifying arrays, 46
\ (backslash)
  creating references, 72
  metacharacter, 65
  in prototype declarations, 72
  reference creation operator, 58
! (bang)
  CPAN.pm eval command, 20
  logical negation operator, 58
  .newsrc entries, 433
  Perl debugger command, 151
  !! Perl debugger command, 151
  != (not equal to) operator, 59
  !~ (pattern match) operator, 60
{} (braces)
  delimiting statement blocks, 48
  metacharacter, 65

-> (arrow) operator, 58, 163
  dereferencing with, 74
-= (assignment) operator, 60
— (autodecrement) operator, 60
-- option (perl), 33
<% %> delimiters, 612
() (parentheses)
  around function arguments, 85
  metacharacter, 66
  operator precedence and, 57
  (?...) extended regular expression
    syntax, 69
% (percent sign)
  dereferencing with, 73
  modulus operator, 59
  prototype symbol (hash), 71
  signifying variable type, 46
  %= (assignment) operator, 60
+ (plus)
  metacharacter, 65
  unary operator, 58
  += (assignment) operator, 60
  ++ (autoincrement) operator, 60
  +? regular expression quantifier, 68
? (question mark)
  metacharacter, 65
  ?: (conditional) operator, 62
  ?? regular expression quantifier, 68
  ?...? pattern match operator, 64
  ?...? Perl debugger command, 150
; (semicolon)
  ending Perl statements, 42
  in prototype declarations, 72
/ (slash)
  division operator, 59
  encoding in URLs, 325
  /= (assignment) operator, 60
  /.../ pattern match operator, 63
  /.../ Perl debugger command, 150
~ (tilde)
  bitwise negation operator, 58
  suppressing output whitespace, 77
  ~~ to print strings in fields, 77
_ (underscore)
  filehandle, 55
  improving number legibility, 44
| (vertical bar)
  format fieldholders, 76
  metacharacter, 66

OR bitwise operator, 62
Perl debugger command, 151
|= (assignment) operator, 60
|| Perl debugger command, 151
|| (logical OR) operator, 61
||= (assignment) operator, 60

A

\A anchor (string beginning), 67
a command (CPAN.pm), 21
A command (Perl debugger), 143
a command (Perl debugger), 143
-A file test operator, 60
-a option (perl), 33
-a option (dprofpp), 154
-a option (perlbug), 155
\a (alarm) sequence, 66
abort() (Net::FTP), 443
abs()
  Perl built-in, 87
  URI::URL module, 486
−accelerator option (Menubutton), 536
accept()
  CGI.pm module, 335
  HTTP::Daemon module, 473
  IO::Socket module, 385–386
  Perl built-in, 87
  socket function, 380, 383
access.conf file, 357
account() (Net::Netrc), 450
account entries (.netrc), 449
$ACCUMULATOR ($^A) variable, 52
activate()
  Listbox widget, 515
activate
  Scrollbar widget, 513
active() (Net::NNTP), 428
active index
  Listbox widget, 514
  Menu widget, 538
Active Server Pages (ASP), 608, 612
active_times() (Net::NNTP), 428
−activebackground option (widgets),
    502
−activeborderwidth option (Menu),
    538
−activeforeground option (widgets),
    502

bang (!) (cont'd)
  != (not equal to) operator, 59
  !~ (pattern match) operator, 60
Barber, Stan, 423
Barr, Graham, 390
base()
  HTTP::Response module, 463
  URI::URL module, 486
base module, 177
$BASETIME ($^T) variable, 54
bbox()
  Canvas widget, 531
  Listbox widget, 515
  Text widget, 518
bcc() (Mail::Send), 401
-bd option (widgets), 503
-before option (pack geometry man-
      ager), 497
=begin command (pod), 78
Benchmark module, 177
-bg option (widgets), 502
-bigincrement option (Scale), 534
binary() (Net::FTP), 443
Binary() (Win32::Internet), 571
binary Perl distributions, 13–14
BinaryRead() (Request object,
      PerlScript), 613
BinaryWrite() (Response object,
      PerlScript), 616
bind(), 88
  Canvas module, 531
  Socket module, 380, 382
bind_col() (DBI), 375
bind_columns() (DBI), 375
bind_param() (DBI), 370
binmode(), 88
-bitmap option (widgets), 502
bitwise operators, 62
bless(), 88
blib module, 180
block of statements, 48
body() (Net::NNTP), 428
Body()
  Mail::Internet module, 412
  Mail::POP3Client module, 418, 420
bookdb.dir, bookdb.pag files, 366
books, Perl-related, 9
-bordermode option (place geometry
      manager), 501

-borderwidth option (widgets), 503
braces {}
  delimiting statement blocks, 48
  metacharacter, 65
  regular expression quantifiers, 68
  { Perl debugger command, 151
  {{ Perl debugger command, 151
brackets []
  metacharacter, 65–66
  Perl debugger command, 152
Buffer property (Response object), 616
bugs in Perl, reporting, 155–156
  (see also debugging)
built-in functions, 85–141
  listed alphabetically, 87–141
  listed by category, 86–87
  socket-related, 380–384
built-in Perl variables, 51–56
button() (CGI.pm), 336
Button widget (Perl/Tk), 506
byte() (Net::FTP), 444
Bytecode backend (Perl compiler), 39
byteperl interpreter, 40

C

C, CC backends (Perl compiler), 39
c command (Perl debugger), 144
-c file test operator, 60
-C file test operator, 60
-c option (perl), 33
-c option (perlbug), 156
-C option (perlbug), 156
C preprocessor (cpp), 33
C<> interior sequence (pod), 80
-C option (perlcc), 40
CacheControl property (Response
      object), 616
callbacks, widget (Perl/Tk), 496
caller(), 89
Camel image, 9
cancel() (Mail::Send), 401
CancelConnection() (Win32::NetRe-
      source), 583
canon() (Mail::Address), 416
CanonicalizeURL() (Win32::Internet),
      563
Canvas widget (Perl/Tk), 524–533
Capini, Aldo, 548

debug()
  Mail::Folder module, 405
  Text widget, 518
declarations, 43
  packages, 160
  private vs. local, 71
  subroutines, 70
  variables, 47
default_port() (URI::URL), 486
defaults() (CGI.pm), 338
defined(), 92
deiconify() (Frame widget), 542
del_group() (News::Newsrc), 434
delay() (LWP::RobotUA), 455
delete(), 93
  Canvas widget, 531
  CGI.pm module, 339
  Entry widget, 510
  HTML::Parser module, 480
  Listbox widget, 514
  Mail::Send module, 402
  Menu widget, 539
  Net::FTP module, 444
  Net::POP3 module, 396
  Text widget, 518
Delete()
  Mail::POP3Client module, 419–420
  Win32::Internet module, 571
delete_all() (CGI.pm), 339
delete_content() (HTML::Parser), 480
delete_label() (Mail::Folder), 405
delete_message() (Mail::Folder), 405
DeleteKey() (Win32::Registry), 589
DeleteValue() (Win32::Registry), 589
delta() (Scrollbar), 513
Deparse backend (Perl compiler), 39
dereferencing, 73, 163
deselect()
  Checkbutton widget, 507
  Radiobutton widget, 508
DESTROY method, 162
Devel::SelfStubber module, 195
diagnostics module, 196
diamond < . . . > operator, 75
die(), 75, 93
−digits option (Scale), 534
dir() (Net::FTP), 444

directories
  file-related functions, 86
  functions for, 86
DirHandle module, 197
−disabledforeground option (widgets),
    503
disconnect() (DBI), 371
Display() (Win32::Console), 550
distributions() (Net::NNTP), 429
division (*) operator, 59
dlineinfo() (Text widget), 518
do statement, conditional modifiers
    with, 50
do(), 93, 371
document object (PerlScript), 610–612
DOCUMENT_ROOT variable, 326
documentation, Perl, 25–27, 77–84
  = to signify in programs, 43
  utilities for, 81–84
dollar sign ($), 65
  dereferencing with, 73
  prototype symbol (scalar), 71
  regular expression anchor, 67
  signifying scalar variables, 46
  special variables (see $ variables)
domain() (Net::SMTP), 394
Domain property (response cookies),
    615
dot (.)
  concatenation operator, 63
  metacharacter, 65
  Perl debugger command, 150
  .. (range) operator, 62
  ... (range) operator, 62
  .= (assignment) operator, 60
double-quoted string literals, 44
Dowd, Sean, 390
downloading
  Perl language source code, 10–12
  Perl modules source code, 12,
    15–25
dprofpp utility, 154
dump_results() (DBI), 372
dump(), 94
  CGI.pm module, 339
  HTML::Parser module, 480
dup() (Mail::Folder), 405
DynaLoader module, 198
dynamic scoping, 47, 71

E

-e file test operator, 60
-e option (perl), 33
-E option (dprofpp), 154
-e option (perlbug), 156
-e option (perlcc), 40
\e (escape) sequence, 66
E<> interior sequence (pod), 80
each(), 94
ebcdic() (Net::FTP), 444
$EFFECTIVE_GROUP_ID ($)) vari-
        able, 53
$EFFECTIVE_USER_ID ($>) variable,
        53
$EGID ($() variable, 53
−elementborderwidth option (Scroll-
        bar), 512
email, 390–422
    folders for (Mail::Folder module),
        402–411
    handling messages (Mail::Internet
        module), 411–414
    header control (Mail::Send mod-
        ule), 400–402
    Mail modules, 390, 398–422
    parsing addresses (Mail::Address
        module), 414–417
    Perl-related mailing lists, 7
    reading (Mail::POP3Client module),
        417–422
    retrieving (Net::POP3 module),
        395–398
    sending (Mail::Mailer module),
        398–400
    sending (Net::SMTP module),
        391–395
embedding scripts in messages, 33
encoding URLs, 325–326
=end command (pod), 79
__END__ constant, 55
end index
    Entry widget, 510
    Listbox widget, 514
    Menu widget, 539
    Text widget, 517
endgrent(), 94
endhostent(), 94
endnetent(), 95
endprotoent(), 95

endpwent(), 95
endservent(), 95
endtag() (HTML::Parser), 480
End() (Response object, PerlScript),
        617
English module, 200
Entry widget (Perl/Tk), 509–512
entrycget()
    Menu widget, 539
    Menubutton widget, 538
entryconfigure()
    Menu widget, 539
    Menubutton widget, 538
EnumerateRights() (Win32::FileSecu-
        rity), 561
%ENV hash, 54
Env module, 201
env_proxy() (LWP::UserAgent), 458
environment variables, 38–39
    CGI-related, 326–328
    DBI-related, 376
eof(), 95
    HTML::Parser module, 478
eparams() (URI::URL), 486
epath() (URI::URL), 487
eq (equal to) operator, 59
eq() (URI::URL), 487
equal sign (=)
    assignment operator, 45, 60
    for embedded documentation
        (pod), 43
    in hash name/value pairs, 46
    for pod commands, 78
    == (equal to) operator, 59
    => operator, defining key/value
        pairs, 46, 62
    =~ (pattern match) operator, 60
equality operators, 59
equery() (URI::URL), 487
err() (DBI), 372
Errno module, 201
$ERRNO ($!) variable, 52
error_as_HTML() (HTTP::Response),
        464
Error() (Win32::Internet), 566
errstr() (DBI), 372
escape_from() (Mail::Internet), 413
escaped sequences, 66
$EUID ($>) variable, 53
$EVAL_ERROR ($@) variable, 52

L

Y

Z

About the Authors

Ellen Siever is a writer at O'Reilly & Associates, where she has also been a production editor and tools specialist. Before coming to O'Reilly, she was a programmer for many years in the Boston area. In addition to computers, her interests include her family, travel (especially if it's in the Southwest), and photography.

Stephen Spainhour is a writer for O'Reilly & Associates. He has contributed to many O'Reilly titles. He is an avid fan of professional tennis (and terrible player), and when he's not checking for tennis scores on the web, he enjoys cooking, electronic music, and watching lots of television.

Nathan Patwardhan is a consultant with Collective Technologies where he works with Unix and programming languages like C and Perl. Nathan has been interested in Perl for several years, his most recent efforts being centered around Perl for Win32. In his free time, he enjoys Etch-A-Sketch and desserts by Swanson. You might occasionally find Nathan on EFNet's #perl or #helmet or checking in on one of the Usenet groups: *comp.lang.perl.misc* or *comp.lang.perl.moderated*.

Colophon

Our look is the result of reader comments, our own experimentation, and feedback from distribution channels. Distinctive covers complement our distinctive approach to technical topics, breathing personality and life into potentially dry subjects.

The animal featured on the cover of *Perl in a Nutshell* is a camel (one-hump dromedary). Camels are large ruminant mammals, weighing between 1,000 and 1,600 pounds and standing six to seven feet tall at the shoulders. They are well known for their use as draft and saddle animals in the desert regions, especially of Africa and Asia. Camels can go for days without water. If food is scarce, they will eat anything, even their owner's tent. Camels live up to 50 years.

Ellie Fountain Maden was the production editor and project manager for *Perl in a Nutshell*. Nicole Gipson Arigo was the copyeditor, and Ellie Cutler proofread the book. Clairemarie Fisher O'Leary, Jane Ellin, Maureen Dempsey, and Sheryl Avruch provided quality control reviews. Seth Maislin wrote the index, and Robert Romano created the illustrations in Adobe Photoshop 4.0 and Macromedia Freehand 7.0. The inside layout was designed by Edie Freedman and Nancy Priest and was formatted in troff by Lenny Muellner, using ITC Garamond Light, ITC Garamond Book, LetterGothicMT, and LetterGothicMT-Oblique fonts. This colophon was written by Michael Kalantarian.

Whenever possible, our books use a durable and flexible lay-flat binding. If the page count exceeds the lay-flat binding's page limit, then perfect binding is used.

More Titles from O'Reilly

Perl

Learning Perl on Win32 Systems

By Randal L. Schwartz, Erik Olson &
Tom Christiansen
1st Edition August 1997
306 pages, ISBN 1-56592-324-3

In this carefully paced course,
leading Perl trainers and a Windows
NT practitioner teach you to program
in the language that promises to
emerge as the scripting language
of choice on NT. Based on the "llama book, this book features
tips for PC users and new, NT-specific examples, along with
a foreword by Larry Wall, the creator of Perl, and Dick Hardt,
the creator of Perl for Win32.

Mastering Regular Expressions

By Jeffrey E. F. Friedl
1st Edition January 1997
368 pages, ISBN 1-56592-257-3

Regular expressions, a powerful tool
for manipulating text and data, are
found in scripting languages, editors,
programming environments, and
specialized tools. In this book, author
Jeffrey Friedl leads you through the
steps of crafting a regular expression that gets the job done.
He examines a variety of tools and uses them in an extensive
array of examples, with a major focus on Perl.

Learning Perl/Tk

By Nancy Walsh
1st Edition January 1999
376 pages, ISBN 1-56592-314-6

This tutorial for Perl/Tk, the extension
to Perl for creating graphical user
interfaces, shows how to use Perl/Tk
to build graphical, event-driven
applications for both Windows and
UNIX. Rife with illustrations, it teaches
how to implement and configure each Perl/Tk graphical element.

The Perl Cookbook

By Tom Christiansen &
Nathan Torkington
1st Edition August 1998
794 pages, ISBN 1-56592-243-3

This collection of problems, solutions,
and examples for anyone programming in Perl covers everything from
beginner questions to techniques that
even the most experienced Perl
programmers might learn from. It contains hundreds of Perl
"recipes," including recipes for parsing strings, doing matrix
multiplication, working with arrays and hashes, and performing
complex regular expressions.

Learning Perl, 2nd Edition

By Randal L. Schwartz &
Tom Christiansen,
Foreword by Larry Wall
2nd Edition July 1997
302 pages, ISBN 1-56592-284-0

In this update of a bestseller, two
leading Perl trainers teach you to use
the most universal scripting language
in the age of the World Wide Web.
Now current for Perl version 5.004, this hands-on tutorial
includes a lengthy new chapter on CGI programming, while
touching also on the use of library modules, references, and
Perl's object-oriented constructs.

Eliminating Annoyances

Windows 98 Annoyances

By David A. Karp
1st Edition October 1998
464 pages, ISBN 1-56592-417-7

Based on the author's popular Windows
Annoyances Web site (http://www.
annoyances.org), this book provides
an authoritative collection of techniques
for customizing Windows 98. It allows
you to quickly identify a particular
annoyance and immediately offers one or more solutions,
making it the definitive resource for customizing Windows 98.
Includes a CD with a trial version of O'Reilly Utilities: Quick
Solutions for Windows 98 Annoyances.

O'REILLY®

TO ORDER: **800-998-9938** • **order@oreilly.com** • **http://www.oreilly.com/**
OUR PRODUCTS ARE AVAILABLE AT A BOOKSTORE OR SOFTWARE STORE NEAR YOU.
FOR INFORMATION: **800-998-9938** • **707-829-0515** • **info@oreilly.com**

Eliminating Annoyances

O'Reilly Utilities: Quick Solutions for Windows 98 Annoyances

Software developed by Mark Bracewell & David A. Karp
1st Edition October 1998
CD-ROM with full online Help
ISBN 1-56592-549-1

O'Reilly Utilities: Quick Solutions for Windows 98 Annoyances is the stand-alone software companion to David Karp's *Windows 98 Annoyances* book. This software provides immediate, automated solutions for many of the key annoyances described in the book, as well as other important new enhancements to Windows 98. Developed in cooperation with David Karp, *O'Reilly Utilities* allows you to immediately improve your productivity with dozens of Windows extensions that go beyond Tweak UI and make common tasks easier, such as group file renaming, file copying, and customizing the desktop. Even better, we've built programs into this package that solve some of the most aggravating behaviors of Windows and other applications.

Web Programming

CGI Programming on the World Wide Web

By Shishir Gundavaram
1st Edition March 1996
450 pages, ISBN 1-56592-168-2

This book offers a comprehensive explanation of CGI and related techniques for people who hold on to the dream of providing their own information servers on the Web. It starts at the beginning, explaining the value of CGI and how it works, then moves swiftly into the subtle details of programming.

Web Programming

JavaScript: The Definitive Guide, 3rd Edition

By David Flanagan & Dan Shafer
3rd Edition June 1998
800 pages, ISBN 1-56592-392-8

This third edition of the definitive reference to JavaScript covers the latest version of the language, JavaScript 1.2, as supported by Netscape Navigator 4.0. JavaScript, which is being standardized under the name ECMAScript, is a scripting language that can be embedded directly in HTML to give web pages programming-language capabilities.

Learning VBScript

By Paul Lomax
1st Edition July 1997
616 pages, includes CD-ROM
ISBN 1-56592-247-6

This definitive guide shows web developers how to take full advantage of client-side scripting with the VBScript language. In addition to basic language features, it covers the Internet Explorer object model and discusses techniques for client-side scripting, like adding ActiveX controls to a web page or validating data before sending it to the server. Includes CD-ROM with over 170 code samples.

Frontier: The Definitive Guide

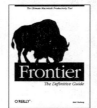

By Matt Neuburg
1st Edition February 1998
618 pages, 1-56592-383-9

This definitive guide is the first book devoted exclusively to teaching and documenting Userland Frontier, a powerful scripting environment for web site management and system level scripting. Packed with examples, advice, tricks, and tips, *Frontier: The Definitive Guide* teaches you Frontier from the ground up. Learn how to automate repetitive processes, control remote computers across a network, beef up your web site by generating hundreds of related web pages automatically, and more. Covers Frontier 4.2.3 for the Macintosh.

O'REILLY®

TO ORDER: **800-998-9938** • *order@oreilly.com* • **http://www.oreilly.com/**
OUR PRODUCTS ARE AVAILABLE AT A BOOKSTORE OR SOFTWARE STORE NEAR YOU.
FOR INFORMATION: **800-998-9938** • **707-829-0515** • *info@oreilly.com*

Web Programming

Web Client Programming with Perl

By Clinton Wong
1st Edition March 1997
228 pages, ISBN 1-56592-214-X

Web Client Programming with Perl
shows you how to extend scripting
skills to the Web. This book teaches
you the basics of how browsers
communicate with servers and how
to write your own customized web
clients to automate common tasks. It is intended for those who
are motivated to develop software that offers a more flexible
and dynamic response than a standard web browser.

Dynamic HTML: The Definitive Reference

By Danny Goodman
1st Edition July 1998
1088 pages, ISBN 1-56592-494-0

Dynamic HTML: The Definitive
Reference is an indispensable
compendium for Web content developers. It contains complete reference
material for all of the HTML tags, CSS
style attributes, browser document
objects, and JavaScript objects supported by the various
standards and the latest versions of Netscape Navigator and
Microsoft Internet Explorer.

O'REILLY®

TO ORDER: **800-998-9938** • *order@oreilly.com* • *http://www.oreilly.com/*
OUR PRODUCTS ARE AVAILABLE AT A BOOKSTORE OR SOFTWARE STORE NEAR YOU.
FOR INFORMATION: **800-998-9938** • **707-829-0515** • *info@oreilly.com*

How to stay in touch with O'Reilly

1. Visit Our Award-Winning Site

http://www.oreilly.com/

★ "Top 100 Sites on the Web" —*PC Magazine*
★ "Top 5% Web sites" —*Point Communications*
★ "3-Star site" —*The McKinley Group*

Our web site contains a library of comprehensive product information (including book excerpts and tables of contents), downloadable software, background articles, interviews with technology leaders, links to relevant sites, book cover art, and more. File us in your Bookmarks or Hotlist!

2. Join Our Email Mailing Lists

New Product Releases

To receive automatic email with brief descriptions of all new O'Reilly products as they are released, send email to:
listproc@online.oreilly.com
Put the following information in the first line of your message (*not* in the Subject field):
subscribe oreilly-news

O'Reilly Events

If you'd also like us to send information about trade show events, special promotions, and other O'Reilly events, send email to:
listproc@online.oreilly.com
Put the following information in the first line of your message (*not* in the Subject field):
subscribe oreilly-events

3. Get Examples from Our Books via FTP

There are two ways to access an archive of example files from our books:

Regular FTP

- ftp to:
  ftp.oreilly.com
  (login: anonymous
  password: your email address)
- Point your web browser to:
  ftp://ftp.oreilly.com/

FTPMAIL

- Send an email message to:
  ftpmail@online.oreilly.com
  (Write "help" in the message body)

4. Contact Us via Email

order@oreilly.com
To place a book or software order online. Good for North American and international customers.

subscriptions@oreilly.com
To place an order for any of our newsletters or periodicals.

books@oreilly.com
General questions about any of our books.

software@oreilly.com
For general questions and product information about our software. Check out O'Reilly Software Online at **http://software.oreilly.com/** for software and technical support information. Registered O'Reilly software users send your questions to:
website-support@oreilly.com

cs@oreilly.com
For answers to problems regarding your order or our products.

booktech@oreilly.com
For book content technical questions or corrections.

proposals@oreilly.com
To submit new book or software proposals to our editors and product managers.

international@oreilly.com
For information about our international distributors or translation queries. For a list of our distributors outside of North America check out:
http://www.oreilly.com/www/order/country.html

O'Reilly & Associates, Inc.
101 Morris Street, Sebastopol, CA 95472 USA
TEL   707-829-0515 or 800-998-9938
       (6am to 5pm PST)
FAX   707-829-0104

O'REILLY®

TO ORDER: **800-998-9938** • order@oreilly.com • http://www.oreilly.com/
OUR PRODUCTS ARE AVAILABLE AT A BOOKSTORE OR SOFTWARE STORE NEAR YOU.
FOR INFORMATION: **800-998-9938** • **707-829-0515** • info@oreilly.com

Titles from O'Reilly

WEB

Advanced Perl Programming
Apache: The Definitive Guide,
  2nd Ed.
ASP in a Nutshell
Building Your Own Web
  Conferences
Building Your Own Website™
CGI Programming with Perl
Designing with JavaScript
Dynamic HTML:
  The Definitive Reference
Frontier: The Definitive Guide
HTML: The Definitive Guide, 3rd Ed.
Information Architecture
  for the World Wide Web
JavaScript Pocket Reference
JavaScript: The Definitive Guide,
  3rd Ed.
Learning VB Script
Photoshop for the Web
WebMaster in a Nutshell
WebMaster in a Nutshell, Deluxe Ed.
Web Design in a Nutshell
Web Navigation: Designing the
  User Experience
Web Performance Tuning
Web Security & Commerce
Writing Apache Modules

PERL

Learning Perl, 2nd Ed.
Learning Perl for Win32 Systems
Learning Perl/TK
Mastering Algorithms with Perl
Mastering Regular Expressions
Perl5 Pocket Reference, 2nd Ed.
Perl Cookbook
Perl in a Nutshell
Perl Resource Kit—UNIX Ed.
Perl Resource Kit—Win32 Ed.
Perl/TK Pocket Reference
Programming Perl, 2nd Ed.
Web Client Programming with Perl

GRAPHICS & MULTIMEDIA

Director in a Nutshell
Encyclopedia of Graphics
  File Formats, 2nd Ed.
Lingo in a Nutshell
Photoshop in a Nutshell
QuarkXPress in a Nutshell

USING THE INTERNET

AOL in a Nutshell
Internet in a Nutshell
Smileys
The Whole Internet for
  Windows95
The Whole Internet:
  The Next Generation
The Whole Internet
  User's Guide & Catalog

JAVA SERIES

Database Programming with
  JDBC and Java
Developing Java Beans
Exploring Java, 2nd Ed.
Java AWT Reference
Java Cryptography
Java Distributed Computing
Java Examples in a Nutshell
Java Foundation Classes in a
  Nutshell
Java Fundamental Classes Reference
Java in a Nutshell, 2nd Ed.
Java in a Nutshell, Deluxe Ed.
Java I/O
Java Language Reference, 2nd Ed.
Java Media Players
Java Native Methods
Java Network Programming
Java Security
Java Servlet Programming
Java Swing
Java Threads
Java Virtual Machine

UNIX

Exploring Expect
GNU Emacs Pocket Reference
Learning GNU Emacs, 2nd Ed.
Learning the bash Shell, 2nd Ed.
Learning the Korn Shell
Learning the UNIX Operating
  System, 4th Ed.
Learning the vi Editor, 6th Ed.
Linux in a Nutshell
Linux Multimedia Guide
Running Linux, 2nd Ed.
SCO UNIX in a Nutshell
sed & awk, 2nd Ed.
Tcl/Tk in a Nutshell
Tcl/Tk Pocket Reference
Tcl/Tk Tools
The UNIX CD Bookshelf
UNIX in a Nutshell, System V Ed.
UNIX Power Tools, 2nd Ed.
Using csh & tsch
Using Samba
vi Editor Pocket Reference
What You Need To Know:
  When You Can't Find Your
  UNIX System Administrator
Writing GNU Emacs Extensions

SONGLINE GUIDES

NetLaw   NetResearch
NetLearning   NetSuccess
NetLessons   NetTravel

SOFTWARE

Building Your Own WebSite™
Building Your Own Web Conference
WebBoard™ 3.0
WebSite Professional™ 2.0
PolyForm™

SYSTEM ADMINISTRATION

Building Internet Firewalls
Computer Security Basics
Cracking DES
DNS and BIND, 3rd Ed.
DNS on WindowsNT
Essential System Administration
Essential WindowsNT
  System Administration
Getting Connected:
  The Internet at 56K and Up
Linux Network Administrator's
  Guide
Managing IP Networks with
  Cisco Routers
Managing Mailing Lists
Managing NFS and NIS
Managing the WindowsNT Registry
Managing Usenet
MCSE: The Core Exams in a
  Nutshell
MCSE: The Electives in a Nutshell
Networking Personal Computers
  with TCP/IP
Oracle Performance Tuning,
  2nd Ed.
Practical UNIX & Internet Security,
  2nd Ed.
PGP: Pretty Good Privacy
Protecting Networks with SATAN
sendmail, 2nd Ed.
sendmail Desktop Reference
System Performance Tuning
TCP/IP Network Administration,
  2nd Ed.
termcap & terminfo
The Networking CD Bookshelf
Using & Managing PPP
Virtual Private Networks
WindowsNT Backup & Restore
WindowsNT Desktop Reference
WindowsNT Event Logging
WindowsNT in a Nutshell
WindowsNT Server 4.0 for
  Netware Administrators
WindowsNT SNMP
WindowsNT TCP/IP Administration
WindowsNT User Administration
Zero Administration for Windows

X WINDOW

Vol. 1: Xlib Programming Manual
Vol. 2: Xlib Reference Manual
Vol. 3M: X Window System
  User's Guide, Motif Ed.
Vol. 4M: X Toolkit Intrinsics
  Programming Manual, Motif Ed.
Vol. 5: X Toolkit Intrinsics
  Reference Manual
Vol. 6A: Motif Programming Manual
Vol. 6B: Motif Reference Manual
Vol. 8 : X Window System
  Administrator's Guide

PROGRAMMING

Access Database Design and
  Programming
Advanced Oracle PL/SQL
  Programming with Packages
Applying RCS and SCCS
BE Developer's Guide
BE Advanced Topics
C++: The Core Language
Checking C Programs with lint
Developing Windows Error Messages
Developing Visual Basic Add-ins
Guide to Writing DCE Applications
High Performance Computing,
  2nd Ed.
Inside the Windows 95 File System
Inside the Windows 95 Registry
lex & yacc, 2nd Ed.
Linux Device Drivers
Managing Projects with make
Oracle8 Design Tips
Oracle Built-in Packages
Oracle Design
Oracle PL/SQL Programming,
  2nd Ed.
Oracle Scripts
Oracle Security
Palm Programming:
  The Developer's Guide
Porting UNIX Software
POSIX Programmer's Guide
POSIX.4: Programming
  for the Real World
Power Programming with RPC
Practical C Programming, 3rd Ed.
Practical C++ Programming
Programming Python
Programming with curses
Programming with GNU Software
Pthreads Programming
Python Pocket Reference
Software Portability with imake,
  2nd Ed.
UML in a Nutshell
Understanding DCE
UNIX Systems Programming for SVR4
VB/VBA in a Nutshell: The Languages
Win32 Multithreaded Programming
Windows NT File System Internals
Year 2000 in a Nutshell

USING WINDOWS

Excel97 Annoyances
Office97 Annoyances
Outlook Annoyances
Windows Annoyances
Windows98 Annoyances
Windows95 in a Nutshell
Windows98 in a Nutshell
Word97 Annoyances

OTHER TITLES

PalmPilot: The Ultimate Guide
Palm Programming:
  The Developer's Guide

O'REILLY®

TO ORDER: **800-998-9938** • *order@oreilly.com* • *http://www.oreilly.com/*

OUR PRODUCTS ARE AVAILABLE AT A BOOKSTORE OR SOFTWARE STORE NEAR YOU.

FOR INFORMATION: **800-998-9938** • **707-829-0515** • *info@oreilly.com*

International Distributors

UK, EUROPE, MIDDLE EAST AND AFRICA (EXCEPT FRANCE, GERMANY, AUSTRIA, SWITZERLAND, LUXEMBOURG, LIECHTENSTEIN, AND EASTERN EUROPE)

INQUIRIES
O'Reilly UK Limited
4 Castle Street
Farnham
Surrey, GU9 7HS
United Kingdom
Telephone: 44-1252-711776
Fax: 44-1252-734211
Email: josette@oreilly.com

ORDERS
Wiley Distribution Services Ltd.
1 Oldlands Way
Bognor Regis
West Sussex PO22 9SA
United Kingdom
Telephone: 44-1243-779777
Fax: 44-1243-820250
Email: cs-books@wiley.co.uk

FRANCE

ORDERS
GEODIF
61, Bd Saint-Germain
75240 Paris Cedex 05, France
Tel: 33-1-44-41-46-16 (French books)
Tel: 33-1-44-41-11-87 (English books)
Fax: 33-1-44-41-11-44
Email: distribution@eyrolles.com

INQUIRIES
Éditions O'Reilly
18 rue Séguier
75006 Paris, France
Tel: 33-1-40-51-52-30
Fax: 33-1-40-51-52-31
Email: france@editions-oreilly.fr

GERMANY, SWITZERLAND, AUSTRIA, EASTERN EUROPE, LUXEMBOURG, AND LIECHTENSTEIN

INQUIRIES & ORDERS
O'Reilly Verlag
Balthasarstr. 81
D-50670 Köln
Germany
Telephone: 49-221-973160-91
Fax: 49-221-973160-8
Email: anfragen@oreilly.de (inquiries)
Email: order@oreilly.de (orders)

CANADA (FRENCH LANGUAGE BOOKS)
Les Éditions Flammarion ltée
375, Avenue Laurier Ouest
Montréal (Québec) H2V 2K3
Tel: 00-1-514-277-8807
Fax: 00-1-514-278-2085
Email: info@flammarion.qc.ca

HONG KONG
City Discount Subscription Service, Ltd.
Unit D, 3rd Floor, Yan's Tower
27 Wong Chuk Hang Road
Aberdeen, Hong Kong
Tel: 852-2580-3539
Fax: 852-2580-6463
Email: citydis@ppn.com.hk

KOREA
Hanbit Media, Inc.
Sonyoung Bldg. 202
Yeksam-dong 736-36
Kangnam-ku
Seoul, Korea
Tel: 822-554-9610
Fax: 822-556-0363
Email: hant93@chollian.dacom.co.kr

PHILIPPINES
Mutual Books, Inc.
429-D Shaw Boulevard
Mandaluyong City, Metro
Manila, Philippines
Tel: 632-725-7538
Fax: 632-721-3056
Email: mbikikog@mnl.sequel.net

TAIWAN
O'Reilly Taiwan
No. 3, Lane 131
Hang-Chow South Road
Section 1, Taipei, Taiwan
Tel: 886-2-23968990
Fax: 886-2-23968916
Email: benh@oreilly.com

CHINA
O'Reilly Beijing
Room 2410
160, FuXingMenNeiDaJie
XiCheng District
Beijing
China PR 100031
Tel: 86-10-86631006
Fax: 86-10-86631007
Email: frederic@oreilly.com

INDIA
Computer Bookshop (India) Pvt. Ltd.
190 Dr. D.N. Road, Fort
Bombay 400 001 India
Tel: 91-22-207-0989
Fax: 91-22-262-3551
Email: cbsbom@giasbm01.vsnl.net.in

JAPAN
O'Reilly Japan, Inc.
Kiyoshige Building 2F
12-Bancho, Sanei-cho
Shinjuku-ku
Tokyo 160-0008 Japan
Tel: 81-3-3356-5227
Fax: 81-3-3356-5261
Email: japan@oreilly.com

ALL OTHER ASIAN COUNTRIES
O'Reilly & Associates, Inc.
101 Morris Street
Sebastopol, CA 95472 USA
Tel: 707-829-0515
Fax: 707-829-0104
Email: order@oreilly.com

AUSTRALIA
WoodsLane Pty., Ltd.
7/5 Vuko Place
Warriewood NSW 2102
Australia
Tel: 61-2-9970-5111
Fax: 61-2-9970-5002
Email: info@woodslane.com.au

NEW ZEALAND
Woodslane New Zealand, Ltd.
21 Cooks Street (P.O. Box 575)
Waganui, New Zealand
Tel: 64-6-347-6543
Fax: 64-6-345-4840
Email: info@woodslane.com.au

LATIN AMERICA
McGraw-Hill Interamericana
Editores, S.A. de C.V.
Cedro No. 512
Col. Atlampa
06450, Mexico, D.F.
Tel: 52-5-547-6777
Fax: 52-5-547-3336
Email: mcgraw-hill@infosel.net.mx

O'REILLY®